AYRTON
SENNA
THE WHOLE STORY

Other books by this author:

MEMORIES OF AYRTON

AYRTON SENNA
As time goes by

INSIDE THE MIND OF THE GRAND PRIX DRIVER
The psychology of the fastest men on earth:
sex, danger and everything else

JUAN PABLO MONTOYA

MURRAY WALKER
The very last word

MICHAEL SCHUMACHER
The greatest of all

AYRTON
SENNA
THE WHOLE STORY

Christopher Hilton

Formula 1 photographs by Rainer Schlegelmilch

Haynes Publishing

First published in April 2004
Reprinted 2005 and 2006

The text in this paperback was previously published in
Ayrton Senna: The Hard Edge of Genius (1990),
Ayrton Senna: The Second Coming (1994),
Ayrton Senna: The Legend Grows (1995), and
Ayrton Senna: His Full Car Racing Record (1995).
The book also contains additional material.

A catalogue record for this book is available from the British Library

ISBN 1 84425 096 2

Library of Congress catalog card no. 2004100806

Published by Haynes Publishing, Sparkford,
Yeovil, Somerset, BA22 7JJ, UK
Tel: 01963 442030 Fax: 01963 440001
Int.tel: +44 1963 442030 Int.fax: +44 1963 440001
E-mail: sales@haynes.co.uk
Website: www.haynes.co.uk

Haynes North America, Inc.,
861 Lawrence Drive, Newbury Park,
California 91320, USA

Page-build by G&M Designs Ltd., Raunds, Northamptonshire

Printed and bound in England by J. H. Haynes & Co. Ltd, Sparkford

Jacket illustrations, front: Preparation (Rainer Schlegelmilch).
Back, top left: FF1600, 1981 (LAT); top right: Estoril, 1985 (Rainer Schlegelmilch);
bottom: Senna v Schumacher, 1994 (Rainer Schlegelmilch).

CONTENTS

INTRODUCTION

Everyone I spoke to reacted immediately and in the same way. 'It can't be, can it?' Lost somewhere in the incredulity, you could hear them doing the mental arithmetic; could hear the realisation that it can be, and is, a decade since Ayrton Senna died at the Maggiore Hospital, Bologna, after crashing during the 1994 San Marino Grand Prix at a corner called *Tamburello*.

'It's been a long year since yesterday afternoon, an afternoon which began hot and dry and sunny and ended deep in mourning. It's been a long year since 1 May 1994 which began with foreboding and compressed itself into 1.8 seconds, a moment which has expanded into all time.'

I wrote those words to introduce a book, *The Legend Grows*, which marked the first anniversary of Imola and I was trying to capture what people felt then. They had the same reaction – 'it can't be, can it?' The passing of a whole decade is much harder to take because, however close you feel to Senna and his career – and the accident which lasted those 1.8 seconds – it has to be much further away. This book is a gesture against that.

I've used the opening words from *The Legend Grows* for a reason. That, and two other Haynes/PSL books – *The Hard Edge of Genius* and *The Second Coming* – have been reworked into a chronological narrative with, to round it off, an abbreviated version of a fourth book, *His Full Car Racing Record*, which contains reports on each of Senna's 235 car races. In the reworking I have added, where appropriate, information which has come to light since the books were published. To smooth the narrative, I have also done some rephrasing: *Hard Edge* and

Second Coming, both written while he was still alive, were obviously couched in the present tense and can seem slightly strange if you read them cold these ten years on.

The first chapter of this paperback is entirely new, and brings the story up to 2004.

Many, many people helped with the four titles and although they were thanked in the original publication I've drawn them together now, plus the sources: Tony Dodgins, Reginaldo Leme, Paulo Casseb, Wagner Gonzalez, Terry Fullerton, Peter Koene, Martin Hines, Rick Morris, Malcolm Pullen, Ralph Firman, Dennis Rushen, Calvin Fish. Kenny Andrews, Eddie Jordan, Dick Bennetts, Martin Brundle, Alex Hawkridge, Chris Witty, Herbie Blash, Peter Gethin, Johnny Dumfries, Peter Warr, Nigel Stepney, Steve Hallam, Lee Gaug, Barry Griffin, Francine Chatelain, Kaspar Arnet, Eric Silbermann, Caroline Horsman, Chuck Nicholson, Martyn Pass, Mike Hill, John Watson, The Rev. Ian Tomlinson, Henri Pescarolo, Derek Bell, Jackie Stewart, Derick Allsop, Russell Bulgin, rallyman Phil Collins, Maurizio Sala, Samantha Harris (BBC), Keith Sutton; Ron Dennis, Peter Stayner and Juliane White (McLaren International); David Chappell, Sports Editor of *The Times*, for permission to quote from their feature by Andrew Longmore on Senna's last weekend; Derek Warwick, Johnny Herbert, Philippe Streiff, Peter de Bruijn, Mike Wilson; Joe Saward (formerly of *Autosport*); John Corsmit of the FIA; Pino Allievi of *La Gazzetta dello Sport*; Reinhold Joest; Gerhard Berger; Professor Sid Watkins; Sir Frank Williams, Ann Bradshaw (formerly of Williams GP Engineering); The Bishop of Truro, Michael Ball; Lake Speed; Martin Whitaker; Owen O'Mahony, Senna's pilot; Betise Assumpcao who handled Senna's publicity, Angelo Parilla; Monica Meroni for active assistance and translation, Roland Christen, Dr Giovanni Gordini of the Maggiore Hospital, the Liverani family, the staff at Imola; Gordon Message, John Love, Bob Dance, Rubens Barrichello, Marcel Gysin, Cor Euser; David

Fern of Donington; David Tremayne, formerly of *Motoring News*; Rick Rinaman, a chief mechanic with the Penske team; Wilma Shalliday, Headmaster's Secretary, Loretto; Brian Hart, Inge Donnell for translations; archivist Martin Hadwen, Lyn Patey, Irene Ambrose, Dave Coyne.

I have quoted, with permission, from *Autosport*, *Motoring News* and *Karting* magazine (and thanks to Mark Burgess for permission to do that). I have also quoted from an *F1 Racing* magazine feature, 'Remembering Ayrton', by Oliver Peagam (and thanks to the editor, Matt Bishop, for permission). I leaned heavily on *Autocourse*, the Marlboro Grand Prix Guide, *The Guinness Complete Grand Prix Who's Who* by Steve Small (Guinness Publishing) and the *Grand Prix Data Book* by David Hayhoe and David Holland (Duke); *Cars and Car Conversions* for a portait of what happened in mid-Wales when Senna went rallying.

I drew background from: *Ayrton Senna, Trajectoire D'un Enfant Gate* by Lionel Froissart (Glenat, Grenoble); *Adriane: My Life with Ayrton* by Adriane Galisteu (Apa Publishing, Adelaide); *Goodbye Champion, Farewell Friend* by Karin Sturm (English language edition, MRP, London); *Le Livre d'Or de la Formula 1 1994* by Renaud de Laborderie (Solar, Paris); *Damon Hill Grand Prix Year* by Hill and Maurice Hamilton (Macmillan, London); *Flying On The Ground* by Emerson Fittipaldi and Elizabeth Hayward (William Kimber, London); *Driven to Win* by Nigel Mansell and Derick Allsop; *Life in the Fast Lane* by Alain Prost with Jean-Louis Moncet; *To Hell and Back* by Niki Lauda (all Stanley Paul).

The TAG-Heuer/Olivetti computerised results provide virtually every lap Senna ever drove at Grand Prix weekends. A videotape, *Senna the Champ* (VSR International) was extremely illuminating, while a video library of the BBC coverage helps too, and so thanks to the Corporation and Murray Walker, Martin Brundle, Jonathan Palmer and the late James Hunt for being there and doing it so well.

Chapter 1

THE SECOND LIFE

Speed exercises a deep fascination. With anything mechanical the fascination sharpens because speed itself can be increased to whatever technology will allow. It is also available to ordinary people – in this case any motorist. The speed limit on Britain's motorways is 70mph but many modern saloons will do 130mph, no trouble at all. Consider: at 130 you are *closing* at 60mph on anyone observing the British limit.

At the 1994 Pacific Grand Prix at Aida a pace car – a Porsche 911 – was used to bring the cars round the parade lap to the starting grid. This was to keep them bunched so those at the front wouldn't have to wait too long for the rear to come up. A Porsche 911 is only getting into its stride at 130mph, of course, but Senna complained that this car was simply not fast enough to take them round at the speed they needed to heat the tyres.

Now consider: for the 1985 Grand Prix of Europe, at Brands Hatch, in the second timed practice Senna crossed the line in his JPS Lotus at 188mph (second quickest to Keke Rosberg's Williams, at 190). He would have been closing on the law-abiding Briton at 118mph.

These are the ranges of speed at which the Formula 1 driver habitually operates. That day at Brands, eighteen drivers were doing 180mph or more. The slowest was Huub Rothengatter in an Osella at 170mph, and when was the last time you did 100mph more than the legal limit?

Incidentally, the white Longines timing strip laid across the track to record drivers' speeds out in the country was still there many years later, long after the last Grand Prix had been run. This strip was worn and bore the black of countless tyre marks burnished like scars across it. Somebody who worked at the circuit showed it to me and said: 'That's where Senna was recorded at over 200mph.' Curious: instinctively he related it to Senna, not to anybody else.

What separated Senna from others was that, even at these immense speeds, he was able to do things which remain astonishing. Somehow it unfolded slowly to him, so slowly that he could apply his mental capacity as a data-logger and remember everything the car was doing. It was a gift, and when even experienced motorsport people were confronted with this for the first time they could not believe it.

Ayrton Senna's life began in Sao Paulo in 1960, grew to the point where he was the most famous racing driver in the world and ended against a wall at Imola in 1994. From that moment, mysteriously, a second 'life' began and has grown to the point where it is something far more potent and practical than the reverence of memory.

He was accustomed to speed because he'd started in a kart at four – the fascination got hold of him immediately – but that only takes us so far. Most of the others started young and in karts, so that they were accustomed, too, but it seems that they could not see it as slowly as Senna and they certainly could not log the quantity of information. In direct comparison, their options were limited.

As our story unfolds, this may shed light on why, from his earliest days, Senna was able to do what seemed to be the impossible – almost to defy normal human limitations. It also raises a question mark over what still seems inexplicable: how, on lap 7 of the San Marino Grand Prix at Imola, the Williams got away from him.

Even now, these ten years afterwards, nobody knows. As I write this, however, the Italian legal process lingers. In January 2003, reports emerged that – although Williams Technical

Director Patrick Head and former Williams designer Adrian Newey had been cleared of manslaughter in December 1997 and an appeal against that was dismissed in 1999 – a further appeal was due to be heard within a year. A French magazine, *AutoHebdo*, carried this headline: THE STORY WITHOUT END.

This was meant, perhaps, to be ironic because the news item underneath it announced the facts of the new appeal, but pointed out that essentially the Italians had been going round and round for a long time to get back to precisely where they had started. Quite unconsciously, however, the headline covered much broader terrain because the Senna era did not end at *Tamburello* or in the Italian courtrooms. On the contrary, it was almost as if he would have a second life after *Tamburello*.

His sister Viviane has said (in *F1 Racing* magazine) that 'Ayrton had asked me to set up something to look after poor children in Brazil.' This was shortly before Imola and was the birth of the Senna Foundation.

'I started to think about it but we never had the second conversation. Then I started to research what we should do.'

She has also said: 'The popularity of the Senna image is as strong as ever, which is amazing. It was while the family was mourning that we decided to continue the creation of the Foundation.' In 1998 its expenditure reached $9 million and the Foundation was able to help well over 180,000 children.

As *The Sunday Telegraph* noted in 1999, 'hundreds of roads and public buildings have been named after him and a vast range of goods – including motorbikes, bicycles, pens, watches and sunglasses – carry the Senna name.' One of the Foundation's projects is to help educate children from poor backgrounds by giving them half a day's sport if they spend the other half in the classroom. Another scheme – delightfully called Speed Up Brazil – is aimed at preventing school children from doing so badly that they have to repeat whole years of their education. On average, only 47 children in 1,000 get through the eight years of their school education in just eight years.

By 2001, according to one source, Senna's trademark was bringing in $6m from licensing. The Senna products, including the comic *Senninha* (Little Senna), were bringing in vastly more.

The reality of helping deprived children is extremely touching. Towards the end of 2003, a BBC crew went to Sao Paulo to film for a documentary on his legacy and the reality touched them hard. They were non-motor racing people and consequently able to be objective (which those who lived through Senna's first life find difficult). That the work of the Foundation should be to honour a sportsman rather than, say, a Secretary General of the UN or a religious figure, took them – I suspect – by surprise.

That Ayrton Senna can still surprise even a decade after Imola is no surprise at all.

Senna's career clearly has potential as a film, and from time to time there have been rumours that one was either being planned or is imminent. Film is a way of defeating time because, as long as a single copy survives, everything and everyone on it lives again each time it is shown. A Senna film would bestow a certain measure of immortality: he, through the medium of whoever played him, would *always* be available, just as the real Senna will always be there on videos of his races and in the clips of interviews he gave.

The favourite to play Senna has long been Spanish actor Antonio Banderas and a couple of years ago the rumours seemed to be hardening. Viviane said there had been discussions with Warner Brothers after a lengthy period of resolving the exact focus of the film. That was a delicate matter because the temptation might be to make a rip-roaring life-in-the-fast-lane cliché of a thing – with an eye on the commercial possibilities – rather than a sensitive portrait of an extraordinary man. Viviane understood that perfectly, because she said of Banderas, 'his proposal calls for a mix of the personal and the emotional, showing idealism and respect.'

There was a headline about this, too: FILM WILL UNRAVEL MYSTERY OF SENNA'S LAST MOMENTS. It was above a long piece about the Banderas film in *The Observer*, a British national newspaper, in September 2001. 'Viviane said the film would tell the world the truth about her brother, especially who and what the family believes were responsible for his death.'

No elaboration was provided.

Script writer Jeremy Lew – who originally set out to put together a Senna film and introduced Banderas to the Senna family – insisted to me that nothing was afoot. He explained the complexities of the Hollywood market place, especially in the light of various take-overs, and that few Americans had heard of Senna or of Formula 1. He still feels that a Senna film would have great appeal on a global scale (especially of course in countries with Grand Prix traditions) but might perhaps be better if it came from Europe. Lew, incidentally, researched and wrote a script in the mid-1990s, and agonised over every nuance. He'd like the chance to revive the project and thinks one day he might.

Many speak of Imola providing a sudden and unstoppable impetus to improve safety in Formula 1, and point out it is a valuable part of Senna's legacy. That has happened at two levels: the physical – *Tamburello* was immediately reshaped into a most innocent corner, for one example, neck braces for drivers as another innovation – and what I must call the spiritual. Imola casts a long shadow and, consciously or subconsciously, much of what is done in Formula 1 is influenced by that. You won't be seeing unprotected stone walls at 190mph corners ever again.

When the great Jim Clark was killed in 1968, people within Formula 1 felt more than a sense of emptiness and incredulity. They thought *if it can happen to him it can happen to anybody*.

The first real impetus over safety was driven by Sir Jackie Stewart. At the time Stewart was mocked and called a coward. He persisted. By 1994 the world was a very different place, politically correct to a degree unthinkable even a short time before – but *Tamburello* brought the same emptiness, the same incredulity and the same thought. That, I believe, is the enduring influence of Senna's death: the vow that, despite all the high dollar commercial and technological ambitions that motivate F1, this sort of tragedy must never happen again.

Those who die in their prime are fixed forever in immortal youth. Time can no longer touch them. Ayrton Senna will *always* be the fit, charismatic and handsome man he was as he walked to the grid on 1 May 1994. He will never be a day older. It has cloaked him in an untouchable, tragic majesty, and this in turn has both created and sustained a deepening fascination with him – and curiosity about him. More than that, he was such a complex man that it has taken all these years after Imola to fully appreciate just *how* complex he was, how many layers there were to him and what they might have revealed.

Now: the first life.

Chapter 2

THE BOY FROM BRAZIL

Geography is important but not decisive in motor racing. If you want it badly enough you can go for it from any starting-point, as 1982 World Champion Keke Rosberg from frozen Finland proved, but an established starting point helps and Brazil is that. People in the sport speak of a Brazilian 'mafia' meaning Brazilians who help Brazilians who help Brazilians to get on. Brazil is a rich-poor country (no contradiction) and if you're among those immediately in front of the hyphen that helps, too. It is also, incidentally, the same size as Australia – and that's the end of the geography.

Ayrton Senna da Silva was born in Sao Paulo on 21 March 1960 to Milton and Neide. They already had a daughter Viviane, who we've met. Another son, Leonardo, would follow.

Senna was known by his surname, da Silva, until 1982 when he decided it was not distinctive enough (too many da Silvas in Brazil, like too many Smiths in Britain) and simply dropped it. Senna, incidentally, was his mother's maiden name.

Viviane says that as a child Senna was always picking fights with bigger boys which, in a sense, he'd continue to do for the rest of his life. She'd claim she once 'intervened' and got a whack from somebody for her trouble. She adds that 'his eyes had real sweetness in them, you know. Everyone said so.' In an interview, she'd broaden this glimpse by saying that Senna was almost stubborn in getting what he wanted and by nature very restless. A normal lad, in fact.

Milton had a successful car components business as well as farms. 'The factory had about 750 employees,' Senna said, 'and my father started from nothing. There were about *ten* [Senna's italics] farms and a total of 400,000 hectares with well over 10,000 head of cattle.' The family lived, as you might expect, in a large house. It was in a northern suburb called Santana. They were, as you might expect, a close family and an Anglo-Saxon mind like mine has to stretch itself to imagine what a haven and a bastion that remains in Latin and Hispanic lands. The family does not close ranks in time of trouble: the family closes ranks all the time.

In the fullness of time, Senna would have a pad in Monte Carlo – almost obligatory for Formula 1 drivers and some not even in Formula 1 – and a house in Faro, Portugal, but home was where it had always been, Brazil, home is where he went back to whenever he could. There, he'd build a complex beside the sea, complete with its own kart track, and delight in water sports with Viviane's sons.

Even as his Formula 1 career began, when he was a maturing man, he'd confess that 'homesickness, evidently I have that. My heart is over there; it's my country and it contains my family, my friends, the people I know, my hobbies. Here in Europe I work, that's all. The other drivers, the Europeans, don't suffer from this uprooting, they can go home in an hour or two as soon as they have a day off. For us it's different and I miss Brazil. My family misses me, I am very attached to my family, my friends, my girlfriend [a TV star] who works there six days out of seven. It's hard but I don't complain. I chose this life, I knew the inherent sacrifices and I accepted them, but in the future I will try and organise my calendar to go back to Brazil as often as possible. It's very difficult because during the season we have testing every week.'

Alain Prost – after the great Marlboro McLaren rift of 1989 which appeared on the Richter scale – may or may not have been accurate when he complained that Senna was back in Brazil with 'Mommy and Daddy' instead of sharing the burden of testing, but in another sense Prost had missed the point: home is not where you escape to, not where you take refuge in, home is where your existence is. Prost, having long decamped France for Switzerland, was conducting a lively, sometimes loveless lament with many of those who professionally ought to have been nearest and dearest to him – French journalists – and had become effectively international, at ease anywhere on Mother Earth. Senna remained Brazilian; only Brazilian juices flowed in him and one evening, when I tackled him about how you can live amongst so much poverty, he mounted a defence lively enough for the man from *The Times* to feel the need to step in, conciliating and mediating in that Foreign Office way you'd expect from a *Times* man.

Today, surveying the immensity of Sao Paulo – population unknown, but comparable to Mexico City and Beijing – it's hard for an outsider to see it in terms of homesickness: the crazy traffic, the chaotic architecture, the drugs and crime, the shanty towns, the pollution. But there's something else about the place, harder to quantify: a tropical feel, a Latin ease within a multi-cultural society, a bustle, fluidity rather than rigidity, smiles on street corners and, whenever you're least expecting it, kindness. Brazil has a character of its own – including cuisine – and Sao Paulo a prestige of its own, because it's the money town for the whole country. Add that it's where you were born and raised, went to school, where friends and family are interwoven into whoever you are, and the homesickness becomes not only explicable but also perhaps inevitable.

Paulo Casseb, the friend, made this judgement, *circa* 1988: 'Ayrton was familiar, very familiar. It means he likes to be all the time near his family. His father is very quiet. It's very hard to explain because he has a strong personality but he's such a fine person that if you come to talk to him for two minutes you feel like you've known him for ten years. Ayrton was a normal child, but ever since he was a little kid he liked to drive a lot. When Ayrton was four his father made his first handmade kart for him. He played in it in the back yard and in public parks.'

It had 1 horsepower.

Neide says that he was clumsy as a small lad, would fall going up stairs and she'd always buy him two ice-creams because he'd drop the first. Learning to control the kart taught him co-ordination, perhaps even delicacy, of movement.

Senna would ruminate among his memories and say: 'I was just doing it for myself, for my own feelings. I hardly knew who I was.'

This feeling of power exercises, I repeat, a powerful fascination, especially when an engine can deliver so much of it. To give a context: no man has been recorded as running faster than 26.9mph, no horse faster than 43.2mph (the *Guinness Book of Records*). In practice for the 2003 Italian Grand Prix at Monza, Michael Schumacher got 225mph out of his Ferrari – and continuing the theme of the previous chapter, he'd be *closing* on the law-abiding Briton at 155mph ...

Casseb gives us the very first example of the inexplicable. 'I recount something which happened when Ayrton was seven. His father had a jeep at the farm, looked after by the man who looked after the farm, and he was very good friends with Ayrton [and therefore presumably allowed it to happen]. One day, Ayrton drove the jeep by himself. Nobody had ever taught him to drive and he was changing the gears without the clutch. His father didn't believe what he was seeing, it was so amazing. Ayrton didn't hurt the jeep. Because it was a very old engine it would have been necessary to push the clutch hard and so Ayrton was going first, second, third and fourth without it.'

There is coincidence here with Jim Clark who wrote of his early years: 'I remember being interested in mechanical things like most boys, although I was not particularly attracted to motorsport. I believe I was first drawn to driving and motor vehicles by an interest in their engines rather than their capacity for speed. As a small boy I was quick to take any chance of jumping up on a tractor and going for a little spin. Because of this almost insatiable mechanical curiosity I probably knew as much about our tractors as the farm workers who drove them.' (*Jim Clark at the Wheel*, Arthur Barker, 1964.)

The kart assumed more and more importance, Senna took it seriously and Milton realised he would have to take it seriously, too. Senna once described graphically how he first competed at the age of eight, which is a conundrum since he ought to have waited another five years: 13 was the minimum age. Senna, however, didn't make mistakes about matters like his races and it must have been so. He'd remember the grid was decided by drawing lots and he drew Number 1. He'd also remember older, bigger boys were in it but 'I was small and light so my kart was fastest on the straights with the weight advantage I had.' The big boys might draw up in the corners but *Senninha* bombed along those straights. Another kart touched him with three laps to go and he went off.

At ten he had a more powerful kart but, of course, could not legally race yet so each weekend he drove at a track called the Parque Anhembi.

In 1973, everything began to change. In early February, Emerson Fittipaldi won the Brazilian Grand Prix at Interlagos, a race in which brother Wilson and Carlos Pace also took part. This, then, was a living tradition, one which could be followed and inevitably it is easier for those who follow. The pathfinders have already been there. Expanding on that, at this Grand Prix Milton brought Ayrton along to meet Emerson – a meeting Emerson still remembers, and which led to genuine, lasting friendship.

The first (official!) race of Ayrton Senna's career was five months later – 1 July – at the little kart track beside the Grand Prix circuit.

A week before, Milton invited a man called Lucio Pascual Gascon – known as Tche – to his office in Sao Paulo. Tche, a Spaniard who had been a military engineer and emigrated to Brazil some quarter of a century earlier, was a famed kart engine tuner. He'd worked with Emerson Fittipaldi and Pace when they karted.

Tche already knew a bit about Senna because he'd seen him practising at Interlagos and felt he had a future. The Spaniard would now work for Senna preparing the kart.

Casseb says 'he won, he won, he won. Since he was a kid the only taste he knew was victory. His father sponsored him because his father was in the car components business anyway. I must say that of all the tracks in Brazil that Ayrton was ever on he's breaking all records. Till now the records haven't been beaten.'

At that first race he met another ambitious youngster called Maurizio Sala. 'Ayrton had been testing without racing. He was a really shy boy, not many friends but a lot of determination. I was a guy who could communicate, I could mix with people no problem, he was the opposite of me. Anyway, I was the new up-and-coming man in karts and I'd won the last few races. At Interlagos he beat me …

'In Sao Paulo my life was about racing,' Sala said. 'The first word I spoke was not "Mama" or "Papa" but "car!" When I was a little older I would drive about at great speed with my sister in our parents' old Fiat. I could not reach the pedals so my sister had to do that while I steered the thing. After going to a kart school I started to race them myself. My father said "I make kart for you." I wait one year, two years: nothing, so I buy one myself. The first year I spent racing with my own small team against Ayrton da Silva. He was always first, me second. Every race da Silva and I blam, blam, blam but Ayrton was just a little bit quicker in those days. I used to have to think a lot to stay with him. Da Silva, then, was spectacular and a bit wild – he did not need to think about his driving so much …

'I had an old Volkswagen [his mother's] and I used to put the kart on the top of it and go to the races. Ayrton was from a different background, he got his first kart because his father gave it to him. He had – well, not an easy life but a better life because of the money. His father was very rich but please understand that that never changed Ayrton's character, it was only that he never had to worry about money. He had his own van with a chauffeur to look after him. He was his own mechanic, him and the chauffeur. He was taking it very professionally, always he did. [The van had a workshop in it.] He had the right equipment, the right engine, the right everything.'

The ordinary racers built their own engines at Tche's workshop but Senna didn't. Tche built his engines and folklore has it that whenever the workshop phone rang Senna answered and explained politely that, sorry, Tche couldn't take the call because he was too involved in working on an engine. He was – Senna's engine.

Tche has said that Senna 'always came to a race to win it. For him, the others didn't exist.' This is the first reference, as far as I'm aware, of Senna's absolute single-mindedness. He would always claim that he was not 'programmed' to come second, third, fourth and it must have been there from early childhood – like the restlessness which Viviane sensed would go against him at moments when he needed concentration and control.

Again in the fullness of time he'd learn to concentrate, and he'd master (mostly) control, but at this stage Tche could only make vain exhortations.

Tche: 'Keep cool, keep cool.'

Senna: 'No, for me it's first place or nothing.'

Tche judged the young Senna 'an individualist, always seeking perfection' and this, as far as I'm aware, is the first reference to how, whatever he was doing, he did it completely and with exquisite attention to every detail.

The child was the father of the man.

He and Tche became close, to the point where Tche's visiting card *still* bears a photograph of the finish of that first race; and Tche *still* wears a Senna T-shirt with a logo about missing him. Once in the workshop, *circa* 1998, we were chatting and he suddenly opened his blue overall top to reveal the T-shirt. 'I wear it because I miss him every day,' Tche said, eyes full of a great sincerity.

There was another member of the Brazilian mafia around in those 1970s days. He'd raced karts against Senna and he'd been to England to race single-seaters. He was called Chico Serra and he'd play a pivotal role in Senna's career, but not quite yet.

'I thought,' Sala said, 'Ayrton was really good, aggressive and on the track he was like he is now [1989]: everything or nothing. He started to win races but he never made a lot of friends. His determination was his main thing. We crashed many times because I was competitive, he was competitive, I didn't want to give way and he didn't want to give way.'

And a memory of Interlagos, a track, grass beyond it and two karts locked in combat, the first bearing the number 27, its tiny front wheels pointing straight towards you, its (slightly) larger rear wheels pointing left, left, left and a helmeted head dipped over a big steering wheel.

Senna. Just behind, another kart, another helmet, another visor, like equipment for a lunar landing, and the four wheels all pointing a different way. Sala. The third kart, whoever that might have been, is a long, long way behind.

I've reconstructed this from a photograph, taken at a race *circa* 1976 and I've reconstructed it because it captures something: there it is, beautiful in its innocence, the urge of combat, one young man leading another and both working the steering wheels so hard. Another thought: the position of Senna's wheels suggest something you can't do at all. You used to be able to do it long ago when Jim Clark worked quite other steering wheels in quite other circumstances: four-wheel-drift. A ridiculous notion at Interlagos, *circa* '76 in a suction-orientated kart.

Isn't it?

'Power comes from my education which, you would say, was privileged,' Senna said. 'I was privileged to grow up in a healthy environment. My family gave me this opportunity and have always been behind me. When I have some problem, some question, I have people whom I trust to go back to. I know a lot has been said about my sister's role in my career [a psychologist, don't forget] but in fact it's my whole family which plays a big role. I am close to my parents, my brother and my sister. My sister has three children, which is the most beautiful thing that can happen to you in life.'

Senna moved to the 100cc international category and in 1977 won the South American Championship in Uruguay. He was also Brazilian champion, of course, and would be so four times. Casseb remembers the flavour of those days: 'He had a lot of support because everybody liked him. He would always talk, he never refused reporters. He was promoting the sport. He was very, very serious as a boy, I think too much serious. He seemed like a child who was thirty years old.'

Sala remembers, too. 'In those days I was a close friend of his – no, not close but we used to go out together, he used to come to my house. Conversation wasn't difficult but it wasn't deep. We never talked about motor racing. He couldn't relax when there were a lot of people around. He went out with my sister Carolina. but he was dedicated in his career and she wanted something different.'

In January 1976, he and Milton travelled the 45 minutes from their home to Interlagos to watch a qualifying session for the Brazilian Grand Prix, opening round of the season. Here Senna saw the great ones of the day, not only Fittipaldi and Pace but Lauda, James Hunt, Jochen Mass, John Watson, Jody Scheckter, Jacques Laffite, Carlos Reutemann and, in the beautiful black and gold Lotuses, Ronnie Peterson and Mario Andretti. Evidently young Senna sat on a wall watching, entranced.

Eight years hence, the 'new' Nürburgring was opened in Germany with a celebrity Mercedes saloon car race starring (truly) Lauda, Reutemann, Watson, Scheckter, Hunt and Laffite, among others. None of them won. Guess who did?

To sum up: Senna had attended a leading Sao Paulo school, *Colégio Rio Branco*, and been an average pupil. Staff noticed two things. First, he was not interested in academic work. He'd ask what mark he needed to pass an exam, apply his formidable intellect and data-logging and get it: not more, not less. Second, that those eyes which had real sweetness in them could often be dream-like, too, dreaming of the karting. He spent long hours around his kart *thinking* it all through, races, opponents, circuits, tyres, tactics. He could afford that time because, as he must have known, when the exams loomed he'd only have to ask what mark he needed ...

From 1973 to 1977, you see, he won a clutch of local and then national championships plus the triumphant venture into deepest Uruguay. He was slender and shy. He was seventeen and, orthodoxy would decree, only exploring the temporary delights of karting before, as the eldest son, he knuckled down into Milton's businesses. That would be the course of his life.

To phrase it in such a way, the course seems natural, authentic, perhaps in South American family terms inevitable – and untrue.

He intended to beat the world.

He expressed it once in the simplest terms. 'I have never changed my motivation, I have always wanted to win, I always want to be the first. It is the best way to thrive in motor racing – if not the only way.'

Chapter 3

FOREIGN FIELDS

'I had never heard of Ayrton Senna before,' Angelo Parilla says. 'A friend of my father had a big company in Sao Paulo producing tables and chairs. He had two sons racing in karting and he was friendly with this Ayrton Senna, who was also racing. Ayrton wanted to compete in the World Championships so he got in touch with this man and this man got in touch with me and asked, was it possible for me to help this young guy?'

The Parilla family made karts called DAP in Milan. They were a small but effective firm who manufactured all components except the tyres. 'I said it was possible and asked for something like $6,000, $7,000 for the equipment, mechanics, everything.

'Before he came to Milan his father rang me up and said Ayrton only liked Brazilian food and even when he was in other South American countries [the Uruguayan venture] he wouldn't eat until he got home! I thought we'd see about that. The boy took the plane and I met him at Milan airport. I didn't know what he looked like but I did know he had two sponsors, Coca-Cola and a Brazilian company, Gledson. He wore a Gledson hat so I recognised him. He didn't speak much Italian and I spoke 10 per cent Portuguese. It was 11 o'clock in the morning and I decided we'd go to a good Italian restaurant to see what the boy did like to eat. It was a Florence-style restaurant where they have good meat. [You have to imagine that what follows must have been enacted with gesturing, pointing and a verbal struggle for mutual comprehension.]

Parilla: 'What would you like?'

Senna didn't know, of course.

Parilla: 'Do you like spaghetti?'

Senna: 'I've never eaten spaghetti before, but I'll try it.'

Parilla ordered spaghetti carbonara [coated with minced ham and a creamy sauce] and the boy wolfed it.

Parilla: 'Do you want wine?'

Senna: 'No. Water, thanks.'

Second course Parilla ordered pork and the boy wolfed that, third course dessert, wolfed that.

Parilla: 'Coffee or cognac?'

Senna: 'No, I don't drink coffee or cognac. Water, thanks.'

Parilla: 'Is there anything else you want?'

Senna: 'Spaghetti carbonara again, thanks.'

Parilla: 'Yes, OK, but you can't have the whole meal again, it's beyond my pocket!'

Thus another friendship was born; and it endured. (When Senna returned to Brazil, evidently he said Brazilian food was terrible.) The first few days, of Senna staying in a modest local hotel, were awkward. In fact, 'it took a few days because he spoke very few words of English, probably 50 words, and we tried it in English and that was a disaster. So we evolved something which was between Portuguese, Spanish and Italian and we found out that that worked. His family was very, very rich and at home he lived like a king. Here in Italy he was staying in a small hotel, could hardly speak a word of the language so the first 10 days were really hard for the boy. Those 10 days were important because he was proving to himself that he didn't have to stay in Brazil for the rest of his life. And whenever he drove the kart, immediately everything else vanished for him.

'He was a strange young man, a nice boy, he looked in good condition, didn't give any trouble at all, very quiet, but he seemed strange because he was an 18-year-old who was only interested in going to the track with the kart and testing it. Nothing else. He wasn't interested in going into Milan to have a look at the shops, even.'

Senna tried the DAP at Parma, a track more than 100 kilometres from Milan. Terry Fullerton, also a DAP driver and

World Champion in 1973, was there and it went like this: for almost a week Fullerton tested and evaluated between 30 and 40 engines and then Senna ran them. Towards the end of the week, Angelo's brother Achille said to Senna 'OK, go for it'. Angelo records that 'Senna did 10 laps and he did the same time as Terry. This was astonishing. Parma is difficult, and he'd not driven before on Bridgestone tyres. He'd been used to Brazilian tyres at home. To drive on Bridgestone soft tyres was not easy, so what he did was astonishing.'

Fullerton says of Senna 'he was immediately quick but as a driver he looked a bit raw and obviously not very polished. He did, however, have natural ability. We used to do a lot of testing at Parma. He came down with us, just someone over from Brazil who nobody had heard of and who was paying. People would do that from far-flung places, they'd be reasonably good but you wouldn't think of getting a result out of them – that happened frequently and it still does. But this guy was quick.

'I remember that day. He asked me about his driving and what I thought he was doing wrong. That's quite amusing, looking back. He was throwing the kart about too much going into the corners, he was losing speed because the kart was sideways too much. He used to speak to the factory in some sort of broken Italian-Portuguese and his English was fairly monosyllabic.'

A Dutchman, Peter Koene, was also a DAP driver and was also at Parma that day. 'He was very fast. He wasn't racing, he was playing in the kart. By that I mean he was driving so easily. For him it was easy to drive, you understand. He was a nice man but not very open. Later on, when I used to speak to him more, it was better.'

In the small karting community word soon spread. A Yorkshireman and driver, Mike Wilson, says 'there'd always been fairly good Brazilians but nobody exceptionally good. First thing I heard was that Fullerton had been doing some lap record times at

Parma with a Brazilian sat about two inches off his back bumper bar keeping up with him. In fact, that was the first thing I'd ever head about Senna. I hadn't actually seen it.'

Before we leave Parma, we need to consider Senna's situation. He was perhaps suffering from the first of many bouts of homesickness. He did not speak Italian or much English – his grades in the latter had been average, no more, at school (the just enough philosophy?). That left him isolated and almost mute. Nor could he expect much charity from his fellow karters.

And, lacking the language, you don't even know what they're saying, about you or anything else. And you're eighteen. It is nowhere near manhood, whatever 18-year-olds think. Perhaps a degree of isolation was born at anonymous Parma, at an anonymous test session, and perhaps it never completely went away. In time, he would master Italian well enough to be fully expressive in it and, of course, master the English language to comfortably fluency, but that would take another seven years.

Gazing ahead for a moment, far beyond the buzzing little karts, the seven years were by their nature long years. After his marriage and divorce – and apart from another Brazilian, Mauricio Gugelmin and Gugelmin's wife Stella – he had only one constant companion. Himself. You can find yourself in loneliness and lose a part of yourself, too, but it hardens the resolve, strips away all distractions, concentrates you upon your primary purpose, and no person I have ever met mistook Senna's primary purpose. None of them (including myself) takes any credit for this. Even if you tried, you couldn't miss it. It was as all-pervading as a car crash, wham, everything all at once and whatever else you care to think, you've been in the crash.

Gugelmin, incidentally, had met Senna 'through karting. The Brazilian championship is very competitive and we travelled around the country to many different circuits. He was just about to enter his first World Championship. I had a sponsor with a big lorry and Ayrton couldn't keep his kart safe in the back of his road car so we arranged to put it in my transporter. He was racing in a different category and we became friends then.'

Parilla remembers that 'a week after Ayrton arrived, Tche flew to Italy. He didn't work on the kart, he just came to support Ayrton like a father-figure. The combination between Tche and Ayrton was very, very close. Tche came at his own expense, and he's not a rich man. Ayrton was lucky that Tche came because he could speak Portuguese to him, and that made him feel more at home.'

The little Parilla team (six or seven plus drivers) set off for Le Mans in a car and two vans and when they reached the town in France, famous for its 24-hour sportscar race, they booked into the Ibis hotel. Le Mans was manifestly not Italy in its architecture, language or food. Senna would have to handle the transition. He did.

Karting magazine described Le Mans as 'a purpose-built track of the traditional Continental sinuous type.' The stranger came to compete with the drivers who'd been around, Fullerton, an American called Lake Speed, and Wilson, to select just three. The Brazilians apart, entries were from Austria, Belgium, Switzerland, France, Germany, Denmark, Britain, Italy, Norway, Holland, Sweden and the USA.

Despite the custom-built track, the event was chaotic. The French officials couldn't cope. A pretty girl in a bikini tried to force entry into the paddock wearing an accreditation pass which bore the photograph of a bearded man, and nearly made it.

Karting wrote: 'The second heat contained the new European individual champion Pierre Knops of Belgium and the extremely rapid Senna da Silva of Brazil using DAP equipment. He was only in this series of heats because of a substantial penalty after a high noise reading in the time trials. It was a nice clean start and the Brazilian rapidly disappeared into the distance never to be challenged.' The reporter added naughtily that 'just like the scene at the guillotine during the French Revolution, the French nurses knitted patiently at the first corner, watching the accidents appreciatively.'

Senna won the third heat, but in the sixth 'an early lead was lost when he had to retire.' In describing the Time Trials section after the heats, *Karting* pointed out that 'the Brazilian Senna da Silva had arrived in Europe just 10 days previous to the Championships. By putting up third fastest time with his compatriot [Mario S. de] Carvalho fifth, Brazil was suddenly a force to be reckoned with and there was the intriguing possibility of the Championship going to a non-European for the first time.'

This second section of Time Trials comprised six heats. 'Initially [G.] Leret had the lead from Senna da Silva in the second heat but the Frenchman appeared too inexperienced at this level of competition and was squeezed out by the Brazilian. There then occurred yet another of those strange coincidences that seemed to dog the whole event, and which, although not significant individually, perhaps are worthy of note when viewed in retrospect. We had the flying Brazilian out front followed by [Toni] Zoeserl and Leret. The leader started to slow so that the gap very rapidly diminished to zero then Senna da Silva parked on the grass. The race director prepared to black flag Zoeserl for knocking off the leader. What is of interest here is that this action was the first and only time the race director seemed interested in taking action for alleged bumping tactics and it would have resulted in a Frenchman winning the race. Fortunately he was persuaded to go to the Brazilian's kart and see for himself that the retirement was because it had seized and not because of being hit. It was a close call and many felt jittery at the thought that the Championship might be at the mercy of impetuous officialdom.'

In the last heat, Corrado Fabi's early lead was 'destroyed by Senna da Silva who dragged [Georg] Bellof with him after the latter had only just made the start following a rapid kart change on the rolling lap. They scrapped around with Fabi taking second place only for him to spin while trying to get back in front.'

The finale comprised three runs. In the First Final Senna finished seventh. In the Second, 'Senna da Silva was really steaming and effortlessly dispatched Leret.' Later, 'Speed led Senna da Silva, Mickey Allen and [Lars] Forsman with all knowing that if the American could hang on to the lead until the end he would be Champion. At one stage the Brazilian drew alongside Speed and gained about three inches only for Speed to coolly shut the door at the next corner.'

Many years later, in a drawl straight from his native Jackson, Mississippi, Lake Speed would remember this.

'I took up karting because it was one of those deals where a kid down the street got a go-kart and every child in the neighbourhood had to have one. That was fun karting. It started to get serious when I was about 13. It was also kinda funny because I only came over to Europe once a year for the World Championships, whereas the others had been racing each other all season long. No, no, I hadn't heard of Senna before Le Mans, I didn't know a thing about him.

'Everyone there was talking about this guy who was a hot runner from Brazil, and he was a factory driver for DAP which meant he was one of their front-runners. You've got to keep your eye on the competition a little bit but, no, I really didn't know him. Me just coming in for the World Championships, I was pretty much an outsider. We were at the far end of the pits, about as far away from everybody else as you can get. We didn't even have a stand to put the kart on, we were using a big trash barrow.

'I had one close encounter with him on the track. I was leading the race and Senna had worked his way up to second. I could *feel* someone behind me, one of those instinct things. Sometimes you just know, or maybe it's the sound that you hear. Past the pit area there was a 180-degree right turn and I just *felt* he's gonna try and beat me there, he's gonna try and outbrake me. I was going as hard as I could go.

'I stayed to the left and mentally I paused, I reasoned, and yes, he was trying to outbrake me, yes, he was comin' by but he was going too *hot* and he went off. If I'd turned in we'd have had a crash. I never saw him again in the race. You understand, with an incident like that, well, the competition is so close anyway and at Le Mans it really, really was close. It gets to people. It got to him and he went for it and I recognised he was going to go for it. If I'd tried to fight him it would have cost me or both of us, but as it was I let him go and he was going too hot.'

When Speed says 'going off' he doesn't mean a tremendous crash because Senna recovered quickly, but ... not for long. *Karting* says he was 'using broad new tyres for each race with the 7.0 size on the rear whilst Mickey Allen was having to use the 6.5s as he didn't have the latest style to match the wide rears. Perhaps this was the reason for the ensuing tangle or perhaps it was a tactical error, but as Mickey challenged the Brazilian so he appeared to be unable to match the adhesion of the other and the resultant collision put them on the grass, with only Allen restarting.'

In the Third Final, now irrelevant because Speed had the title, 'Mueller, Allen and Senna da Silva were having a mighty fight which resulted in more than one collision.' Speed finished in fourth place, de Bruijn fifth, Senna sixth, Wilson 18th.

What really happened at Le Mans? 'There were superior compound tyres supplied by Bridgestone,' Parilla says, 'and we tried to get a set for Ayrton but Bridgestone refused. They said it was too late, it wasn't possible, this and that, so I bought a set – they weren't the best, they were medium good I would say – from another Italian team, Bira. We paid 800,000 lire (around £400). We saved the specials for the Finals and before them, in the second heat, Ayrton ran standard compounds and was leading immediately. He went away from everybody, went away at probably 10 metres a lap, which was astonishing to see. He was unlucky because the engine blew up.

'In the First Final he started 16th on the grid and finished seventh. When he came in he said "I need a different sprocket, then I can go a lot quicker." We changed it and in the Second Final he was (almost) leading then he had the accident with Allen. In the Third Final he had to run on standard compounds because by then the specials were really destroyed. He was disappointed because he could have won the World Championship. My personal opinion is that the first year he came to Europe he was absolutely unbeatable [if he had the right tyres, the engine didn't blow and he didn't crash]. He knew nothing about Europe, he knew nothing about the European drivers but he was in absolutely 100 per cent perfect condition. *And after Le Mans he realised he was good enough to win.*'

During Le Mans, Lake Speed, Mike Wilson and Peter de Bruijn spoke not one word to Senna. De Bruijn says 'we were in different teams, of course, he was racing for DAP, me independent. I always stayed by myself, I never drove for an official factory. In karting we were all a little bit close in that maybe drivers would talk, maybe not, but you certainly wouldn't spend all day together.'

They'd start speaking to him and he to them, and – in 1989 and 1993 – he'd show Wilson such kindness that even years after Imola the Yorkshireman couldn't bring himself to watch a Senna video, of which he has several, to the end.

After Le Mans the Parilla team returned to Italy and flew to Sugo, Japan, for a race there. 'In Sugo he was really quick,' Parilla says. 'In Timed Qualification he came fourth but as usual with him he had a big problem with the front tyres. They were good for three or four laps and then he destroyed them because that was his style of driving. In the Final he ran second, had more problems with tyres and finished fourth. We knew he'd return to Europe the following year because he wanted to win the World Championship. It was the biggest thing he wanted. In fact, he flew from Japan to Brazil and we flew back to Italy and we brought his driving overalls, to keep for him for the following year.

'And the following year, a week or two before he was due to arrive, we took the overalls to have them cleaned so he'd look proper. When he arrived and saw them he started to cry. He didn't expect people to care about him like that. He was a nice guy, a really nice guy who became a sort of son to us. He stayed with us, not in a hotel. My house was small, my brother's house was small, so he stayed one week with me, one week with my brother and we sent him for one week to our mother!

'He arrived in May and was with us five months, more or less. He never contacted home and nobody from home called him. I don't know if it was deliberate, I don't know if he was proving his manhood. A few times, a very few times, I tried to ask him about his mother, about his father, but there was no reply really. It's a strange story. It was also something which astonished me. I'd say "look, you want to call, you can call" but no, he didn't want to. It's normal to call home now and again. Was it part of becoming a man? I just don't know. Strange, really strange.'

'He came over again and did much more of a season,' Fullerton says.' He was at a big meeting which they held at Jesolo [a resort on the Gulf of Venice] every May. It was the biggest race after the World Championships. He also competed at San Marino, Wholen in Switzerland and Parma – as well as the World Championships.'

It's little short of amazing that shy and largely mute Senna, who remained a stranger and – in European terms – promising, but no world beater, should have created so many memories of Jesolo. I propose to examine it in some detail.

'By this time,' Fullerton says, 'he was recognised as being very good. He was very single-minded about his racing although in international terms he didn't have that much experience. For example, testing. The way to test is not to go for the fastest time. You try six or seven engines to see which stay consistent so that you get a proper comparison between the engines and you know which one is best. Then, when you've sorted that out, you put them to one side and test the chassis. He wouldn't do that, he wasn't tuned in to doing that. Once he and his mechanics had found a good engine they'd want to put that on, go out and try to get a time.

'Very often in unofficial practice he'd do very good time, then in official practice he'd be surprised when I beat him. I'm sure it was inside him that he had to be the quickest. He kept making that mistake: to be quickest when it doesn't matter and, because of that attitude, you're not quickest when it does matter. I think he learned that over a period of a couple of years. It perplexed him – because he was tackling it the wrong way. He used to come over to the tent where I kept my times to compare them with what he had done. "Why do you keep looking at my book?" "You don't want me to?" "No, not really, I don't." That was it. I never saw him in my tent again.'

Martin Hines, a leading British karter, reflected that 'Senna was a dedicated racing driver but most people are like that, really. Selfish. They want to go out and win for themselves and because they want to win they keep their secrets to themselves. They're not being nasty but they're not going to divulge things they've learnt. I've always been under the impression that people are not born to be absolutely naturally talented drivers. Perhaps what happens is that you're driven [no pun intended] towards motorsport because that's in your blood, but once you get there it's the sort of person you are which determines how successful you will be: at the end of the day it's an absolute gut feeling that you've got to win no matter what the others do. All winners are selfish.'

If Ayrton Senna did not know that already, he did the moment he left Terry Fullerton's tent for the last time at Jesolo in May 1979. He would not forget the lesson. It did not, of course, affect the primary purpose and we can illustrate that with his own words which, although spoken five years later, capture it exactly. 'Physically I was at the end after the Spanish Grand Prix but because I had won I recovered quickly. Winning is the best medicine to regain strength. In the evening I had fully recovered and I drove the race again in my mind. I wanted to enjoy my victory once more that way.'

The witnesses at Jesolo …

Fullerton: 'I've seen him do silly things when he wasn't quickest. At Jesolo for the Champions Cup: at that stage I'd won it every year for about four years and he wanted to win it very badly, that and the World Championship. He wasn't quite quick enough and he still didn't have the experience to know quite what was going on. The track at Jesolo used to get grippier by the half hour during testing. Unless you altered the kart to cope with that you wouldn't go fast enough and it was dangerous because the kart would go on to two wheels.

'I remember the last test session. The track had got grippier, he hadn't adjusted his kart, he was too eager to get out on to the track, he went up on two wheels on a fast corner – right by where I was standing so I could see he didn't lift off – the kart went over and he had an enormous accident. He went into the fence flat out. It was a horrendous moment. The run-off area was so short, then there was an iron fence. He'd have been doing sixty, seventy miles an hour. He hit the barrier first with the kart behind him. He was very badly winded. That was inexperience. It really messed him up. He obviously didn't do a good time after that.'

Mike Wilson: 'At that time the tyres we were using were very, very sticky and it was easy to lift the kart on to two wheels. On the Friday – the race was on a Saturday – he went on two wheels on the fastest corner of the circuit and that also sent him into the fence. So he was injured before he even started the race.'

Parilla: 'In practice he did a lap, two laps, he came in and said "one front tyre is bigger than the other." I said "no, no, impossible." He said "yes, one tyre is bigger than the other." We checked and he was right: one tyre was bigger – by a *millimetre*. Also in practice he had a big crash. My wife took him to hospital, they checked him over and nothing was broken. He came back and raced. We put him in the driving seat because it wasn't possible he could put himself in it. He held position two or three in the race – but after the crash we'd moved the engine from one frame to another, and that had to be done quickly because there was no time. The mechanics did not discover that the carburettor had been damaged on the bottom and ...'

Fullerton: 'In the race he had another horrendous moment. He was overtaking, trying too hard. He dived up the inside of someone and got catapulted out of the kart ...'

Wilson: 'The way my kart had been set up I had a few problems, my kart was slidey. Once I got better grip from the tyres my lap times got better and better, whereas Senna was really quick for the first five or six laps. He was behind me so, down the straight, I held the inside line to try and keep him behind – I wasn't zig-zagging – knowing that if he did get past it would be difficult for me to repass him. He pushed me a couple of times to try and get me out of his way, just touched the back bumper bar to knock me wide, but I managed to keep the kart on the inside. Then at the end of the straight – where there was a fast right-hand corner to a hairpin – he lunged down the inside as I was turning in to the corner. All of a sudden, he was there and it was absolutely impossible to avoid touching each other. Unfortunately we did touch and he turned over and ploughed into the fence. He went completely over two or three times.'

Peter de Bruijn: 'It was good to race against Senna, really good. I found him very hard with himself. I saw races he went off the circuit, was taken to hospital, came back, raced again. I remember at Jesolo the mechanics had to lift him into the kart to race. It was difficult to believe what he demanded of himself. I think, that time at Jesolo, he crashed four times. I understand he was hard on the team, hard on the mechanics but hard on himself, yes, but that is the way I see a racing driver must be. If you want to succeed, and also succeed in everyday life, you must accept that you have to give 100 per cent, and that is what he was giving.'

Fullerton: 'The kid was loaded with ability but he didn't have any fear, which kids of that age tend not to have. That was the year he was married to a Brazilian girl. She had an hour-glass figure ...'

Of Liliane, more in a moment.

Wilson: 'Afterwards, we had an argument at the circuit and then we also had a bit of an argument in the evening at the prize giving. It was in the centre of Jesolo and, if memory serves me, I'd been third. When we had the accident I suffered a puncture which didn't help, you know. I went up for a trophy and, as I was coming back with it, I walked in front of him, not particularly knowing that he was sat there. He turned around and said "you stupid idiot" or something like that. I replied "eff off," that sort of thing, as people unfortunately do. From that accident we were never really friends.' Not yet.

At Jesolo, he was asked about the extent of his future. 'A kart driver to reach Formula 1?' Senna mused. 'For the moment I do not think about it. Brazil already has Nelson Piquet [with Brabham in Formula 1] and is keeping precious the heritage of Emerson Fittipaldi' – World Champion 1972, 1974, still driving for the Copersucar team.

The race at San Marino, Parilla explains, 'really was at San Marino: a street race, a difficult and dangerous circuit. Ayrton was leading the Final, like usual, by a long way and lapping slower karts. There was a big accident at the chicane, karts everywhere, ambulances. It looked like there was only one path through the wreckage and Ayrton went into it but he couldn't get through and stopped so the whole circuit was blocked. The organisers decided that was the end of the race and he'd won!'

The World Championships were at Estoril in 1979.

'He had a big crash,' Hines says. 'He and another driver were absolutely neck-and-neck alongside each other in every corner and eventually they touched. It was a major accident. Senna was lucky to get away with it.'

Senna himself took up the commentary: 'The accident was in the third semi-final where I only needed second place to take pole position for the first final. So I stayed in second place, chasing, right on the tail of the leader and suddenly his engine seized, I hit him and rolled over. I re-started and finished eleventh. The leader was ... Fullerton! That accident eventually cost me the title. The Championship was decided on places in the semi-finals.'

In fact, Senna finished second overall to Peter Koene at Estoril. De Bruijn began speaking to him, the distances diminishing, but 'when I did I saw him as a strong competitor, a very strong one (chuckle). He was very, very fast at times but he didn't use the brakes properly. That was a lack of experience, because he made quite a lot of tactical mistakes. In racing he was a hard man, to talk to he was polite and nice, very polite actually.'

He was eighth after the opening heats.

The karting rules had changed. In the finale, a driver's two best finishes counted from the three Finals with the grid positions for the First Final being used if a tie-break was needed. That grid, pole to the right:

                                    De Bruijn (NL)

                   Wilson (GB)

                                    Schurman (NL)

                   Yasutoshi (J)

                                    Giugni (I)

                   Koene (NL)

                                    Senna (BR)

                   Nielsen (DK)

In the First Final Senna took the lead 'to a roar from the crowd'
who were Portuguese, of course, and connected to Brazil by an
umbilical cord, as it were. *Karting* reported that Silva passed
Koene into the lead. Silva enjoyed seven laps of lead until de
Bruijn tigered back. Suddenly this intense pace and close
competition – in effect we had a solid 20-kart long queue –
resulted in Silva slipping back so the three Dutchmen [de Bruijn,
Koene and Harm Schurman] held the first three places in the
Championship!' De Bruijn won, Koene second, Senna fifth.

In the Second Final, de Bruijn had pole and a win would give
him the Championship, as Senna well knew. Not surprisingly de
Bruijn was in the lead as they snaked through the first right-then-
left bend closely followed by Koene, Schurman, Sugaya
Yasutoshi and Silva, *Karting* reported. 'In characteristic
flamboyant style, the Brazilian took them one by one until he was
behind the leader – the master blocker [de Bruijn, whose] hand
shot up indicating he had a problem: a broken chain. For the last
six laps it was the DAP team with the nervous twitch, because
Koene was pressing Silva hard and both were driving DAPs. One
incident could so easily have eliminated both. With three laps
left, Koene got past Silva without an entanglement.' Koene won,
Senna second.

The organisers deliberated for an hour and a half to be sure
they understood the permutations. If de Bruijn won the Third
Final he'd be Champion. If Koene won he'd be Champion. If

Senna won he'd have a first place and a second, but so did Koene – and Koene had it on the grid place tie-break from the first leg.

Karting reported that 'the track surface temperature had dropped 10 degrees Fahrenheit. No team orders were given, just Peter and Ayrton walking quietly together to discuss that – because, as there was no way the latter would be Champion, there was no objection to him winning the Third Final. All that mattered was that they shouldn't wipe each other out in a brief moment of glory to let de Bruijn through.'

There is extreme doubt about this. The evidence points to the fact that Senna *did not know*.

Because the organisers had deliberated for the hour and a half 'it was almost dark. The enormous stands were packed with fans jeering and whistling at the delay, with a former British team manager proud of his part in winding-up the spectators with cat-calls and stamping,' *Karting* reported. 'De Bruijn led but a mechanical problem halted him. A yellow DAP sweater, waved at Koene, was the signal that he could relax if he wished.'

Koene had already given Senna an 'easy opportunity' to go past. 'The spectators knew the drivers' nationalities, if not the subtleties of the points scoring system, so when Silva took over the lead there was a tremendous roar of appreciation for the Brazilian. Responding to the encouragement of the public and mechanics waving anything that bore the DAP name, Silva adopted a dashing driving style, with rapid flicks and swoops, in the twilight.'

Senna won, Koene sixth, but no escaping the tie-break. If the rules had not been changed, Senna would have been World Champion, the only title in his career which he contested and did not win. Specifically:

	Koene	Senna
First Final	2	5
Second Final	1	2
Third Final	6	1

'He lost just by the rules,' de Bruijn says. I explain to de Bruijn that this irritated Senna (or worse) long after. 'You say he was still upset about it 10 years later well, yes, that must be. At Estoril, the two drivers who should have won it [de Bruijn and Senna] did not win it! You have a depth of feeling. All the good drivers have that. There's nobody who goes home laughing if they've lost. When I lost in 1979 I did not race again for three months. I was completely fed up with everything. Your whole career is to beat the best, to win the World Championship. You can be five times second but it's better to be one time first, no? So when something like that happens, when you think you're going to win and you don't, it's difficult to express what feelings you get. I still have the same now (1995). I run a lot of drivers in karts and every time we lose I feel sick. I think it's normal.'

'Of the three Finals, he won one, I won one and we had the same points,' Koene says. 'To win, all I had to do was finish in front of another de Bruijn. I did it but Senna thought he was World Champion. About five minutes after the end of the race everybody knew it was me. He was very disappointed. I can't remember if he spoke to me. I didn't know him well. That began the next year.'

Senna said 'it was the year the rules were changed. Previously, if it was still a tie it was decided on your results in the Third Final. Now it was decided on the semi-final results.'

In a magazine called *Kart and Superkart*, a journalist wrote: 'Silva crossed the line the jubilant winner of the last Final, thinking he had won the World title. The scenes were something else. Everyone, including me, was wandering round thinking da Silva was World Champion and indeed da Silva was ecstatic with joy in his pit, but down the other end of the pits Koene was being hugged and kissed by all and sundry, obviously realising *he* had made it. The scene changed dramatically a few moments later when da Silva had had the situation explained to him, and was inconsolably sobbing in the back of the DAP pits, where a DAP mechanic was also in tears – either of joy at a DAP win or of sorrow at da Silva's misfortunes! Between the two stood Angelo Parilla, not knowing whether to laugh or cry in his greatest moment of triumph.'

Parilla remembers that in the 'First Final, Ayrton felt something wrong, he was checking the engine all the time and he was fifth. My brother checked the engine and found the problem. Ayrton started sixth in the Second Final and finished one metre behind Koene. He started the Third Final like a rocket and at one stage he was going away at 20 metres a lap. At Estoril they used the grandstand which they use for the Formula 1 Grands Prix and it was full, 10,000, 20,000 people. You have to realise this was Portugal, you have to realise the links with Brazil, all the crowd were for Senna. He was going along the straight in front of the grandstand punching the air. My brother and I knew he wasn't Champion but he didn't know. He finished the race, he was jumping around, he was kissing everybody. Between my brother and I, we said we have to tell him. I said: "Look, Ayrton, you're not World Champion, you're in position second." The boy cried like I've never seen anybody cry in my life.

'I still say he wasn't second at Estoril but he *won*. Normally, if people have the same number of points, who wins the Last Final is Champion and it had been like this for ever and ever. They changed that and it was decided by a grid position – crazy, crazy, absolutely crazy.'

To all intents and purposes, Senna remained another karter, albeit a fast and determined example of the species. He wasn't. Perhaps the first authentic piece of Senna mythology lies here. Reflecting, de Bruijn says 'for me the most interesting thing with

Senna in karting was that – maybe because I had problems in finding grip – he always had a lot of it. He was constantly going onto two wheels and having to control the kart like that because of too much grip, but he could control the kart on two wheels. The control was not the problem for him but it was for most of them, they could not do it (chuckle).

'In those days, if you had big grip you slid a lot. I tried to find grip by using the settings on the kart, but he gained a great deal of it by pushing very hard. He was one of the first to run wide settings on the rear, for example. I was running narrow for grip and he already had too much! That showed he had a certain style, a certain way of driving. This grip must have come from the way he drove because the others did not have it. I don't know how to explain it, I just don't know. Probably it was the way he pushed the kart into the corner – he told me later that he never understood how it was possible we were running *our* settings! He did not understand how I could drive with the narrow. He'd thought about those things, like he always did.'

De Bruijn is reiterating the accepted wisdom: wider = less, narrower = more. 'I presume he was at least five, six centimetres wider in the rear. He could only handle that because of the way he drove and it was fascinating to watch.'

Mike Wilson explores the mythology. 'What Peter de Bruijn says is correct, but I don't think Peter knew that Senna used a wheelbase which was 101cm and the karts we were using were 104: the shorter the wheelbase the more grip the kart would give you. If Peter or I had gone out with the wider settings on the 104cm the rear would have been so slidey it would have been impossible to keep it on line. The shorter wheelbase gave him a *hell* of a lot of grip in the corners so his settings went wider and wider.

'His kart was the same length from bumper bar to bumper bar as the rest, but what they did was move the rear axle 3cm forward, and in doing that they redistributed the weight. The seat position is the heart of the kart. He liked it like that because he always used it like that. In Jesolo, when he went on to two wheels and into the fence, it was because he was using the short-wheeled kart. I don't know why he liked it like that. Probably his style of driving. Even now you get people wandering round the paddock watching what others do then setting up their karts the same as the fast boys do. It is wrong. Everybody has his own style of driving to get the best out of what the kart can give him, and that is what Ayrton was doing.'

You see it for what it is: not copying the fast boys but going his own way.

Parilla says that 'Ayrton's speed was difficult to believe. The frame would jump like *this* or like *that* and he would stay full throttle. That's something natural, absolutely natural. It is true he liked the wide setting and this was, I would say, five or six years before anybody else discovered it was what you needed. When a race started he was immediately quick. I remember once at Jesolo he pulled far away from everybody in the first lap and in karting it's usually only one or two metres. Not with him. It came from the setting that he had and the power in himself that he had. In karting there was no comparison with him, no comparison, like he proved later in racing cars.'

To which Martin Hines adds: 'Terry Fullerton was rated as the best kart driver in the world for many years, and the only driver I ever heard Terry have a good word for was Senna. He was the only one that he really did rate. He was brilliant, at the end of the day he was brilliant.'

To which I add that, when he had become Formula 1 Champion and had measured himself against Piquet, Niki Lauda, Prost, Nigel Mansell and anybody else who cared to have a go at him, he was asked on Brazilian television who was the best driver he'd raced. The interviewer muttered *Piquet? Prost?*

'Terry Fullerton,' Senna said.

Chapter 4

CHANGE OVER

In 1980, Senna came back to Europe for the third time and contested the Champions Cup at Jesolo again. 'By halfway through the race I realised I was reeling him,' Fullerton says. 'I could see that he was looking across the hairpin at me getting closer and closer. Then I got this feeling I was going to be sick. Maybe it was the physical exertion, the adrenalin, but when your mind is tuned into something like that everything else seems secondary.'

Fullerton did catch him, they touched wheels, Fullerton (literally) held on and won. They were by the swimming pool next day but Senna 'just sat in a deckchair not joining in the fun. All of a sudden he jumped out of his seat and pushed me into the pool. After that the smile came back to his face.'

The World Championship was at Nivelles, Belgium, which de Bruijn describes as one of the most complete tracks: 'fast but with slow parts and very difficult because you can't have gears on the karts, you know, so to go fast round these slow corners wasn't easy.'

Karting reported that 'the hopeful programme spaces for Mexico, Peru and Uruguay failed to materialise and there were many attempts to slip drivers into other countries at the last minute. The angry parents of a Dutch driver made an enormous scene when he was denied acceptance as a Japanese.'

De Bruijn competed and so did two future Formula 1 drivers, Stefano Modena who won the Time Trials section (Senna tenth) and Ivan Capelli. In fact Senna spun in the Time Trials but recovered quickly. He was ninth after the Heats.

In the First Final, *Karting* said: 'Silva overtook Gysin with the Brazilian waving his fist, apparently over baulking by the Swiss.

Meanwhile Fullerton now had the lead followed by Silva and Gysin. The front eight were condensing into a solid column and Gysin's thrust past Silva sent the Brazilian spinning off.'

Gysin can't remember the accident's circumstances or when he first met Senna. He does remember a comradeship forged and united by desire. 'You are rivals in this sport and you just want to win. Our rivalry was not to the extent of killing somebody, but we certainly wanted to win. That was of the utmost importance. I thought highly of him. Although we were rivals, there were always small problems, not big ones, and we were always rubbing each other up. I find it difficult to explain. It really was the little things.

'Before Nivelles, I'd never had an accident and it was what we call a *carambolage*, a coming-together. No bones were broken or anything of that sort. When I look back, Senna had to improve himself as a kart driver as we all had to improve ourselves. Apparently he was a loner. He might have belonged to a team but he remained a loner. He could not accept to be second or third. He wanted to stand apart from the others. Again, I find it difficult to explain what exactly I mean by a loner. He didn't like it when he couldn't be number one and he didn't show it but we all knew. If you even try and hide your disappointments it's quite something.'

Koene remains slightly awe-struck by a moment at Nivelles. He thought he saw *levitation* at a corner. 'It seemed as if Senna lifted the kart, turned it in mid-air and *then* took the corner. I knew then that he was very, very special.'

Senna won the Second Final. He made 'an attack on Gysin (in the racing sense) and took over the lead with a waved thank you.' Going into the Third Final, and the rules the same as 1979, six drivers could win the Championship: De Bruijn, Gysin, Jorg Van Ommen (West Germany), Alan Gates (South Africa), Senna and Fullerton. At the first corner de Bruijn and Gysin were together, a fractional gap from Silva and Van Ommen (*Karting*).

De Bruijn remembers 'I took the lead in the beginning and after some laps Gysin overtook me but I did not try and fight with Gysin because I knew Senna was just behind and for sure it would be a hard race. My decision not to do anything was based on the hope that Gysin and I would pull away from Senna and we did, by 50, 60 metres.'

It was a risk because, as *Karting* pointed out, 'if they stayed in this order Silva would be the Champion. De Bruijn, however, took back the lead and the front pair separated away from Silva, who had earlier chopped Gates.' So de Bruijn took the Third Final and the Championship, Senna second overall. *Karting* reported that 'Silva had come close to getting the title and was less than happy at coming second. How he must have wished that Gysin could have stayed in the lead for the last few laps!'

De Bruijn says that 'afterwards, Ayrton was disappointed but every driver is like that. It was especially true in his case because he'd lost it the year before as well. Now he'd had to win the Third Final or me not win it.' In fact Senna could have taken the title by finishing third, provided de Bruijn didn't win. 'Ayrton had had the pressure of six drivers being able to take the Championship, so he was disappointed, sure, but that's normal.'

The 1980 South American Championships were in Uruguay again and Angelo Parilla went there. 'We had a good time, no, we had a *really* good time. Ayrton was one and a half seconds quicker than everybody else. It was a nice place, a nice hotel and we never went to bed before 4 o'clock in the morning! He had a number of friends with him, some from Argentina, some from Brazil, and he was enjoying himself.' And here it was, the side of the man so few saw.

Senna was already thinking of single-seaters, the next step from karts, although the missing World Championship gnawed at him. Most unusually in a young, ambitious driver who shouldn't look backwards, he'd interrupt his single-seater career in both

1981 and 1982 and return to contest the Championships. Moreover, in 1981 he'd do three kart races and in 1982 he'd do two.

Some of the precise details of how Senna came to race in cars are misty, others quite clear. For instance, Sala has said: 'Ayrton started in karts [only] because his father gave him one and the kart took him towards motor racing. I don't think that in those early days he wanted to be a Formula 1 driver or if he did he never let us know. But he was determined to do things perfectly and that's what he did in karts. He won everything in South America.'

The Brazilian heritage helped Senna because, as I've said, another Sao Paulo karter, Chico Serra, had been to England racing single-seaters with the van Diemen factory team in Norfolk (in 1977) and now began to mention the name Senna to Ralph Firman, running van Diemen. If you were going to race cars, this was the best place to start.

It was time for Senna to make the decision: to go upwards, stay in karts or get out of the whole thing. There were no other options. Many people assume this is a natural and inevitable decision because most kids start in karts, it's relatively cheap (then, anyway), it's (literally) thumping good fun as well as a valid way to find out if you are any good.

Actually karting was not and is not a kiddies' playground – in the late 1970s one driver a year was being killed – nor was it a playground in another sense, which was why Fullerton was testing six or seven engines before turning a knowing eye to the chassis. Most Formula 1 drivers started exactly here and I won't bore you with the list except to say that between 1978 and 1980 Senna had raced, as we have seen, against Stefano Modena, Ivan Capelli, Aguri Suzuki, Stefan Bellof and Corrado Fabi.

Karts can be, if you wish, an end in themselves, a complete world. The next step is on to a ladder and in 1980 the ladder had specific rungs: Formula Ford 1600 leading to Formula Ford 2000 leading to Formula 3 leading to Formula 1. The air gets more rarefied and harder to breathe the further up you get. A lot of kart people stay contented kart people, like Martin Hines. Few, entering single-seater cars in Formula Ford 1600, intend to stay there except for the minimum time, which is one season. They're already gazing up the ladder towards interesting commodities like fame, fortune and immortality – as well as, on one rung or another, finding out how good they really are, how high they can climb.

The ladder is why the decision is so big. You are very probably committing the next decade of your life to it and this is not something to be done lightly. For a start it's going to cost a packet and you might end up broke very quickly, although that was one factor Senna didn't need to worry about. Milton was eminently able to finance a season of Formula Ford 1600 for his son if he chose to do so.

Soon enough a shy, quiet, polite, self-contained young man would present himself on the doorstep of an office beside Snetterton circuit, a most modest place in the quiet and rural county of Norfolk, and ask for a Formula Ford 1600 drive. His wife with the hour-glass figure would be a sensation, no less, in such parts.

Reginaldo Leme was a TV commentator based in Sao Paulo: 'For the first year in England it was at least fifty per cent of his father's money.'

'Ayrton went to college in Sao Paulo (business studies),' Casseb says. 'His father wanted him to stop racing and help him in the factory so Ayrton went there in order not to disappoint his father. But his father felt he was really unhappy so he decided to give Ayrton another push.' We shall hear Senna's own revealing account of what happened at a later moment, but before we reach the change over from karts to cars we need to listen to the three karters we've already met because, in retrospect, each has something of significance to say.

Hines: 'A kart reacts so quickly because it is so small and light '

Koene: 'If somebody handles a kart well they can handle a Formula 1 car. I thought he would end up in Formula 1, yes. I thought that was his intention. He was as good as that. When I got to know him better he was still very close, he didn't speak before the races, only during qualifying. I saw him years later when he was driving Formula 1 at Zandvoort and I spoke with him and he was very nice, very normal, you understand.'

Fullerton: 'The last time I spoke to him was one day at Silverstone in '83. He looked quiet, confident but he hadn't changed that much. I think he'd grown up a bit. He'd had a good feel for a kart. I'd sensed he was going to go on with this as a career. When I heard he'd started to do cars I was sure he'd get to the top.'

It was a sentiment shared by someone else. Ayrton Senna.

A small, functional office butted on to a factory near the London to Norwich Road. The modest racing circuit was not far away. It had all the feel of a rural, pastoral place, reflecting its setting: East Anglia is a labyrinth of lost lanes where, through tall hedgerows, you can glimpse old barns or thatched cottages nestled into the sleep of centuries. You're much more likely to hear the hum of a combine harvester racing to finish the harvest than the shriek of a racing car itself, unless you go to the place in the fields beside the London road. It is called Snetterton.

Early spring '81. The young man standing before Ralph Firman seemed confident. However far he'd travelled to be here – half the world – Firman scarcely felt he was a stranger, even at this first meeting; felt, in fact, that he knew him already.

Firman, a stocky man of great presence, would explain the Chico Serra connection and how 'we maintained a good contact with him. He talked a lot about a driver called Senna and he kept saying "he's coming, he's coming." For whatever reason it took him two years to come. I'd not seen him until he walked into my office but I did feel I knew him because Chico had been telling me how good he was.'

That very, very first impression: the confidence.

'We had dinner at a restaurant, The Doric, in Attleborough, a nice restaurant, English-stroke-Italian,' Firman says. Attleborough is typically Norfolk, a market town moving at its own pace and The Doric one of a row of venerable houses facing a small green. It had a feel of quality about it: a pleasant bar and beyond that tables in a stately wood-panelled dining room.

'His English was very poor but I'd got used to that kind of thing, particularly with Brazilians.' Serra apart, Firman had run Carlos Pace, Roberto Moreno and Raul Boesel. 'We sat there and we did a deal. Like any driver with van Diemen he settled in Norfolk, rented a house. We always arranged things like that for new drivers. It was a nice little two-bedroom bungalow just south of Norwich.'

Another impression was gathering in that dining room in Attleborough: Senna knew precisely what he wished to do, and that was win motor races: not compete in them, win them.

Senna brought to England his young bride Liliane (née Vasconcelos de Souza) who, it would seem, didn't like the food, the climate or her husband's total absorption with 1,600cc Formula Ford cars. Senna never spoke about this and Liliane, who remarried after the divorce and has two children, has never done either, so far as I am aware.

Senna did however confess to Angelo Parilla that he himself found 'a big problem with the weather and the food was a big problem, too. He loved the food in Italy, he loved everything in Italy. I know that staying in England was particularly hard for him but he knew it was necessary and he did it.'

Senna remained in England (although wintering in Brazil, of course) until 1985, through Formula Ford 1600, Formula Ford 2000, Formula 3 and Formula 1 with Toleman and Lotus.

In 1981, he would contest – or, more accurately, taste – three 1,600cc championships scheduled to go on simultaneously during the season: the P&O, sponsored by the shipping company; the Townsend Thoresen, another shipping sponsor; and the RAC – the Royal Automobile Club, guardian angel of domestic motorsport.

He'd meet many new circuits although they soon became familiar. There are many meetings but few circuits so you find yourself returning and returning. Between 1 March and 29 September – the span of the season – Senna would drive Brands Hatch five times, Mallory Park four times, Snetterton three …

This is of enormous benefit to the young driver because once he becomes familiar with Brands Hatch he can forget about simply finding his way round and start on the more important business of refining himself immediately prior to exploiting himself and, just as important, familiarity becomes an equalisation. All the kids know their way round so direct comparisons between them become valid, especially since they all have the same Ford 1600 engine.

The cars are twitchy little tyrants and, with all that fearless, youthful ambition fuelling them, the races often move from Armageddon to Götterdämmerung and back again. Derek Warwick, looking back as an established Formula 1 driver, once said: 'I don't know how we did it in 1600, I don't know how we steered them in straight lines, I don't know how we dared.' Firman offers a judgement on that, too. 'Put it this way, they're difficult to handle and go quickly with.'

He was now into another world and a complex one, a world with several clearly defined elements which interlock. An example. In Firman's office, and quite by chance, Senna would meet a Norfolk man whom he would meet again and again. He was called Calvin Fish. 'He knew of me. I was at the factory one day – I was driving a van Diemen engine. This was before he ever drove a car for Ralph. Ralph said "I've got this Brazilian over, he's called da Silva, he knows your name well." Ayrton had obviously read about me. He was extremely polite. It's difficult because you're not a Brazilian and there was a language barrier. We used to laugh about it a little bit. I think he spoke more English than sometimes he'd let on, but if the situation demanded it he'd suddenly say: "I don't understand what you're saying".'

At this moment, van Diemen did not have their 1981 car ready. A mechanic, Malcolm (Puddy) Pullen, says 'I think we were short of parts or something. We decided to put him out in the last year's model just so he could learn to drive.' Pullen's thought processes were as you might expect, and understandably so: Senna was 'just another foreign driver, you know, like you get.' This did not survive Senna's first session in the car at Snetterton. 'He had something about him and it's hard to put your finger on exactly what. It was *something*. He had this very professional approach, he was very precise about everything. He'd come in and say "the car does this, the car does that, and so on".'

Firman was watching closely, too. Speaking in 1989, he told me 'you find some people who come out of karts – which have got a fair power-to-weight ratio and quite grippy tyres – and take to it straight away, others take longer.' That first time, on a quiet day against the rural, pastoral backdrop? 'It was obvious he was very, very good. I could see he was going to be an excellent driver. You can tell by the way a driver handles the car, by the way he controls it. He was fairly quick from the word go. He started in a less-than-perfect car (the '80) and, like many drivers, he was too keen to go quickly too soon, but I had no doubt the guy was going to win races. He was self assured, calm, he was very hard and demanding, but not in an unpleasant way. He was very sure, which I think he's always been. He hadn't been in the car much before the first race.'

We must not pass over Snetterton itself too quickly. It is – and I am not being unkind – a place to dream, perhaps, but not a place to make your dreams come true. That will have to be done elsewhere, on the great and famous circuits.

Senna recollected. 'For sure the karting enabled me to go fast. It is much, much easier than FF1600 where, apart from the basic car control, you cannot use the experience you get from a kart because they are so slow – there is no grip.'

This is not a contradiction. Karts are twitchy little tyrants, too, and a wonderful place to learn the delicate nuances of control; the lessons remain valid in FF1600 where, as Firman has said, handling and speed are an elusive combination; and we shall have the evidence of another driver to corroborate that, too, soon enough.

Here are a young man's first successive steps into motor racing, the meetings arriving quickly. There are hints of future greatness in them, as there were with the karting, but you have to look closely.

1 March 1981. The Club circuit at Brands Hatch – a round of the P&O Championship and the only round Senna would contest, thereafter concentrating on the TT and RAC. Brands was an awkward place to begin, all downhill-uphill loops and corners, adverse cambers and an alarming rush along the start-finish straight to a drop at Paddock Hill so sharp you can leave your stomach behind. He qualified in mid-field, behind the other two van Diemen works drivers, Enrique (Quique) Mansilla and Alfred Toledano; and behind, also, a crisp, neat businessman running a Royale-Nelson more as a love affair than a career. He was called Rick Morris.

'In the race he drove very aggressively and very wildly and I thought: Oh, it's another Brazilian. We'd had a trail of people like that, Chico Serra and Roberto Moreno and so on. He was wild at Clearways. I have a distant impression of that.'

This is an unfolding right-hand curve of a corner from the Club circuit on to the Grand Prix circuit, but so wide that it permits several permutations as you feel for the apex. Once you're familiar with it you find the apex every time, but when you're unfamiliar ...

'Obviously he was wild,' Firman says defensively, 'but he matured, both as a person living in England and as a driver.'

Pullen, on the pit-lane wall watching as the small cars – capable of 125 miles an hour – darted by during the twelve laps of the race, found himself making a different kind of judgement. 'I felt he was working his way into the racing without making a fool of himself, I felt he was building himself up.'

Enrique Mansilla (van Diemen) 10m 18.1s
Rick Morris (Royale-Nelson) 10m 19.5s
Dave Coyne (van Diemen) 10m 20.4s
Alfie Toledano (van Diemen) 10m 24.6s
Ayrton da Silva (van Diemen) 10m 26.1s

The British magazine *Autosport*, which must be one of the most comprehensive and well-informed of its kind in the world, carried this astonishing paragraph constructed by a journalist who can't have seen Senna before and constructed only on the evidence of that fifth place eight seconds behind the winner: 'Making an impressive FF1600 debut at Brands Hatch was Brazilian 100cc kart star Ayerton [sic] da Silva. Undoubtedly we shall hear more of this young man.'

Thruxton. The first round of the TT Championship. *Autosport* reported: 'All eyes were on Ayerton da Silva who engaged and got the better of Mansilla in a thrilling all-angles tussle.' Morris won, Senna third.

At that meeting a diffident young photographer moved quite by chance into his life. In 1981 he was as Senna was: making his way into his profession. He was called Keith Sutton. 'I was working for a Brazilian magazine and they asked me to take pictures of Brazilian drivers racing in England. At Thruxton I did a lot of shots of him, portraits, action, everything. Liliane, his wife, was extremely attractive, you know. She spoke very little

English. At Thruxton she'd walk through the paddock and everyone would stop what they were doing. She had the Brazilian shape, the Brazilian bum. She was very nice.'

Brands Hatch. Second round of the TT. Pullen says 'the new car was finished and he had that. It was a wet race and he just drove away into the distance. You could see he was going to be a winner. I mean, he was a winner. At Brands he was overjoyed – like I was. There is no feeling on earth like winning for the first time. As he went over the line Liliane nearly picked me up off the ground. She was ecstatic, nearly in tears.'

Keith Sutton had gone to Brands and 'Ayrton recognised me from Thruxton, remembered I'd been taking pictures there. He said "are you a professional photographer?" "Yes, of course." "I need pictures doing. Can you help me out?" "Yes, of course." He won his heat, then he won the race and there I was on top of the rostrum doing the shots – fantastic light, him and his wife. Brilliant. Basically that was it. I tried to get to as many Formula Ford races as possible, doing shots for him. He paid me for the pictures. I was just doing prints from the negatives.'

Thereby hangs a tale. A young driver from Bristol, Steve Lincoln, was in that race which Senna won. I knew nothing about Lincoln but I'd wanted to talk to him for a previous book. He seemed to have vanished, and all I could discover was that he came from the Bristol area. A mention of him in the book produced – by chance, and many years later – a sad postscript. It came from Roger Orgee, a former driver who eventually 'ran my own F3000 team until about 1996, when it all went wrong. I was in Formula Ford 2000 and Steve was a young enthusiast. We got him in a car and I helped him quite a bit. He was very, very promising and I think he won the South West Championship in Formula Ford then got into it at the national level. He was incredibly quick, but he hadn't got any money and one day he just turned round and walked away from it. He was strong-willed like that. He went to work for London Life, I think, on the sales side.'

That wet and distant Brands day, he and Senna were on the same track with, in overall terms, the same chance. There were two heats (Lincoln fourth in Heat 1, Senna winning Heat 2) and a 15-lap final. Senna won it in 15m 07.2s, Lincoln third on 15m 17.6s. The *Autosport* report is not precise. 'The final began in atrocious conditions but it seemed to matter very little to the Brazilian, who fought off challenges from Andy Ackerley who spun off trying to outbrake the Brazilian on the outside line into Druid's and Steve Lincoln, who fell foul of the conditions – worsened at this stage by a setting sun – at Surtees [corner].'

This suggests that Lincoln was pressing (or trying to press) Senna before Toledano got through after whatever happened at Surtees. If that's the case, they must have been separated by a few yards. Sport is a beautiful mistress but a cruel master. Senna would become a global presence, Lincoln – so promising – would have a career almost nobody remembers. He died of cancer at the end of 1992.

Coyne explains that Senna 'kept himself to himself. He didn't really speak to many people, although he learnt English quite quickly. He knew he was good. He wouldn't give anything away but he was a pleasant person. He had good equipment, good everything, and it was unusual to find someone with the talent to be able to use it all. That's what he did.'

Senna was already thinking ahead, far, far ahead. He needed Sutton's pictures to publicise himself in Brazil so that, one distant day when he might be looking for sponsorship and his father was no longer paying the 50 per cent, getting it would be much easier. He knew Moreno and Boesel in Formula 3 and Nelson Piquet in Formula 1 would command most of the column inches in the Brazilian press and so he'd have to push himself in. If you've been dallying with the notion that he wanted the pictures for reasons of vanity or to put in a scrapbook, forget it. He intended to make history, not record it.

Already, too, he had begun to wreathe a kind of mythology around himself. He'd go to the pub with the boys, but rarely speak. Many found him shy although – obviously – that ceased as soon as he was in a car.

'We'd go testing and he'd do a particular time, say 1 minute 30 seconds,' Pullen says. 'Ayrton would then reason "I can go two-tenths quicker there, three-tenths quicker at that corner but there's no point because we're only testing. When we are qualifying for the race I'll go five-tenths quicker." He always would. That amazed me. He would never put everything on the absolute limit in testing because, as he pointed out, you might go off and once you go off that's the end of your testing for the day. He always knew how much quicker he could go. Instinctive talent? That's right.' Liliane was endearing herself to the team, too. 'She used to bake these amazing banana cakes and bring them down to the workshop for the mechanics. I'd never eaten anything like them – delicious. It was a treat for us. I think it must have been a Brazilian recipe.'

Mallory Park. He took pole and *Autosport* wrote: 'Mansilla made a storming start from row two and drove all the way around the outside line at Gerrard's [a big curve] to take the lead in opportunistic style, while da Silva held off Ricardo Valerio, Toledano and then the works Royale of Morris. Valerio and da Silva swapped positions a couple of times in the opening laps before the Mexican dropped back to fourth on lap 4 and left da Silva in second place ahead of Toledano. Over the next few laps da Silva homed in on the leader, cutting a lead of several seconds to just a length by lap 11. On the last lap da Silva made a faster exit to Gerrard's than Mansilla. He came up alongside but was unceremoniously edged off on to the grass by the Argentinian and angrily had to settle for second place with Toledano right on his tail.'

What followed is still recounted in hushed tones and one witness, who forbade me to use his name, says 'their tempers began to bubble.' The two drivers had to be forcibly pulled apart, someone arm-locking Senna round the neck to do it. Keith Sutton found something thrust over his camera lens so he couldn't take more than a couple of pictures.

Senna was second again at Mallory two weeks later, this time behind Morris who 'nipped' through near the end and won by 0.1 of a second after a frantic race. The pace was so 'fantastic' that the lap record, which had stood secure since 1974, was broken by Toledano (who did 49.40s and clipped 0.2 of a second off it).

Snetterton. Wind dragged rain over the flatlands, where Senna squeezed out a small but commanding lead and held it from Morris. During that race an affable Formula Ford 2000 team manager was 'walking along the grass not really paying much attention. I saw this little black and yellow car in the lead but only by a few yards. It was Senna, just another Brazilian, people were saying. It started to rain and I looked on the next lap and he was half a lap ahead. Everyone else had slowed down and he hadn't. I thought: *My God*. I walked up to him afterwards and said: "I'm Dennis Rushen." His wife was there, the lady with the hour-glass figure who used to wear jump suits. I said that I ran a 2-litre van Diemen team and "if you want to do 2-litre in 1982 you can have the whole British and European season for £10,000." I plucked that figure off the top of my head. It was a really cheap deal but, I mean, anyone who can do that in the wet is special. Very, very special. I hardly spoke to him any more throughout the season.'

Oulton Park. 'I was on pole by quite a margin,' Morris says, 'half a second or something, and up the hill to the double-apex right-hander Senna came up the inside of me and literally banged me out of the way. We'd have been doing about 90mph, third gear. You come up, you brake, you turn in. It's not an accepted overtaking place, especially on the first lap. But he did it. His front wheel was to the side of my car, I was already moving out of the way and he put me on to the grass.'

Morris remembers that 'two things' were 'very characteristic of his driving: aggression and force. But everyone drives aggressively in Formula Ford 1600. The trick is to get away with it, skilful enough to get away with it.'

As Morris has already said, 'we'd had a trail of people like Serra and Moreno and I always got on well with those guys. Ayrton was the first Brazilian I didn't really click with in the way I had with all the others. I mean, we used to have a laugh but he wasn't a laugher, he was very serious, he seemed introverted, he seemed unsure and I never knew whether it was an arrogance or an introversion.

'People behave soberly for various reasons and I couldn't make up my mind. We got on well, there was friendship, but that was later, in 1982 not 1981.'

This is interesting because others will say it too: there was no friendship while you were in direct competition with him because he did not wish friendship then. He wished to beat you and any form of sentiment might dilute that. If he did like you – and he seems to have liked most people – he pressed that far down within himself and ignored it. It made for loneliness. He accepted that it would. In this sense, he was not an ordinary person at all. And he was only twenty-one ...

Mallory Park. A good start, a six-second lead held comfortably to the end. Firman is not a man given to extravagant words but he is insistent about this: 'From about the middle of the season I thought he was going to be World Champion. It wasn't any particular moment, it was a gathering impression.' Funny. Pullen felt that, too.

Knowing eyes watched Senna's fledgling career unfolding, among them Alex Hawkridge of the (fledgling) Toleman Grand Prix team, who quickly concluded that Senna was dominating the races as no man had since Jim Clark. Small Formula 1 teams, as Toleman were, constantly scanned the horizon for potential talent because they didn't have the budget to buy already created stars. Here was the talent. By Senna's third race – Brands, and the first win – the adjustment from karts had been decisively made.

Silverstone. Morris recounts with particular relish, 'that 1600 race is a legend of Silverstone, quite amazing. He got away and I was stuck in the pack. I caught up with him with about four laps to go and we were towing round together. He was very quick into the corners – another characteristic of his driving, quick to the apex, sort out the consequences afterwards – but I was coming out quicker. My style was slow in, quick out – because in 1600 you can scrub off the speed if you're not careful.

'I went to overtake him on the back straight on the last lap, going into Stowe Corner. I went to the inside, he moved to the inside, I moved to the outside with him alongside me and we were at full bore: 125mph. He had me on the grass – not an uncommon thing in 1600 halfway down the straight. I had two wheels on the grass. I backed off, I followed him and we came under the *Daily Express* Bridge towards the chicane.'

The whole approach has been changed beyond recognition now, made into a coiling snake called the Complex. In 1981 you came under the bridge [the *Daily Express* Bridge] and flowed straight ahead to the chicane. The chicane was like a circular traffic island and tight. It was the eye of a needle and positioning all-important. Once you got the inside line, logic insisted that you had it all to yourself. No room for two.

You must picture a couple of small rockets hammering towards it. 'I went to the right, to the inside,' Morris says, 'he blocked me there and he thought he'd won the race.'

Picture, now, the rockets nose to tail, Senna positioned to snake through, the right-hand line feeding him directly into the chicane. Morris again: 'I went to the outside and I waited until he braked, then I came right across his bows from the outside. I went straight across the chicane' – the kerbing formed a hump and the whole car bounced – 'but inside the yellow penalty line.'

Morris won.

'Ayrton was unbearable. Apparently he went past the pits going like this [shaking his fist], he was shouting at Ralph [Firman] when he got back, there was talk of protests; but, you know, I'd got the corner. I was so wound up about the incident on the straight. Outside line at the chicane on the last lap isn't exactly a healthy thing to try. Perhaps that's why I got away with it – because he wasn't expecting it. I didn't speak to him that day but we talked about it later. We laughed about it later.'

The race report is just as intriguing. Senna did take a clear lead and Morris had caught him by lap 5 – it was a ten-lap race. 'Morris spent the rest of the race working out where and how he could pass the Brazilian. On the second last lap Morris scrabbled through on the inside but then coolly let da Silva past again as they braked for Woodcote. All the way round the final lap da Silva doggedly clung to the inside line and this left Morris with only one option: to try the outside line into Woodcote. Morris gave it a go, whereupon da Silva left his braking as late as he dared and left Morris with seemingly nowhere to go. Did he give up? Not a bit of it. Rick used every bit of his Formula Ford experience to bounce his Royale over the chicane kerbs ...'

Morris 17 minutes 1.85 seconds; Senna 17 minutes 2.72.

We are now ten races into the season and the sequence is worth setting down. Senna had been fifth, third, first, second, second, second, first, first, first, second. Firman understood perfectly what was happening. 'Why he won so many races is because he did it on the first lap: pole position, soon as the lights go, bang, he's away. He pulled 10, 15, 20 yards clear. In two or three laps you'd find other drivers circulating as quickly, but they'd lost the race. They'd never get the gap back. That's the sign of a driver: a man who can just do it from the word go.'

It became a strategy, a tactic, a constant. It imposed enormous strains on the drivers trying to pull the gaps back because, as they were forced to conclude, they had to stay with him on those crucial first and second laps, but to do that they had to pit their nerve and skill against his nerve and skill in the most direct way, and he had lots and lots of both. Why doesn't everybody do this? Because they can't.

Donington Park. 'I'd always thought he was fairly good,' Morris says. 'At Donington I got fastest lap although a typical thing happened, I'd got stuck in the pack after the start. I was fourth or fifth or whatever. Ayrton did have the ability to put in the most amazing first lap – unbelievably good starts, tremendous opening laps. I started reeling him in, reeling him in, reeling him in. I got to within ten feet of him and I watched him through the corners. I was impressed. He was kicking up dust every time he came out of Coppice [the corner on to the main straight], he was using not only the track but the rumble-strips and two or three inches of dirt beyond them – and not on one lap, on every lap. That was unusual because one of the hardest things to do in Formula Ford 1600 is drive consistently. They are pig-awful things to drive. And lap after lap after lap off the track by two or three inches …

'I was using the rumble-strip and I might have used the dirt every once in four or five laps if I went too fast but he was doing it deliberately.

'He got very annoyed with me at that meeting for mucking up his practice. I had a problem and I was going to come into the pits. I don't know whether I hadn't seen him or whatever. I'd moved over to the right with my hand up, slowing down, I moved into the first part of the chicane as Ayrton was coming round. Obviously I spoilt his line, however unintentionally. He came to me. He said: "Rick, you spoil my lap." I said: "Sorry, Ayrton, I didn't mean it."'

Brands Hatch. 'The RAC 1600 men gave their all in one of the most hectic 15 lappers seen all year,' *Autosport* wrote. 'Setting-up problems in practice confined series leader da Silva to the third row whereas his team-mates Mansilla and Toledano shared the front. A truly sensational start by da Silva saw his yellow car arrive at Paddock alongside Mansilla's blue one, Ayrton having displaced four cars instantly, seemingly without contact! The Argentine gave not one inch at the notorious right-hander [the stomach-churning drop, remember] but he had to relent at the hairpin [Druids], da Silva forging ahead immediately. The brilliance of the former karter once free was a joy to behold: Deft flicks of opposite lock through Paddock – such elegant car control can only be natural talent – took him further out of reach until dramatically the van Diemen slewed sideways beyond instantaneous recall at Clearways with three laps remaining. Ayrton resumed fourth with a water hose adrift.'

Senna now began a cascading, imperious run of six straight victories: at Oulton on 25 July (plus fastest lap), the same at Mallory on the following day; at Brands on 2 August he made a 'storming start,' completed lap 1 six lengths in front and stayed there (although Toledano set fastest lap); at Snetterton on 9 August he faced the penultimate round of the RAC Championship and by then only he, Mansilla, Toledano or Morris could still win it: halfway through, it rained. Senna, 'tip-toeing,' looked 'master of the difficult conditions.'

Here is another theme, and it too will run through. His car control was so sensitive that others might flounder amidst the waves which cars churn; he never. It would lead directly to a performance in a storm at Monaco so consummate in its bravery and touch that people still speak of it – but that was four years away; another at Estoril in a deluge – but that was five years away; another at Montreal – but that was eight years away.

Now, at Snetterton, others proved the depth of the risk in the wet, and that set what Senna did in its true context. Half a dozen of them plunged off 'like a bomb had burst.' Senna won by a couple of seconds from Mansilla; and set fastest lap, of course. He had 105 points, Morris 95, Mansilla 75. He could not be caught. He was champion.

Donington Park. He beat Morris by almost a couple of seconds.

Thruxton. He was in full control by the third lap and that gave him the Townsend Thoresen title. Marcus Pye of *Autosport* was in that race and remembers: 'Senna did seven or eight laps to within a hundredth of a second each time. You almost felt you were watching sleight of hand because it did not seem possible in an FF1600 car. The nature of the car wouldn't allow it. OK, you can do it in Formula 1, maybe, with big tyres and so forth – but an FF1600!' (Coyne says 'however difficult the cars were to control, Senna was consistent, that was the thing.')

Between that race and the final TT round, at Brands Hatch on 29 September, Senna went to Parma to contest the World Karting Championship. The engine capacity had been increased from 100 to 135cc, an unpopular move. Certainly, de Bruijn says, Senna 'did not like it. The other thing was that Dunlop tyres dominated. He could not beat the other Dunlop runners because he did not have the engine and I could not beat them because I did not have the tyres. That is to say, I had good equipment but not the good tyres.

'Nobody knows this, but on the last morning he came to me and offered me his tyres – you weren't restricted, you could do that – to enable me to win. Unbelievable. He understood that he couldn't win, he understood that I arranged everything in my team myself against the big factories and, actually, he was a little bit in the same situation with DAP, a very small team. So he made the offer. I said, "what is this?" He said, "yes, I'd really like you to win more than the others!" He was like that and in other ways we were similar. He didn't talk all day, he was business-like, doing the things you should do, the things you have to do. It's usual that there is a certain distance between drivers because otherwise you cannot go for it 100 per cent on the track with them.'

Wilson says that 'we started saying hello to each other in 1981, but only if we happened to walk past each other.' Here are the distances. 'When you're racing, whether it's karts or Formula 1 – whatever kind of racing it is – you can say "yes, he's a friend" but really he's just a friend to say hello to, because when you are on the circuit you don't have friends. Everybody's out there to win and you can't afford friends – you can't, you can't. You must not put yourself in a position where you think: "I'd better not overtake him because I know him so well."'

De Bruijn gives another perspective. 'At that stage in a driver's career you don't know how good they can be in a single-seater. I had a year in Formula Fords and I do know that when you arrange good things around you, and with the experience that you have in pushing yourself to win, then you can. I was not surprised by what he did in single-seaters, not at all. If you're good in karts, 99 out of a hundred will be good in cars, but only the *very* good ones – Prost, Senna, Mansell, Patrese – come to the top. In karting you have many good drivers but not so many extremely good ones.'

Senna would say: 'I was one of the favourites and I was in a good position to win. But then the material I got was no good, the engine and the frame. They changed the regulations to allow 135cc engines and my frame was not strong enough for the engine. I could finish only fourth. I was very upset.'

The opening time trial told him the worst, only sixth quickest. In the heats he was third three times and in the final fourth twice, taking him to that fourth place overall.

Brands Hatch. He was second to Morris.

Keith Sutton was to receive a short, sharp shock. 'Brian Jones [the suave on-circuit commentator who also did the interviews on the rostrum afterwards] said to him: "Well, Ayrton, you've done very well in Formula Ford 1600, you must be looking forward to Formula 3 next year." [It would have been an acceptable step up the ladder, missing the Formula Ford 2000 rung.] Ayrton said: "No, I finish with racing, I'm going back to Brazil." I'm stood there and I just couldn't believe it. He was a bit disillusioned because to continue he needed sponsorship and his father needed help on the farm and that was it.'

'When I left I was unhappy for a number of reasons,' Senna said. 'I was very disappointed. One of the main reasons was that, as you know, in order to find a sponsor you need good publicity. That is especially important in Brazil because it is so far away. Of all the Brazilians who have come to England I was the first to win two championships in the first year, the RAC and the TT. I won 12 races; I qualified on pole position 14 or 15 times – in 18 races. These were very good results but I couldn't get good press in Brazil and without that I couldn't find a sponsor. I knew that I needed a sponsor before I could move into Formula 3 and I tried very, very hard. I was competing for space in the newspapers with Moreno and Boesel, who were winning in Formula 3, and also Nelson Piquet was winning the World Championship. After all that there was no room for FF1600.'

He did go home, missing the fabled Formula Ford Festival at Brands Hatch which is traditionally a chance – if you win it – to reach a larger audience within the world of motorsport. Small wonder: it attracted an entry of nearly 250 FF1600 cars.

'He had completed his two championships and for whatever reason he decided he had to go back to Brazil,' Firman says. 'His father wanted him to go back, his father had only given him the one year, that's right. We had no contract to do the Festival. Having said that, he did say he would let me know whether he could do it or not. In the meantime young Tommy Byrne [an affable Irishman currently with van Diemen in FF2000] had come up and said "I will definitely do it for you." To be fair, Ayrton phoned me from Brazil and said he would do it, but I declined. I couldn't really mess Tommy around when he had committed himself.'

Sutton says 'I am sure Ayrton would have won the Festival. The guy who took over his car, Byrne, did win it. Ayrton sent me a letter saying thanks for all your help. His English was still really poor.'

So it was over, finished, done with. He'd be remembered as a talented kid who went away. Rick Morris puts that into its context. 'Fernando Riberio, for example, was very introverted and got God and when I beat him he threatened God would kill us all. At Hockenheim he'd been thrown out of his team and we were sitting there after practice sipping beers and he hadn't got a car to drive because Royale had taken it away, and the Lord was coming and we were all going to be killed. At the start of the race he had his overalls on and his helmet in his hand, still convinced the Lord would provide him with a car.

'At the end of 1981 Alfie [Toledano] gave me a great big Mexican hat, Quique [Mansilla] gave me a present – I can't remember what it was now – but Ayrton wasn't on that level. Ayrton was much more remote, much less friendly. You'd go up to the van Diemen pits after practice and ask how it went, you'd talk to the drivers. Some were very emotional afterwards, others would go away and hide in the truck. Riberio would sit in the truck and play a flute. Ayrton would just sit. He was always insular, a little bit lost maybe, certainly not gregarious.

'Raul Boesel – because of his German stock – was more straight-back-on-the-horse-with-leather-boots, Roberto Moreno was more of a monkey-on-a-stick, Ayrton was more calm, controlled, authoritative, slightly arrogant. I think it was a combination of different country, loneliness and dedication. He was always very dedicated, much more than the other two [Mansilla and Toledano].

'I remember when he got his first Mercedes – 1983 or '84 – and his showing it to me at Brands Hatch. He was inordinately proud of it. He said: "Come and have a look at my car."'

This wasn't vanity, any more than Sutton's photographs had been. After all, a Mercedes carries a certain cachet, but a Ferrari it ain't. No, it was something more profound. Son of a rich father, he had earned the Mercedes himself. It is entirely possible that he regarded the Mercedes, gained by his own talent, as representing his true manhood, his true independence.

Another memory from Morris. 'It happened in the paddock at Brands. I had my new son Stevie with me on my shoulders and Ayrton was very attentive, "how are you, Stevie?" and so on. He was always happy to talk, he just wasn't smiling-talking.'

But we're still in October 1981. 'I decided to buy a house so I never had the determination to be a full-time racing driver,' Morris says. 'I was quite happy driving what anybody would put in front of me.'

The implication is clear: he'd have spent the money on such a career, not a house, if he did have the determination. Senna himself obviously didn't have the determination either, because he'd gone. Nor did Steve Lincoln, who'd become an insurance underwriter. The way the world goes.

It was quite natural Senna had been so attentive to Stevie, quite natural for a family-loving South American; and that was ironic in its way. As Ayrton and Liliane da Silva boarded their Varig flight for Brazil that late autumn, all was not well with them as a couple.

Chapter 5

RETURN OF THE PRODIGAL SON

The plane had lifted off from a place called Foz do Iguacu, famous for its waterfall and kart track, 500 miles from Sao Paulo. Ayrton Senna had been there as a celebrity guest for the Brazilian Championships. He didn't take part and neither did Sala, who was looking for sponsorship to get to England. (Mauricio Gugelmin won.) Now, on the plane, Senna and Sala sat together. 'He said to me he had retired and he was working for his father's company. I could feel he wasn't happy, that he wanted to be in racing again. I think in his mind he said: I dreamed of England, I went, now I want to go back.'

Dennis Rushen remembers that 'there was a lot of pressure from his father, who didn't want him to race and said this is silly and so on. Over the winter, Ralph Firman and I discussed someone to replace Tommy Byrne in Formula Ford 2000 and Senna was the man to have. Ralph did more than I did to get him back. Ralph used to ring him and say: "It's great over here!"'

'When, in 1981, we'd decided to go into Formula 2000 we'd contacted Rushen Green to run our works car,' Firman says. 'Now, in 1982, Ayrton decided he did want to compete in it. He rang me up ...'

Rushen remembers the meeting. 'We sat down in the office, him, myself and Ralph and Ayrton said "yes, OK, but Dennis told me I could do the lot for £10,000." Ralph went mad – "what?!" – but Ayrton hadn't forgotten what I'd said to him that day at Snetterton and we had to do it for that figure. He had some Brazilian money from a company called Banerj.'

What did happen?

'My father simply made me free to decide what I wanted to do,' Senna would say, 'and after I decided we agreed together (father, myself, the family) that this was simply *Go* and we would not look back any more, just look ahead. That happened after my first season – 1981 – after I got back to Brazil. At the end of 1981 I had tried to help my father in his business, from that October to February 1982. That month I made my mind up and again together we decided to go for it. For sure without my father's help life would have been a lot more difficult, but we also agreed as a matter of principle that the day I was in a position to, I would pay back all the investment. That happened when I got to Formula 1.'

At the time, 1982, he'd said he was 'very excited' to be back. There was however a problem: Rushen and the boys decided that Ayrton da Silva wasn't easy to pronounce and made a very British decision. They nicknamed him Harry.

He had come back alone. We must approach his marriage in one context and one context only: how it materially affects a proper portrait of the man.

Liliane has already moved in the background like a mute bit-part player, gorgeous to behold but, to us, a total stranger.

I propose to offer you the words of four men and then leave it all until the fleeting words of a fifth later on, and dwell on it no more.

The first is Brazilian, and will remain anonymous. 'She was from a very good family, accustomed to servants, she was completely unprepared for being a housewife in a house in Norfolk.'

The second is Keith Sutton. 'I think he had a few problems with his wife at the time. He'd only been married since the February before. She was very nervous. I could see that. She seemed to be very nervous about his racing. I don't think he could cope with that kind of pressure. I mean, he was totally dedicated to being in racing. I think he realised he had made a big mistake and he came back without her.'

The third is Sala. 'I met Liliane only once. I think Liliane was his first love and when he decided to come to Europe he was a little bit afraid to come by himself and he took her with him to have support, but in the end he didn't have the support he wanted from her.'

The fourth is Calvin Fish. 'His wife was good looking and that's just another sacrifice he made to get where he's got. She seemed very friendly. You'd see them at the track. He'd be in the car testing, she'd be watching. Even back then I always believed that his goal was to be Formula 1 World Champion. He really believed he could do that and when you're racing against a guy, you don't know the depth of his feeling. It was like this was the one goal. I felt it even then, I really did.'

Senna himself talked motor racing, rationing out his thinking. He was also looking beyond the FF2000 season. 'Last year I won many races in FF1600. If I am lucky I can do the same this year in two-litre. Then I don't need to do Formula 3 this year. If I was to do Formula 3 then I must win to get good publicity, because people will be looking to next year and I must keep the sponsors happy. To win in Formula 3 you must do many miles of testing in the car – that is for sure – but really there is not enough time.'

There was the option, perhaps, of Formula 2 (as it was then: another rung). Listen to a 21-year-old talking: 'It is true that a Swiss man contacted me by phone and he said that Maurer [a German team] were interested in me for F2. He said that he had a sponsor and that there would be no problem with the money, but he changed his tune by the second time that we spoke and I knew then that there was no security, no real chance. I don't really want to do F2 anyhow, because I think to do well depends too much on what tyres or what engine or what chassis you have. I think that in Formula 3 it is much more even. I hope that if I can go well and win races in Formula 3 then I will be able to jump straight into Formula 1, like Raul Boesel. If you can be competitive in 1600, in 2000 and maybe Formula 3, why not in Formula 1?'

Here is the young man's second sequence of steps into motor racing. He is doing more than gathering experience and confirming the reputation he made the season before. He is creating an impetus which would propel him a great distance in the years to come.

'He didn't come over until the start of the season,' Rushen says. 'I can't even remember him testing. The first race was at Brands Hatch. He jumped in and I gave him a crash course in what wings and slicks were all about. I said: "This is a wing …"'

For the non-technical, wings can be adjusted on a car to improve performance but Formula Ford 1600 cars didn't have them, so Senna was experiencing them for the first time. More than that, wings introduce drivers to the various *possibilities* of a car.

He won by 14 seconds, beating – among others Fish. In 1989, Fish told me: 'He creates this mystique about himself, not letting people get too close to him. It's strange because obviously you reflect on how you raced against him and how his career has gone since. You admire the guy now for what he's achieved and what he's achieving but when you're competing against a guy you don't admire him, you respect him. You don't sit back and say. "Well, this guy is great" because if you do you won't be able to race against him.

'What stands out in his character is his single-mindedness about racing, the incredible intensity of it. I wonder whether he really enjoyed it at the time. I wonder if the intensity takes away the enjoyment. He comes from a different culture and I don't know how they express themselves. They may do it in a different manner, but I never really felt he was enjoying himself.'

What he did was win: at Brands on 7 March, at Oulton on 27 March. Keith Sutton was at Oulton and 'I saw him there. I said: "Look, you've got the talent to make it, we're both on the same level in our different careers, we both want to do well, why don't we get people to know you by doing press releases and sending them to all the Grand Prix managers? I work for a lot of foreign magazines. I can send them the releases and pictures and obviously if you're doing well they'll print them." He said it was a good idea and we came to an arrangement. He was paying me.

'It had never been done before – press releases to Grand Prix managers, Bernie Ecclestone, Frank Williams, Peter Warr [of Lotus] and everybody else and he was only running in Formula Ford 2000. I had headed notepaper done for him with his helmet in all the colours. I wasn't a journalist or a writer or anything, I just wanted to help him because I saw the talent and I thought it might help me.'

Oulton Park. He took pole, battered the two-year-old lap record after 'rocketing away' at the start, set fastest lap and beat Fish by ten seconds.

Silverstone. He won.

Donington Park. He won.

'Ayrton's closest friends were Mauricio Gugelmin and his wife Stella,' Rushen says. 'He lived with them and Stella was like a mum to him, if you like. So we were at Donington and Mauricio was in Formula Ford 1600 at Snetterton. I also ran a man who worked for Mazda and he got me a Mazda. Ayrton won the race and he came walking over with the garland around his neck and he said: "We can get to Snetterton to see Mauricio in his race. It's going to be in an hour and a half's time. We can make it." I said: "But it's two and a half hours between here and Snetterton." He said: "I'll drive."

'So I sat in the front passenger seat and Spider the mechanic sat in the back seat and we got from Donington to Snetterton in just over one and a half hours – a time that could not be done. Fortunately I had a book with me which I put up in front of my eyes because I really didn't want to see some of the things that were happening.

'I understood then that the guy had a belief in his own ability – that he was blessed from above, if you like – that, say, no tractor would come out in front of him. He'd overtake and there would be something coming the other way and you'd think: this can't be done. He'd go at roundabouts flat out and he'd sort it out when he got to them. Spider was pure white and he was nearly sick. When we got to Snetterton, Spider said: "I'll never drive with you again." I just went into a corner out of the way.'

Snetterton. He won. It is worth dwelling on this race. Several cars at the back of the grid tumbled into a crash on the first corner. By then Senna had long gone, and as he crossed the line to complete lap 1 Kenny Andrews, Senna's young team-mate, was fractionally behind him, Fish fifth. They all moved through the debris of the crash. Almost immediately Senna slowed and Rushen was understandably puzzled. 'Ayrton came round first, then he came round seventh, the lap after that he slowed down as if he was coming into the pits but he didn't. Then he started picking people off.'

Andrews was equally puzzled. 'I was leading the race by about 15 seconds and I saw him in my mirrors. He was a long way away and I thought: *this is it, I'm going to win, I've got this one sewn up.* He caught me very quickly and overtook me.'

Rushen will never forget the end of that race. 'Ayrton won but he didn't stop after the line, he stopped about 300 metres down the road. He got out and said: "I've got no (expletive) brakes." We looked and a flint had come up and sheared his front brakes, so he'd driven the whole race with only rear brakes.'

'Afterwards we were having a discussion in the office,' Andrews says. 'I asked Ayrton: "Where do you think I'm going wrong?" He said: "You brake too early for the Esses, I was braking later than you and I only had the rear brakes …"'

Silverstone. He won, and that was six pole positions, six fastest laps, six victories. Rushen summarises it simply. 'We had Nelson engines and one of them was brilliant so we had not only overkill in the shape of the best driver but we had the best engine. We were winning the races by up to 17 seconds. It was quite amazing. But at that time he hated being away from Brazil, he hated England and he would not drive the car until his gloves and balaclava had been laid on the radiator to warm them up. He couldn't take the cold, hated it. He wouldn't test in the mornings because he didn't want to get out of bed – but, I mean, all Brazilians are like that. They don't want to get up.

'We had Dunlop tyres and by Dunlop's own admission it was a bad tyre. You could grain it in about six laps. When we tested, all we did was have a huge stack of tyres to see if we could find a good set. If we did, that could be worth a second, a second and a half over everyone else.

'We found out very early Senna's testing ability. He could be on his own lap record at Snetterton within four or five laps and he was so accurate that it was pretty obvious driving the car was the easy bit. He had so much time to tell you the left rear tyre was doing such-and-such on such-and-such a corner, and that was absolutely unbelievable. It's obvious now [1989] he's good, but if you worked with him then you could already see how good he was.

'I'll give you an example. One day Ayrton was testing at Snetterton – you know, to find a good set of tyres – and Gary Evans, then a young driver, was there in a Formula Ford 1600 car. Gary came in and said the car didn't feel right, the engine didn't feel right and he was painfully slow. I said to Ayrton "would you mind just hopping in this and see what's happening?" He goes out and he needs no time to adjust. He'd just been on wings and slicks and now he isn't. The third or fourth lap out he was as quick as Gugelmin who was also there, in the works van Diemen and they're always the best cars. He just did it. Unbelievable. Then he came in and said: "Yes, the car is awful." I've never seen anybody else be able to do things like that.'

Fish sensed, and then saw, that Senna 'was susceptible to pressure.' Fish would judge that in subsequent years Senna would overcome it and 'understand that on a certain day another car will be in better shape' and he wouldn't be able to beat it. 'But in 1982, when you were challenging him – and when I say challenging I mean wheel-to-wheel, overtaking him or leading him (sitting at one car's length behind him was a different deal altogether) – it was as if he shouldn't be put in that position. He personally felt he was head and shoulders above everyone and simply shouldn't be in that situation. He felt as he was in a different league to everyone else. When it came to "I may get beaten today" he didn't know how to handle it. He'd either put you off the track or maybe crash trying to overtake you. It was very strange. Maybe it was a phase he was going through. Whenever it got to that point, it was panic, he'd go completely to the *nth* degree to get back in front.'

On 18 April he contested the F2000 round at Zolder. He took pole by a clear second, led.

Autosport reported that 'on pole position, by a clear 1sec, was da Silva, his Rushen Green-run van Diemen once again completing only a minimum of laps and being handily quickest in each session.' *Autosport* added that 'sadly' the confrontation between Senna and Cor Euser, a Dutchman and reigning European FF1600 Champion, 'ended almost before it had begun as da Silva's Nelson engine let go after only three laps of the race and he had to relinquish his lead to Euser.'

It made Euser briefly famous. 'I didn't even know the guy,' he says, 'because I wasn't that much involved in racing. To me it was just a hobby. I'd won the European FF1600 mainly because of my Dutch friends who arranged everything around me. I had a 1979 Delta and Senna had a 1982 factory van Diemen. My car was prepared by myself and some truck mechanics! After I won at Zolder, everybody was stunned. They said "how can you beat Senna?" and I said "who is this guy? I don't even know him."

Ayrton came over and said "terrific job." That was the first time we'd met and the first words he spoke to me. My English was so bad I asked my mechanics what "terrific job" meant and they told me. The ice had been broken and we started to speak to each other in our bad English.

'I tried to get friends with him but he was a difficult person to form a relationship with compared to the other drivers from England. It was easy to do that with them but Senna was – how do you say it? – different. I raced for fun but it was his profession, his job. Maybe he deliberately didn't want to make friends with people. He was a little shy and there was a small group of people he did talk to. After the Zolder race he spoke to me because he thought I was something special – I'd won the race. He could seem a snob but if you spoke to him he wasn't.

'Toine Hezemins, who was a Daytona 24-hour winner and main importer for Rotax go-kart engines for the whole of Europe, remembered Senna from karting and said: "You have to watch this guy, he's incredibly good." I said "well, I've beaten him!" Hezemins offered Senna £50,000 for a contract to be able to promote him and Senna wanted £75,000 or so and didn't do it. I was shocked to hear that type of money. I asked Hezemins "why don't you sponsor me?" and he replied: "It's two different ball games the way he follows his profession and you pursue your hobby."'

Mallory Park. He didn't take pole but won.

Zolder, another round of the European Championship. 'It was the weekend when [Gilles] Villeneuve was killed,' Rushen says. 'We got there in the morning and Ayrton said he'd been offered a contract by Toleman and one by McLaren. "I want to go over and introduce myself to Nelson Piquet." He wandered off on his own and he came back really crestfallen. I said: "What's the matter?" "He just snubbed me. I'll beat the bastard one day." He could let things like that get really inside himself, to somewhere bitter and intense. That hurt him a lot, it really did.

'I had the only (road) car and he wanted to go and see this girl somewhere. I said: "Right; if you win, you can take the car and I'll find my own way back to the hotel, but if you lose you've got to drive me all the way back." He said; "Yes, fine, yes." He was 13 seconds in the lead and the next lap he didn't come round. He walked back holding his helmet and as he went past me (he'd spun off) he said "sorry." I made him drive me back to the hotel ...'

Toleman did make an approach. As I've said, Alex Hawkridge was running the team then. 'I'd seen him win Formula Ford 1600 races in 1981 like it was just an everyday event. He was clearly an outstanding natural talent. We approached him and asked him if he was interested in a sponsored Formula 3 drive – and he wasn't particularly. Chris Witty, who was our sponsorship man, made the approach ...'

'I went up to him and spoke to him,' Witty says. 'That was the initial approach. I knew that, at the same time, Ron Dennis was sort of sniffing.'

Hawkridge takes it up again. 'We arranged a meeting. At that point he'd already been speaking with others in Grand Prix racing. He got introduced through the Brazilian machine, as it were, but it was all very long-term, nothing immediate and of course he hadn't done Formula 3 at this point. He turned down our offer of a sponsored drive. Then the rules were changed and he had to qualify for Formula 1 through results in a lower formula, and Formula 3 was stipulated as the minimum entry level. The "Superlicence" had just been established. We said: "Look, Ayrton, you can handle Formula 1 no problem," because we thought he could. "All we've got to do is get this definition of a Superlicence out of the way in half a dozen Formula 3 races and then you can come and be our Formula 1 driver." He turned that down cold on the basis that he needed more experience, he wanted to learn about racing and in his view there were no short cuts to that.'

Witty vividly remembers Hawkridge saying: '"Look, if you sign an option form we will sponsor you in Formula 3, we will give you a Formula 3 budget" – because we reckoned he was worth it. He said: "No, no, no, I can cope with finding my own money." We kept working on him, I mean, I used to meet him in his Alfasud at the Hangar Lane gyratory system [on London's North Circular road] and pass pieces of paper to him ...'

'He took the view,' Hawkridge says, 'that the car determines your performance so much in Formula 1 whereas in the junior formulae, where the engines and tyres and chassis and power are so similar, individual performance makes you shine. He wanted to prove himself the best – and he was desperately anxious to prove that point to himself as well as everybody else. It was kind of ridiculous because he stood out so far as being the exceptional talent of the decade to anybody who bothered to look: and he wasn't just occasionally that, he was systematically that. He qualified fastest, he got the jump at the flag, he got the first corner, he automatically won the race. Since I'd watched Jim Clark in my childhood, nobody had dominated motor racing in the way that he did.

'Along the way we spoke to people who were involved with him, Ralph Firman, Dennis Rushen – Dennis was an old friend of mine and he told me just how amazing the guy was.

'It wasn't an aspiration to ever get into Formula 1, it was an ambition to dominate Formula 1. That's all he contemplated. It wasn't "I want to get into Formula 1, I want to be a Formula 1 driver and now I've made it," he never thought in those terms. So when it came to actually trying to negotiate with him it was against a background where you were interviewing a candidate who only wanted to be considered by a team which had a Formula 1 "World Championship-winning car". The negotiations with Ayrton were difficult ...'

Senna expressed this sentiment, or compulsion, in a single sentence. 'I could never be just another Formula 1 driver.'

During my interview with Hawkridge, he paused as if the enormity of it still lived with him. 'When he was in Formula 2000 he was not interested in getting any toe on the Formula 1 ladder at all. That was a constant right through the negotiating. I respect Ayrton for this: he made no secret of the fact that he's completely self-centred and it was an overwhelming ambition to be World Champion.'

Hawkridge judged [1989] that Senna would change 'as a consequence of being World Champion [in 1988], I think he'll be a more contented individual. I don't think he'll be any less competitive because I don't think he can be any other way. He will be someone who will be more pleasant to be with, less unnerving to be in conversation with.

'Anyway, he turned down an option to get paid for a Formula 3 drive and said no, if he couldn't do it on merit he wouldn't do it at all. I said "well, this is merit because you're good enough." He said "ah, but there are conditions attached, I've got to drive for you, I want a choice if I win the Formula 3 Championship. I think I'll have a choice." He was not wrong, he was completely right and he had the self-confidence to do it. He had the self-confidence all the way through the piece to know that that would happen. He was never likely to rush into anything.'

I have quoted Hawkridge at length, and in doing so interrupted the flow of the narrative, because the whole episode is so instructive, startling and very likely unique. Every driver you meet on the edge of Formula 1 is actively hustling to get into it any way they can. You do not under any circumstances anticipate that you will go straight into a team which is poised to make you World Champion.

Senna did.

And please remember we are still at Zolder in May 1982, he still hadn't even driven a Formula 3 car. He would, though, within a few weeks, courtesy of Eddie Jordan, now into running his own team.

Oulton Park. Fish was leading, Senna in second place and Andrews third. Andrews remembered it as if the enormity of this still lived with him. 'We were up each other's gearboxes, within inches of them. Cascades is the flat left-hander going down the hill, it's very tricky and on about the third lap Senna's rear right tyre exploded. He was flat in fourth gear, doing 125mph and the car snapped sideways. He was broadside on a negative camber corner – and there is no way you can get out of that. I lifted immediately because I thought *this was going to be a big shunt and I won't be able to miss it*. Then I saw his ability. He controlled the car until it was pointing forwards again. I was in awe of that control. He went through the next corner on three wheels and the corner after that and then he pulled over and let me by. I'd have gone off, Calvin Fish would have gone off.'

This episode made Dennis Rushen smile when he reflected on it. Senna, you see, 'came into the pits with just bits of rubber hanging off the wheel and said: "I've got a puncture …"'

At that Oulton meeting, incidentally, Fish had pole (and took 0.1 seconds off the lap record) *and* Senna took part in a Sunbeam Tl celebrity race. There were two seasoned drivers among those against him, John Brindley and Chuck Nicholson.

'I don't think I even spoke to him,' Nicholson says. 'He had one of the faster cars – they weren't all the same – but that made no difference to what happened. I remember he made a perfect start and quite literally we didn't see him again at all. He made no semblance of a mistake, obviously, just vanished into the distance. He broke the lap record! It was a seven-lap race and he did it in 9m 50.2s, Brindley, who was second, in 9m 57.3s. So Senna was pulling out a second a lap, that's a great deal round Oulton, and Brindley was known as a very, very fast driver. Of course, at that stage Senna was only regarded as a promising newcomer but I said to somebody afterwards: "Promising? This man is going to make it."'

Fish reflects that 'initially in 1982 we were in a very close-knit community. I had my own team but we were both based at

Snetterton. At midday everyone would go down to the café and have lunch, we'd be eating table-to-table and then on a Thursday afternoon we'd be on the same racetrack. When we'd go to Europe the transporter trucks would leave at the same time. We were constantly in each other's presence but he always felt it was necessary to detach himself a little bit. One of my best friends is Tommy Byrne but when it comes to race day we go at it as hard as we can. After the race we go and have a beer. But Ayrton didn't feel – rightly or wrongly – that he should be doing that.

'Basically, underneath, Ayrton was a nice guy but he had to put on this front which didn't let anyone get too close. Now and again he'd join in when we were playing the video games – the mechanics would be there, too – but more often he'd leave and do something else. Underneath he wanted to play the video games but he had this plan and the plan said that that wasn't the way it was done. He felt that if he let you too close to him he would lose that little edge he thought he had. He was taking it incredibly seriously.

'My car was a match for his but that wasn't enough. You had to do your job right, you had to qualify on the front row, you had to have a great start, and Ayrton would take tremendous chances – well, not chances but he'd go for it on the first lap when the tyres weren't up to temperature and the car could get out of shape. He'd put in a dynamite lap. Gradually, when I was finishing second to him so many times – and we were trying to beat the guy to the championship – we started looking at the lap times and they were basically similar. What he was doing was taking that chance when the tyres were cold, pulling out a lead of maybe a second (and we're only talking about 10- or 12-lap races) and I'd run the rest of the race sitting exactly one second behind him. I don't think he was controlling the races. It was the advantage that he'd pulled out immediately.'

Sutton knew Senna's career was gathering momentum. 'He was winning every race and by the middle of the season people started to take notice. Frank Williams was contacting him, Toleman were contacting him. I got home from somewhere one day and my mother said "there's been a telephone call for you. Bernie Ecclestone's been on the phone." I couldn't believe it. "What does he want?" "He wants to talk to you about Ayrton." Then I had a letter from Peter Warr at Lotus, and one from Frank and I put them in contact with Ayrton.'

Senna stepped into Jordan's Formula 3 car 'at Silverstone on the Club circuit in midsummer,' Eddie Jordan remembers. 'He was clean-sweeping in two-litre and I rang him up one day. I had started the team at the end of 1981 and 1982 was my first full season. I was running James Weaver and we were having big difficulties getting money together. I wanted to move into driver-management and I was looking for young talent. I rang up several of the top promising young guys to give them a test, although Senna was one of the few I did it for free. Normally I wasn't likely to do things like that in those days.

'He said his father had just come across from Brazil and he was driving for Rushen Green and he needed to get permission. Could he come on a Wednesday afternoon because he'd be at Mallory Park doing a couple of laps in the morning? I said OK, and he came down.

'Weaver had done a pole position time the previous weekend which was, I think, 54.2 seconds (in the morning qualifying). Ayrton arrived and he did twenty laps and he looked amazingly good. It was in the afternoon, please remember, and in the crisp morning air Formula 3 cars always go that bit quicker. The warmer it gets, the more the barometric pressure increases and the engine suffers a bit. So to equal the time set in a morning represents a slightly quicker time.

'He came in, made a couple of adjustments to the car – it was driver-tuning, really, he wanted to tune it for himself. It had some slight understeer and he moved it just ever so slightly, he didn't change anything seriously. We had set the car up exactly as

Weaver had raced it. He didn't do anything with tyres. He went back out again and after another ten laps he equalled the time we had been on pole with. After another ten laps – it was his first time in a Formula 3 car, don't forget – he became one of the first drivers to get into the 53 seconds on the Silverstone Club circuit. That was astonishing, absolutely amazing. Whatever adjustments he had made we kept and Weaver went on to win three races very soon after that. We won with Senna's adjustments at Donington, Jerez and Nogaro.'

Jordan added – he was speaking in 1989, remember, not today: 'As a person I think he lacks something. He would never have driven for me because, to be honest, I think he was keen on the Ron Dennis thing [at McLaren]. Perhaps I didn't have the pedigree. I would say that even then he was looking as far ahead as Ron. The inkling was there. That said, I have nothing but the highest regard for the boy. What he did in our car was a joy and I was thrilled. I feel honoured that he did it.'

Brands Hatch. Fish, who had a new car, took pole but Senna beat him to Paddock and, as a contemporary account says, 'Fish lost part of his nose-cone as a result.' Senna set fastest lap and won by a couple of seconds.

Mallory Park. He won.

Brands Hatch. He won.

Hockenheim. The next round of the European Championship. Reginaldo Leme, working for the big newspaper in Sao Paulo and TV Globo, the Brazilian channel which carried the races, met him for the first time. 'He introduced himself to me in a hotel in Heidelberg [favoured haunt of the Formula 1 fraternity] "I'm Ayrton Senna, I'm planning to race until Formula 1," he said. I felt in him very big ambitions. I knew his name very well but I didn't know him personally. We went to dinner together and he talked a little bit about racing, about his plans. I remember that after this I felt his talent was so good, that his plans were so good, his objectives so good that I introduced him to the journalists I knew well, British, French, Italian. I said to them: "For sure we'll see him in Formula 1." He appreciated that. Sometimes he asked me to do that.'

He took pole, 'cooked' his clutch on the start line and then became sucked helplessly into mayhem at the first chicane when Cor Euser, in the lead, overdid it and barrel-rolled.

Euser explains: 'My car was parked in the open and it rained the night before. We had to drill holes in the floor of the cockpit to let the water out. That night, too, some children were playing around the car and they changed the brake balance so badly that I had a very big crash on the first lap. That's how I went racing at that time. I got a new Delta which wasn't as good as the '79 and Senna beat me time after time. I always finished second. I didn't have the equipment to compete with him and his ability was a little bit better or his team were more professional. I don't say if we'd had the same equipment I could have beaten him, but I could have run closer to him. He wanted to have the pole and he wanted to have the fastest lap and he wanted to win the race and he wanted to win the Championship. I wasn't ready for that kind of thing. I was a hobbyist! We'd still speak but it was "how are you?" sort of thing.'

Oulton Park. He won, overtaking Andrews on the first lap.

Zandvoort. He won despite missing the first practice with clutch problems. He hadn't been to the circuit before and now had only thirty minutes to feel his way round.

Pole.

At the start he missed second gear and was second. He stayed there for a lap, out-braked the leader, Jaap Van Silf Hoat, at the corner called Tarzan and won from Fish.

Snetterton. He was – wait for it, wait for it – only second. It was his first defeat in a race he had finished.

Castle Combe. He won.

Snetterton. Senna's balance went into counterbalance. 'He had me off,' Fish says. 'We were the local racers, it was a big local race, all our friends were there, we were both on the front row. The strange thing is that when you race with Ayrton at that level he almost takes you away from the rest of the field. It was him and me – I'm not putting the other guys down – but it really was him and me. That's what he brings out of you: the best. You have to squeeze yourself to find that last little bit and when you look in the mirror the rest of the field has disappeared. Anyway, Ayrton took the lead at Snetterton, my team was "hooked up" a little bit better and about six laps into the race going down the back straight I was fastest and I moved out of his slipstream to go by him. He moved over and kept pushing and pushing and pushing.'

One account says they were both 'weaving back and forth' across the straight. Fish: 'I was alongside the guy and he pushed me right on to the dirt. I went off the track. We were both young, we were both going for it and what I should have done was lift off, tuck back in behind him and had a go somewhere else – but at that age you keep your foot down. It wasn't as if he left me a car's width at the end of the straight. I'll try and intimidate someone to the point where they lift off but I won't push them off.

'Back then it was "this guy can't be passing me!" – it was like that all the way across the track. I bounced ten feet up, it was all very spectacular and everyone was watching. I landed OK but I had to retire because the clutch was full of dirt. It was a time when I had started to close a little bit on him in the championship and it was important to get every point I could. Of course, it gave him 20 points and I didn't score any and it was a big deal. Everyone said: "Hey, you need to do something about that" and the marshals' reports said that number 11 pushed number 74 off the track and we put the protest in and it was one of the biggest splits Ayrton and I had.

'After that he was very angry with me. He felt that I should have gone and had a word with him. I don't think it would have made much difference, I don't think he really would have listened. Well, he would have stood there and listened but it wouldn't have made any difference. We felt that if something official was done and if the same situation arose he wouldn't do it again.'

Rushen is candid, despite his enormous affection for Senna. 'Ayrton put Fish on the grass and kept him there all the way to the Esses. It was down to the stewards and this, that and the other and Ayrton said: "They pick on me because I'm Brazilian," but I mean he was well out of order. He was so intense, he wanted it so much.'

Fish is candid, too. 'He was angry that we went through the official channels. He got fined something like £25 – typical RAC – and then we went to another tribunal and they upped it to £200 but they let him keep his points so it didn't help us at all. It changed the relationship between us because we then went off to Europe on a three-week trip and we stayed in the same hotels, and their mechanics and I used to get on really well, but Ayrton was still angry and didn't want to be around any more than he had to be. That put more strain on it.

'He put racing on such a level – in the way he went about things – that I'm really not sure he was enjoying himself.' Fish added that Senna might have subsequently reflected that '"hey, I had a great time," but from the outside you wondered about that. He was very solemn, you know, and the people who were associated with me used to look at him and say "he's not really a happy kind of guy" although on certain occasions he would come out and he could be funny, actually. He had a good sense of humour – when he let it come out.'

This is confirmed by Keith Sutton. 'He did the race at Snetterton and I went up to spend the weekend with him. That was good fun, him and Mauricio Gugelmin in the house at Norwich.'

The three-week trip took in Hockenheim (again), Austria and Denmark. 'When we went to Europe we travelled in the car, just him and me together,' Rushen says. 'We got very close. We'd talk about many things. He was very shy and didn't want to talk to people much but the people he liked – for example Spider his mechanic, and myself – he had all the time in the world for. He pushed other people out of the way to come and talk to us because he felt comfortable with us.'

Hockenheim. He took pole, set fastest lap, won but there's a curious background tale about this race. Two English women, who did not know each other and did not know Senna, travelled to Hockenheim to watch the Grand Prix. The FF2000 was a supporting event on the same programme. I quote them to show the immediate effect Senna could have on total strangers.

One was called Lyn Patey. 'I sat in the start-line grandstand with the colourful panorama of the Stadium section spread in front of my awed eyes. The death of Gilles Villeneuve was the reason I was there. The day after Zolder I woke with the dreadful realisation that I'd never seen him race on the race track, only on TV. I made a resolution. This would never happen again [with great drivers]. I decided to give myself a birthday present by booking a trip to Germany. With mild curiosity I watched some funny little cars lining up on the grid. My attention was caught by a pretty yellow helmet in the car on pole. The commentator gave the driver line-up and suddenly a strange, exotic name was ringing round the Stadium. I remember thinking it sounded wonderful and resolved to keep an eye on its owner. He didn't let me down: lights to flag, smooth as silk, miles ahead. Afterwards I fought through the crowd of Brazilians and others to reach him. I held out my hand and he grasped it and had a big smile. We shared a few words and then others demanded his attention. I walked away feeling suddenly sad.'

The second was Irene Ambrose. 'Still in shock after Pironi's accident the day before [Didier Pironi crashed his Ferrari and was trapped, but survived, crippled] I was huddling in the grandstand by the Stadium entrance overlooking the twisty bit. I remember vaguely seeing the Formula Fords come out and, as the leader pulled away, my lasting impression is of the commentator's triumphant "Senna da Silva" reverberating around the concrete. Something must have clicked into place then.'

He and Rushen drove on to Austria and the Österreichring. During the journey he said to Rushen: 'Who do you think is the best, me, Chico Serra or Nelson Piquet?'

Rushen: 'I dunno really.'

Senna: 'Well, I've got a big advantage over them. I've been driving karts from four years old.'

Rushen adds that 'he was really honest like that – a lot of talent plus the fact that he was lucky enough to have been driving for so long. That makes a big difference.'

Österreichring. He took pole with a 'staggering' lap and vanished into the distance, beating Fish by 24 seconds. This meant that in the next race (Denmark) he could clinch the European Championship. He said to Keith Sutton 'I'd like you to come, I'll pay for your air fare and your hotel.'

'That was pretty decent of him,' Sutton says. 'I flew out to Denmark. That was just a superb weekend. It was also a very fraught weekend, there was a lot of tension.'

Rushen reflects that 'there was something magical about that event. We had already won the British Championship and this European one meant a lot. I remember sitting on the grass in the paddock discussing with Senna whether we should put half a degree of rear wing on or not and it became an obsession. Should we, shouldn't we? Suddenly I said "hang on, we don't normally act like this, we're getting all twitchy about this."'

Jyllandsring. Pole. Fastest lap. He beat Fish by 2.5 seconds over the 25 laps. 'He was crying,' Rushen says, 'Ayrton was crying. He told me that: he was crying on the last lap. He went a bit wild afterwards.' Sutton – 'We went out for a meal and he was thrilled.' Rushen – 'It was the first time Ayrton got drunk ... on two vodka and tonics. There was a motorcycle in the street and he got on it and did wheelies.' Fish – 'It's hard to explain to the average person how close you are, living in the same hotels and so on. After he'd won the Championship he did come out and it was the first time anyone had seen him drunk. It was fun, it was good to see him let his hair down. We were all in a bar and we all had a few drinks and obviously that was difficult for a Brazilian who was used to being a Coca-Cola man. It was nice: there was camaraderie now that it was over, we'd done our best, the Championship was settled. I don't have any bitterness. He took away a lot of the glory that some of us others might have had and there's a fine line in this sport between really achieving success and being one of several people who do a good job.'

He won at Thruxton on 30 August and Fish is illuminating about that. Senna, he says was 'very shrewd, extremely clever' even if you forget about the fact of how quick he was. He thought 'way ahead of time. At Thruxton I was leading by a couple of seconds and we came up to lap the back markers at the complex. I decided the gap between me and him wasn't big enough to sit back and follow them through so I went inside on the first corner, the guy in front didn't see me, blocked me and I did have to follow them through. I lost a bunch of time through all three corners. Ayrton read it perfectly. As we came out of the complex he swept by and beat me. It was a day when he had one of his biggest smiles after the race because he knew he shouldn't have won but he still managed to do it.'

Silverstone. Joint pole with Fish, and he took a small lead which he built on.

Mondello Park. He won.

The last race of the season was at Brands Hatch. Rushen won't ever forget that, either.

'Just before Brands he went to do the World Kart thing [the Championship in Kalmar, Sweden] and it was a disaster. He finished 14th and it was rubbish, everything was wrong. He came back and you could see his attitude was bad.'

At the very start of the season Senna had confided that 'I have already been to Italy and DAP have built a brand-new frame. It is completely different. The engine is still not too good yet but we know where the problem is and the new parts will be ready soon.' Clearly there were other problems but Senna had still hungered for the championship. *Karting* magazine reported that 'timed practice began at 9.30 on Saturday morning with the air temperature on the low side under a ten-tenths cloud cover. All went well until da Silva stopped on his first lap with a flat tyre and was not allowed a re-run as he had passed the start flag.'

Ten drivers spun out at the first corner of Heat 2 and 'overshadowing the efforts of the front-runners … was the meteoric progress of da Silva, his engine smoking copiously as he carved forwards from the very back of the grid to gain 22 places by race end. The young Brazilian remains as unassuming as ever, despite his successes in Formula 2000, and continued to affirm that it is karting that represents the great challenge.'

In Heat 3 'da Silva performed yet another of his miracles, once again climbing no less than 23 places on his long-suffering DAP.' In Heat 6 'da Silva again made up a tremendous amount of ground.' In the final itself 'the amazing Mr Silva made up half a lap deficit and then got all the way up to 14th.'

Peter de Bruijn remembers: 'I went off, got back on the track and we did the whole final together battling for 13th, 14th place!

I spoke to him quickly afterwards, he was already in Formula Ford 2000 and we talked a bit about that because I'd raced the Formula Fords myself in 1979.'

Mike Wilson, who won, remembers the prize giving. 'Obviously the first three were on the podium. The fourth driver came and shook hands with the first three and then stood by their side, the fifth man came and shook hands with the first four and so on and so on and it came to Senna, 14th, and he didn't shake hands with anybody because he was so upset. He really wanted to win the World Championship. At the time I thought the worst words you can think of, but looking back and knowing him more, knowing what kind of character he had, I'd have probably done the same thing myself if I'd been in that situation. It affected him so much not to have achieved it because he probably realised it was his last chance.'

It was. He was deeply disappointed and, as Rushen says, his attitude was bad for Brands Hatch.

'It all became a story of the front wings,' Rushen says. 'I said: "That's where we want the front wing." He disagreed. The qualifying session lasted twenty minutes and he came in three times to fanny around with this front wing. He didn't normally do that and he'd hardly done any laps. The fastest time was 46.5 seconds but three people were on that and he did it last so he started on the second row (Victor Rosso and Fish were the others) and halfway through the race he broke the lap record but it was too late to catch Fish. We had an argument – the only time we ever fell out. I said "[expletive expletive] what was that about?" He said: "You [expletive expletive]." That was the only race where his attitude was wrong.'

So what did happen? 'He decided,' Rushen says, 'that he was in a race and all of a sudden he wanted to win it. You could visibly see him speed up.'

Morris was there as an interested spectator. 'I distinctly remember Ayrton and Calvin Fish going into Paddock that time

Fish beat him. Fish had a better engine but – going into Paddock – the difference between the two drivers was noticeable, how Senna would catch up on pure skill.'

He had raced 28 times and won every one except six – and of those, four times he didn't finish (engine failure, spun off, puncture, crash). He was only actually beaten twice, at Snetterton and that final 2000 at Brands.

'He was always on a roll,' Fish says. 'When people start winning it's hard to get them out of the habit. There's no such thing as luck. You make your own and if ever there was a situation like that – I'm thinking of the complex at Thruxton when I was blocked – Ayrton would make his own. When you race against somebody you don't analyse them strongly, you analyse how you can beat them. You don't get into their abilities because, if you do, you're beaten before the race starts. Looking at it now, he had tremendous car control, tremendous natural ability and the ability to find things which could be turned into his favour. He was extremely intelligent in manipulating his own destiny, always being with the right teams, having the right equipment and having some control over all of that.'

Andrews the team-mate says that 'when I raced with him I thought a lot of people didn't understand. He was very shy and people got the impression that he was a difficult person. The thing was, when he was at a racetrack or driving the car he was absolutely dedicated. Away from the racetrack he was great fun, he was as good fun as anybody.' Andrews found him 'the most dedicated person to anything I have ever come across' and didn't think he could 'be knocked for that,' although people looked from the outside and said he was 'arrogant. I didn't find him at all like that. There were a lot of practical jokes. He was forever tying my shoe laces together when I was asleep. But when people were talking he couldn't answer because he didn't understand the English language brilliantly.' Andrews found him straight: "if you asked him a question you'd get a straight answer, no nonsense. He was helpful to me, he was a good team-mate.'

Roger Orgee, friend and helper of Steve Lincoln, saw one of Senna's victories at Brands Hatch. He was standing with Peter Browning, a well-known racing official. 'Peter said "this is a future World Champion." He was about fifty yards in front of everybody and just stayed there. He was one of those guys who stood out straight away.'

Nor was the 1982 season over.

Chapter 6

STARLET WARS

The tall man had a face which was almost florid. Down at the end of the transporter, beyond the tools and the workbenches, a small modern office had been created and he sat within it, hands resting on the table in front of him. He had a becalmed presence but eyes which, from time to time, were surveying you in small bird-like darts. Dick Bennetts wielded words in a phlegmatic way, as most team managers do, and he discussed the calms and storms of motor racing dispassionately. To you it may be heady, hedonistic, exotic, nakedly exciting, a cocktail of extremes. To him this was a job and all the incidents merely factors in his big equation.

'I'd met Ayrton Senna in the middle of 1982,' he would say, his voice still carrying the traces of a New Zealand accent. 'It was quite a laugh. The year before he'd driven with Mansilla – the young Argentinian – and he didn't rate him very highly. We had taken a few races in 1982 to get Mansilla into the winner's circle and we almost got the Formula 3 Championship. Ayrton's reasoning was that if he didn't rate Mansilla and we could make Mansilla a winner we must be a pretty good team.

'We did the non-championship Formula 3 race at Thruxton at the end of 1982 and Ayrton drove in Mansilla's car. He got into it and virtually without touching it he was flying. He said the car felt very, very good and he just wanted one small adjustment because it had a little bit too much understeer for him. He put it on pole by a mile, won by 13 seconds. We reached a verbal agreement after the race and he signed in January.'

The race was televised by the BBC and anyone involved in motor racing, including Grand Prix moguls, would certainly be watching.

Senna said: 'the most important thing for me was Formula Ford 2000. I didn't think it would be possible for me to race this year with a good team in Formula 3, but by the beginning of September I had already clinched the 2000 Championship so I decided it was a possibility for me to do this televised F3 race. I went home to Brazil in order to enjoy a little bit of the summer, the sunshine and also to meet my sponsors and talk about this race and about next season. I arrived back in England two weeks before the race and did some tests at Thruxton and Snetterton. I went well in the car and I found it was very good to work with Dick Bennetts. We seemed to understand each other well so I was looking forward to the race. Obviously the TV race was very important for me and now that I have done well I hope it will help me to find the budget for next season.'

Senna was the only man to get into the 1 minute 13 seconds in qualifying. He did it in both sessions. He took the lead from the flag (of course) and 'I was just making sure nothing could go wrong and that I didn't make any mistakes.'

Dick Bennetts ran West Surrey Racing, an extremely professional team. In 1983, they would contest the 20 rounds of the Marlboro British Formula 3 Championship: a thorough testing ground for a young driver because it stretched from March to October (so he'd have to master many different kinds of weather again). It would be fought out on six different circuits. Moreover, Formula 3 represented the last step before Formula 1.

'Ayrton brought some sponsorship over with him, so he'd got a bit of money,' Keith Sutton says. 'I think it was at that time that Ron Dennis contacted him and said he'd pay for the full season of Formula 3, and Ayrton turned it down ...'

(Much later, Ron Dennis would recount to me why Senna turned him down. Dennis wanted him to sign an option for the McLaren Formula 1 team, but of course, that did not guarantee him a Formula 1 drive when the time came, but would prevent him from driving for other teams. Dennis retains the utmost respect for someone just out of Formula 2000 who had the self-confidence to *know* he would do so well in Formula 3 he'd have several options open to him.)

Already journalists writing their previews to the season were posing a single question: who can beat Senna and his Ralt-Toyota? (If you're more of a general reader, let me explain that racing car constructors build the cars – in this case the Ralt company – which Dick Bennetts and other teams bought. Teams use engines made by major manufacturers, in this case Toyota. As we shall see in a moment, another team had a Ralt-Volkswagen. This holds true in Formula 1, hence McLaren-Mercedes, Williams-BMW, and so on. The point about FF1600 and FF2000 was that they all had Ford engines, and the drivers had a much more equal chance.)

Already Senna had tested the car twice and gone fast. Now, as the first race approached – Silverstone, 6 March – there seemed only one rival, Martin Brundle, a young man from Norfolk with a lovely, dry sense of humour. He, too, was in a Ralt-Toyota, but with Eddie Jordan Racing.

The ingredients were present for a season which would become nearly poetic; it would move to pinnacles so extreme that in the end it captivated all motor sport in a way which had not happened before or since at the level of Formula 3.

'I knew nothing of him personally,' Brundle would say, his voice still carrying faint traces of a Norfolk accent, 'although I'd heard a lot about him. I'd seen him win a Formula Ford 1600 race in 1981. Now all I heard about was this guy who was going to dominate Formula 3 and because he virtually hadn't driven in Formula 3 it seemed a bit strange. The talk was of who's going to get near him and I found that strange, too.'

Nor could Senna expect a fond embrace from Jordan. 'He knows I gave him a free drive in 1982 at Silverstone and he hardly spoke to me in 1983 at all and I was fighting my balls off to beat him. It's only recently [1989] that he nods and says "hello, Eddie." I don't like that so much. I gave him that first [F3] drive, I don't harm people, I help them. He is very much the professional, he is not a talkative person. I certainly wouldn't go out of my way to befriend someone who didn't want to be friendly with me. I'm not saying I'm perfect – far, far from it – but I paid and I know how difficult it was for me to survive in those days. As it's happened, he's turning out to be perhaps the greatest driver we've known ...'

These are a young man's final steps towards Formula 1.

Silverstone. In earlier testing, Senna and Brundle had battered the Club circuit record (53.94 seconds) set the season before. In qualifying for the race itself the wind blew down the straights full into the cars and a driver called David Leslie in a Magnum-Toyota took pole. This was as amazing then as it is now and would not be repeated. In 21 races, Senna took pole 16 times.

Senna was second quickest, Brundle fourth, Fish fifth and Johnny Dumfries, then twenty-three and in a Ralt-Volkswagen, sixth. Leslie held Senna to Copse Corner – Leslie had the inside line, of course. Senna drove round the outside of him and after five laps his lead grew to 3.28 seconds. At the end, after 20 laps and 32.16 miles, he was seven seconds ahead of Brundle.

Davy Jones once explained to me: 'Although I was as quick as Senna and Brundle, as a race progressed I might make a mistake, miss a gear change, but those guys wouldn't. Even at Formula 3 it was a very high level. For example the old Stowe Corner you took flat out in fourth, you arrived in fifth, changed down, then flat. Well, Senna wasn't even lifting, he was flat in fifth.'

The question came back immediately: *Who could beat Senna?*

Thruxton. Pole from Brundle and an 'exquisite' start. In the wet – it had rained earlier – he was quicker through the corners, Brundle quicker along the straights. Senna described it like this:

'I could see that I was faster through the corners but I also knew that I had to conserve my tyres. I knew that whoever could make their tyres last longer would win. And my engine just would not pull more than 5,000 revs.' Brundle set fastest lap. Senna, rarely a conservationist at this stage of his career, won. He had influenza. 'I did not feel good but I was not making mistakes in the car so I felt it was OK. But I'm not sure I was going as well as I could have done.'

Silverstone. Pole. It was wet again. Brundle would say from the heart: 'He is incredible. He always seems to find just a bit extra.' At Stowe, Senna took him on the outside. 'Quite brilliant,' Brundle said. The race was stopped after six laps by a downpour; a second six-lap 'heat' was run later, Brundle led again and this time Senna took him on the outside at Becketts. Brundle: 'It was incredible. He had two wheels on the grass but he still kept going.' Bennetts: 'Ayrton got beaten off the line and then just drove round the outside. Martin was staggered, as he admitted afterwards.'

Thruxton. Pole and victory although he had 'flu (again) and Bennetts wondered about letting him race. At one point he was third, took Brundle, took the leader – Davy Jones – on a power play and finished a second ahead of Brundle. 'Why doesn't he ever make a mistake?' Brundle wondered wistfully.

Irene Ambrose was at Thruxton. 'I made my timid way into the West Surrey awning clutching my entrance ticket, the only bit of paper I had. A slight, dark-haired boy [he was 23!] sat on a couple of wheels, smiling at me as I approached. Feeling ludicrously nervous I thrust the ticket at him and asked for his autograph. The smile deepened and as I gazed into those dark brown eyes I thought they looked very old in such a young face. He controlled the race perfectly and, feeling proud, I made my way into the paddock to congratulate him. He was still grinning widely as he shook my hand and thanked me.'

If you were an opponent, he was the hardest man in the world to beat. If you weren't, he was touchingly normal.

Coyne, for example, 'joined Ralph Firman in 1983 to do FF1600. 'Ayrton, who knew Ralph well, would come across and sit and talk to me, basically trying to help me, and that was nice. The moment you stopped being a threat he was totally different.'

Eddie Jordan watched Senna's progress with a knowing eye. 'Senna had this tactic of doing the opening couple of laps in a blistering way and it broke the opposition. He was the one who started it. Other drivers actually couldn't cope with it. A lot of them were trying to find themselves at the beginning of a race. Senna demoralised them all during the first two laps. He made a fantastic effort' – Jordan added that you could see him doing the same when he reached Formula 1 'but in Formula 3 he raised that to a new level. If you couldn't keep up with him you were finished, you'd never catch him back. Martin Brundle finally got around to accepting that if you couldn't stay with him you'd be beaten anyway.'

After Thruxton he flew to Brazil because he needed to relax, did relax and was back for round 6 at Silverstone saying he felt better. He took pole and won.

Thruxton. Pole, fastest lap from Brundle, win. Irene Ambrose sat 'in the grandstand to watch qualifying. He seemed to be taking a different line through the chicane each time, getting wilder and wilder until the little Ralt twitched ferociously in protest. After that he became smooth and consistent. "What were you doing out there?" I asked in my innocence. He was sitting on his tyres again, bent over slightly, hands clasped between his knees. "Just finding my limits," he said, smiling.'

A strong wind made it 'impossible' to set the car up perfectly at both the complex and the chicane. Meanwhile Bennetts confirmed that Senna was in discussions with the Williams Formula 1 team. 'He's trying to speak to as many people as possible.' This would lead to a test session but was not intended to lead to more.

Brands Hatch. In qualifying, *Autosport* said: 'Yes, Ayrton had done it again – his seventh successive pole – but it was the manner in which he achieved his position that provided the talking point of the morning. Quite simply the Brazilian's car was sensationally fast through Paddock Hill Bend. "It's right on the limit at that corner," confided Ayrton, "and I can tell you that it feels quite dangerous!" A dab of the brakes, a flick down into fourth gear and throw the car to the right, hard on the throttle: that was Ayrton's recipe for success. And he was quite visibly the fastest through that particular corner. Once, during the second session, he missed his down-change, turning into the corner without any positive drive, but even that presented only a minor problem, the Brazilian sliding wide out on to the "old" circuit [which runs alongside] and quickly bringing the car back under his total control. His progress was very good to watch.' The margin Senna-to-Brundle in the race was just under three seconds, and that was number nine.

Silverstone. Pole, fastest lap, victory, the margin to Brundle nearly 10 seconds.

Bennetts says 'of course, the bubble has to burst' and it did at Silverstone (round 10) two weeks later. To clarify this, rounds 9 and 10 were both at Silverstone, although round 10 was also a joint round of the European Championship.

'Senna was clearly very good in qualifying, so he was on pole more often than not,' Brundle said, exploring the context of the season from its start. 'Usually I was alongside him on the grid a tenth or less behind him but he seemed to catch me out for pole quite comfortably, really. But because you are side by side on a Formula 3 grid – no stagger – it's not that important. It was all about the first corner. He was very aggressive into the first corner. He'd take all the risks a man could take on the initial two laps to put a gap between himself and his pursuer, which basically was me. In the first race he'd beaten me comfortably, in the second race I'd got on his tail at Thruxton, I'd followed him the whole way and given him a hard time. After the race he responded in a slightly surprising way by telling my mechanics that it had been too close for comfort and he'd have to do something about it. It really interested me when he said that. I realised for the first time that I had made him aware of me. We never chatted much during the whole year so I can't even remember the first time I spoke to him.'

At the joint round at Silverstone you could choose in which championship your result would be registered. Bennetts outlines the thinking in their camp. 'We had such a big points lead over Martin that we chose not to do the British part.' In other words, Senna went European.

Very few Formula 3 races endure in the popular memory. By definition, Formula 1 casts its long shadow over them; these young drivers were serving their apprenticeship and would only be properly measured when they ascended, when they found themselves wheel-to-wheel with such as Niki Lauda and Alain Prost rather than (to select two names at random who were at Silverstone that June day) Max Busslinger and Carlton Tingling.

This race endures.

In the first qualifying session, in the wet, Senna was second quickest. It forced Brundle to gamble. 'You could choose between European tyres or British tyres – they were for the British Championship, they were much harder and slower. I made a decision to go for the British points because it was my one chance to catch up some of the ground lost to Ayrton. Although I was the fastest British runner I was only 12th on the grid. I thought what's the point of that? I need to be at the front of this field. I made a spontaneous decision and to this day I don't really know why I did it. I decided to mount European

tyres with a few minutes of the second qualifying session to go.'
(Technical note: Brundle had run in the wet on Avons, was now
changing to Yokohamas.) 'I said: "Mark me up a set of Europeans,
I'm going to go for it." I put it on pole.'

Brundle 1 minute 23.99
Senna 1 minute 24.08
Dumfries 1 minute 24.63

'All of a sudden I was in charge and it was one of the best
decisions I have made in my racing career. I put some extra wing
on, which was another flyer [risk] to get more downforce on the
basis that if I got away I wanted to be flat through Stowe and
Club, which the European tyres would allow you to do. Once I
got in front I was going to do a Senna. Nobody was ever going to
catch me. And off I went ...'

Brundle was in the lead at Copse, Senna second, Dumfries third.
They crossed the line like that for the first lap ... and the second.
Dumfries felt that 'Senna seemed to be in a bit of trouble with his
tyres and I caught up with him and we started to battle. I got a good
run out of Becketts, I was alongside him going down Hangar Straight
and he put me on the grass. I kept my foot on the accelerator and I
got back on the circuit. Do I blame him? No. I would like to
honestly, actually hear a driver say he has never put anyone on the
grass. That's fair. But it was interesting because he was under
pressure from me and he was also trying to catch Brundle.'

Senna did have tyre troubles. A contemporary account: 'Senna
had gambled on running three different types of tyre, including a
harder "SH" on the front left against the advice of the Yokohama
technicians in an effort to ensure that it would still be in good
condition at the end of the race, but he was soon in trouble with
excessive understeer.'

Senna would explain that 'after two laps the left rear wasn't
working at all. There was just no grip.' Bennetts would explain

that 'we opted for open tyres and we had an accident. Martin was on Yokohamas, Martin was leading, Ayrton put a wheel off at Club Corner and must have had a puncture because when he got to the chicane he lost it; to which Brundle says: 'So away I went. In an attempt to reach me he ended up in the catch-fencing at the chicane and that was the turning point, really.'

Enter Eddie Jordan: 'Senna made a mistake at the chicane, he went on to the top of the chicane and spun into the guardrail.' Jordan pauses, and you can hear his voice changing gear. 'We broke Senna that once at Silverstone – I'll never forget it. It was a hard-fought season and we established ourselves (as a team) with the Brundle-Senna battle, mainly because Brundle kept at him. We were beaten nine times in a row but we were all determined we were going to beat him.' He explained that Brundle was a very talented driver 'but you have to fill his head with the right kind of vibes. The thing about it is, we worked on him so hard that eventually he felt he was as good as Senna. It became personal, it was so competitive it was unbelievable, never have we seen a season like it. We got lots of TV and we got lots of credibility out of it.'

Bennetts says that 'that began a little series of setbacks. Ayrton was just never happy to finish second. There was such determination that we often had pole position and fastest lap, but he'd be beaten off the line and would run second – worth seven points (six for second place, one for fastest lap) – but might then crash trying to take the lead, losing the six points.'

Cadwell Park. By now the duel was starting to draw big crowds. That gave it a feeling of importance, but Cadwell was to be something different altogether. 'You have to find your limit,' Bennetts says. 'If you are winning everything, there is still a day when you must face the fact that you will be beaten and I think it doesn't hurt a driver to have one or two accidents (to show he *has* found his limit, not of course to hurt him).

'The classic example was Cadwell Park. We already had pole position and he wrote the car off with about two minutes of qualifying left. He was on pole over Brundle and if memory serves Brundle was eight-tenths behind [it was Senna 1 minute 22.57, Brundle 1 minute 22:58]. Ayrton said: "I can go another four or five-tenths quicker, just reduce a little bit of the understeer." We did that and apparently someone timing out on the course had him four or five-tenths quicker, but he didn't complete the lap. He destroyed the car on the Mountain – it's a very tricky little area and it goes uphill quite steeply. He got it wrong through there and went off. He hopped out. A marshal was knocked over and Ayrton, I'm told, was more worried about the chassis than the marshal.' (In fact, as Senna made clear to me, 'I never realised the situation with the marshal!' and this is undoubtedly correct.)

He'd strayed slightly wide coming out of the right-hander at the foot of the hill, kept the power on but ran out of road and struck the marshal's post virtually head-on. The car was wrecked and the marshal had to be treated for bruises and shock. He didn't race.

Snetterton. He qualified only fourth and had no idea what was wrong with the car. Neither did Dick Bennetts. Brundle took the lead, Senna inevitably behind him, Brundle pulled away, Senna nibbled and nibbled and by lap 12 – half distance – had caught him. Going along the straight to the S-shaped corners, Senna decided that the only way to overtake was to seize the inside line. He crept up on the inside with two wheels on the main tarmac throwing dust and stones at the car behind (Jones). Into the left-hand kink Brundle moved across on to the normal line, but Senna had his foot hard down. Spectators saw a 'tell-tale puff of smoke'. Senna's front wheel ran up and over Brundle's rear wheel. Senna spun across Jones and into the tyre-lined Armco backwards.

'Let's put it this way, I was less than white, less than pure in the incident,' Brundle says. 'He asked for a tribunal and they got a load of spectators in who saw the incident and let's face it, there we are at Snetterton, Norfolk, my home track. By now the war with Senna was pretty common knowledge and the tribunal was asking local people to make comments, so I didn't get fined or my licence endorsed. The relationship at that point was at its lowest. We didn't speak very much. I got on with him very poorly because he very much felt that it was Brundle and Great Britain versus Senna.'

Cor Euser has an interesting sideways glance at that. Euser raced Formula 3 and found Brundle more remote than Senna 'and Brundle speaks good English! I don't know why Brundle acted like that but probably he wanted to win as badly as Senna did and it's a question of keeping the distance with your opponents. That's what I have in mind when I say that *if I speak to someone they might get information out of me and that's why I don't speak to them.* If you push somebody off the track and he's your friend he will be your enemy after the race, simple as that. We are all human beings, but that's a calculation you have to make.'

Anyway, it was certainly Brundle and Norfolk versus Senna. 'Gradually our points lead was being eroded and up to then I'd never really sat down and had a good talk with him,' Bennetts said, because Senna was 'a very intelligent young guy. Some other young blokes you give them a bollocking every time they have an accident but with Ayrton being intelligent you know he really didn't mean to have it. But eventually, when I saw our points were eroding away, we sat down and had a chat. I said: "Do you realise this: it's better to finish second, you can't win every time." He found that extremely difficult to accept. There was only one place for him and that's first. He did realise his championship was slipping away.'

Between Snetterton and the next race, Silverstone (round 13 of the 20), Senna tested the Williams Formula 1 car at Donington. He did 70 laps, best time 60.90. What impressed

Frank Williams most at the time 'was that he got into the rhythm very speedily. He'd never driven anything as quick as a Formula 1 car but you'd never have thought so. I'm looking upon it as a kind of long-term investment in the future. There's no way we can handle him next year because of our current situation. I think Bernie Ecclestone's going to offer him a deal.' (Ecclestone owned the Brabham team and was monitoring the situation closely.)

'He came to see me a while ago,' Williams went on, 'asking for advice, saying that everyone was offering him 400-year deals and so on, the usual stuff. I told him that I couldn't really advise him but if it would help him to get the feel of the thing he could have a run in one of our cars whenever it suited him. I wasn't acting philanthropically – I hope he'll remember we treated him fairly.'

Reflecting much later, Frank Williams would say: 'After the first few laps it was obvious he was very talented, oh sure. In 21 laps he got down to a time which was about a second quicker than Jonathan Palmer [the team's test driver] and a second is a big difference over the 60-second circuit. He stopped and said: "I think the engine's going, so I'd better pack it up." The engine showed no signs of distress although it was sent for a re-build. I really think he said what he said because he was pressing on too hard – there were a couple of pictures taken at the time of him braking into the chicane with his left wheel half off the ground. I think he felt he should slow himself down by stopping! He was very good, but I didn't come back to the factory and say to Patrick Head: "we've got to get this guy whatever happens." Maybe that was an error ...'

Silverstone. Pole, fastest lap, victory, Brundle chasing all way.

Donington Park. Pole but Brundle got away first, held the car steady to the first corner and then held it steady to the end. This was the first time Senna had been beaten when he'd completed a race.

Oulton Park seemed to confirm that Senna still could not accept second place. Brundle was in the lead and, as he says, 'we had a coming together which was really his fault. He took a slide up the inside of me, I mean never in a month of Sundays was that going to work – I would have had to turn off the circuit to avoid the accident.'

Jordan remembers that 'Senna made an absolutely suicidal dive up the inside and the two of them went off, which was sad.' Amplifying Euser, Jordan felt that 'possibly Ayrton didn't speak to us because it might have taken an edge away. He was mega-competitive, he knew I was up to all sorts of tricks to try and beat him. We had protested him, he had protested us. After Oulton, he got fined and had his licence endorsed.'

Senna's view: 'I was right up his gearbox and I was going much quicker than him. I just braked late and went for the inside. I'm sure he didn't see me and he closed in on me when we were already going into the corner.'

(Meanwhile, rumours said that he had been offered a contract with Brabham.)

Silverstone. Pole, and the race margin to Brundle a second and a half. Senna 116, Brundle 94, Jones 60.

Oulton Park. Pole, Brundle took the lead, Senna after him, Jones after him. On lap 8 Senna tried to go outside Brundle at Druids and slithered off, buckling the front end of the car.

Thruxton. Pole but now, for the only time in the year, genuine bad luck struck at Senna. Brundle led, Senna overtaking in the complex on the gravel when Brundle locked his brakes, Brundle overtaking just after the chicane because Senna took a ragged line through it. As they completed the second lap Senna peeled away into the pits, travelling slowly. The engine had failed. Senna 116 points, Brundle 113, Jones 67 – and Brundle mused that if he won the last two races he'd be punished by his consistency. He'd have scored in 18 of the 20 rounds and you could only count 17 finishes.

Silverstone. Jones pole, then Brundle, then Allen Berg, a Canadian, then Senna who'd spun 'wildly' at Abbey Curve backwards, touching the railway sleepers. The race? Brundle from Senna all across Silverstone's broad acres and 20 laps. On the last lap Senna toyed with taking Brundle on the inside at Beckett's but decided against. Brundle 123 points, Senna 122.

By now, Senna's diary was filling quickly with intriguing entries.

On Sunday, 23 October he'd go to Thruxton to contest the final and decisive round of the British Formula 3 Championship. The following week he, Brundle and Stefan Bellof would test the Marlboro McLaren at Silverstone. In the second week of November he'd test the Toleman, again at Silverstone. A couple of days later he'd test the Brabham at the Paul Ricard circuit in the south of France. That would finish on Monday, 24 November and he'd fly back to Britain in Bernie Ecclestone's own plane in time to catch a flight for Macau and the international Formula 3 race there.

First, Thruxton, set in the gentility of English pastureland. There was mist, hanging and lingering, insinuating itself around Church Corner – a very apt name – where the cars would have been going at top speed. They waited for the mist to clear. They knew that Brundle had a one-point lead after 19 rounds. They knew that, because of his consistency, Brundle was having to drop points and what he needed was simple now: to win. It was 23 October 1983.

They couldn't see a proper, straight-up no-nonsense example of mechanical machinations which makes motorsport so devious, infuriating and interesting.

'We didn't know for a long time,' Dick Bennetts says, 'that Brundle had an engine done by Novamotor Italy. Our Novamotor engine had been rebuilt in England and we weren't given the latest developments. So for Thruxton we sent the engine to Italy, to where Brundle's had been done. Ayrton drove a car down with the engine in the boot. That's not unusual. We send a lot of our drivers to meet engine builders. We still didn't get the same modification as them, but it was rebuilt.

'My honest view is that if we'd had the same spec engines midway through the year Ayrton possibly wouldn't have had so many accidents [i.e. wouldn't have had to push so hard]. But we didn't know about it until two or three races from the end of the championship. I'd found out by looking at their car in scrutineering. They had a different pulley on the engine. It got me thinking. I rang Novamotor and they said "it's just a one-off development". So we had our engine rebuilt, but we couldn't get one with the special pulley. What we did have was 1984 sidepods and Eddie was upset then.'

Yes, Eddie was upset then. He says: 'This is a fact – we went into the last round of the Formula 3 Championship one point ahead in a total long series. When you think back, when you see what Senna has achieved, I reckon as a little team – as we then were – running one car we were magic. I was furious with Ron Tauranac. It was one of the reasons I left Ron. He upset me because we fought so hard and he brought an unfair advantage. In the wind tunnel he had found a new underbelly. They weren't flat bottoms, there were wing sections underneath. OK, maybe Ayrton deserved to win because he was the best, but we didn't deserve as a team and as a customer to be treated unfairly. I admire Ron but I have never ever forgotten that he brought it in. This was a completely new underwing. We used to get some stuff to try for him and Dick Bennetts used to get the same. Dick got his hands on this and he persuaded Ron that he should be given the opportunity – because he had tested it – to have it exclusively for the last race. Why Ron did that for him I don't ever know.'

Bennetts: 'Well, all I can say is that Novamotor gave him an advantage by giving him an engine which had a different cam pulley arrangement and we didn't have one.'

Brundle: 'At a race before it was wet and what I was doing was short-changing, second, third, fourth coming out of the chicane. That's how I went so far off into the distance – but I was pulling too low revs. We went into the last round with an engine which was basically tired because I didn't have enough money to do anything about it. Senna went to Italy – I know because Stefano Modena is my current team-mate [1989] and he's told me Senna stayed with him. He had an engine pulled apart, put on the dyno all under his supervision, decided he didn't like that, had another one put together, put on the dyno and decided he did like that.'

Senna: 'Not so. I simply took our engine to Italy, they rebuilt it in one go, straightforward, nothing else much, which proves that for half a season we were at a disadvantage to Brundle.'

Brundle: 'He brought it home personally [in the boot] so he had a new engine for Thruxton. Also, Ron Tauranac had got two new parts ready for 1984, a push rod front suspension and new sidepods with five per cent more downforce. So I got the suspension and Senna got the aerodynamic package and the aerodynamic package was the thing to have.'

Now, this early morning of 23 October, the mist did begin to clear. The cars were able to go out at 9.28 for the first practice session. Wintry sun peered through the dispersing mist. Senna did a handful of laps, eased the car into the pits, Bennetts adjusted the wings, he went back out. The American Jones had done 1 minute 13.63. Senna responded with 1 minute 13.55 – and the record was 1 minute 13.55. Not that that mattered. Brundle did 1 minute 14.03 and the session finished. Years before, local residents had obtained a High Court injunction to stop motor racing during the hours of worship. Now the bells from two churches with the same name – St Peter and St Paul, one near the circuit, the other in the nearby village of Kimpton –

tolled across the flat land. In the second session Senna brushed aside the record.

Brundle: 'To be honest, we're scratching. The engine is pinking like mad for some reason and there's also too much oversteer.'

The faithful had seen all this but now, quietly, discreetly, the man from 1982 – Dennis Rushen – moved unseen by them into the paddock. 'I have a lot of time for Dick Bennetts, he's a good guy. Dick's a brilliant engineer but if he has a weakness it's that he's not too good with drivers. Towards the end of the season he was having problems and he phoned me up and he said, "Harry keeps telling me to [expletive] off every time I say anything. Would you come down and have a word with him?" I went to Thruxton and I got him in the transporter. I said: "What the hell are you doing? There's one race to go for the championship and you've got to get out there and do the job." He accepted it quietly. But that's how he can be. You've got to handle the guy. Harry wants to have his own way and you've got to let him have his own way or let him think he's having his own way. It's important to do that.'

With this piece of man management concluded, Senna took his place on pole position. He faced 15 laps, only 35.34 miles but long enough for an enormous amount to happen. Somewhere nearby his father, a man of obvious dignity and presence, watched intently.

Irene Ambrose 'knew he was going to win and I wanted to be there. It involved getting into London at the crack of dawn, getting a train to Andover, switching to a branch line "somewhere in Hampshire" and the very long slog, dodging traffic down windy country roads to the circuit. The day went quickly …'

Senna made a perfect start, Jones tucked in behind him, Brundle tucked in behind him but at the complex Senna was already a couple of lengths ahead. Brundle attacked Jones, urged his car alongside but Jones held him off. They came through the chicane feeding them on to the start-finish straight but Senna was gone. After two laps he was two seconds ahead.

What Brundle, hounding Jones, didn't know was that Senna had taken a risk. He'd taped up the oil radiator outlet to heat the engine more quickly. 'It worked perfectly. The oil was up to proper temperature within a lap or so rather than the usual six or seven.'

But now – it was lap 6 – with the water temperature rising he leant an arm out to tear the tape away. He couldn't reach it. Surging towards the chicane he had to make a decision. Could he afford to wait, the temperature climbing and climbing? He unbuckled his safety belt – and he'd taken care to practise this many times the week before.

He angled his body forward, opened the air flap but the chicane was on him. He thrust himself back into the seat but there was no time, no time at all to clip the belt up again. He had reached the chicane. 'By the time I looked back up, I was almost up to the chicane. I thought I'd lost it for a minute. All of a sudden I was not part of the car, I was sliding around inside.'

A memory returns of that day: Senna, buckled up again, moving away, moving away, Brundle flicking and darting behind Jones but trapped – Senna relentlessly keeping on moving away, moving away. The lead became seven seconds and still memory holds: Brundle at the chicane, the snout of his car probing at Jones. In the end, it became the most simple of all motor racing stories: he had the will but lacked the speed.

Senna eased back for the last couple of laps and on the final one his hand was held high out of the cockpit in salute. He'd won it. He stood on the podium with both arms raised, both fists clenched.

'I struggled, I really struggled,' Brundle says. 'Davy Jones beat me and it was one of the few times in the year when I didn't finish first or second. I hadn't got the power, I hadn't got anything. I saw Senna have a big wobbly moment while he was taking the tape off, but then he won and he won fair and square. On the podium, and in front of his father and mother, he was very magnanimous and after that there was an interview with both of us and he was busy telling the whole world that I was the best British driver who had emerged since Jim Clark. I think we ended up realising we had done each other an awful lot of good. If he'd won the championship at a canter – sure, he was Senna, he was going upwards anyway, no problem – that wouldn't have been the same thing. Me being near gave it an awful lot of credibility. We had national and international coverage, we had done a lot for each other. We elevated each other straight into Formula 1.'

Ambrose went to the West Surrey truck and 'it was getting dark. Eventually I got my chance and dived in to congratulate him on his victory. Anyone who ever glibly said he was cold or unfeeling should have seen him that evening. He was as genuinely overwhelmed as anyone I have ever seen. As I trudged out of the circuit I was torn between awe and the elation of knowing I'd witnessed history being made – and being grateful for it – and the knowledge that with Formula 1 beckoning it could never be the same again.'

Bennetts says that 'there was no point' in Senna doing Formula 3 again in 1984. 'He sought my advice a little bit, not too much. He pretty much had his own thoughts on things, he was a very intelligent man for his age. I didn't know the Formula 1 people that well in those days.'

That night Senna, his father and mother, the Bennetts, some members of the team and Keith Sutton, went to a restaurant at Shepperton, near where West Surrey Racing were based, to celebrate with a meal. He was very happy and it was, Sutton says, 'a really nice evening.'

Next, the McLaren at Silverstone. Marlboro invested in the infrastructure of motor racing and, courtesy of McLaren, they gave the three promising young drivers their taste. Marlboro and McLaren did things properly, John Watson came along and drove a few laps to set a time – a yardstick with which to measure the youngsters.

'I was so impressed by the whole thing,' Brundle says. 'I'd never driven a car with anything like that power. I mean, the fastest thing I'd ever driven was a Formula 3 car with 150 horsepower and suddenly here I was – 550 horsepower and it was absolutely no problem.'

Memory's mechanisms are a mystery to me. I remember so clearly Silverstone that day: how emptied it was, how intimate. You could stand beside the car, chat to whomever you wanted. It was cold enough to need anoraks, cold enough to leave Brundle with one hand in a pocket, the other nursing a polystyrene cup of coffee. I remember – how can memory be this exact? – standing just inside the pit door with Brundle's father, a patrician of a man. The instant Brundle moved away – that impossible growl-howl of the engine when you're close to it – I remember shouting (you have to): 'I hope he comes back!'

'Yes,' his father shouted as the red and white McLaren flowed down the pit lane. I don't remember Bellof being there at all that day but he was, he was. Years later, I came across a photograph of the pit lane, Brundle in the car and the McLaren mechanics making final adjustments. On the far side of the car, Brundle's father stands gazing as if he is looking at a beautiful painting. He has binoculars round his neck. There are precisely two people on the pit lane wall and Senna nowhere to be seen. Behind the car I am standing with Bellof and we are both laughing. I repeat: I have no memory of this whatsoever, never mind what was amusing us so much.

'We all did roughly the same lap times, Brundle says, 'about a tenth apart. We had already blown dear old Wattie's set-up time completely out of the window although he didn't need to impress three young drivers. He'd done it all before. Every time I came in they cleaned the flies off the car, every time I got in the car on went a Brundle and a Union Jack sticker [on the side of the cockpit]. They were so professional I just wanted to kiss Ron Dennis's feet for allowing me 30 laps in this wonderful piece of machinery. Senna managed to blow up on his first run.'

He did – it wasn't his fault, of course – but before that, to quote *Autosport*, 'he quickly got into the groove but incurred a finger-wagging from Ron Dennis for trying to go too quickly too soon and was hauled out of the car to cool off for a short while.'

Meanwhile out there, out at the back of the circuit, a small, rather jolly man watched. He was called Herbie Blash and he was Brabham's spy. 'I went purely to watch Senna. We had Brabham and Senna in mind. I was timing Senna, he did a lap – a 1 minute 11 – and then the engine blew up. It happened where I was timing him so I could see – and none of the McLaren people could – exactly how quick this lap would have been. When the engine blew he never made it past the point where they were timing the cars, so they never got the lap. Obviously I informed Senna. He said he knew it was quick but I was the only one who knew how quick it was. I didn't inform McLaren ...'

Brundle says that 'after my laps I got out and I was so excited about it. Meanwhile Senna was negotiating a second run, much to my annoyance. I was a simple country boy from Norfolk. I'd got myself in a Grand Prix car and I hadn't got management around me, I hadn't got anybody around [except dad], it was just me doing what I did naturally. Senna was there with managers and all that sort of thing. I was impressed by that, you have to take your hat off to the guy; and he was negotiating a second run ...'

Senna: 'I had absolutely no managers. It was myself and my father, that was all.' And negotiating a second run? 'I did it all myself and the simple reason was that during my first run something didn't work well. I can't remember what it was now ...'

After that second run, incidentally, Senna said: 'The McLaren is quite an easy car to drive and I know I could have gone much quicker. The steering is lighter than on my Formula 3 car, although I wasn't really comfortable. My right leg was squashed [against the monocoque] and the blood wasn't circulating properly, I couldn't feel the throttle well because of that.'

Next, the taste of Toleman. Chris Witty remembers 'he tested the same day Brundle drove the Tyrrell. Ayrton had the TG 183, the thing that Derek Warwick had been driving. It was at Silverstone, a nice, bright, cold day but the engines love it when it's crisp in autumn time. He got in this thing and instantly he was on the pace and he ended up about a second quicker than Warwick had done in the Grand Prix. Mind you, Brundle went quicker that day than Rosberg had done in the Williams at the Grand Prix. Rory Byrne (the designer) said: "This is the guy." He had the ability even at that stage and at that age to know what a car was doing, know what he wanted a car to do and converse with an engineer. Rory said: "He's brilliant, we've just got to have him."'

Next, a taste of Brabham. Blash, the team manager, had returned silently home from Senna's McLaren test at Silverstone a disciple. 'I knew him from Formula 3, because I'm a friend of Dick Bennetts [they drank in the same pub in Shepperton!] and after Silverstone, we were really keen to sign him up. He tested for us at Ricard. He was very quiet – very, very quiet. He wasn't pushy in any way. He did a very professional job for somebody who you'd have thought was looking at the big world of Formula 1. He took it very calmly, jumped in the car, came back, gave us very good feedback, very good information. From there you could see the guy was going to be a World Champion.'

This was part of a general Formula 1 test, all the big teams and drivers present. Brabham had four hopefuls there: Mauro Baldi, Senna, Roberto Guerrero and Pierluigi Martini. Michele Alboreto went fastest in the Ferrari, 1m 2.5s, and this is what the hopefuls did: Baldi 1m 7.80s, Senna 1m 7.90, Guerrero and Martini 1m 8.60. You can make too much of these things, but Baldi had driven two full Grand Prix seasons (Arrows 1982, Alfa Romeo 1983); Guerrero had, too (Ensign, 1982, Theodore 1983), so that a fairer comparison for Senna's time would be Martini's.

Next, Macau. The distant Portuguese enclave was linked to Brazil by the umbilical cord just like Estoril. It was notable for casinos, slums and paddy fields.

'There were several magical moments in 1983 and Macau was one of them,' Bennetts says. 'It was the first time there had been a Formula 3 race there. Ayrton arrived very late Wednesday night and jet-lagged. He'd been testing the Brabham. When he went out on Thursday morning for qualifying he hadn't seen the track before – others among the entry had been there in Formula Atlantic.

'It's a four-mile Monaco-type street circuit, it's got a long straight and two and a half miles on very twisty, narrow, bumpy roads. He brushed a wall in qualifying, damaged a rim – he was that close – and then he put it on pole. No, it didn't surprise me because of his raw talent. The race? He just cleared off and won both heats. My belief is that a lot of it is the ability of concentration, the power of concentration. If you apply your mind to a lot of things you can do them. He had total dedication and concentration and talent as well. Some guys are very quick at learning circuits, others will drive round for two years and still not find the right line.'

This was Senna's debut at a street race. In first qualifying Guerrero (Ralt-Toyota) did 2 minutes 22.85 seconds, Senna and Brundle both on 2 minutes 23.47. Senna had only three laps before he brushed that wall, damaging all four wheels but not the car itself. In the second session he bent a gear selector and, losing time for repairs, had only three laps again. It was enough. He did 2 minutes 22.02, Guerrero next on 2 minutes 22.18.

Guerrero took the lead in the first heat and quite naturally reached the hairpin – only 150 metres from the starting line – still in the lead. If he 'covered' this, nobody would catch him afterwards. Guess who took the lead from him? 'He came past me down the alley between the two corners,' Guerrero said. 'I couldn't believe what he was able to do on cold tyres.' Senna won, went to bed for an hour and a half – he still had jet lag, the weather was extremely hot and 'I wasn't feeling well.' The second heat: Flag to flag.

Irene Ambrose 'stood outside a TV shop in Tottenham Court Road, London, for about half an hour watching Senna win Macau. I walked away with a sense of rightness I experienced so many times later.'

Bennetts says that 'because it was all new to us we went out and had a very good night. Teddy Yip of Theodores, you know, put on a wonderful spread in the Lisboa Hotel after the race – a fantastic spread.' The party went on until three in the morning. 'We got to bed about four-thirty, five, which you don't do in England when you're racing.'

The overall situation in Senna's career: McLaren had no vacancy (they were running Lauda and Prost), and Williams had no vacancy (they were running Keke Rosberg and Jacques Laffite); Riccardo Patrese was leaving Brabham for Benetton, and Italian company Parmalat – sponsoring Brabham – wanted another Italian to replace him, hence Martini and Baldi at the Ricard test. Staying in Formula 3, as Bennetts has said, was not an option. It is a precise commentary on the complex nature of motor racing – and the interwoven, overlapping vested interests which make it function – that, at the tail end of 1983, the young driver with the richest potential for decades might find himself with no drive at all.

Chapter 7

TOLEMAN

The room was large for an office. You could have held small conferences there. It had a view of suburban England, a solid, timeless, becalmed grey stone church, semi-detached houses fringed by trees. During the day you could hear the hum of an ordinary English shopping street not far away, just up there by the traffic lights. Brentwood, on the very outer reaches of London, was functional, just as Alex Hawkridge's office was. The office was also deep within the heart of the headquarters of a company called Toleman, then well-known for an extremely anonymous activity. They delivered cars from ports to salerooms. (An employee once said: 'We can't even advertise. Who cares who delivers their cars?')

Ted Toleman was an incorrigible adventurer who couldn't resist offshore powerboats or the Paris–Dakar rally. One day in the late 1970s, while he was buying me an extravagant lunch at his extravagant country club he began talking of his Formula 2 team. The conversation drifted easily into the realms of conjecture and Formula 1. They made it in 1981, won their first points in 1983 and that year Derek Warwick joined Renault, which offered the chance of becoming World Champion.

It was to fill this vacancy that Senna journeyed to Hawkridge's office. Hawkridge charts the background: 'He got engaged in this contest with Martin Brundle in Formula 3 and both of them knew that one of them would drive for Toleman the next season. They were the two drivers. If Ayrton hadn't signed and Martin had been prepared to, Martin would have been our driver for 1984. Ayrton knew that. So it went to the guy who got the championship, in essence that was it. We did the deal here in these offices. It was well into '84, it was real last-minute stuff. There was Bernie Ecclestone, Ron Dennis, Lotus ... I think he'd had a pretty liberal sprinkling of promises. Along the way he'd had contact with just about everybody. As the pre-season progressed to a crescendo he was acknowledged to be somebody that they ought to be interested in. Formula 1 is such a closed world that I don't think anybody apart from us was actually serious.'

Peter Warr of Lotus was. He had had Senna in *his* office, but what happened next illustrates the conflict of interests which operate within Formula 1. The main backers of Lotus were John Player Special and at Brands Hatch for the Grand Prix of Europe in late 1983 Player, a British company, was the sponsor of the race, too. 'One of our drivers, Elio de Angelis, put his car on the front row,' Warr says. 'Nigel Mansell was on the second row. The next morning I opened up the British papers and the headlines were screaming MANSELL ON THE SECOND ROW! John Player said we'd better keep the Brit, and we did.'

Hawkridge explains that 'we had to be serious for different reasons from the others. We couldn't hire a superstar [money] or even a current experienced driver on a minimum retainer – our cars wouldn't get a fair showing in the hands of an average Formula 1 driver. We had to go for young talent. That was the only way forward for Toleman. We had to have somebody good enough to progress the car and we knew Ayrton was capable of doing that. Martin would have been, too. Either of those guys would have done justice to our product so, to be honest, I wasn't really bothered. The pluses and minuses were about equal. I don't think there was any difference in speed between them. I don't think there was a great deal of racing difference between them.

'I have to say that on balance results speak for themselves. I believe in the performance system: Ayrton won the Formula 3 Championship and Martin came second. Even Martin can live comfortably with that.'

He can. He said: 'It all came down to the Toleman drive, really. I was in Alex Hawkridge's once and they made it quite clear that they wanted me to drive for them, but that Senna was top of the list. I think Senna was going to Brabham at the time but Piquet wouldn't have him, so he came back and got the Toleman drive.'

Herbie Blash confirms that and expands on it. 'I was sad in one way but in another way we were more than happy to keep Piquet because he was our World Champion. Piquet said no [to having Senna] and Piquet was involved with our Italian sponsors [Parmalat]. So it was very difficult to say: "Oh, I felt really sorry for Senna." Bernie was the one who told him.'

Witty 'saw a lot of Ayrton in 1983. I was the one who used to go to the Formula 3 races and keep tabs, talk to him and generally try to woo him – because certainly when he started going well in Formula 3, Ron Dennis came on pretty strong. Then it got to the situation where Bernie wanted him. That was quite good fun. I mean, that was Bernie in some ways wanting to prevent him going to Ron – Bernie is very persuasive. But at the end of the day it suited Bernie not to have him because of Bernie's package [Piquet, Parmalat.] You can understand why.'

'I don't think Ayrton had any choice,' Hawkridge says. 'We were his last stop but the issue for him was: *before I sign for this team rather than retire from motor racing altogether I have to be absolutely sure*. He said in conversation before we'd signed the contract: "If the car isn't good enough and if you stop me changing to another team I will leave racing. You cannot force me to drive a racing car. Either you make a term in the contract to allow me to take up anther chance if it comes along or you give me no option but to leave racing if I don't think your car is competitive. I'll stay with you if possible and I'll give you a hundred per cent every time I sit in the car." What can you say to a guy who says that to you? You can't say "that's unfair, Ayrton," you can't say "that's not the way we do things in Formula 1," you can't make a guy give you a hundred per cent – but he did every time, he gave us everything he had.

'Would he have retired? I never know with Ayrton. He was a self-assured, confident negotiator.' Hawkridge judged it was the 'same dilemma' for the others who Senna dealt with in the future. You just didn't know 'how far' he believed what he said. Hawkridge didn't doubt him.

'The negotiating was completely one-sided. He got what he wanted. It wasn't money, money wasn't a problem at all, it was the conditions of the contract and in particular the buy-out terms of the contract – the one area where I disagreed with him. I'm talking about the terms of the contract as we understood it. But I can appreciate the overall problem because you were dealing with a Brazilian who was working in a foreign language with a legal document which is resting on lawyers on the end of a telephone. That's what we had. We were sitting in this office with an open telephone line to his lawyers in Brazil. I didn't have our lawyers. I reckoned it was unfair enough as it was, so I was anxious that it was fair to him, anxious that it was something he could live with and that we would never have to use.

'In other words, if it became a usable document then the relationship between us and our driver was finished. We approached it on that basis but nonetheless he was very particular about every single sentence, wanting to know exactly what it meant and adding words throughout the agreement. With his lack of command of the English language he did a hell of a job to meet his requirements. It was an insight into him.'

All this was centred on the buy-out clause, intended (by Toleman) never to be used. It said: 'If Senna wants to leave he has to tell us before he signs for another team and pay us a certain amount of money.' In due course, when Senna did use it, his action gave Grand Prix racing one of its regular convulsions.

'The meeting went on well into the early hours of the morning, thrashing out the interpretation of the words. He would accept some explanations, he would insist on others being changed.' Don't think, Hawkridge mused, that he was just a good racing driver – he was good at whatever he did, a man who would 'excel at anything' he put his hand to.

Senna was candid. Toleman 'was the best offer, the best situation that I could have at that time. Toleman was coming up, it was a new team. They really believed that I could learn with them and do a good job. They were prepared to commit themselves a lot with me so I felt it was the right thing. Taking everything together, I'm sure it was at that time, given the conditions.'

Just before we journey to Brazil in late March, 1984, we must consider tyres. Because a Formula 1 car is what it is, a small difference magnifies itself. If you are a casual tele-spectator, you might imagine that all tyres are virtually the same: they aren't. It is an accepted axiom within Formula 1 that you virtually cannot win on uncompetitive tyres. This would become central to Senna's first season and would give Formula 1 another of its regular convulsions. Three companies were supplying the 15 teams.

Michelin: Brabham, Ligier, McLaren, Renault.
Goodyear: Alfa Romeo, Arrows, ATS, Ferrari, Lotus, Tyrrell, Williams.
Pirelli: Osella, RAM, Spirit, Toleman.

The big boys, then, were grouped around either the French or American companies; the small boys around the Italian company.

At Jacarepagua, the circuit for the Brazilian race, Witty remembers that Senna had 'asked for something like 35 passes, some ridiculous number, and Bernie said to tell him the facts of life. He thought he could have as many as he wanted.'

This may well have been a misunderstanding. When I quoted Witty as saying this in the manuscript of *The Hard Edge of Genius*, which Senna corrected, he was clearly upset at the implication that he'd asked for more than his due. It offended his sense of honour. He wrote: 'To my mind the number of passes was as usual very restricted and what we decided was on the basis of what we had in our hands – so people were going in and out under a system where everybody had an opportunity to see a little bit of Formula 1. Don't forget this was my first Grand Prix and it was in Brazil.'

By everybody, he includes members of his family who, as Witty says, 'idolised him. Ayrton was a demi-god, even to his family. It's almost like a little cage in Brazil and they didn't actually come into the area where we had the car. His mother sat there nearly all day in the shade and I thought this was idolisation of the eldest son ... but, I mean, he was a pretty good kid to idolise.'

To those who imagine the Prodigal Son was selfish and self-centred, please listen to Keith Sutton. 'I'd kept in touch with him over the winter and he said he wanted me there at his first Grand Prix – Brazil, of course. He said he'd look after me. He did, my flight to and from Rio, my hotel.'

He qualified on the eighth row of the grid but lost turbo boost pressure on lap 8. Witty had noticed something in Brazil, apart from his family, and it presaged, he believes, the beginning of the end – already. 'I think it actually started as early as that Grand Prix. He appeared with a Marlboro patch on his overalls and a Munroe shock-absorber patch. His contract said he could have anything he wanted, but he had to clear it with the team, and he hadn't. Alex brought Ayrton up to Brentwood and there was Peter Gethin, myself and Alex, and Alex tore into him. I actually saw a tear in the kid's eye and I thought: "Oh, Christ, he's being belittled." Alex was really laying into him a bit, and I think Ayrton thought: "Should I really have to go through with this?" Technically, Ayrton was wrong, but the problem with him was that if you gave him an inch he'd take six. I mean, he was fairly good at making sure he got what he wanted, but I felt we were a bit hard with him.'

Gethin remembers that meeting at Brentwood. 'Ayrton was crying, in fact he was crying quite a lot. I saw him suddenly realise what was going on and it was like a drawbridge going down in front of his face. In that moment he went from Senna the child to Senna the man.'

In South Africa he qualified on the seventh row, finished sixth. He'd had to drive part of the race with no nose cone: he'd hit something, probably a stone, which made steering exhausting, and at the end had to be helped from the car. He had not, of course, driven anything like 72 consecutive laps in a Formula 1 car before; and as a point of interest Martin Brundle, after an extended pre-season test in Brazil in the Tyrrell, had to be helped out, too. Only time in the cockpit prepares the body for the special strains.

'Ayrton was very difficult to cope with,' Witty says. 'He knew what he wanted and always got what he wanted. Alex, as I've said, was pretty strong with him in the early days, maybe a little bit too strong, and Ayrton thought: "Right, I know where I'm going, sod you guys." He did have a sense of humour although he was unbelievably intense. He just knew that if you are going to be successful you've got to detach yourself from the distractions. That would no doubt be the same for a tennis player or whatever, but it seems to me particularly so in Formula 1. If you are going to deliver you've got to give it one hundred per cent.

'I remember Zolder vividly. We had the old dog which was, well, the double-wing thing from the year before. He'd driven it in Brazil and retired, he'd driven it in South Africa and got his first point, he came to Zolder and he knew that we had the new car sitting back in the factory and he was a bit upset.' Toleman were negotiating with Michelin, having decided that they were going nowhere with Pirellis. 'We felt politically that we should transfer all the allegiance of the new car on to Michelin. He said the old car [the TG 183] was an absolute dog to drive. I thought

Opposite: *The young man beginning his journey to conquer Formula 1: Hockenheim, 1984.*

Left: *Push-starting a career: Karting at Interlagos, Senna in pink.* (Courtesy Tche)

Below: *He was fast in FF1600. This is Mallory Park, 1981.* (LAT)

Right: *FF2000. Team talk before he wins at Thruxton, August 1982.* (Bruce Grant-Braham)

Far right: *Summer 1983, F3, thinking of Formula 1?* (Bruce Grant-Braham)

Below right: *Leading Martin Brundle at Silverstone, 1983 – and winning.* (Bruce Grant-Braham)

ALL PHOTOGRAPHS ARE BY RAINER SCHLEGELMILCH EXCEPT WHERE STATED.

Above: *Glimpses of 1984. Bitter Imola, where rain in qualifying kept him out of the race.*

Right: *Quick on the draw: Brands Hatch, the British Grand Prix and Senna is already out between the two columns.*

Below: *Too quick on the draw: the crash at the start of the European Grand Prix at the Nürburgring, Senna nearest the camera.*

Glimpses through the rain, 1985. Senna's first victory, in a storm at Estoril.

Imola, and the Sunday morning warm-up was wet.

Rain at Spa, and Senna sets off for victory.

But dry in Hungary in 1986 – where he was second behind Nelson
Piquet.

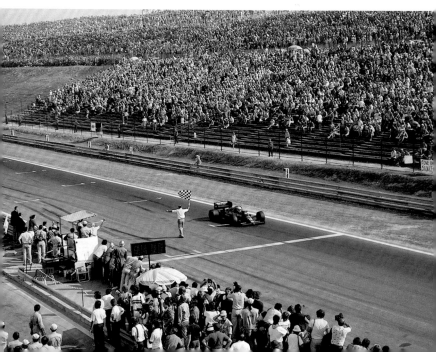

Plenty to contemplate in 1986 … including going off in the French Grand Prix. Senna apologised to his mechanics.

he'd do five laps. The guy did the whole race. He finished seventh, subsequently promoted to sixth when Stefan Bellof was disqualified [allegedly, Tyrrell added lead ballast to the fuel]. To me it said so much for the guy that he knew the car was a dog, didn't want to drive it, but did the job.

'People found him difficult to get on with and one thing in the early Toleman days, he was very sceptical of journalists, particularly those in Formula 1 that would suddenly want to become your best mate.

'We had Stefan Johansson later that year, Stefan is a big mate of mine but he's too nice. That's why Stefan had about four second places and 23 third places. There were great social scenes and, when he got to McLaren, Stefan was quite happy to be in the shadow of Alain Prost – but he wasn't a winner.' Senna was.

Now, as we move towards the next race, Imola on 6 May, the tyre situation was becoming acute. As Hawkridge says: 'We'd been with Pirelli, we'd always been with Pirelli, we'd never had an opportunity to run on anything else. We believed that our engine wasn't the problem and we had a reasonably competitive package – well, a hell of a competitive package. We were convinced that tyres were our problem. Pirelli had stopped listening to us long before, we could make no progress. We said: "There's no future in this relationship, we've lost all confidence" – and this was the team talking, because my relationship with Pirelli was an arm's-length one; but the morale in the team was so bad over the tyre issue that the team would have gone downhill. It was a make-or-break position. We either had to find an alternative or stop Grand Prix racing. It was our Waterloo. We had to obtain a different tyre manufacturer and prove once and for all whether our team had any competence or not. If, having changed, the car was not competitive, that was a reason to stop. If the car was competitive it was no guarantee of success, but at least it was a way forward.'

Hawkridge approached Michelin.

'The first time we ran on Michelins I went to the test. That was when Ayrton impressed me more than on any other occasion. By agreement with Michelin we would run their previous year's tyres which, by their own acknowledgement, were uncompetitive. We were made no promises that we would ever have the same tyres as McLaren. McLaren had some sort of golden vote that would exclude us from getting comparable equipment. We ran on their old tyres, cross-matching different compounds. Ayrton was able to keep improving the car. It amazed even the Michelin technicians.

'This was Dijon, after the race at Imola. We decided to change to Michelins the race after Imola. The reason was we didn't want to embarrass Pirelli on their home ground. So we had an agreement with Michelin that no announcement would be made. That was a Michelin request. The drivers [the other was Johnny Cecotto] were frustrated as hell – Senna in particular, having run on the Michelins. He was transformed. "This is a different ball game, now we're with the front runners." I tell you, within five laps of running on Michelin tyres he said "we're on the pace."'

But not at Imola. Toleman took a drastic step – there were suggestions of a financial dispute between them and Pirelli – and didn't run in the Friday qualifying session to 'pre-empt any hostile reaction from Pirelli' (*Autocourse*).

The Tolemans did go out on the Saturday but a fuel pressure problem prevented Senna from doing a lap any faster than 1 minute 41.585 seconds. It was not enough to get him into the race.

'The decision had nothing to do with me, that was a team decision and was between the team and Pirelli, so there was nothing I could do about it,' Senna would explain. 'I was not upset that we changed, I was upset that we didn't have the opportunity to race in Imola because we did not run during the first day of qualifying and ended up not qualifying, I was upset for that but during the season it was a good decision because the Michelin tyre was a better tyre.'

Hawkridge said that 'we were never off the pace from that point on. Look at the results, look at the qualifying, look at the race performance on year-old tyres and you'll see that the only people who could beat us were McLaren. Ayrton? I mean that guy had an absolute knowledge of where he was at, what he was capable of and he also knew the car was good. He was right to be pushing for a change, he was the guy who motivated and made that change happen. He made full use of it when it did.'

Witty 'spent a lot of time with him when he failed to qualify for the San Marino Grand Prix – which is the only time in his life he did fail to qualify. Ayrton and I went off on the Sunday. We had to be at Dijon on the Monday morning to test a new car [the TG 184, with the Michelins] and we went off to Linate Airport in Milan, missed the plane and decided we'd take the car all the way. We drove together, we talked a lot about marriage and about my marriage and I asked him about his brief marriage, and we got on pretty well. He said to me: "How do you find you get on with your wife when you are travelling all the time?" I said: "I find it very difficult." (Witty and his wife later divorced.) I said: "It is difficult because when they're not working they want to be with you," and he said for him it was difficult, he'd married very young and he knew that what he needed to do needed no distractions. I think it was just a question of incompatibility at a very early age.'

Friends would find themselves drifting away, too, among them Keith Sutton. 'With all the Formula 1 pressures, all the Formula 1 people and contacts coming up to him, I kind of lost touch with him; and he started earning lots of money whereas I was only going up steadily.' Circa 1989 he still sent me a Christmas card every year to my good friend Keith, but that was about it.' Sutton would 'say hello to him and everything' but it wasn't the same 'as in the old days. In those days we'd go out for a drink, music, girls, and we'd talk about what young men of the same age talk about. But after that, I don't know, I lost him.'

Between Imola and Dijon, Senna contested a celebrity race to open the new Nürburgring. John Watson was among the other drivers. 'It was just before Mercedes launched their 190Es and everyone in the race had an identical one. Obviously the race was a good chance for publicity for Mercedes and the track. The field was a celebrity one with a host of Formula 1 drivers past, present and future. Ayrton took it very, very seriously. He thought that if he could beat Lauda, Prost and Rosberg it would bring a lot of attention to him. He'd be noticed by a wider public. You have to remember that at this point he was only an up-and-coming driver. My own view of celebrity races is that you do your best to win, of course, but it's not exactly the end of your career if you don't. Senna's attitude was that he had to win it. That day was cold and wet and he did a bloody good job.'

He did. He covered 12 laps in 26 minutes 57.58 seconds. Lauda was behind him, 26 minutes 59.16, and this is the rest of the field Senna beat (in finishing order): Carlos Reutemann, Keke Rosberg, Watson, Denny Hulme, Jody Scheckter, Jack Brabham, Klaus Ludwig, James Hunt, John Surtees, Phil Hill, Manfred Schute, Stirling Moss, Alain Prost, Udo Schutz, Jacques Laffite, Hans Herman, Elio de Angelis. Alan Jones retired.

'It showed us,' Watson concluded, 'what this guy was all about.'

Immediately after the race, Senna said to Russell Bulgin, a journalist and friend: 'Now I know I can do it.'

At Dijon, Senna qualified on the seventh row on the Michelins. He was openly enthusiastic but had only one set of qualifiers and, at the very moment he chose to use them, Lauda left oil on the track. In the race, he was up as high as ninth, fell back a place before the turbo went on lap 35.

Monaco can be a deeply infuriating motor race because it is around the streets and you can't usually overtake. Senna was again on the seventh row after qualifying.

It rained. This is worse at Monaco because the churning walls of water are running at you along narrow, armco-clad corridors.

Prost led, Mansell overtook him on the tenth lap and Mansell led a Grand Prix for the first time in his life. It lasted five laps. He hit the armco and hit it hard. In these circumstances Senna attacked the circuit.

Lap 1: ninth. lap 2: ninth. Lap 3: eighth (overtaking Laffite). Lap 4: eighth. Lap 5: eighth. Lap 6: eighth. Lap 7: seventh (overtaking Manfred Winkelhock). Lap 8: seventh. Lap 9: sixth (Alboreto spun). Lap 10: sixth. Lap 11: sixth. Lap 12: fifth (overtaking Rosberg). Lap 13: fifth. Lap 14: fourth (overtaking Arnoux). Lap 15: fourth. Lap 16: third (Mansell crash). Lap 17: third. Lap 18: third. Lap 19: second (overtaking Lauda). They crossed the line and Senna was 34.355 seconds behind Prost. The hunt began in the walls of water.

Lap	Prost	Senna	Diff	Gap
20	1:56.684	1:56.170	-0.514	33.841
21	1:56.264	1:57.551	+1.287	35.128
22	1:56.144	1:55.226	-0.918	34.210
23	1:57.618	1:54.674	-2.944	31.266
24	1:56.873	1:54.334	-2.539	28.727
25	1:56.641	1:55.650	-0.991	27.736
26	1:56.848	1:55.253	-1.595	26.141
27	1:59.669	1:55.232	-4.437	21.704
28	2:00.193	1:56.628	-3.565	18.139
29	1:59.436	1:56.666	-2.770	15.369
30	2:02.598	1:59.008	-3.590	11.779
31	2:03.766	1:59.433	-4.333	7.446

At this point Jacky Ickx, the official starter, decided to stop the race. The decision remains controversial. Why did he do it now and not a long time before? Certainly for several laps Prost had been gesticulating from the cockpit to have it stopped. At the end of lap 32 – and with 46 laps left – the red flag was shown and Prost slowed. Senna, moving like a thunderstorm within a thunderstorm, caught and passed him on the finishing line and thought he'd won. Unfortunately the positions were calculated from the end of the previous lap – 31 …

'Monaco was a quirk,' Hawkridge says. 'We were supposed to be running on the year-old Michelins but they didn't have year-old rain tyres. Come the race, surprise, surprise, Michelin said to McLaren: "Sorry, we have to give Toleman tyres and we only have one sort of tyre. We can't send them out on dries." Suddenly McLaren had this youngster called Ayrton Senna in a ridiculous car called a Toleman on the same tyres as they had and they were going to lose the race.

'If some diligent official [Ickx] hadn't jumped out and stopped it just before Prost was overtaken … well, the race had been horrendous for the preceding 15 laps and when it was stopped the track was by no means in its worst state. Everyone who was there shared the sentiment, I think, that Ayrton was robbed of his first Grand Prix victory. He took it completely calmly, he wasn't [visibly] upset. I'm sure he was disappointed but he showed no emotions that were uncontrolled at all. It was not a racing driver reaction of thumping his helmet and banging the car or anything, he just said: "Well, what do you expect? This is the Establishment we're taking on." That was his attitude to it. "They're not going to let me and Toleman blow their doors off at Monaco." He had Prost completely sussed. He wasn't driving over the limit, within the laps to go he would have easily overtaken him.

'Monaco was the highlight of our racing career. It was a hell of a race. We could believe it was happening. We knew it would happen, we absolutely knew.'

Hawkridge makes this overall judgement: Senna would always run his own race, he didn't do anything else. He didn't compete with other people. 'The word competition actually means seeking together' – and he didn't do that. He rose above other people. He had to prove that he was in his *own* race, that he was in a different class.

That sodden night in Monaco, when darkness mercifully drowned the whole dripping mess, Hawkridge knew something else. 'It was pretty clear that we had the makings of a bloody competitive Formula 1 team.'

However he contained his feelings Senna was 'very, very angry because we were almost leading after a hard race and suddenly it was stopped halfway through. Maybe I would have taken the lead and crashed myself after another five laps and have nothing, but I believe we could have won. After some time just reflecting, I thought it was a fantastic result because of the way the thing developed. I probably got more publicity than if I had won.'

Later Senna spoke to Angelo Parilla.

Parilla: 'Ayrton, the first 10 laps were bad. What happened?'

Senna: 'The car was impossible to drive, there was too much power (in the wet) so I turned the turbo boost down. The more I turned it down, the better the car drove. At the end of the race, the boost was totally closed. No boost at all!'

From this moment on the perception of Senna was altered. He had thrust himself on to the big stage and almost taken the leading part, too. One day he clearly would, perhaps even tomorrow.

It rarely happens like that.

Montreal was anti-climactic. He qualified on the fifth row, finished seventh two laps behind the leader (Piquet) – the car never on the pace. Detroit was anti-climactic. He qualified on the fourth row, crashed on lap 21 (a broken rear wishbone). And they all went to Dallas. In retrospect it was a mistake to have a Grand Prix there – a new circuit, of course, which the drivers didn't like much at all, and when Can-Am cars had used it on the Saturday after Formula 1 qualifying they tore the track surface to pieces. Quick-set concrete laid overnight didn't set and the warm-up was delayed then postponed altogether.

'It was red hot and the track was breaking up at every corner in practice,' Hawkridge says. 'They were actually laying cement between sessions and quick-drying concrete and all kinds of things in a disastrous situation. I walked with the FISA delegation and I could kick the tarmac out with my foot – ridiculous.

'The track was strewn with marbles and it was quite clear nobody would go out and improve their time on it. Peter Gethin was our team manager then and Ayrton came walking out of the garage, overalls on and his helmet on, and Peter said: "You ain't going out in this." Ayrton went absolutely berserk, just absolutely blew his cool completely, just total emotion, he went absolutely crazy with Peter Gethin. He wanted to go out. Peter came to me and said: "Alex, what do you think?" I said: "Peter, you're team manager, I don't interfere in those things but I'll talk to Ayrton and I'll certainly reinforce the decision you've made." So I went to Ayrton and I said: "Look, Peter's the team manager, he has to decide, he's got that job to do and that is his job." Ayrton said: "Well, if you don't change it I'll act accordingly." I think we actually lost Ayrton at Dallas that day because we didn't agree with him.'

Gethin did not hear Senna say the words; what Gethin did hear was the Toleman going round the track when 'I turned my back.' Despite everything, Senna had gone out. When he came back 'it was the only time he had a mouthful from me. He walked off up the pit road like a spoilt child.'

'My understanding is very clear,' Senna would say. 'I had been on the circuit the previous day and also that morning – so to me nobody at that time was in a better position to judge the situation with the circuit. I am happy to agree with somebody else's point of view as long as it is shown to me and explained to me in a dialogue, but not as an order imposed, as at Dallas.'

Gethin remained, however, a staunch admirer. Speaking to me in 1989 he said: 'Ayrton is the best driver I have ever encountered and the most single-minded. I think he knows how good he is. I think he's a terribly ambitious bloke, I think he's terribly mercenary in terms of he'll put everything aside to do what he wants to do. His one thought in life is motor racing and winning motor races. I think he realised early on how good he was. I'd have put a lot of money on him becoming World Champion even in the Toleman days. He is shy outside motor racing and basically I think he's a nicer bloke than he appears to be. He's just terribly hard on himself and anyone else around him who is going to give him something which is going to be winnable in, whether it's a Ferrari, a Toleman or a Lambretta. I thought he was the best driver I'd seen since Jim Clark. He's got everything.

'I liked the bloke, overall I liked him. I thought he was a very tough little man, a very hard little man, who knew what he wanted, where he was going and where he was going to end up. If he said to me he was running for president of Brazil I'd say yes and wouldn't be surprised if he became so. We had times when it was very difficult [the tyres] but, you know, that's life. Sometimes you have to make decisions, whether they are good or bad. In that tyre business, in all the things I saw and heard going on, I thought a stand had to be made. I had a great admiration for Alex.'

That day at Dallas – and from the third row of the grid – Senna was fourth at the end of the first lap but kissed a wall, needed four new tyres, kissed a wall again and retired on lap 47 (out of 67) when the driveshaft went. Of the 26 starters, 12 retired 'hit wall' so Senna was not alone.

Between Dallas and the next Grand Prix, Brands Hatch, Senna was asked to drive for the Newman Joest team in the World Sportscar Championships, the 1,000 kilometres of the Nürburgring. He would partner Henri Pescarolo and Stefan Johansson in a Porsche 956.

'At that time I didn't know him at all,' Pescarolo said. 'Reinhold Joest had been told there was a very good young Brazilian driver, you should try him. Joest said: "Why not?"'

'I have a friend who knew Senna,' Joest says, 'and this friend said "give him a chance, he wants to drive one time in sportscars" so that was the whole thing. I had never met him before. He came to the Nürburgring and I found him a real gentleman. He was 100 per cent intelligent and not only in car racing but also in other points. You could talk with him politics, religion, a thousand things. He knew what he was talking about. He was also very sensitive. He came, saw the car and watched the car.'

Pescarolo says they 'were allowed to have three drivers in the team. I met him in the pits while we were waiting to start practice. He was very shy. He wasn't speaking to anybody because he didn't know anybody.' (Sportscars are an off-shoot of single-seaters in one sense – Grand Prix drivers past, present and future do take part in them – but are a separate world altogether in another sense.) 'He didn't know the car and it was the first time he'd driven a big car like that.'

Johansson and Pescarolo took the morning session. Senna went out in the afternoon – inevitably it was wet – and did but a single lap. He brought the Porsche smoothly into the pits and earnestly enquired what all the cockpit dials and switches did. (Truly. And he'd done a lap without knowing, as we shall see in a moment.) They told him and, as Pescarolo says, 'he was competitive straight away, you know. After a few laps he was doing a good time. I wasn't really surprised because I'd been told he was promising, but he coped with the big car, the big engine and it looked very easy for him.'

Joest gives the context, however. 'Sure there was a big difference between a Formula 1 car and a sportscar, but the 956 and the 962 (which another team, Skoal Bandit, ran at the Nürburgring) were, I think, the best sportscars in the world at the time. They had a lot of ground effect and so on. They were heavier to drive but the ground effect was the same. In feeling, the Formula 1 and sportscars were nearly the same. Senna was quick immediately.'

He was seventh fastest in the wet and eventually the Porsche qualified eighth.

Quentin Spurring wrote this in *Autosport*: 'Joest Racing lost its way in the morning session with the Le Mans-winning 956B, over-experimenting with the settings. Johansson and Pescarolo monopolised the car in dry practice, leaving new recruit Ayrton Senna to learn the car in the afternoon. Until then, Ayrton had never driven a closed racing car in his life and had not even sat in a Porsche 956. After his first lap in the car, he was back in the pits asking for directions around the cockpit dials and switches. After that he settled down, finding the car much lighter to drive than he had anticipated. Soon he was showing the almost uncanny smoothness and consistency for which he is becoming known in Formula 1, and it was he who set the respectable wet session time.'

The race was unhappy, and wet, too. Pescarolo began, had a puncture, they lost eight laps with clutch problems and towards the end water was getting into the electronics.

Spurring wrote that 'the interesting Johansson/Senna/Pescarolo combination had worked the delayed Joest Porsche nicely into the top 10, but a lot more time – a crippling eight laps – had been lost when the clutch packed up. Now the car was running in a distant 12th position, and, in common with several others, it was getting water on the electrics.'

They finished eighth.

Pescarolo: 'Because he didn't know anybody, he stayed in his part of the pit, speaking very little. After the race he disappeared, that's all.'

Actually, he didn't.

'We had problems,' Joest says, 'and the drivers couldn't use the full turbo boost. Senna went on the outside line to overtake another Porsche and that was very impressive but, you know, when it's raining it's sometimes better that you don't have too much boost. After the race, Senna spent three hours with me and he gave me a list of 30 or 35 points, saying 'OK, you need to change this, you need to change that.' Some were small things and some were bigger things. It meant his life was his job and that was automobile racing.'

Those who disliked Senna, or called him arrogant, would see this unique de-brief as another example. He'd driven only one race in the Porsche and yet sat down and told its owner what was wrong with it. I don't think such an opinion is true and I sense Joest doesn't, either. Senna was simply good enough to know this car (and perhaps *any* car) could be improved and felt it a duty not just to say so but point out how.

Ordinary people don't do this. Ordinary people can't do this, even if they wanted to. (Not much later, Senna confided to Angelo Parilla that 'it was my first and will be my last time in sportscars. They're too big, they've too much weight, I don't like those.')

During 1984 Senna, who was involved with a watch company, went to the annual Swiss watch show in Basel and during this visit had a long lunch with journalist Roland Christen and a couple of other people. 'We were able to talk properly,' Christen says, and thereby hangs a tale. Senna did not forget Christen. We shall see.

Meanwhile, Angelo Parilla says that 'as soon as Ayrton went into Formula 1, that first year with Toleman, he discovered Formula 1 was a different story. And he didn't like Formula 1, he didn't like anybody in Formula 1 – so he had to make another face to show to the world. When I saw him being interviewed, it was not the same person that I knew. But if he came to Milan and stayed a few days with me or my brother he was the same person again. I asked what happened and he said "I hate Formula 1 and all the people in it."'

At Brands for the British Grand Prix he was on the fourth row, worked his way carefully up to third place and stayed there. He tracked Elio de Angelis (Lotus) and every time de Angelis squeezed out a little lead he came back at him. With five laps left Senna took him on the inside going towards Paddock on a power play which had the crowd on their feet. And that was third place.

In Germany his rear wing failed after four laps (when he was fifth), in Austria the oil pressure went on lap 35 when he was fourth. Brian Hart, who produced Toleman's engines, recounted one of those interesting little stories which float briefly round Formula 1 and then die but give you instant insight. During the Austrian Grand Prix, out there in all the loops down the slopes, Senna saw a car ahead, recognised it and its driver, noticed the car was travelling slowly and reasoned (1) it's probably dropping oil and (2) the driver is too lazy to park it and walk back. There was oil. Senna went round it. Prost, charging along, didn't and spun off in a mad carousel into the armco. I mention this not to criticise Prost (who probably had no chance to see) but to try and show you how Senna's mind worked at 250kph.

'Then,' says Hawkridge, 'the unbelievable happened. Michelin announced their withdrawal. We had put all our eggs into their basket – bearing in mind that we'd blown Goodyear off in Formula 2, so we'd already shut one door and we'd shut another by changing from Pirelli to Michelin. Then the Michelin door shut. Michelin's withdrawal was nothing, I'm sure, to do with our performance, it was for purely commercial reasons. That company is so professional that I don't doubt it was anything else. Ayrton knew of it beforehand, he knew there was a likelihood that it could happen. We believed that it couldn't happen to us. We'd been through enough! They just couldn't! I suppose it was wishful thinking. We didn't have anywhere else to go and I'm sure at that point that was it as far as Ayrton was concerned – but I think if you are realistic it goes back earlier, to that incident at Dallas.'

They went to Zandvoort. It was to be in no sense an ordinary weekend. 'There were,' Hawkridge says, 'tremendous up sides to Ayrton,' but he wasn't 'a team player' and the warnings were 'there for anyone to see. The first we heard was when two journalists arrived in our motorhome with a press release on Lotus paperwork telling us Ayrton Senna had signed for them. I mean, it was so embarrassing. We had umpteen guests and sponsors, we were negotiating a multi-million-pound sponsorship which could have taken us into the big time at that meeting. So it destroyed our credibility – that we didn't know what the hell was going on within our own team.'

Lotus had a proper sit-down luncheon under the awning against their motorhome to make the announcement, while immediately outside it Witty whispered through to me: 'Remember every word that's said. I want to know afterwards.' Hawkridge, a little further off, was pacing about incandescent with rage. Ted Toleman wandered a bit further off again. His habitually benevolent face seemed bemused. Nor was it so easy when Nigel Mansell came in under the awning. A glance told him we all knew he was being replaced by Senna.

'It was embarrassing for me when Ayrton came into the motorhome,' Hawkridge says. 'I tackled him on it and he said: "I'm sorry, I have not agreed to this." Then he changed his position. He wasn't saying he didn't have an agreement with them, but he hadn't signed an agreement with them. Then, from that, he hadn't signed an agreement with them so they weren't authorised to put out a press release, but that was over a period of several weeks, not that weekend.

'I don't blame Ayrton or Ayrton's management for keeping their ears permanently to the ground because everyone's doing that, it's part of the lifestyle. I don't even blame Ayrton for deciding his future wasn't within Toleman. He had the right to do that, the clear and expressed right. What he didn't have the right to do was enter into an agreement with anybody else before he'd advised us and released himself from his contract through an agreed payment. The payment wasn't that large, for Senna it wasn't even an issue, and in fact, he paid the money that was due.' Senna was 'an honest man, not dishonest, genuinely not dishonest – but liable to interpret events liberally.'

In Holland he was ninth on lap 19 when the engine went.

And they went to Monza …

Hawkridge remains unrepentant. 'We took the car off him. The reason was a simple one: we had to settle the issue of whether we were going to end up in court because he had clearly breached the agreement, no doubt about that. Journalists at the time saw and read his agreement. There is no doubt about whether it was right or wrong, it was patently wrong. We weren't on about money, we were on about the humiliation that he'd caused us, and the embarrassment, and the fact that he'd probably put us out of motor racing forever; breached the credibility to such an extent that Toleman could no longer continue in motor racing and get support from sponsors and suppliers. He'd accomplished that in one hit – all the credibility I'd been working flat out for years to achieve. He didn't just cost us the possibility of Formula 1, he cost us the possibility of being super-competitive with a major engine manufacturer. It was a catastrophe. I felt he shouldn't be allowed to get away with that. He wasn't worried about courts or legal fees or whatever: the one thing that hurt Ayrton, the one thing he couldn't tolerate, was to be stopped from doing what he loved, which was driving a Grand Prix car round a Grand Prix circuit. We just stopped him driving.'

Senna went to see the Parillas, based at Milan. Angelo says that 'he came to us three or four days before Monza and stayed. We said "we can take you to Monza" but he said "no, I don't want to go to Monza. I'll watch the race on television."'

In fact, Senna did go to Monza, and tried to defuse the row by saying that all he wanted to do was drive and not have any more 'aggravation'.

Hawkridge says 'Senna went out there [to Monza] and I'd told him before he went that he wouldn't be driving. He laughed. He didn't think we were serious at all. I wasn't there on the first day of practice, and I wasn't in England either so I wasn't contactable. I got home on the Friday evening and the phone lines were melting. Bernie [Ecclestone] wanting me, Marco

Piccinini [of Ferrari] wanting me, [Jean-Marie] Balestre [of the governing body FISA] wanting me. There were so many names I'd have been 24 hours on the phone ringing them all back. I spoke to Peter Gethin and I asked what had happened. He replied: "Just what you said would." Then he went on to say Bernie had totally supported our position – but you'd expect that from Bernie, wouldn't you?'

Yes, I would. Ecclestone had worked flat out for years to give the whole thing credibility and cannot have welcomed anything hinting of anarchy.

'It was the only way you could get through to Ayrton,' Gethin says. 'I do think he needed taking down a peg or two and that was the only thing that he did understand. It wasn't a matter of fining him.' Gethin points out that Senna didn't like to be fined but driving was 'his one kick in life ... above everything else. Most drivers I knew liked the odd girl or two, but I think Bo Derek for Ayrton was a Ferrari,' and that's the way he was.

Hawkridge describes how 'Piccinini tried the conciliation role. He said: "Are you really sure?" He couldn't see what all the fuss was about. Here was a guy who had just regally screwed us and all we were doing was saying we don't really require this driver's services which, under our contract terms, we were allowed to do at any point in time. The first time we wanted to exercise it – massive outcry, all this lobbying, all this pressure for us to do something we didn't want to do. We put Stefan [Johansson] in the car and he came a glorious fourth, which frankly, proved an enormous point. I'd have been very unhappy had we not proved it: that the car was on the pace ... and on year-old tyres.'

It is time, high time, to listen carefully to Ayrton Senna. 'Basically, to me, I was giving indications to the team, and particularly to Alex; that I had in mind the desire to leave since the Grand Prix at Montreal. The reason was simply to give the team a better opportunity to find the best choice for the next season, even if in doing that I was putting myself in an uncomfortable position. But to my mind it was the right thing to do. The whole thing at Zandvoort was disgusting. I was very annoyed with Peter Warr – no release, no news was supposed to go out at all. Before anything could be said it was my desire and duty as a professional to inform Toleman that I was 100 per cent leaving, plus where I was going – so it was a bad start in my relationship with Warr, but this is Formula 1 and I have learnt from it.'

It is also time, high time, to listen to Peter Warr's side of this. We have heard how, at the European Grand Prix in late 1983, 'I had already had Ayrton in my office discussing driving for us in 1984 and we were not far from having an agreement in principle. As it was Elio put the car on pole at Brands Hatch, Nigel was on the second row confirming the resurrection of Lotus to its role as one of the leading teams after the depths of despair following the death of Colin Chapman. Our astonishment at the newspaper coverage the next day was only exceeded by the pleasure of John Player because the headlines were not TEAM LOTUS BACK ON POLE but MANSELL ON THE SECOND ROW! This convinced the sponsor that, against the team's wishes, we had to retain Nigel for 1984 and we suspended negotiations with Ayrton.

'Convinced as I was that Ayrton was the man of the future we stayed in touch and built up a dialogue to the point where serious negotiations were in train.' Following a 'furtive' meeting between Warr and one of Senna's advisors at Dallas, 'during the summer months of 1984, meetings were taking place between us and Ayrton and his new manager Armando Boteilho. These culminated in a very protracted series of meetings going on late into the night with Ayrton's lawyer Tony Clare, one of the most careful and meticulous of men. His very fastidious approach to matters, whereby every "i" had to be dotted and every "t" crossed, all guaranteed that what happened at Zandvoort could not have happened had there been no prior agreement in place.

'We were aware throughout that Ayrton was only able to sign for us as a result of having a buy-out clause in his Toleman contract, which had been shown to us with only the amount of the buy-out deleted. Incidentally, the eventual fee in our new contract with Ayrton was almost exactly ten times the figure on the table the previous autumn!

'Now the scene shifts to Zandvoort. Team Lotus's contract with John Player had a renewal date in August and the option to continue lay with them. Prior to this, however, a new sales and marketing director, Brian Wray, had been appointed and replaced the rather gentlemanly way of doing business with that company with a Harvard Business School approach of "stack 'em high, sell 'em cheap" which negated a great deal of the classy, upmarket black and gold image we had been cultivating with their leading brand. Wray had to be convinced of the value of the motor racing sponsorship and came to Zandvoort having been promised' – although not by anyone at Team Lotus – 'one of the by-then traditional motorhome lunches with the British press so they could get to know him and he would have an opportunity to impress them with a release of team news which would have them all running for the telephones to file the story. From that point on, Team Lotus and I had very little control over the situation.

'It is true to say that Ayrton knew of our intentions to make the announcement that weekend, but it is also true to say that he had requested the opportunity to inform Toleman first, as a matter of courtesy and to let them know that he would be exercising his buy-out option. But then another factor came into play.

'At that time it was a not altogether agreeable practice for some journalists to align themselves with certain drivers, acting as their unofficial or official spokesmen – or even managers. Others doubled up their duties as pressmen with being PR representatives of teams. All this meant that any prior knowledge of news stories had little chance of remaining confidential.'

Zandvoort was 'a case in point. As a result, the embargo of the Team Lotus press release was ignored by a few and by the time their colleagues had seen them moving about the paddock with a "hot" piece of paper the damage was done, the story out and the Team lunch became the forum for some animated discussions. I had little or no control of the accelerating events but it was a matter of some regret that our relationship with our new driver had got off on a wrong and seemingly unprofessional footing. Nonetheless, Ayrton seemed to understand and accept the explanation offered. So the pressures on Hawkridge and Co. were no greater than those on us and his somewhat hysterical reaction plus his supposedly "blow by blow accounts of my words, statements and conversations" were bewildering to say the least. Until I went up to him on the grid that Sunday at Zandvoort I had never met or even spoken to the man before!'

Witty, who felt he had a relationship strong enough to talk frankly to Senna, did so. 'When it came to the bust-up, I was sitting with him once in the Toleman offices at Whitney [where the racing team was] and I said: "I'm asking you a question personally. Why are you doing this, why are you going to Lotus? Without you, we become a hell of a lesser team." He said: "The problem is, when I joined the team I had a lot of belief in the management and I questioned the technical ability of the team. Six months later I have total faith in the technical ability of the team, but I question the management."'

Senna was back for the Grand Prix of Europe at the Nürburgring but crashed on the first lap. And they went to Portugal where he was another driver, really, just one of many moving around the maze of the paddock or sheltering in the arbour of their motorhomes, and this would not be his day or theirs. It would belong – forever – to either a certain Niki Lauda or a certain Alain Prost. Lauda, back from the dead these many years, was poised to win the World Championship. In the simplest terms, even if Prost, his team-mate at Marlboro

McLaren, took the Portuguese Grand Prix and Lauda finished second, Lauda had the title by half a point.

But that was only the most obvious of the dimensions: there was, too, a swell of emotion for Lauda. You only had to glance at him to see why: the still-seared ear, the areas of molten skin fossilised now, the damn near macabre moment whenever he took off his cap (rarely) and only a strange plateau of tufts of hair remained from the fire at the Nürburgring in 1976. Nor was it purely emotion. Lauda had become the drivers' spokesman over safety.

This October day in 1984, as the clocks moved towards 2.30 and the race, he was already an historical figure, to some a mythological and superhuman figure, twice champion already but in another era, the 70s, and now surely about to do it again. The fact that he'd retired between 1979 and 1982 and had scarcely even watched a race on television was one dimension; the fact that he'd come back and mastered turbo engines to this extent was another.

He'd qualified 11th and that was yet another dimension, particularly with Prost on the front row. Lauda was going to have to do some overtaking and it was making the other drivers tremulous. What if, even inadvertently, they baulked him, brushed against his McLaren, sent it spinning off? Could they, as racing drivers, move tamely out of his way? Or dare they, if they could hold Lauda, stay in front of him, be the one to rob him? I'd already broached this delicate matter with a driver and he had said: 'Well, what would you do? I'll tell you what I'll do – get the hell out of his way. History isn't going to remember me as the clown who cocked up the championship.'

Exactly. Probably it was a commonly-shared sentiment. Some, of course, would calculate it in a more refined manner, put on a bit of a show, lay on a bit of the old cut-and-thrust and then get the hell out of his way. As Lauda himself realised, it looked better for them on television like that; and the cameras would certainly be tracking him. And from nowhere, as it seemed, a breathless whisper travelled through the paddock. *Marlene's here*!

Marlene Lauda never went to the races, Marlene Lauda thought all the drivers were crazy, races were crazy, the whole ethic of the thing, the whole desire for the thing was crazy, and there she suddenly was, regal as Habsburg – that stately progress with friends in attendance as she moved along the back of the pits, that defensive Royal Family perma-smile. Marlene was at Estoril to witness the consummation. In its rarity it was a news event all by itself; and another dimension.

Ayrton Senna da Silva is walking briskly down the alley between the canvas walls towards his Toleman car deep in the pits up there, up the slight incline from the paddock. He is 24, he is of course in his first season in Formula 1, a rookie and with a small team. He stops to answer my question: 'Well, what are you going to do?' For an instant he seems not to understand. He shakes his head – bemusement, not an answer. I explain the question more pointedly: 'Will you get out of Lauda's way?' His eyes invariably looked straight into yours and they were doing that here, posing their own question: 'How can you ask me something as silly as that?' To the original question he didn't have to stretch his English vocabulary at all. He covered it in one word: 'No.'

He finished third.

'The climax was that we were running two cars in the top four at Estoril [a trick of memory. Johansson got no higher than sixth, but never mind] so we went out with our best, most competitive position,' Hawkridge says. 'In fact – and this shows the character of Ayrton and that our relationship really wasn't as bad as everyone would imagine and how realistic he was – we said we really wanted to do some comprehensive tyre testing. "We haven't had a chance to do any all year and we want to test some other drivers. Ayrton, will you stay over after Estoril and run the car each day and set a pace? Then we can measure the other drivers." He went out and on his fifth lap he took the lap record apart. He was like a second and a half inside the lap record on the same tyres he'd used in the Grand Prix the day before. He came in and he said: "This is what I've dreamed about, it's the first time I've driven a Formula 1 car on the limit" and he was the happiest I'd seen him all year.'

So he'd been nursing the Toleman all that time …

'He went out and he had no worries, no responsibilities. If he'd written the car off – it would never happen – but if he had it wouldn't have affected Toleman and it wouldn't have affected him. He blitzed around and made the McLarens look like lemons. (Prost had been on the front row of the grid, remember.) He showed what he was capable of. Stefan had stepped in and done the job and Ferrari hired him on the strength of that, but what Ferrari didn't see was what we'd seen Senna do after the last race. We knew what he could do and he knew. Nobody else knew.'

They were soon to find out and, as a matter of record, that Monday Senna did 1 minute 21.70 seconds. It equalled Piquet's time which had taken pole in the Portuguese Grand Prix and it was on a set of race tyres, albeit of a soft compound. Piquet of course had been on qualifiers …

'I remember doing a deal with Sergio Taccini, the Italian sportswear company – in fact a bonus deal because we'd had them as a sponsor, but Warwick had moved to Renault and they wanted to stay with Warwick,' Witty says. 'They said to me: "We'll do a deal with Senna" but they didn't think he'd be on the podium many times so it was a high bonus. At the end of the season, I think he'd earned more than Warwick had done!

'We knew that the guy was good. He destroyed Cecotto mentally, right, he didn't really get a chance to destroy Johansson because Johansson was only in for three races. In a funny sort of way Stefan accepted the role that he played later with the Alboretos and the Prosts. At the Portuguese Grand Prix we had three cars, right, and Stefan went out in his race car intending that maybe he would use the spare, but Senna was very clever. I don't know whether he did it on purpose but I think it was in the back of his mind. He went out and did about three laps in his race car, there was a problem with it, he gets into the spare, monopolises the spare for the rest of the warming-up session.

'It was very clever tactically the way he got guys like Rory Byrne and the team to work around him, very difficult if you were a number two driver to do anything about it. Ayrton wasn't really a whinger but everything had to be right. But you don't mind if he turns it into lap times like he used to do.'

Witty would remain 'an admirer of Ayrton' because he thought he'd 'been able to touch him a bit. I spent a year working with him.' Witty could see 'a hell of a lot in the guy' and why he was so good at his job. I only really thought that afterwards, when he was about to leave. He obviously felt that the Lotus thing was better for him. [He did.] I wonder – it's like a million and one things, isn't it? – if he had stayed with Johansson, would we have got the Goodyear tyres over the winter? If the whole thing had worked, if it hadn't been sold to Benetton, if, if, if …'

John Love worked for Toleman and he and Senna were 'quite close, because he lived in Reading with Mauricio Gugelmin and Mauricio's wife Stella, and I lived at Newbury. I didn't usually work on his car because I was doing tyres and composites and fabrication. In fact I did work on it once and that was at Zandvoort. A team-member's father died and he had to fly home. Ayrton was very young when he came to us and he was self-opinionated and a lot of the team took, well, not exception to that, but they felt that he was an upstart and nobody really talked to him much. He could appear bloody-minded and didn't seem interested in other people's opinions. To me, he was more a friend. I think people thought he was an upstart because they didn't really know him at all.

'Even when he was so young, he knew exactly what he wanted and where he was going and, because of that, he had this air of too much confidence. People didn't like that. He could focus absolutely on one thing until he had overcome it and had it under his control. He certainly had two faces (but was not two-faced: that's a clear distinction). He did have a good sense of humour and so on, but if you only saw the implacable face you couldn't judge that there was another one. Most people saw him at circuits or in the factory, where he was always deadly serious. At home he was completely different. There was only once when I remember having a joke and fooling around and that was at Zandvoort on the Thursday morning. I was chasing him round the paddock trying to kill the little bugger! I can't remember what he'd done.

'When it was to be announced that he was joining Lotus he did warn me in the morning that there was a load of crap going to happen in the afternoon. After that, Toleman wouldn't let him drive at Monza although he showed up at the circuit. Then he went back to Brazil. I had to go to his house every day and pick up his mail and send it on.

'He and Mauricio and Stella were all very close. To my knowledge, he never really watched any other driver racing except Mauricio. Again at Zandvoort, I remember after the Grand Prix there was a Formula 3 race and he stayed back for it, he sat on the wall and watched Mauricio do the whole race and Mauricio won and he was absolutely delighted. They were very, very close.

'In English, he understood more than he could speak. If it was something to do with the car or the racing he explained himself well, but if you were having a normal conversation that's when he would struggle; but he never forgot, never forgot. I always used to get a Christmas card and a birthday card from him years after he'd left Toleman.'

When Senna journeyed to the Toleman factory to say a final good-bye in winter 1984 he wept. He always seems to have found leaving difficult. Gordon Message, who worked for

Toleman, remembers 'he came down to the factory to say goodbye and he was very emotional. He knew everybody there because he'd jog or cycle to the factory regularly to see what was going on. He obviously had to go to Lotus, but that didn't lessen his emotion. Maybe in later years he hid that side of him because he may have thought it made him vulnerable. Some drivers do feel like that. I didn't start going to the races in 1984 until the French Grand Prix at Dijon (fifth race) because before that my job was to make sure the cars were ready to be transported to the races. It meant I only got to know him in the second part of the season. I found him intense, very intense – in the way that Michael Schumacher is today, but maybe more intense than Schumacher.'

If there were distinct rungs on the ladder to Formula 1 – FF1600, FF2000, F3 – there were also distinct rungs within Formula 1: Toleman the small team leading to Lotus, who might bring Senna wins – and championships. It was what he'd always wanted. Now he thought he was going to get it.

Chapter 8

WARR ZONE

'If you're inclined to the view that, well, perhaps Elio de Angelis wasn't as good as we thought he was, why Johnny Dumfries didn't make it, they had no chance. The guy was driving at a super-elevated level.' These are the words of Peter Warr and they represent a homage to Senna. We have heard many homages already but this one is more important.

Lotus had had their World Champions – Clark, Graham Hill, Emerson Fittipaldi, Jochen Rindt, Mario Andretti – and were still, in 1985, a big team.

What really happened when Senna left Toleman for them is absurdly simple, no mystery at all. He knew Lotus could give him the World Championship, he knew Toleman couldn't. Lotus, Senna concluded, was 'definitely a better opportunity'.

'The first time I met him was at the factory,' mechanic Nigel Stepney will say. 'I didn't really have a lot to do with him because I was working on Elio's car and he was in the other one, but you could see that when he was in his car he was totally oblivious to everybody else. He could wind himself up into a very great intensity. You could watch him standing there or sitting in the car concentrating and somehow he was completely different to anybody else you could meet.'

Warr's evaluation of de Angelis – killed in a testing crash after he'd left Lotus – is not insensitive and must not be seen as that. Warr is evaluating only the driver, not the man, and he is entitled to do that, just as anyone can evaluate any driver killed. You could barely speak of motor racing at all in an historical sense if you didn't. Many, many are gone now, Clark, Hill, Rindt ...

And Colin Chapman, too. He died in 1982, not that long after de Angelis won in Austria, and this had been Lotus's first victory since 1978. Chapman was a turbulent, self-made strong man and quite possibly in the originality of his thought, a genius. He founded a company which made racy road cars as well as racing cars. From 1958 to Chapman's death, Lotus won 72 Grand Prix races. To Peter Warr came a difficult, uneasy inheritance. He hired a designer, Gerard Ducarouge, who built an entirely new and competitive car in five weeks.

In 1985, Warr was three years into his inheritance and now he'd got Senna. It was a coup. Senna, meanwhile, wintered in Brazil and contracted a viral infection of the inner ear so that he could not blink his right eye. It inflamed part of his face. 'It helps you to realise how weak you are,' he said, 'how inadequate you can be. You control yourself more, be careful, give more attention to yourself, your mental and physical condition, everything.'

Stepney says that 'when he first came to us Elio had been there a while [since 1980], Ayrton'd only been in Formula 1 a year and Elio was a bit worried, I think. Everybody used to like Elio but Senna came along and – I don't judge he did it on purpose – after a while had the whole nucleus of the team working for him. It just happened.'

In the winter of 1984–85, Senna, Gugelmin and Stella had gone back to Brazil, leaving John Love to go round to their house and 'fire up the Mercedes which Ayrton had bought. He'd left it in the garage. I'd take it out for a drive to keep it in running order. It was a new Merc and it was his pride and joy – he'd bought it with his own money and although the family were rich, buying it himself meant a great deal to him.'

Enter Bob Dance, the Lotus chief mechanic who was a central pillar of the team and had been for decades. Toleman, Dance says, were 'a small team and Senna had his sights set on bigger things. Lotus were strong and during 1984 he decided Toleman wasn't quite the place he wanted to be. He was very keen to join us and of course we were very keen to have him, too. He had obvious potential and Peter Warr was no fool. He picked a good man. I'd met him before at the Formula 1 races and he seemed a friendly sort of chap.'

In those days, Formula 1 had a traditional pre-season test session in Rio in February so, as Dance says, 'we started life with him out in Brazil. He was down-to-earth and pleasant and his family were pleasant. We met them and his younger brother was around, his sister not so much. He did the testing and he was impressive considering he'd just joined us. It's easy to forget that he hadn't won a race yet and we really didn't know.

'What I found *immediately* impressive was this: we had Renault engines and we had the Renault engineers with us and a lot of little crystal display units had been taped in the dashboard area reading off about ten things the engineers wanted to know. Bear in mind it was his first run in a Lotus. He said "you see all that there [the displays]. Don't expect me to come in and tell you what all of them are saying because I can't, but what I can do is tell you what half are saying on one lap and the other half on the next lap. Is that good enough?" He was already off and running.

'At the end of one afternoon, I said: "Give me a lap in your hire car" and he took me round. He was on home ground, of course, and he said: "You see this section here, if the wind is blowing in a certain direction" – left to right, or whatever it was – "that really makes you move across the track, you have to watch out for that." It was obvious to me he was very astute and he thought about it all, every aspect of it. Then, on the other side of the coin, he was also a good sport with the lads. There was more practical joking then than now. Lotus was very strong under Peter Warr, good morale, and Ayrton didn't escape the odd practical joke, but he also came back with practical jokes as well. He played a trick on me.'

In sequence: Lotus pulled the cream cake trick on him – 'sniff it, Ayrton, to make sure the cream hasn't gone sour' – and as he did they'd pressed his nose into it. He made his response when he was good and ready.

Senna: 'Have one of my sweets.'

Dance: 'What have you done to them?'

Senna: 'No, no, nothing, they're good. Have a sweet.'

Dance: 'OK, I'll eat one, no problem.'

Dance says that 'it made all my mouth blue, and when I went to pee in the toilet for the next few hours I peed blue as well. It was hilarious. Yes, we used to have some fun with him. He took all the boys out down the coast, he said: "I'll drive, I'll take you." People don't visualise this, don't visualise him like this. He'd eat with us and that sort of thing. But as you come up in your career – and it seems particularly so in Formula 1 – there's more and more media hounding you and your life ceases to be your own. All the time, you tend to have to go into hiding. You want to sit down in a restaurant and eat with your friends but you can't: people wanting to know if there's any chance of an autograph, people wanting to talk, people wanting you to speak to other people. In the end perhaps it overwhelms you a bit. I think he did take a decision to be two people: the private person and the public person.

'He was very much a flyer of model aeroplanes and he'd bring his kit along. When he'd done his day's testing he'd go out onto the straight by the pits and go flying with his models. He was very good at it. He could throw them around the sky. In Brazil, he'd chase the buzzards with his radio models or he'd get one up around the local microlite boys! It's fairly laid-back over there and they enjoy themselves.'

That test session in Rio wasn't all so innocent. Senna and Mansell (then Williams) had a disagreement on the track, Senna claiming Mansell baulked him, Mansell explaining he was on a fuel economy run and if he'd slowed it would have wrecked the figures. Later in the day, on the last corner, the disagreement became physical. Senna struck the rear of the Williams, was airborne, landed heavily and damaged the Lotus. Senna said: 'I was much quicker than he was. I'd been trying to get past for half a lap. I'd tried one side then the other. When I went through down the inside he just chopped across my nose.' To which Mansell said: 'The first thing I knew was when I felt this big bang at the back. I'm in Brazil, and he's Brazilian. The back of my car is damaged, the front of his car is damaged. I rest my case.'

Senna qualified on the second row for the Brazilian Grand Prix at this same circuit in April and was third on lap 48 when the electrics failed.

Then – Portugal, a lap of 1 minute 21.007 and his first pole position in Formula 1. That was done in the second qualifying session. The first session had been wet. Steve Hallam was a senior team member and, he says, 'Ayrton set an unbelievable time when the track was in that condition, unbelievable.'

Senna 1 minute 21.708
De Angelis 1 minute 22.306
Lauda 1 minute 23.670

'So he had provisional pole and the next day he simply consolidated it,' Hallam says. On the Sunday it rained hard. Of the 26 who started, only ten would be running at the end.

The story of the Estoril, run in those 'diabolical' conditions, is hallowed ground in motorsport. On the parade lap Mansell and Martini (Minardi) spun. At the green light, Senna seized the lead and moved away from de Angelis.

Lap	Senna	De Angelis
1	1:52.748	1:55.398
2	1:46.338	1:46.259
3	1:44.693	1:45.515

While Senna continued to build on this, the treachery of the conditions is revealed by a fact: by lap 30, seven drivers had spun off. On lap 43 of 67 Alboreto (Ferrari) moved into second place but 58.066 seconds behind Senna who, you'd have thought, would now cruise home, only increasing his pace if Alboreto mounted any sort of threat from the distance. Wrong. Alboreto did cut the gap to 55.433 seconds in another couple of laps. Senna went quicker than Alboreto for each of the next 10 laps, increasing the lead to 1 minute 12.639 seconds and when, on lap 56, Alboreto responded by cutting it to 1 minute 10 seconds Senna promptly accelerated again, forcing the lead to 1 minute 17.203 seconds on lap 60. *Then* he eased off, winning it by 1:02.978. It was devastating.

Senna was completely and typically candid. 'They all said I made no mistakes, but that's not true. On one occasion I had all four wheels on the grass, totally out of control ... but the car came back on to the circuit.'

When he'd won it the sodden mechanics raised their hands in salute and Peter Warr danced like a man who had vindicated his professional life.

He was goddamned fast: pole at Imola, pole at Monaco, front row in Canada, pole in Detroit. 'Ayrton was almost two seconds quicker than anybody else,' Hallam recalls, 'and Joe Ramirez of McLaren said: "OK, which short cut did he take?!"'

Stepney, too, says that 'the street races stand out most vividly in my memory. He was simply so much quicker than anybody else. They all take risks but I don't believe he took bigger risks than the others. He had not just speed but a purity, he cut every corner finer, he went closer to the barriers; and he didn't do this for just one lap but lap after lap after lap, he could do it for a whole race, he drove like that all the time. That's the difference.'

He put the Lotus on the front row in France, only the second row at Silverstone, only the third row at the Nürburgring ... only the seventh row in Austria (the car didn't like the bumps on the track), only the second row in Holland, pole at Monza despite an amazing lapse. He had not, of course, driven Monza before and 'on the first morning I arrived at the chicane flat in fifth because I'd forgotten it was there!' He was on the front row at Spa, pole for the European Grand Prix at Brands Hatch, only the second row in South Africa. Oh, and he won Spa by 28 seconds from Mansell, and was second in the European.

John Watson drove the Marlboro McLaren (Lauda was ill) at Brands. 'In qualifying I was coming down from Westfield Bend and I was on an in lap – going to come into the pits. Round Dingle Dell dip into Dingle Dell I saw this car coming very quickly behind me. Just at the bottom of the dip Ayrton came through on the inside – I'd left him room. I witnessed visibly and audibly something I had not seen anyone do before in a racing car. It was as if he had four hands and four legs. He was braking, changing down, steering, pumping the throttle and the car appeared to be on that knife edge of being in control and being out of control. It lasted maybe two seconds.

'Once he had checked the speed of the car and he'd got the right gear, what he was trying to do was maintain boost pressure. On a turbo you lift off and the power goes away very fast. He got to the point of the track where he wanted to make his commitment to the corner. The car was pitched in with an arrogance that made my eyes open wider. Then – hard on the throttle and the thing was driving through the corner. I mean, it was a master controlling a machine. I had never seen a turbo car driven like that. The ability of the brain to separate each component and put them back together with that rhythm and co-ordination – for me it was a remarkable experience, it was a privilege to see. I was so moved that I went down to the Lotus pit and I said to Peter Warr and Gerard Ducarouge "I've just seen something" and they said "yes, yes, we know."'

We might dwell, in contrast to this, on the final race, Adelaide, where Senna gave a chaotic performance, crashing and banging, and his maturity was called directly into question. He defended himself stoutly enough, analysing each incident and then, broadening it, added: 'The drivers have different lives outside racing so we never see each other. At the race track we have the opportunity to talk but when I am there I find I have so much to do with my team that I hardly find time to eat. My attitude is to make my car as quick and as safe as I can and then try to drive it as well as I can. That's the way I see it and I suppose that's not good when it comes to forming relationships with other drivers.'

He had 38 points and fourth place in the Championship. De Angelis, on 33, was fifth and leaving for Brabham.

Postcripts to 1985.

The first is from the Swiss journalist Roland Christen. 'A Japanese friend was starting 350cc racing in Japan, a bit like the kind they have in California. The cars look like racing cars. He wanted publicity for this and was producing a brochure. He needed a foreword from a Formula 1 driver. I wrote the foreword, wishing the venture well, but the idea was to get a driver to read it and if he agreed with what I'd written, we could use his name. At Monte Carlo during the Grand Prix I approached several drivers and they wanted money, some as much as $10,000 – just for reading a foreword, saying "yes" and lending their name to it. One driver even referred me to his business manager! I began to get a bit desperate and we thought we'd have to pay. I decided to approach Senna – the great, upcoming Ayrton Senna – and I was prepared to go to, I think, $20,000. He didn't ask for money at all! He read it, approved it and said: "This sort of thing is good for the whole sport, our whole sport. I'm happy to be asked."'

The second is from John Love. Toleman were bought out by Benetton and raced no more after 1985. 'Just after Monaco in 1984,' Love says, 'Toleman got Michael Turner (a leading motorsport artist) to do a watercolour of the finish of the race. All you can see is Prost and Senna, everything else grey. Ayrton signed it. When Benetton took over they had a clear-out and I got the watercolour. I've still got it. It's funny-peculiar because I'm not the kind who keeps racing memorabilia. This is all I have.'

Lotus needed Senna more than he needed Lotus, and he proceeded to exercise a veto over who would be his number two driver. Senna's defence: 'The principle was that in '86 they would concentrate behind one driver. Otherwise we would have compromise situations.' In this, Senna was uncompromising. Derek Warwick, available because Renault had dropped out of Formula 1 altogether, was an obvious candidate. Senna said no. Senna: 'It was bad, bad. Until then I had had a good relationship with Derek.'

This did not endear Senna to the British motoring press, who by sheer weight of numbers as well as diversity present collectively something of a force. Who the hell was this upstart Senna, with only a couple of seasons behind him, making decrees? Why doesn't he serve his apprenticeship, keep his mouth shut in deference to people who know better. Worse, Warwick was immensely popular.

Senna's words come back. 'I could never be just another Formula 1 driver.'

He intended to be *the* Formula 1 driver.

(While the indignation was gathering strength, someone – I won't name him – said calmly and clinically: 'Senna is doing the right thing. Lotus are no longer big enough to field two front runners, they'd dissipate their strength.' This is not only interesting, it is accurate. Senna was not frightened of competition, never had been, never would, but he was frightened of the dissipation.)

The choice fell upon the Earl of Dumfries, known as Johnny. 'It was far from ideal circumstances,' he will say, 'but it was a chance to get into Formula 1. For sure it had negative sides to it, but I would have been stupid to turn it down. If I could turn the clock back I still would have taken the drive, but I'd have behaved in a different way if I'd had more experience then. I think I was too naïve at the time, I didn't capitalise on opportunities. Most people are pretty naïve when they get into

Formula 1. I didn't have time to capitalise on the experience of my first year.'

You see it clearly: Dumfries was happy to be there at all, which is what we discussed when Senna was having discussions with Toleman. The whole lot of them are going to be happy to be there at all at the beginning – except Senna. (Don't forget Hawkridge: 'He intended to dominate Formula 1.')

Dumfries says 'I wasn't particularly sociable with the other drivers when I'd been in Formula 3 [in Senna's year, 1983], I just didn't want to be. I was there to beat them, not socialise with them. So I didn't really get to know him until I came to Lotus. There are lots of guys who are touted as being brilliantly promising drivers. I don't pay too much attention to what I read in the press and I think Senna always suffered from being written about too much.'

People tended to 'write about Senna in extremes,' which Dumfries found 'a bit unfortunate for him but, by the same token, I don't think it really bothered him either.' The impression Dumfries gained was that Senna was the sort of person who didn't need a lot of friends and probably had a small group of them who he trusted. He didn't want 'to go out and make lots of them.'

What Dumfries had 'was strictly a working relationship between us and conducted on that level. I don't think I was compared to him. He knew that I was the number two driver. I was in my first year in Formula 1 and he was in his third, he had established himself in the team. He'd always be clever in picking the team he thinks is going to be best for him. That is an asset because as driver you tend to become too emotionally involved and sometimes it's difficult to make rational decisions.

'What tended to happen was that the team would polarise around him. I'd sort of split off with my own race engineer and we'd do our own thing. I didn't want to feel I was hanging on the edge of their circle. I can't be bothered with that. So I'd go off and we'd discuss what we thought was the way to go. If you do that there's always pressure – there's pressure generated from inside yourself. I wanted always to be as quick as possible in the car.'

Stepney became Senna's mechanic in 1986. 'For me it was good because you knew you were in with a chance, and as far as I'm concerned there's not much point in going to the races unless you are in with a chance. He expected everything to be right and in those days at Lotus it was hard in any specific car to get it absolutely right to the point he wanted. In some respects he expected a lot more than you could actually do for him. You could see he was going to win the World Championship. He was that kind of person.

'He knew the weak points of the car and he could read the car mechanically going round a circuit. He knew what the limit of the car was – not just in driving it but the actual car itself. He had to have the brakes a hundred per cent, the gearbox a hundred per cent and if he had one doubt about the gearbox he'd make you take it out – if he'd missed one gear he'd make you take it out. He was into everything on the car.

'He would stand for hours looking round the car, just generally looking. He knew a lot about the car. You could never hide anything from him. If anybody ever did and he found out, he didn't like it.

'I remember at Detroit he'd done his warm-up lap and had come to the grid and we were checking over his car. The rear skids – the plates under the gearbox – had disappeared because he'd gone over a manhole cover [endemic at Detroit, a street circuit]. We were told not to tell him. It might have damaged the car because it could have damaged the gearbox, but we couldn't put new skids on.

'It wouldn't have affected the car but because he didn't know about it he kept on driving over the same manhole cover on the same line. If somebody had told him he would have changed his line and missed it. He'd have said: "Yes, I know where that happened and I'll miss going over that point again." After the race he heard about it and he said: "Next time tell me, I want to know everything."

'His precision was unbelievable. When we had the fuel metres – fuel in the turbos was always on the limit – you'd listen to his debrief and he'd be going round the circuit and he could tell you at what place he was point one of a litre plus or minus on the lap. He could tell you when that figure changed – before or after the bridge, on certain corners, at different parts of the circuit. He was that intense.

'You'd got this gauge in front of you and it was changing the whole time. If it changed earlier than he anticipated at, say, the bridge – he knew he was using too much fuel. He remembered it and this was through the whole race. His mind? On a debrief he could spend five or ten minutes telling you about one lap, every bump, every entry, every exit, every line he'd taken through the corner. I think he wore Ducarouge down with his memory power and his explanations of what he'd done. He'd stay until eight or nine o'clock at night and he wouldn't simply go even then, he'd always come and say goodbye. He wouldn't just clear off, he'd speak to everybody and not only the people working on his car but the people working on the other one. Whether it was a general interest or an interest to see what was happening on the other car I don't know.

'He was a very good guy to work with. He was the kind who could pull out a second and that second would come from him, not the car. Say he'd be half a second off pole. Next minute he'd be sitting there on his last set of qualifying tyres, out he'd go and find a second, just like that. He did that so many times in '85 and '86 in the final five minutes of qualifying: sit there, wait, do it. I can't explain that. I think only he could explain it.'

Let me put this into racing performance: across 1985 he had taken pole position seven times, now he would take it eight times. Only Lauda (1974, 1975) and Piquet (1984) had more, nine; the eight equalled James Hunt (1976) and Mario Andretti (1978). It beat Clark, seven, in 1963.

The first pole of '86 was in Brazil. 'He worked hard to get that one,' Hallam says. 'He was absolutely exhausted after the lap. We were dealing with Piquet in the Williams, Ayrton went out on his second set of tyres and he gave everything from himself for that lap. I remember seeing him on the back straight slumped in the cockpit when he'd done it – not slumped so much as hunched. He'd given everything.'

In the race Senna finished second to Piquet, Dumfries ninth and three laps behind. 'I had the fourth quickest race lap,' Dumfries says, 'but it was very difficult to repeat that speed in a race again. I don't know why, but it was very, very frustrating.'

After Brazil the journalist Bulgin was made redundant by the magazine he was working for. He rang Senna and said he wouldn't be going to the next race, and explained why.

Senna: 'How will you manage?'

Bulgin: 'I'll be all right, I've enough to pay the mortgage.'

Senna: 'If you ever need money, anything, contact me.'

(Looking back on this, Bulgin said that 'Senna was the only person who offered me help rather than commiserations.')

That next race, Spain, was a classic: Senna beat Mansell by 0.014 seconds – but first qualifying.

Peter Warr has a revealing anecdote about that. Senna had an unassailable pole time of nearly a full second over Piquet as the second session neared its end. Senna did his lap and Warr said OK, *that's pole, you might as well get out of the car, no point in having another go*.

Senna insisted he wanted to stay in the car and did stay in it, eyes almost shut, for about a quarter of an hour. Then he announced to Warr that he would like to go out again because he'd been playing and re-playing laps in his mind and was convinced he could do a certain time, which he named to the fraction. Warr (wise in the ways of motorsport and actually a fan – if I may put it like that – apart from being a leading player) understood the nuances of the moment, understood that this is how a real driver behaves: you take the maximum from the car and, if you feel you haven't done that already, something inside you compels you to try again *for your own fulfilment*. And if a driver is not fulfilling himself in a car, what is he doing there? Warr ordered new tyres to be put on the Lotus, out went Senna and came back having done exactly the time he said he'd do.

In any qualifying session, watching Senna was awesome and fascinating. Those who worked with him try to explain it as best they can. He could divide his thinking into compartments: the weather (which he monitored carefully), what the opposition had just done, the surface of the track, the time remaining in the session, how the engine was, how the gearbox was, how the balance of the car was, which set-up would be optimum. He could then bring all these factors from the compartments and make a complete, living picture of how he would exploit each factor and create a great harmony from them. If you saw him sitting in the car in the pits waiting to go out, if you looked carefully at his eyes, they were *studying the picture*. It is exactly what Peter Warr saw Senna – eyes half closed – seeing at Jerez.

Incidentally, it is this sort of thing which gets a team solidly behind the driver. They slog and labour to create a fast machine – an intricate, time-consuming and fraught activity – and the driver repays them by making it the fastest machine on the track. *He fulfils them as he fulfils himself*. Incidentally, also, this pole position (Senna 1m 21.602, Piquet 1m 22.431) was the hundredth by Lotus and Hazel Chapman, Colin's widow, was there to present Senna with a cut-glass trophy. He handled the occasion with his accustomed ease and sincerity.

After the race, 'physically I was at the end,' Senna would say, 'but because I had won I recovered quickly. Winning is the best medicine to regain strength. In the evening I had fully recovered and I drove the race again in my mind. I wanted to enjoy my victory once more that way.'

He explained also how he managed to get such good starts. 'I may look slow but people don't know what a Grand Prix is. There are so many things you have to do, think about and even learn in those few hours before the start. For me the only way to be stronger is to concentrate deeply. I try to remember everything, every small detail of my preparation. You must think of everything in this enormous turmoil at the start. It is wrong to recognise people except your mechanics perhaps. I run the whole picture in my head. I inspect the surface of the track. That is important to determine your tactics in the race and your choice of tyres. I believe I am the only one who does that.

'I go through a sort of check list like a pilot except we have nothing on paper. After the warm-up lap I check everything once more. People always think the start of the race is something terrible, that your heart beats like mad, that your brain is about to explode but it's a totally unreal moment, it is like a dream, like entering another world. Your spirit goes and the body sets itself free. When you accelerate there is only one thing that matters, not to fall behind, to take the lead. Really the most beautiful moment is the moment when the light turns red. Everything in me is programmed then, everything is discharged, bang, bang, bang, the tension, the waiting for hours, minutes, it all disappears.'

So now you know.

A wheel bearing went on lap 11 at Imola when he was fourth; he was third at Monaco, second at Spa, fifth in Canada, won Detroit.

Stepney puts that into context. 'When he won he didn't celebrate much, no, as far as he was concerned that was the job that was meant to be done.' Stepney was convinced then, and subsequently, that nobody knew where Senna's limit was in the car. Even when Senna became locked into an extraordinary duel with Prost at McLaren, Stepney judged that 'for sure' he'd 'got a lot left in him, because he wouldn't push the car for the sake of pushing it – he'll be conserving his tyres. You learnt so much about that from him just because of the way he explained how he looked after them.'

He would, Stepney concluded, only use a car as much as necessary. At Detroit and places like that he blasted off into the distance but he still wasn't pushing it any more than he had to. Stepney felt that 'even at Detroit' Senna still had plenty in hand.

In France he spun off, marched back and apologised to the mechanics. At Brands Hatch the gearbox went on lap 27; he was second behind Piquet at Hockenheim, took pole in Budapest. 'He was quick all the way through there,' Hallam says, 'and he was always saying "no grip, no grip, we've got to improve the car!"' He was second behind Piquet in the race, the engine went on lap 13 in Austria, the transmission went right at the start at Monza, he was fourth in Portugal, third in Mexico, the engine went on lap 43 in Adelaide. He had 55 points and was fourth in the table.

John Player were very serious sponsors. Their promotions executive, Peter Dyke, was an almost Rabelaisian figure, knew the journalists well. It was Dyke who acted as master of ceremonies at a Media dinner at Cascais, not far from the track at Estoril on the eve of the Portuguese Grand Prix.

The place might have been a minor chateau. Through high arched windows you could see manicured lawns. Waitresses flitted here and there dispensing drinks from trays. Dyke loomed, slightly larger than life.

The conversation ebbed into silence when Senna came in. Instinctively people found themselves looking at him – as if he was a presence, not a mere person. It was awkward for him: so many faces turned to his. Dyke covered it by making an announcement: 'Gentlemen, I think you already know Ayrton' which broke the silence. By good fortune I sat next to him at dinner. He drank one glass of mineral water in careful, rationed sips and towards the end asked timidly for another. When the white wine was brought and the waitress worked her way along the table he covered his glass with the palm of his hand and smiled politely at her.

I wondered about the perfect lap? 'It is like tying both ends of your tie so that they are exactly the same length. Experience tells you that you can do it, practice tells you that you can do it – but you can't.' For someone who was said to have a limited command of English, it wasn't bad, was it?

(Later, I have to report, I wondered about how he could live in Brazil with money amongst widespread poverty and his defence of his own country was so perceptive, so rational and so vehement that the man from *The Times* thought it prudent to change the topic of conversation. As you might expect, he achieved this effortlessly by saying something like 'tell us please, Ayrton, about last year, when you won in the rain here.')

You and I don't know what it feels like to be gazed at, to be a moving exhibit, to have artificial silence and a couple – or a dozen, a hundred, 100,000 – faces always peering into yours every minute of every place you go until you close the hotel bedroom door. It must be damn near intolerable, must drive a strong man towards screaming and if Senna seemed withdrawn that was one way of coping: you see the faces in a haze, or as you might see trees, not separate trunks but as woodland.

Senna confessed as much. 'It is very pleasant to be able to go to a restaurant without having to book a table even when the place is very busy. On the other hand, when I want to be alone and people won't let me I am annoyed.'

That autumn a van crawled up a tree-lined 'road' in mid-Wales, hit a tree and brought it down. Among the passengers was a Ford and rally sport dealer called Mike Hill. 'We had to go and get a hand saw from a local farmer to cut it into pieces. Guess who was up there on the bonnet doing it? Ayrton Senna. We'd been told he was miserable and arrogant. Nonsense. He was a hell of a nice guy.'

Journalist Russell Bulgin had had a most original idea: why don't we see what Senna can do in a rally car or, to be precise, several rally cars? It was an idea Senna liked a lot and when Bulgin rang him he opened his diary, found two free days and said 'whichever day you want.' So they went to what Hill describes as 'a rally stage which was no longer used as that, but typical mid-Wales, gravel, bends, hills.'

Senna took the wheel of a Ford Cosworth Sierra, a 300bhp turbo-charged rally car. 'The first corner he flung the car in and went off into a ditch,' Hill said, 'but he didn't do that again. He seemed so natural, he learnt so quickly.'

That car was the treasured property of Phil Collins, who had been rallying since 1978. 'I'd never met the guy before,' Collins said. 'It was a week before the final round of the Sierra Challenge – which I needed to win – so I was a bit nervous about anything going wrong. We strapped him in the passenger seat. I gave him a ride to show him what it was about. He was scared witless, he was letting out gasps, the usual stuff from someone in a rally car for the first time. He took over and I was the passenger. I talked to him about the difference between tarmac and the loose stuff. I gave him as much simple theory as I could.

'The first corner was a fast right-hander, almost square, and he did everything wrong, he approached it from the outside, he had understeer, we went into the ditch and bounced along over a row of saplings. "I'm sorry, I'm not thinking, now I know what you mean." There wasn't a mark on the car. Away we went again. Being the nice guy he is he was careful not to damage the car, but gradually over two runs he became far more professional at it.'

He drove a Metro Clubman, insisting on having Bulgin in the passenger seat. Bulgin wrote: 'What you notice most is his right foot. It is never still. Senna is literally tapping the throttle through its half inch of travel. Continuously. The rev counter doesn't flicker, but he's dancing on the accelerator with tiny movements. This car is getting very sideways. Then you tumble it. He's using the throttle to keep the front end working, to give him some – as he puts it – bite.'

He was fast in the Metro, fast in a four-wheel Escort, fast in a Nova. Senna would say that 'here it's much more natural because you have to improvise all the time, you have to have a lot of judgement. There is no room for error. Otherwise you go off the road.'

Collins was spectating: 'I could see he was enjoying it, attacking corners sideways, there was a bigger plume of dust being carried behind the cars – and then he said "I would like to drive your car again …"'

Collins demurred.

'Come on, let me.'

Collins finally did what a good man would do and agreed. 'Senna was brilliant. He was braking with his left foot, bringing the power in at exactly the right place, throwing it, and I felt totally safe. And that Sierra was not an easy car to get the most out of, a wide power band, turbo lag. "Perfect," I said, and when I got out I said: "This boy is something else." There was nothing to add to that.'

Bulgin wrote: 'Senna's last try in the Cosworth is wonderful. He takes the final left-hander in three jolts of oversteer, running the car up the shale piled on the track edge to straighten its exit. The engine note doesn't waver, the hands pummelling the steering wheel. He looks like a rally driver: a brave rally driver.'

Hill remembers Senna saying 'he was very surprised at how much traction the Cosworth had on different surfaces and amazed at how much grip the Metro had. He just got better and better at it. I formed the impression that, given a couple of events, he'd be right up there.'

'We didn't have a budget from the magazine for the job and if Senna had asked for £1,000 for the day I don't know what we would have done,' Bulgin told me. 'I asked him what he did want and he replied "I don't want anything. I came here to learn." I said "well, at least let me fill your Mercedes up with petrol." He said "no, no, nothing thank you."'

And a last memory of mid-Wales, from Collins. 'When it was over I said "now you have driven my Cosworth let me come and have a go in your Formula 1." He said "it is not a problem for me … [pause, slow smile] … but it is not my car …"'

I suppose that everybody knew 1987 would be a decisive season in Senna's relationship with Lotus. It would be his third, and if he didn't win the World Championship, or come extremely close, his hunger for it would inevitably take him to another team where he could win it.

'I think,' Bob Dance says, 'there was a danger we were going to lose him at the end of '86. I think he felt Lotus weren't good enough for him – in the sense of where he wanted to go. At the time we weren't looking as good as McLaren and he was setting his sights higher still. Lotus was not progressing, it was stagnant, shall we say. I believe what kept him with us for '87 was the active suspension we'd have. He thought it might give him an advantage over the rest and he put a lot of effort into it. He could tell you what the car was doing anywhere on the circuit, he could talk for as long as you liked about what his car was doing in a race. He would watch the race afterwards on the TV in the motorhome or in the hotel and he'd analyse his own performance, tell you what he thought of his own performance here and there during the race. He was very critical of himself.'

Lotus had produced a prototype 'active' suspension in the early 1980s: computer technology allowed the system to give the car a level ride. Peter Wright, the Lotus Technical Director, would say 'we can take information from up to 20 different sensing systems at the rate of just over half a billion inputs per lap.'

Senna was 27, nearing that point in his career which is a balance of youth, experience and the need still to do it. He could exploit the Lotus fully, but if the Lotus was inherently incapable of taking the Championship he could do no more. Even Senna was constricted by the art of the possible. Nor would the season be in any sense easy: Piquet and Mansell at Williams, Prost at McLaren, Alboreto and Berger at Ferrari, and he had to beat all of them.

He was at home at Lotus. 'At the end of a race you'd have a bit of a laugh and a joke,' Stepney says. 'He was a practical joker but he picked and chose his moments when he'd do that. We'd have water fights, stuff like that.' People looked at him and said he was cold but 'you know, he had a sense of humour, a very good sense of humour.' Stepney added (in 1989): 'It takes a long time to get to know him and I don't know him fully.'

Before we examine 1987, listen to Senna himself on how he drove a Lotus. 'I used to cover the palms of my hands because if I didn't I'd get these terrible blisters and that made steering difficult. I don't do that any more now. My new car is lighter, easier to handle. I clean the visor. It is strange but something like that can cost you your victory. I perspire a lot during a race but I have a tube through which I can drink. A tube like that must be fitted carefully so it doesn't come loose. That happened to me once and I almost lost the race. In my head I consider every detail. It's never finished. The smallest error in checking, the smallest error in setting the wing mirror could cause a catastrophe. On the circuit it's too late to think of that. I check if all the buttons are in the right place, if they work or not. There is so much to think about, there is never enough time – or room in your mind – to process all the information adequately ... and then it gets tiring.

'Whenever I think it's one of those days when nobody can touch me I call out through the radio link "I'm fine." I think they like to hear that. When I cross the line first it is an overwhelming feeling.'

Moreover, Lotus now had Honda engines instead of Renault. Peter Warr discusses this in retrospect. 'I'm not sure that even now [1988] we have all the facts and figures and data together, but maybe it served us a little bit badly because the Renault engine was a better engine than Senna made it appear. Maybe it was only because he was driving it so fast that its fuel consumption was bad. Maybe it was because he had this throttle control technique – blip-blip-blipping in the corners. The reason we have suspicions like this is because he keeps on coming up as the worst of the four Honda drivers on fuel consumption [Senna and Prost at McLaren-Honda/Piquet and Satoru Nakajima at Lotus]. That's partly because he's going the quickest and partly the blipping of the throttle.

'People were saying "well, the Lotus is a good car, Senna is a bright up-and-coming driver but they are handicapped by the Renault engine which hasn't got the fuel consumption" but who knows if the truth wasn't this: the engine was absolutely fantastic and very powerful, the chassis wasn't that good and Senna was having to drive it above the level of which it was capable of being driven to be competitive – which was why the fuel consumption was bad.'

Lotus got Honda engines for 1987 and with them came a pleasant, experienced man – Nakajima – to partner Senna. He would be immediately useful. Lotus tested at Donington, Senna brought the car into the pits after a couple of laps and said: 'There's something wrong with it because it's vibrating, it feels like it's going to shake itself to pieces.' Nakajima got in, did a couple of laps, came back and said 'no problem. That's the way the engines always are.'

'I greatly valued my collaboration with Renault,' Senna would say. 'The motor racing people are very competent at Renault Sport and we obtained excellent results on pure performance. But at that time Renault's involvement was on the decline. Honda were investing totally, with maximum means and a Japanese mentality of taking-it-to-a-conclusion.'

Lotus had the new and active suspension, created by Ducarouge, and it seemed to be in the Chapman tradition, promising a technological leap ahead of all the others. The system, however, was fiendishly complicated and needed modern computing power to have made it work regularly. When it did work it was that leap, hence Senna's enthusiasm.

Brazil: the active suspension brought problems and Senna spun during the Friday qualifying session. He was quicker on the Saturday and started from the second row of the grid. He had a strange sort of race: in the lead by lap 8, in the pits with handling problems on lap 14 pitching him back to eighth, charged; was second on lap 39, stopped altogether on lap 50 with an oil tank problem.

Imola: pole. In the end he simply couldn't catch Mansell in the Williams and finished 27.545 seconds behind.

Belgium: row two of the grid. Mansell took the lead, Senna following. After a crash, the race was re-started and Senna led, Mansell following. They reached the corner called *Pouhon* – a left – and as they came out Mansell was very close. Along the short rush to *Les Fagnes* – a right – Mansell moved out and, as he drew alongside, was on the racing line. The two cars went into the right-hander together and their wheels touched. Mansell said he thought Senna had missed a gear or the engine had 'hesitated' and he moved left to overtake. 'The next thing I knew, I was being pushed off the circuit.'

Senna judged it a different way. 'I can tell you that nothing happened to my car at the previous corner. I took it flat. Maybe you find the car in front of you appears to slow if you hit the boost button on your steering wheel and have an extra 100bhp. But I couldn't believe what he was trying to do – overtake on the outside at a place like that. I tried to get out of the way, brake as much as possible, but you can only do so much in a situation like that. I was committed to the corner – there was no way I could stop.'

They spun off as if they were locked together, Senna came to rest in the sand trap, Mansell limping back out and on. Mansell went as far as lap 17, came into the pits and his eyes were ablaze with anger. He strode to the Lotus pits and seized Senna.

'When a man holds you round the throat, I do not think he has come to apologise,' Senna commented afterwards. Three Lotus mechanics were needed to get Mansell off Senna, who regained his composure and wandered to the wall to watch Nakajima finishing fifth.

Monaco: Mansell on pole, Senna beside him on the front and what would happen when they reached the right-hander at *Ste Devote*? Nothing. Mansell got there cleanly first, held the lead until lap 29 when the waste-gate went and Senna ran comfortably to the end, finishing 33 seconds ahead of Piquet. Prost now led the table with 18 points, Senna three points further back.

Detroit: Mansell on pole, Senna beside him on the front and what would happen when they reached the left-hander at Turn One? Nothing. Mansell got there clearly and cleanly first, held the lead until lap 34 (cramp) and Senna ran comfortably to the end, finishing 33:819 seconds ahead of Piquet. Senna 24 points, Prost 22.

France: second row of the grid. Senna didn't like the balance of the car and ran a percentage race to finish fourth. Senna 27, Prost 26, Piquet 24, Mansell 21.

Britain: second row of the grid. This time he was hampered by fuel consumption and drove a percentage race to third. Senna 31, Mansell 30, Piquet 30, Prost 26.

Germany: Lotus tested there ten days before the race and at high speed Senna had a tyre deflate. Warr was so concerned that he rang Goodyear in Ohio to warn them they might have a tyre wear problem similar to the one which had – with shocking speed – caused one of Mansell's tyres to explode at Adelaide, the last race of 1986. It turned out to be an ordinary puncture. Mind you, it was a hell of a moment: Senna had been moving out of the stadium complex towards the first chicane and the Ferrari speed trap clocked him at 206mph. The left rear deflated, tearing the rear suspension off the car; and the car kept on in a straight line for 600 metres. The active suspension had been battling to compensate for the deflation.

Senna pondered his future. He'd already spoken to Ron Dennis at McLaren before the season and now, in the German Grand Prix, finished third but a lap behind Piquet and Johansson. He made a judgement: the Lotus could not compete with the McLarens and Williams. A few days later Warr received a letter from Senna's English solicitors saying that he wouldn't be with them for 1988.

(Senna: 'Before the letter was sent I told Peter Warr myself during the weekend at the German Grand Prix as a matter of education' – i.e. information and common decency.)

On the Saturday after the German Grand Prix, Warr flew to Nice and had a long talk with Piquet. On the Wednesday – just before the Hungarian Grand Prix – Piquet flew to London and signed. 'I hadn't spoken to Nelson before that Saturday but I felt we had to act,' Warr says. (Senna: 'Nothing was signed but all the negotiations had taken place and I believed in Ron's word on the deal.') Now Warr again: 'It was quite obvious that Senna thought he was going to be the first to sit down in the game of musical chairs and that everything else would then follow. I wasn't prepared to wait for him – and run the risk of having to choose from the left-overs at the end of the season.'

Senna did not know the team had hired Piquet. He only heard about it when he reached Hungary. 'It amazes me that a company as big and famous as Lotus should behave so unprofessionally. They could have called me on Wednesday – the day he signed – to let me know. Instead I found out here on Friday morning.'

Hungary: third row. He finished 37.727 seconds behind Piquet. Austria: fourth row. He finished fifth, two laps adrift. Piquet 54 points, Senna 43, Mansell 39.

At Monza, Dennis confirmed that Senna had joined McLaren. Senna saw it as a 'great opportunity for me. From a personal point of view I am very happy to work with Alain [Prost]: two top drivers working together can only make a team stronger.' Significantly McLaren were getting Honda engines. Honda liked what Senna did – a lot. He was on the second row for the race, took the lead on lap 24 and lost it on lap 43 when he slewed slightly off – tyre wear – and couldn't catch Piquet, although the difference was only 1.806 seconds at the end.

He got no points in Portugal, was fifth in Spain and the Championship had virtually gone. When he spun off in Mexico (clutch) it had gone. He was second at Suzuka, second at Adelaide – then disqualified because the brake ducts on the Lotus were irregular. It constituted a sad end to three years.

Of Lotus he'd say: 'I knew the team from the inside, it was a team which counted for me. I made friends there.'

I never did discuss the question with Peter Warr because it seemed hardly necessary. Everyone knew why they couldn't hold Senna, none more than Warr himself. His face was wistful, full of quiet resignation, as we moved around the topic, not through it. There was nothing to say.

Prost had won the Championship twice with McLaren, and now, as we've said, Honda engines would be added for 1988. Since 1984 the team had won 25 races – and taken Lauda to the Championship, too. For Senna, it was the main chance; perhaps it was always where he had been going and all the rest merely an apprenticeship, although that's a hard judgement on Toleman and Lotus and the good men at both places. He was still twenty-seven, it was still an age to retain big ambitions.

Dance explained [in 1995] that 'it's fair to say we got the feeling that he wasn't happy with his results. That was not by any means down to his driving. On occasions, our car was unreliable and it wasn't a Championship-winning car. He could see greener grass as other teams got bigger. Lotus didn't get bigger with them. The race shop was virtually the same as it was in say 1980, but if you go to Williams or Ferrari or McLaren they've come on in leaps and bounds: the number of staff employed in development and testing, their equipment, everything you can think of. They've had millions and millions pumped into them year by year. That isn't obvious at Lotus and that's one of the reasons why it's gone down.

'When Ayrton left us, he didn't come and see everybody because, unfortunately, we'd dropped him right in it in Australia. Adelaide is very heavy on brakes and we did all the usual stuff with larger ducts, putting on a flexible tube to get more air to the brakes. At the end of the race – Ayrton finished second – we were disqualified for over-large ducts, so he went off in a huff. Basically, it was because we had really let him down, I guess.

'How do I equate Senna with Jim Clark? Oh dear (chuckle). You have to equate them in their different eras. Clark could drive and win in virtually any car. Senna didn't have that opportunity, so we only really saw him as an open-wheeled racing car driver (long pause). He had a reasonable mechanical knowledge and I think his model planes helped him in that. Clark had a reasonable mechanical knowledge, not a great knowledge. They were both (pause) … yes, intelligent young men. They had the desire to win. Coming second wasn't for them. When Senna was preparing to do a qualifying run, he'd watch his TV monitor, his car would be ready to go and he would decide for himself when it was time to go out. You knew he was going to qualify first, put the car on pole. That was the object of going out in qualifying. He expected 100 per cent from the people who worked with him and he always gave 100 per cent himself. He wasn't likely to have off days, even though he was a Latin. Some are very temperamental. I didn't class him as that type of driver. Clark was the same. In their respective eras they are equals, if I can put it like that.

'What is *it*? It's mental and physical condition, it's a natural ability. What makes a good pianist? What makes a good artist? They've that little extra, whatever it is, but it takes them to the top. As racing drivers, they have perhaps that little bit more daring but they know they can push that little bit further because they can control their situation. They have a very fine balance. Usually the quick men are good in the wet. Senna's second race for Lotus was in terrible conditions at Estoril, diabolical afternoon, cold, miserable, standing water. He had one "off" but he didn't go off to the point of losing direction across the grass: he still had the car heading the right way and he wanted to win. It's the will to win, isn't it? He should have been an astronaut or a test pilot because of the involved work you have to carry out, not just a driver. He was capable of testing military aircraft, land them, tell you exactly what was going on, how they handled, everything.'

At Lotus, in an uncompetitive car, he had 57 points and third in the Championship. The final words go to Warr: 'Ayrton Senna's time with Team Lotus was undoubtedly a very, very exciting period in modern motor racing. The thing that really marks him out is that he was the first driver since Jimmy Clark to arouse the sort of emotions that Clark did within the team. He was certainly the first driver since Ronnie Peterson to have people as excited about some of the things he could do with a race car – you know, things you just couldn't believe.'

One postscript. A 15-year-old from Sao Paulo, Rubens Barrichello, 'was trying to get into the World Karting Championships. The karts were the thing Ayrton liked most all the time. That's why he had a circuit built on his ranch. My father rang him to try and get some help in understanding about the World Championships better because up to then I'd only done the Brazilian and South American. Ayrton was a great help. He phoned his old team, DAP, and I raced for that team. At that time, I was becoming a professional driver in karts, well not exactly a professional but I'd been racing them for six years, seven years. I met him when I went to Rio and he was testing for the Brazilian Grand Prix. He was a big hero of mine. By 1987 he'd already done things that nobody could imagine. He'd raced in Portugal and won (in the storm, 1985), he'd been on pole in Monaco, things like that so yes, yes, he was a person that every driver would like to be: not just if you were from Sao Paulo but the whole of Brazil.'

Whatever, Alain Prost, World Champion with McLaren in 1985 and 1986, was waiting for him there. He did so as *seigneur* – people spoke of McLaren as Prost's team. John Watson met Senna at an Austrian health spa and warned him to tread carefully at McLaren; remember it's Team Prost. Senna replied that he intended to beat Prost physically and mentally, and at the first opportunity.

Behind the press release optimism, the choreographed publicity photographs, the honeyed words to journalists, the hands being shaken for the cameras, a terrible storm was coming.

Chapter 9

THE FIRST CHAMPIONSHIP

*B*ologna. Tuesday, 22 March 1988, evening. McLaren International's Falcon 20 landed from Heathrow; a freighter bearing the McLaren MP4/4 racing car had landed earlier.

Steve Nichols, who headed up the design team, looked for the transporter to take it to Imola. There had been a misunderstanding. The transporter was not there, it was at the track 30km away. They phoned, waited until it came and they reached the track at nine, fussed around, went to their hotel. Nichols had what he remembers as a 'fitful night's sleep'. A question gnawed at him: what if the car is a 'turkey'? It hadn't run yet, McLaren had not run a Honda engine yet, building the car had been a rush and the new season was two and a half weeks away.

Continuing the style of the chapters from Formula Ford 1600 to Formula 3, here are Senna's steps towards what he'd always wanted.

Imola. Wednesday, 23 March. Nichols: 'We arrived, warmed up the car, Prost went out and did the first laps and I mean it was just incredible. Within three laps and before we'd changed anything, he was only a few seconds off his previous best time at the track. He came in, the engine was checked all over, out he went again and he was doing competitive times.'

Prost's best: 1 minute 28.5.

'We changed to Senna and by lunchtime he was quicker than any of the other teams had been in the whole test. By the end of the day our drivers had done times two seconds quicker than the Ferraris, and they'd been the quickest in the previous two days.'

Senna did 1 minute 27.6. Berger – in one of those Ferraris, of course – had done 1 minute 29.90. At least, Nichols concluded, the car is not a turkey.

Senna made no public comment. There was no need. The car had made the comment. Something else had happened that day at Imola, however, and Jo Ramirez would recount it years later. There had been a dispute between Senna and Prost because both wanted to be the first to drive the new car. Senna was clearly doing what he told John Watson he would do: asserting himself immediately. Ramirez sensed a certain animosity between Senna and Prost – already.

Brazilian Grand Prix. Rio, Friday 1 April. Senna and Prost were quickest in the untimed session and both said the handling wasn't quite right. The temperature crept up towards 40 degrees and in the afternoon Senna did 1 minute 30.218, Prost behind Mansell (Williams), and Alessandro Nannini (Benetton) on 1 minute 31.975. Senna: 'We have not had any serious problems. Our car is virtually brand new and we are still finding out about it, so it is only to be expected that we will be adjusting both the chassis and the engine.'

Saturday, 2 April. Senna was right. He thrust in 1 minute 28.096, then Mansell (1:28.632), then Prost (1:28.782). 'I was quite lucky with the track but the most important thing is that we seem to be more competitive in spite of the inevitable minor problems that are to be expected with a brand-new car.'

Sunday, 3 April. It rained, the rain stopped. Senna brought them round slowly on the parade lap to the green light – was he trying to make the others overheat? – and the moment they formed up Senna's arms were out of the cockpit being waved like flippers. Behind him smoke belched from Ivan Capelli's March as if it was a bonfire. Senna had a gear selection problem. The start had to be abandoned. Worse, a fan rushed towards Senna's stationary car and had to be manhandled away by a posse of men in yellow shirts. They were not gentle with him. Senna would start from the pit lane in the spare car. He watched as the cavalcade went by and came from that pit lane fast. By lap 2 he was up to 19th, and now he moved in a hurry: lap 3, 17th; lap 4, 15th; lap 6, 13th; lap 7, 11th; lap 8, tenth; lap 9, ninth, lap 10, eighth; lap 12, seventh; lap 13, sixth; lap 16, fifth; lap 17, fourth; lap 19, third; lap 20, second.

Prost lay ahead. Senna slipped back sixth when his pit stop went wrong. The engine stalled, frantic hands were waved and he was stationary for 32.01 seconds.

On lap 31, an official in a lime green uniform and wearing headphones wandered rather sheepishly out on to the rim of the track. In his right hand he held a small black flag. In his left – and arranged in front of him like a matador's cape – he held a wide black board with the number 12 on it. As Senna passed him the official wandered back on to the grass. It was over.

Senna came in, talked for a while with the mechanics from the cockpit, clambered out, went into the pit lane mêlée taking his driving gloves off. He had been disqualified for changing cars after the green light for that first, aborted start – technically it was not a new race so he wasn't allowed to. 'Why wait until now?' Senna wondered. Actually Ron Dennis had been arguing his case with the officials, and that explained the delay. Prost won from Berger.

Monza. Tuesday, 19 April. He tested, did a 1 minute 28.94, did that again across an extended test of 42 laps, and also did a complete spin at 160 kilometres an hour, thumping the barrier.

San Marino Grand Prix, Imola. Friday, 29 April. He was second behind Prost in the first session for the grid; and faster than Prost on the Saturday. 'The pop-off valve fitted to my engine was giving trouble so the Honda engineers had to fit a new one. Although I knew the valve was not operating correctly I did not come into the pits immediately because I was worried that it might rain.' (Pop-off valve, a way of controlling engine power.)

Ramirez recounts a revealing anecdote about that. The drivers changed in the transporter and ordinarily Prost was first out because Senna folded his clothes so carefully and dressed with the same care. Senna was doing this when Prost, going out, saw the timesheet and murmured to Ramirez – not intended for Senna's ears – '[expletive], he's quick.' But Senna did hear because, when Ramirez turned towards him, he winked. Ramirez judged that a profound psychological moment: Senna on his way to replacing Team Prost with Team Senna.

Sunday, 1 May. Nichols: 'Although we had gone well in testing, Imola is thirsty, it was supposed to be the sort of place where a normally aspirated car would win. Everybody was thinking: will we be good here?' Senna took the lead and was not to lose it. 'We set a quick pace – so far as the fuel allowed, we were racing. This was a question-mark race for us. I never really felt confident we would finish. I thought: there's another race gone for me. The balance of the car was beautiful, the engine fine, the consumption good but quite early I had smoke and a burning smell coming into the cockpit. Later the gearbox started to feel loose.'

Senna stopped just beyond the line, 2.334 seconds ahead of Prost.

Nichols: 'It wasn't absolutely bone dry.' (Geoff Lees, Honda test driver in Japan, would explain that 'fuel consumption can be calculated to within 200 metres over the full distance of a Grand Prix. It is that precise.')

Monaco Grand Prix, Monte Carlo. Thursday, 12 May. Senna took provisional pole with a staggering 1 minute 26.464 and there was only direct comparison, Prost on 1 minute 28.375. Now Senna said something staggering: 'We had a problem with poor engine braking in the morning untimed session which the Honda engineers were able to cure for the afternoon but we still have a slight delay in the power pick-up from slow corners.' Slight delay? Hmmm. On the Saturday Senna challenged credulity with 1 minute 23.998 and again the only direct comparison was Prost, 1 minute 25.425. Prost said: 'Fantastic. There's no other word, is there?' Senna: 'To be honest I can't tell you if I got an absolutely clear lap or not. It's all so frantic here that you can't separate individual laps in your mind. But to be really quick you have to use all the road and you have to take big risks, yes.'

Sunday, 15 May. He led to lap 67, lost concentration just before the tunnel and hit the armco. He was out. 'Monte Carlo was the turning point in the Championship. It was nothing to do with the car or the equipment: The mistake I made changed me psychologically and mentally. I changed a lot inside. It gave me the strength and the power to fight in critical moments. It was the biggest step in my career as a professional, a racing driver and a man. It brought me closer to God than I have ever been. I was feeling easy in front. It was a hundred per cent perfect weekend. Suddenly I lost concentration, made a stupid mistake and threw everything away. It made me reflect about a lot of things. I had good help from my family and other people who gave me power and strength. It has changed my life. I am the same person but my mental strength has changed.'

Prost won, and the Championship stood at Prost 24, Berger 14, Senna 9, Piquet 8.

Ramirez has recounted how he contacted Senna in Senna's Monte Carlo apartment five hours after he crashed and Senna was still in tears. The Ramirez anecdote is well known but stands in amazing juxtaposition to what follows.

'What special personal memory do I have of Senna?' Pino Allievi of La Gazzetta dello Sport, the Italian daily sports newspaper, muses. 'I have a memory of a man with two personalities. The year he crashed at Monaco he had invited me to have breakfast in his home on the Friday. I was there, I think, from 9 o'clock until 11.30 and I came to know a different man. That apartment was not, as you might imagine, typically French, it was a Brazilian apartment put in Monte Carlo. I remember the colours, the pictures, the walls, the furniture, the carpets, everything was Brazilian. The maid, a black grandmother if you like, she was Brazilian of course. Senna lived very happily in that atmosphere and so we spoke freely, off the record.

'I gained a very, very good impression, but of a man totally different than the man I knew through motor racing. Then the following day during second qualifying he was totally different again and that's why I say two personalities, a man with two faces. One was when he was absolutely detached by the motor racing. When he was on the track he was capable of hating people like he did with Prost, because with Prost it was hate. With Mansell it was the same situation, and with Piquet. When he was far away from motor racing he changed.

'The thing that I regret is that he never compromised between his private life and his public life. He could have been better-known as a *man*. The biggest effort he made in his life was to hide his true face. He was a nice man with a complex personality, with many complexes. In a way he was a bit like [Silvio] Berlusconi [controversial Italian politician] but in a positive, not a negative way: invented by the society of image. Like Berlusconi and other people in other areas – Enzo Ferrari is an example – he worked all his life to keep his face private, to promote his image. He was *obliged* to give the public a positive image of himself. He was up there on the screen and he was obliged to hate Prost, obliged to say nasty things about Mansell. He was like an actor on the screen. I think he was troubled, because he never had the courage to show the public his true face and that was his biggest limit.'

Mexican Grand Prix, Mexico City. Friday, 27 May. Senna took provisional pole, took pole itself on the Saturday. Prost won the race, Senna second. 'The pop-off valve opened unexpectedly when I took second gear at the start. After that I did not want to risk using too much fuel so I decided not to chase Alain.' Prost 33, Berger 18, Senna 15, Alboreto 9. 'By the time I got myself into a rhythm Alain was already some way clear. He drove very fast today, never backed off and he deserved the race, sure.'

Canadian Grand Prix, Montreal. Friday, 10 June. Senna went quickest from Prost and again on the Saturday. Prost took the lead and held it to lap 19, Senna always directly behind him. They came to the left-right kink, Senna darted out, ran briefly alongside Prost and reached the right turn on the inside ... on the racing line. It settled the race. 'For all 69 laps we were on the limit of the fuel so Alain and I were pacing each other. In some places he was quicker and at others I'd gain on him. I knew that I had to be patient. Passing him is never very easy but when I saw the chance I made my move and everything came good.' Prost courteously and prudently moved out of the way. Prost 39, Senna 24, Berger 18, Piquet 11.

USA-East Grand Prix, Detroit. Friday, 17 June. Senna quickest, then Prost. 'The tyres were most effective only in the first two or three laps but apart from that everything is going fine.' Everything did not go fine on the Saturday; the track started to break up and Berger and Alboreto were quicker than Senna, although his Friday time was enough to give him pole, his sixth on the roll. 'It was very slippery,' he said. That six poles equalled the record of Stirling Moss (1959–60) and Lauda (1974).

Sunday, 19 June. Senna gave a consummate performance, led from flag to flag in what Osamu Goto, Honda project leader, called 'a survival race'. Goto added: 'As we had anticipated, the temperature was exceptionally high at 34 degrees, which is hotter than it was in Brazil in April. Our priority therefore was reliability and in fact the McLarens started the race with 140 litres of fuel instead of the permitted 150 litres. This gave the brakes a slightly easier time in the first few laps, and that gave them an advantage.' Twenty-six cars set off into the contorting 'tunnels' between the armco and after the 63 laps only eight were running.

Senna was exhausted. 'This race is very hard, both mentally and physically. You're racing against the heat and the walls. When the crew told me to come in for a tyre stop (on lap 42) I did not want to do so. But when I saw that Alain had stopped (lap 39) I was happy to do the same.' Prost 45, Senna 33, Berger 18, Piquet and Thierry Boutsen 11.

Silverstone. Monday, 27 June. Senna tested and told me: 'I have to be as close to perfection as possible because Alain is always like that, too – close to perfection. I have to be exact in setting the car up, exact in every decision I make. We are in the same factory team. If I want to compete with him I have to give the same as he does. For me it is important to have a competitive car like I have now. It is the first time in my career I have been in such a situation and I feel quite happy. With Alain, I expected it to be as it has turned out and I can't see any reason why it should change. In other words, harmony not friction.'

That was the mood of the moment, certainly for public consumption, and I had the impression they were still feeling each other out, shadow boxing, if you like.

Silverstone was a more rudimentary place then. Senna was sitting on a deckchair in the pits. He was between runs and, unusually, not preoccupied with some aspect of the car. I set my tape recorder on top of my briefcase rather than hold it towards his face. I had placed the briefcase, side up, directly in front of his feet. As he began to speak he also began to tease the briefcase with his toe, gently but rhythmically, so that the tape recorder wobbled and then rocked to and fro – but it did not fall. He stopped, let the tape recorder settle, began again and you thought *this time it has to fall*. It didn't. You have to wonder how someone speaking a foreign language (English) could simultaneously do that with such precision and sensitivity. Oh, and simultaneously he was grinning hugely, too.

Later I go off to Stowe, where there was a wooden platform inside the corner, a superb vantage point because you could see a panorama of cars coming out of Becketts Corner into Chapel Curve, all the way to the *Daily Express* bridge on the other side of the track. After a few minutes Senna arrived in a hire car, hopped nimbly out – he was wearing a Marlboro anorak which makes him look broader – skipped up the platform steps and watched. You sensed that he did not wish to be disturbed. He wanted to see what the others were doing and how they were doing it: he wasn't spectating at all. His eyes tracked each car, locking on to them, his head moving in time with them. It was as if he was using the eyes as binoculars, using his mind to disassemble the cars as they passed.

He skipped down the steps and I assumed he was going off to his hotel. It was late afternoon, anyway, and only three or four cars circulated. He'd already seen them. The hire car moved off along the wide, undulating runway which was inside the circuit and led towards the distant paddock, but Senna swivelled off on to the wide grass verge flanking Hangar Straight. Halfway along a man sat hunched over a speed trap. Senna stopped, got out, walked directly to him, stooped, looked at the speeds, started to ask questions …

Tuesday, 28 June. Prost arrives, says firmly that he has to be perfect because of Senna and insists that they are functioning as a team, not factions within a team. Senna meanwhile was out at the back of the circuit flying his model aeroplane, the one he'd kept in the boot of the hire car yesterday. (The McLarens incidentally, were testing rather than trying to blitz lap times; Prost did 1 minute 12.500, which was slower than Berger's 1:12.120; Senna did 1:18.596, slower than Piquet, Boutsen, Nakajima. Alboreto, Warwick and Mansell. Not that it mattered.)

French Grand Prix, Paul Ricard. Friday, 1 July. This time Prost was quicker than Senna (although, Prost said, the handling seemed 'a little bit nervous'). Astonishingly it happened again on the Saturday, so that for the first time in 1988 Senna did not have pole.

Sunday, 3 July. Prost took the lead, Senna hounding him, Prost had a troubled tyre stop and when he emerged Senna was in the lead by 2.9 seconds. Prost hunted Senna and overtook him in a great, incisive swoop at the right-hand loop of *Beausset* – Senna momentarily baulked by two back-markers, Prost seeing this, screwing everything out of the engine and taking the inside line. Prost: 'I think Ayrton lost downforce when he was following another car through the fast corner because he ran wide on to the dirt. I caught him there and then I braked very late at the next corner.' Senna: 'I cannot remember exactly when, but the gear lever began to feel spongy. I started to miss the odd gear, I had a problem with my gearchange when I was leading and it just got worse and worse. Alain behaved very correctly.'

British Grand Prix, Silverstone. Friday, 8 July. The miracle did happen, Alboreto and Berger quicker than Senna and Prost. Senna: 'We have a lot of understeer at Copse and Becketts which is losing us time.' The miracle endured on the Saturday, Alboreto and Berger again quicker. Senna spun twice – complete rotations at high speed – and continued as if nothing had happened at all. Both spins were at Stowe. 'The car was not handling very well there and I was more on the limit than I had been yesterday.' Actually, it was a glimpse of Senna's mastery, the spins so controlled that he might have been doing them as party tricks to entertain the crowd.

Before we leave Saturday, in the morning untimed session Senna's engine needed changing. This was achieved in 1 hour 50 minutes and Senna thanked the mechanics very sincerely indeed.

Sunday, 10 July. It rained, tumbling from a slate-grey sky and this sky had the look of permanent, unmoving cover. It rained all day. The race would be dangerous, as all wet races are, but more dangerous here because Silverstone is fast. Berger took the lead, held that to lap 14 when Senna dipped left and moved past. Prost, hobbled by mechanical problems (he'd eventually retire), was on the edge of the track about to be lapped. Picture it: a back-marker and Prost poised to turn into the sharp left-hand corner just past the bridge and Senna inside them. They would turn across him …

Senna's car twitched under braking and he slithered towards Prost who had to turn sharply away. 'Alain and I almost touched. It was a bad moment because the visibility was so bad. Then we had some unexpected problems with the fuel consumption which was worrying until I got the situation under control. At the speed Berger had been running I couldn't make the finish on fuel. I was pretty sure he couldn't, either.' Prost 54, Senna 48, Berger 21.

The harmony of the season was being broken. The French press savaged Prost – he's a beaten man, hasn't even the stomach for a wet race any more – and Prost was very indignant indeed. He said that the car's problem had made no difference to his basic resolve, which was to cease the moment he felt it was too dangerous to continue. Ron Dennis was angered by the criticism of Prost and said he had the two most professional drivers in the sport and if they ever decided to stop he would give them his full support.

All unnoticed, McLaren and Honda had won their eighth successive race, an absolute record for a single season.

German Grand Prix, Hockenheim. Friday, 22 July. Senna quickest, Prost next, but a radical change on the Saturday, Prost then Berger then Alboreto, Senna tenth. Tenth? 'We took the decision to concentrate on a race set-up, running with a full fuel load. From my point of view the worst that was going to happen was that Alain might knock me off pole position, but I wasn't too worried about that at this circuit [where you could overtake], so we figured it would be more worthwhile running through some chassis settings.' Senna did keep pole – Prost couldn't get within a second of Senna's Friday time.

The traditional after-session press conference was ugly, the press room crowded by a couple of hundred journalists and photographers who milled and mewled waiting for Senna and Prost. As the wait lengthened, one journalist, enraged by the delay, set off to find Dennis to protest. When Senna and Prost did come they protested that they had had a debrief and they had been harassed by journalists who wouldn't wait for the press conference, had been made to say the things they would have to repeat at the conference.

Senna let Prost speak, and we glimpsed a face of Prost we rarely saw, moving towards bitterness. Then Senna asked for the microphone. His voice was almost trembling and made so by the profundity of what he wanted to say. 'Since my childhood I have been taught that it is not honourable to ignore people and therefore when journalists come up to me I try to answer their questions.' In other words, you're crowding me all the time. Why can't you wait until the press conference?

The pressure was gathering around the two men who were, anyway, the only people journalists wanted to talk to virtually the whole time. Eight races (including the German Grand Prix) remained. The pressure could only increase, and very likely day by day.

Sunday, 24 July. It rained, but not like Silverstone, the sky not so leaden, so intimidating. A wet race, yes, but it might become a dry race. Piquet risked dry tyres and any doubts he must have had about that were resolved at the first chicane when his Lotus found itself in closest acquaintance with the tyre barrier and out of the race.

Senna made a flying start, Prost did not. 'In these wet conditions I was not very confident – which was why I did make a bad start,' Prost said. He was fourth as they crossed the line to complete lap 1, second by lap 12. 'Alain was pushing hard to get back at me so I just concentrated on maintaining the gap,' Senna said. 'With wet tyres over a full race distance and no pit stop it was a bit difficult.' He added: 'The conditions were changing constantly, particularly out in the forest where it was much wetter than in the stadium.' Deep into the race Prost spun, recovered and finished 13.609 seconds behind. Prost: 'I kept up the pressure until I spun. I think my wet tyres were a bit more worn than Ayrton's and the brakes were not perfect either – but that was because we had expected the track to dry out much more as the race went on.' Prost 60, Senna 57, Berger 25.

Hungarian Grand Prix, Hungaroring. Friday, 5 August. It was damp and over-cast and Prost went quickest, Senna only fifth. 'At the end of the session, when the track was almost completely dry, it was just a matter of getting a clear lap and I didn't get mine.'

Saturday, 6 August. The sun came out and Senna came out with 1 minute 27.635 – pole, of course – Prost only 1 minute 28.778 and a place on the fourth row of the grid. He'd had a vibration in the engine of his race car and used the spare. Senna: 'It was hard work and it is going to be a long, hot race. It's good to be starting from the front row because overtaking is so difficult.'

Sunday, 7 August. Senna led from start to finish, Prost squeezing up to second by lap 47. The gap: under two seconds. Now Prost harried and hounded Senna. They turned on to the straight. Two back markers were hugging the left. Halfway down the straight Senna moved out into the middle of the track and Prost – screwing power from the engine just like Ricard – went to the extreme right, surging, surging. The corner at the end of the straight: a right-hander. Prost, almost level with Senna, would have the racing line.

As they reached the corner Prost did have it and was fractionally ahead. He took the corner, but his impetus flung him wide as he tried to angle the car to the next corner rushing at them, another right-hander. Senna went through on the inside like a thief, and that was the decisive moment of the race.

'Alain was pushing hard and he was quicker than me. He managed to go through and we avoided each other – I held my breath, for a moment I thought we would both go off the road.' It was tight at the end, Senna winning by 0.529 of a second. 'Hardest I've worked all season,' he said. Senna and Prost 66, Berger 28.

It was Senna's sixth win with McLaren and all manner of records were moving rapidly into focus, but most immediately the biggest number in a season: seven, by Prost in 1984 and Jim Clark in 1963. Senna had Belgium, Italy, Portugal, Spain, Japan and Australia to equal and beat it.

Somewhere in Britain. Tuesday, 16 August. Prost tested Honda's new V10 normally aspirated engine at a circuit sealed against prying eyes. Senna was at Monza testing the Honda turbo engine.

On Thursday Prost tested the V10 at Silverstone, then flew to Italy to test the Honda turbo. Senna flew to Silverstone to test the V10. He crashed 'heavily' at Copse and did considerable damage to the car. This made Peter Warr wonder out loud how Senna was coping with a normally aspirated Formula 1 engine. He had not of course driven one since he'd had a brief go in them in 1983.

Belgian Grand Prix, Spa. Friday, 26 August. Senna quickest, Prost next. 'The engine was working well. The last lap with the second set of tyres was really good and I think I might have been able to go quicker on a later lap if I had not been forced to back off because of Tarquini's incident.' (Gabriele Tarquini in a Coloni car shredded a tyre and was limping towards the pits on three wheels.) Saturday was wet. Prost didn't go out at all and Senna was fourth quickest.

Sunday 28 August. Senna led from start to finish, Prost half a minute behind. 'Today was not as hard as Hungary, for example, but the car's handling deteriorated because of the oil on the circuit and I had to keep it consistent. Although I have to carry on the way I have been doing, I must agree that Alain is in a difficult position now for the World Championship.' Senna 75, Prost 72, Berger 28.

Five races left and in the next Prost was to conjure a masterstroke which argued very forcibly that he did not accept Ayrton Senna was going to be World Champion. Before we leave Spa: McLaren had taken the Constructors' Championship, Senna had equalled the record for pole positions in a season – nine – and, of course, equalled Prost and Clark's total of wins in a season. He had five races left to beat it.

Italian Grand Prix, Monza. Friday, 9 September. Senna was quickest, Prost next. one-tenth of a second lay between them, and that over 5.80 kilometres. Senna: 'I only used one set of tyres on the race car because I wanted to make sure that everything was OK with the spare car that I am using this weekend. The traffic was not too bad, but I made a mistake in the spare car and went straight on at the chicane.'

Saturday, 10 September. Senna took pole from Prost and that broke the nine-in-a-season total of Peterson (1973), Lauda (1974 and 1975) and Piquet (1984). Senna dedicated the record to 'his team and all those had helped him get it.'

Sunday, 11 September. Senna went off into distance, Prost grappling with a misfire. Prost sensed he wasn't going to finish the race and wondered ... and wondered ... what might happen if he turned the boost up and pushed Senna hard. Fuel was marginal, as they say. If Prost pushed Senna hard, would Senna – not knowing the magnitude of the misfire – respond, guzzle fuel in an attempt to hold Prost off and run out before the end? A provocative prognostication. Prost acted on it, dropped out on lap 35 and because Nakajima (in the Lotus Honda) also had a misfire, Goto 'instructed Ayrton to slow down for the sake of safety', but both Ferraris were chasing him hard now and 'Ayrton once again had to increase his speed.' With just under two laps to go Senna could see the Ferraris in his wing mirrors, drawing closer and closer. He was not, he would insist, worried.

Going into the chicane Jean-Louis Schlesser (Williams) lost control and Senna thought he could nip through. Instead, Schlesser came back and punted Senna hard. The McLaren was pitched across the track and came to rest straddling the kerb. Senna was out of the race. How much fuel did he have left? No-one has ever answered that question. All Honda would say was that 'Ayrton did not wish to apportion blame for the accident.'

Portuguese Grand Prix, Estoril. Friday, 23 September. Senna was quickest, Prost next but Prost took pole on the Saturday – only the third time Senna hadn't. And on the Saturday, Prost began to apply psychological pressure in the most obvious way. With 15 minutes of the session left he changed into his civilian clothing, slung a purple pullover across his shoulders and made his way to the pit-lane wall to watch. He was saying to Senna: *I've done 1 minute 17.411 and I know you can't beat it.* Senna couldn't. Now Prost compounded the pressure by saying: 'I was not terribly interested in getting pole. There was no point in taking any more risks just for the sake of a tenth of a second. It's the first time in a long while that I have been completely satisfied with the set-up of my engine in qualifying specification.'

Senna: 'With my first set of tyres I had already done 1 minute 17.8 seconds when they were worn. Normally on my second try I would have expected to go even faster. Unfortunately, it was impossible to get a clear run.'

Sunday, 25 September. Senna took the lead at the first corner but as they rounded the right-hander into the long pit-lane straight Prost was directly behind him. As they reached the start-finish line Prost jinked right and drew abreast. They were doing 190 miles an hour. Senna now moved over, forcing Prost toward the pit-lane wall. A cluster of pit boards were dragged backwards, people ducked – if the cars had touched they could have cannoned anywhere. Prost: 'It was very dangerous. I could do nothing – if I'd backed off I might have hit his rear wheel. If we have to take risks like that to settle the World Championship ... well, I don't care about it, OK? If he wants the Championship that badly he can have it.'

Senna said only that he was angry because Prost almost forced him on to the grass at the start.

The pressure had reached Senna. His anger had taken him to a moment where his judgement went completely, and he did something bordering on the crazy. I repeat: if he had hit Prost the cars could have cannoned anywhere. Prost won the race, Senna – worried by high fuel consumption and oversteer – was sixth. Prost 81, Senna 76.

Afterwards in the quiet of the motorhome Prost and beckoned Senna over. 'Ayrton,' he said very softly, 'I didn't know you wanted the World Championship that badly.'

And that was the harmony broken.

Spanish Grand Prix, Jerez. Friday, 30 September. Senna was quickest, Prost fifth. Senna: 'It is quite difficult to get the car to work here. We changed the chassis set-up quite a lot after the morning session, which made an improvement, and I was lucky to get my one clear lap when I did because the car and engine were working well.'

Saturday, 1 October. Senna pole, Prost next to him. Senna: 'We have to concentrate on getting the chassis set-up to be right through the full distance. Let's hope the computer works accurately and we can use the engine to its best performance.'

Sunday, 2 October. Prost led from start to finish and Senna, who was getting minus readings from his fuel gauge, nursed his car home fourth. Prost 84, Senna 79.

Now we must look at mathematics. In the World Championship you could count only your 11 best finishes and Prost was already being punished by that. Spain was his 12th, and all he could discard were second places (worth, of course, six points). Senna was in a much stronger position. Spain had been his 11th, but he could discard the single point from Portugal, then the three from Spain. It meant this: if Senna won in Japan he became Champion.

But before we leave Spain we must listen to the words of Osamu Goto because they were to create a furore. After the Grand Prix he said: 'There is no difference between the turbos and the aspirated engines here. However, we controlled the drivability, response and consumption of our engine – consequently Alain was able to get a good result by his effort. Now, with two races to go, Honda will be ready to give our drivers an equal chance to win, and we hope for more good competition at Suzuka and Adelaide.' It was an unfortunate choice of words because it implied that Honda had not been doing that already. What it meant was: Honda will keep on giving their drivers an equal chance to win.

Paris. Monday, 17 October. From Jean-Marie Balestre, President of FISA to Tadashi Kume, President of Honda: 'As you know, the Federation Internationale de l'Automobile (FIA) comprises 92 member countries representing 72 million motorists. The greatest marketing experts consider the FIA Formula World Championship to be one of the world's major competitions, along with the Olympic Games and the [football] World Cup. Each Grand Prix is watched by several hundred million spectators.

'This year the manufacturers' World Champion is Honda Motors Co [sic] and I should like to congratulate you on this great success. However, there are still a few World Championship events to be run in 1988 and all the world over eyes will be riveted on the Japanese and Australian Grands Prix, the results of which will be decisive for drivers.

'We should make every effort to ensure that utmost technical objectivity reigns over these two competitions and that equipment (car or engine) of equal quality be available to the two drivers of the Mclaren [sic] Team, otherwise the image of the World Championship, present and future, would be tarnished.

'I thank you in advance for helping the FIA to achieve this end of giving the necessary instructions to all the Honda technical executives who may play a part in these two forthcoming events.'

Balestre expanded on this to Brazilian journalists. 'I do everything to obtain guarantees from both Honda and McLaren that Prost and Senna are treated equally during the final two Formula 1 Grands Prix. It isn't that I've any cause for doubt; just that, this year, we have found ourselves faced with particular circumstances with the domination of one team.' If Balestre found that equal treatment was not being given, 'serious sanctions would be taken.'

Japanese Grand Prix, Suzuka. Thursday, 27 October, Press Room (on notice boards). Tadashi Kume to Jean-Marie Balestre:

'I thank you for your letter of 17 October.

'I would like to congratulate the FIA, the FISA and yourself, as president of the FIA, for the successful efforts put forth in establishing the Formula 1 World Championships, and the prosperous condition of motorsports today.

'I believe that motorsports should be conducted in the spirit of fair play and safety, in order to obtain the interest and emotional involvement of spectators and people concerned.

'Honda Motor Co. Ltd sees fairness as the highest requirement of its philosophy for conducting business, and sets this quality as an ideology in its corporate dealings. From the outset, Honda, as a Formula 1 engine supplier with such a background, has been careful to supply engines having identical levels of performance and technology to racing teams and individual drivers who contribute their highest levels of skills, incorporating the firm attitude of our policy.

'As you mention in your letter, the Formula 1 Championship for this year is drawing to a close, leaving just two events to be run: the Japan Grand Prix and the Australia Grand Prix. We also appreciate that this year's series of races has been a most exciting and significant championship.

'For the last two races, Honda will continue to supply identical engines which will allow the drivers to give supreme demonstrations of their skills, as we have always done, in line with our basic philosophy.

'Finally I would like to express my sincere gratitude to you for consistently performing your important role as president of the FIA.'

While this was reverberating (and it did reverberate), somewhere over the polar route two men were asleep in their seats in a Jumbo. One was Robin Green, the other Dennis Rushen. They had both sensed that Ayrton Senna was going to become World Champion at Suzuka. They would both be there to see it.

That Thursday night Prost didn't sleep more than an hour. 'I should have taken a pill, I suppose, but the later it got the more I was afraid to in case I was drowsy through the morning.'

Friday, 28 October. In the untimed session Prost was quickest (1 minute 44.620) from Senna (1:44.848). In the timed session it was Senna 1:42.157, Berger 1:43.548, Prost 1:43.806. Senna's time was achieved – and it was an achievement – on his first set of tyres early on. 'Unfortunately on the second set I could not get a clear lap before the tyres were too far worn.'

Saturday, 29 October. In the untimed session Prost had a fuel leak and his overalls were soaked. He moved quickly into the pits, climbed quickly out of the car and began dousing himself with water. Petrol burns.

That had been the spare car. Now Prost took his race car and ran on full tanks. The engine was fine, just fine. At lunchtime Prost felt optimistic. In the timed session he was on the track within five minutes of the start and put himself alongside Senna on the front row. Then it rained – more of a drizzle, really – after ten minutes. The rain stopped at 1.30 and Gugelmin lost control of his Leyton House March. It hammered into the armco. Taking the car away needed 16 minutes. A few minutes of the session remained and inevitably it would be a cavalry charge.

Prost went for it but was baulked by Stefano Modena (Euro Brun); Senna went for it and somehow found a clear lap. 1 minute 41.853. With two minutes left Prost made a final assault; he got a clear lap, too, but exiting the chicane took second gear instead of fourth: 1 minute 42.177. Senna had his 12th pole position of the season.

Sunday, 30 October. In the morning warm-up Senna did a 1:46.372, Mansell 1:46.745, Boutsen 1:46.885, Prost 1:47.063. It had been sunny then but now grey cloud was moving across. In the afternoon light rain stabbed and with 15 minutes to go teams were readying wet weather tyres. The rain passed. It was still a dry race although the track might be greasy at the beginning.

On the parade lap Senna and Prost set off as if it was the race itself – but that was only to see what the track surface was really like, how the cars would behave on it. They slowed. They came to rest on the grid, the twin columns stretching away behind them. Ayrton Senna faced the great moment of his life, the moment he had fashioned his whole life around. He needed to cover 51 laps – 185 miles (298 kilometres) all the way back to where the car now rested, and be faster than all the others. The red light came on, quick as the blink of an eye. Three seconds later it blinked to green. Senna knew the clutch was 'sensitive', let it out and the car hiccoughed about four metres forward. Both his arms were out of the cockpit, flailing the air, warning – and pleading with – every one of the 12 cars in the column behind travelling in a wild rush towards him: *miss me, miss me*.

Prost had gone. Berger, directly behind Senna, pitched the Ferrari left, taking the middle of the track to go past. Piquet, behind Berger, pitched the Lotus right and it slithered towards the pit-lane wall under the power of acceleration. Piquet caught that and was gone.

Inside the cockpit of the McLaren, Senna thought crisply and clinically that 'it was all over for me. I dropped the clutch and got the car moving again and then the engine stalled again.' The car was drifting forward because the track sloped.

The middle of the grid – Alboreto, Patrese, Gugelmin – were flooding by as Senna's engine caught.

'I staggered away. I was really lucky.'

He was also lost in the pack, 14th, as they wheeled and turned into the first corner. Prost was in the lead far, far away with Berger harrying him. Prost drew Berger away from the pack and only Capelli could stay with them. The rest were back there over the hill.

On lap 1, Senna had moved up to eighth, overtaking five cars (Mansell had nudged Warwick and gone into the pits.)

On lap 2, Senna overtook Patrese and Nannini. That lifted him to sixth but it didn't seem important. Senna was cutting through the field like a man prepared to risk everything to vindicate his life. No man was as incisive in dealing with traffic, the car wielded as a surgeon might wield a knife, but it had to take time: even Senna couldn't overtake everywhere. As he crossed the line to complete that second lap many hands in the crowd flicked their stopwatches. The gap Prost-to-Senna: nine seconds, and Prost had a clear road, no obstacles at all. The feeling he had was 'perfect'. There was, as he drew further and further away, an 'occasional gear selection problem' but nothing too serious. 'I was controlling the pace, taking care of the fuel.'

On lap 3, Senna overtook Boutsen and that was fifth. The stopwatches flicked again. The gap Prost-to-Senna had gone out to around ten seconds.

On lap 4 he overtook Alboreto just before the chicane – he flung the car on to the inside line, the McLaren's wheels almost caressing the grass at the side of the track, and that was fourth. The stopwatches flicked again. The gap had gone out to 12.936 seconds.

On lap 5, the gap went out to 13 seconds. Senna would hold fourth place across laps 4 to 10 and 'I started to find my rhythm, I was going quicker and quicker.'

On lap 10, the gap had steadied to 11.628 seconds and Senna moved on Berger. He took him on that lap and was third. Meanwhile something interesting was happening up front. Young Capelli was challenging Prost and what Prost couldn't afford was second place, especially since Senna would then be directly behind him – and charging. Worse for Prost, the sky was darkening. No man on earth could make a racing car go faster than Ayrton Senna in the wet. On lap 14 Capelli was right with Prost and those spitting drops of rain had begun to fall from folds of white-grey cloud. As they crossed the line to complete lap 15, Capelli angled the March out and drew level with Prost, and just got ahead before Prost responded.

Still Senna was coming, coming, coming – and as Prost held off Capelli at the end of the straight there he was, within sight at last, rounding the corner at the other end of the straight. From lap 16:

Prost	Senna
1:51.379	1:49.115
1:55.865	1:53.254
1:57.550	1:58.101
1:56.330	1:51.507

They were together now, Prost, Capelli, Senna and suddenly Capelli pulled over to the right of the track, his engine gone. It was raining harder. And there was Prost, filling the road in front of Senna, and there were three back-markers filling the road in front of Prost. At the end of lap 27 Senna nipped out and took Prost – on power – along the finishing straight. As it happened, Prost had missed a gear.

Could Prost stay with Senna, then get back at him? He clung from lap 28 but 'the gearbox problem got worse, which was frustrating because I'd make up time on Ayrton then lose it again with a single missed change. But the worst problem was definitely the traffic.'

With five laps to go, Senna's hand was repeatedly out of the cockpit, the index finger stabbing towards the heavens. *Stop the thing now, he was saying, it's raining and the track is extremely slippery*. The irony of that. He'd have won his first Grand Prix at Monaco in '84 if they hadn't stopped it and given it to … Prost.

Senna's tyres glistened. Prost was shed now, lost somewhere back there.

Even James Hunt, commentating on British television, caught the mood – perhaps unconsciously – as Senna moved with a certain majesty round the final, triumphant lap. 'Unless there is an act of God, we are looking at the new World Champion.' That was one aspect which was never going to worry Ayrton Senna. God was with him in the cockpit and on that last lap, he'd say, he *saw* Him.

As he rounded the last corner he raised a fist – only shoulder high – and shook it in a tight, taut gesture of exultation. As he crossed the line both hands were out, and that was another, more expansive gesture of exultation. In the crowd Brazilian flags waved and fluttered. And still he kept shaking his fists, bang, bang, bang all the way to first corner. Then – it was almost a private moment, almost unseen – he let his neck muscles go slack, let his head fall gently back against the hump of the cockpit. He'd done it.

He faced the television cameras and his eyes were veined red. He must have been crying. 'It was,' he said, measuring each word, 'a lot of pressure. I still can't believe it.' At the press conference he added: 'Even after I got the lead it was very difficult with the back-markers. They did not behave very professionally with Alain and me.'

He came from that press conference, Ron Dennis at his side, and he saw Rushen. 'Ayrton was overcome with emotion, well and truly overcome. In the early days we'd taught him swear words because that's a natural thing with foreign drivers. One particular expression he thought was great but he'd say it at all the wrong times. He'd send me Christmas cards with the words on. So as he went by at Suzuka I said "you're still an [expletive expletive]" and he didn't know whether to laugh or cry.'

Later, he sat on the pit-lane wall. Keith Sutton: 'There was only a French photographer and myself still there. He was doing an interview with Brazilian television and actually watching a re-run of the race on a big screen at the same time. The light was fantastic, a beautiful sky. We were taking pictures with the flash. It was very emotional. And he did the interview with Brazilian television and the television chap had been very close to him when he started, a bit like me. He said: "Now you're World Champion the pressure will be off. You have been very, very dedicated and you have pushed a lot of people aside during years, a lot of close friends. Will this change?" Tears rolled from his eyes.'

Prost described racing Senna in 1988 as 'relatively sporting' and the Championship as 'conventional' although he'd scored more points than Senna. Rules were the rules. Prost did claim Senna enjoyed unconditional support from Honda because they – or Mr Honda himself – preferred Senna's 'Samurai' style. This became a problem, because Prost knew that each year in each team one driver will enjoy a psychological advantage over the other, even when the team are scrupulous about equal treatment in equipment. Prost concluded that the real importance of this can be expressed by a percentage: 80 per cent of doing well is mental. It led to a question for 1989 which could not, and would not, be avoided. Which of these two men had the stronger mind?

A postscript. Mike Wilson won the World 135cc Karting Championships at Laval, France (beating among others de Bruijn and Forsman). 'I went to Paris for the annual motorsports awards, and of course Ayrton was there because he'd won the Formula 1 Championship. I went up first to get my trophy, because they started with the smallest category, which was karting. When I was walking back with it he stood up from his table, came over, put his arm around me and said: "Well done. I see you're still winning!" I said: "Yes I am, but obviously it's not as important as yours although it is important to me." He said: "The really important thing, whatever you're doing – whether it's karting, Formula 1, whatever, even playing cards – is to be the World Champion because that means you are the best in the world. Even in karting it is a great, great achievement." That was nice, very nice.'

Chapter 10

RIDERS ON THE STORM

Alain Prost craned his craggy face towards the microphone and said: 'Ayrton has a small problem. He thinks he can't kill himself because he believes in God and I think that's very dangerous for the other drivers.'

In a direct response for *The Hard Edge of Genius* Senna wrote next to the quotation: 'That's his own thoughts, his own conclusions and words. They don't reflect my thoughts and my beliefs at all.'

Adelaide, November 1989 and it had come to the first of two cold autumns. Bitter cold it was, conducted in great outpourings and great silences, compounded by crashes, judged by tribunals, fed by accusations and counter-accusations. Carefully constructed friendships were broken apart, fines levied, appeals heard, the behaviour of some of the leading players publicly questioned, the integrity of Formula 1 hacked and hammered around day by day, FISA itself seen as inconsistent. There were even motor races, too – and strange creatures they were, each chilling it more and more until in the end a permafrost covered the whole thing.

The season began hot, of course, in Rio a few seconds after the start of the Brazilian Grand Prix. Senna, on pole, put the power down and the McLaren slewed slightly into the middle of the track towards Patrese in the Williams. Berger thrust the snout of his Ferrari up into them trying to get in between, couldn't, flung the Ferrari right to take Senna on the inside as they all coursed down to the first corner, a right-hander. As Berger drew alongside, Senna twitched right – making Berger twitch even further right, two wheels almost off the track. Patrese now turned into the corner and that sandwiched Senna, who still had

Berger on his right – and Berger did have two wheels on the grass. Senna and Berger touched; Senna had to go into the pits, losing a whole lap, and would finish 11th. 'Really, the car ran perfectly – apart from that corner where the only way out of the problem would been to go straight up in the air. Patrese and Berger trapped me and I lost the nose section. That's all there is to it.'

Berger quite naturally saw it the other way. 'Senna chopped across twice to try to make me back off but he shouldn't try that with me. Never in my life will I back in that situation.' (Senna said much later, reflecting on it: 'My honest view is that three cars tried to do the same corner at the same time and there was only room for one.')

At Imola Senna won. 'The car wasn't going too well under heavy braking at first and with Alain pushing hard it took a while to settle into a rhythm, but once the gap reached six seconds I was able to maintain that pace and after Alain spun the pressure was really off.'

Behind these most innocent words the whole season began to break up taking with it whatever harmony had existed before. What happened looked innocent, too, a simple, safe overtaking move at a corner called *Tosa*. Berger had crashed, survived a dreadful fire and the race was re-started. Prost took the lead, held it round the curve of *Tamburello* and positioned the car in the centre of the track on the short surge to *Tosa*. Senna jinked left, went round Prost on the outside – *Tosa* was right then left – and had the racing line. He was in the lead. He did not lose it.

Prost was visibly angry after the race and said he didn't want to say much at all, which was itself instructive because invariably Prost was eloquent whether he'd won or lost. What he did suggest darkly was that an 'accord' had been breached. Accord? What accord could that be? Only later did details emerge: whichever McLaren got to the first corner first would not come under attack from the other McLaren until the race had settled down, and demonstrably Senna had overtaken there. Prost was so angry he did not attend the post-race press conference (and was fined $5,000) but vanished in a helicopter.

McLaren tested at a track called Pembrey near Llanelli, Wales. Ron Dennis would say: 'They had agreed that whoever made the better start would exit the first corner ahead. Alain made the better start, but Ayrton took the corner, which was not consistent with the agreement they had made. A subsequent discussion between them at Pembrey resulted in an apology from Ayrton. The problem is now resolved.'

It wasn't.

Senna would look deep into himself before he explained, patiently and laboriously, the case for his defence in this curious matter. 'Yes, there was an accord, and not only at Imola but elsewhere. It was also present several times last season and it was he who proposed not to attack in braking for the first corner, not me. At Imola we had spoken about it.' Senna explained that Prost had made the same proposal at Imola the year before. 'It was his idea. I had never found myself in this kind of situation before and I said OK. We respected this agreement for several races. Then, as our relationship deteriorated, we stopped doing so. This year after the winter breaks we were on more friendly terms again. Then came Imola. I remembered the agreement of the previous year and I put the question: "what shall we do about the first bend?" He replied: "the same as '88." So that was the situation. Only, I think there is a divergence of interpretation of the concept of this accord and then, above all, a disproportion between the consequences of the overtaking move and his reaction after it. At the re-start he got away a little better than me but I was immediately on his tail to profit from the suction. I thus gathered speed and I made my move well before the braking area. My overtaking move was begun, in my opinion, well before the first corner and as a result outside the terms of our accord, What should I have done? Lift off in a straight line because I was going faster than him? We're in races, yes or no? And I braked later than him, I was better placed, that's all. Never have I wished to betray our accord, not for one second did I think it was dishonest [and, subsequently and poignantly], the agreement has always been that no overtaking manoeuvre would happen *under braking* [author's italics] at a first corner. My overtaking was initiated by slipstreaming Prost during the straight and by the first corner we were side by side!

'After Imola Ron Dennis spoke to me about it for a long time and I explained my point of view. He told me Prost had taken it very badly, that he was disgusted, that he wanted to retire, etc … Ron was very disquieted at the idea of our reunion at Pembrey. Ron exercised an enormous pressure on me to smooth things over. At first I didn't want to because I didn't find that correct. But he insisted and he said to me: "If you say sorry it's forgotten, everything is back in order." And I did it. It was stupid because it meant I had changed my opinion on the concept of our accord and on the overtaking move. Now, I have never changed my opinion. I said sorry for the good of the team, to calm it down, because I was almost compelled to. I wiped a tear away because at that moment it was harming me. Ron did a good job convincing me to accommodate things but it wasn't easy. Perhaps I have the air of a very cold, frosty person but that's wrong, you know. I have a heart and I received a very gentle education. Perhaps I am strong as far as my job is concerned but I am no less a human being because of it. The three of us were there and Ron said: "That will stay between us, we won't speak about it any more, OK?"'

Two days later Prost told the French sports paper *L'Equipe*: 'I do not wish to drag McLaren into difficulties caused by the behaviour of Senna. McLaren has always been loyal to me. At a level of technical discussion I shall not close the door completely but for the rest I no longer wish to have any business with him. I appreciate honesty and he is not honest.'

As words go, they don't come any stronger.

When Senna arrived at Monaco 'people were speaking only about it [the interview in *L'Equipe*]. I am persuaded that in acting like that Alain wanted to implicate me, make me carry the can, make me culpable, in a phrase: put the pressure on me. I decided not to react.'

Only later, in a sudden, heartfelt sentence would Senna say, conjuring finality: 'Since that day at Monaco it's finished, I don't want to hear any more talk about that guy.'

He could isolate himself from it, of course, retreat to his private places, and that is what he did. On the Saturday at Monaco Senna produced one of the great laps in qualifying – 1 minute 22.308 seconds, while Prost could do no better than 1:23.456. Typically, Senna conceded that it 'was obviously a very satisfying lap. I had a little too much understeer on my first set of tyres but everything was fine when we put on the second set. On my second lap with them I got a clear run and recorded my best time, despite making a slight mistake at Casino Square [!]. The engine was fantastic.'

So was the boy himself.

Flag to flag, as they say, in the race. 'At the start I didn't want to push too hard but when we came to lapping traffic I began to pull away, perhaps rather more than I expected but it was just as well because I suffered gearbox problems in the second half of the race, losing second gear then first. It made the car extremely difficult to drive in traffic but I kept pressing on as hard as I could because I didn't want to give Alain any indication that I was in trouble.'

Senna would say that, in Mexico, Prost 'tried to speak to me. I refused. I didn't want to fall into a trap. I didn't want to speak to him any more, it didn't interest me.' Senna won Mexico and took his total of pole positions to 33, equalling Jim Clark. He beat it in the United States Grand Prix at Phoenix. 'I feel rather light-headed, with no weight on my shoulders now that I have established the new record. I take the record from Jim Clark, a man I never saw racing but who by his results was obviously a very special driver. It is a big moment for me.'

In Canada, Senna drove one of the great races in a storm which recalled sodden memories of Monaco '84 except that here it dried. After four laps, Senna – leading – came in for slicks, was fifth when he emerged. He was up to third when the rain began again, up to second when Boutsen pitted and actually started to attack Patrese for the lead. The rain was heavy, Patrese was on wet weather tyres and Senna was still on the slicks. Even Senna could not maintain this almost fantastic assault – no other man on earth could have mounted it at all – and drifted back; even Senna would need wets and on lap 21 pitted again, sixth when he emerged and almost sixty seconds behind Patrese, leading.

He bided his time and then he charged, a proper, classical motor racing charge. It was almost hypnotic to watch, this certainty of control. Patrese pitted for more wets and Warwick (Arrows) found himself in the lead, Senna coming hard at him. Senna took him and seemed to be cruising it. The track began to dry and Senna went on and on in lonely isolation up front until with only three laps left, the engine let go. 'For the last twenty laps I had a blistered left rear tyre. The engine gave no indication there was a problem. I just felt it tighten up and that was it.'

At least France was dry. Senna did not take pole – inevitably if it didn't go to him it went to Prost – and didn't even complete the first lap of the race. 'I was just changing from first to second when the drive simply vanished. There was nothing more I could do about it.' Senna parked the car and walked away.

He took pole at Silverstone, took the lead but 'I had difficulty selecting third gear on the downchange almost from the start. Four or five laps before I finally spun off I almost went off at the same place. Eventually I couldn't get the gear and that was that. I could not take the corner in neutral!' That start, incidentally, had had dramas all of its own as Senna moved past Prost, who suggested that if they'd been 10cm closer 'we'd have crashed.'

As Prost and Mansell passed Senna's marooned car Mansell waved congratulations to Prost, whom he could clearly see grinning in the cockpit. How did Prost feel? 'Happy.' Nor can we ignore the reaction of the crowd who waved their arms in pleasure that Senna had gone off, a most un-British reaction and one which, if truth be told, demonstrated how far Senna then was from a place in their affections.

In Germany in the Friday morning session he crashed. 'I made a mistake and spun off. The spin was my fault. I put a wheel on to the kerb under braking and the car snapped round on me. It was a stupid mistake. It was quite a big impact and I had a slight headache.'

He took pole a fraction more than a second faster than Prost and was lucky in the race. With three laps to go Prost, leading, lost top gear and Senna was by in an instant, swift as a knife thrust. 'I did not have any particular strategy to pass Alain. I was concentrating first on getting as close to him as possible. I was easing towards him, I felt I was close enough to profit by any mistake he might make, then he had a problem.'

Hungary belonged to Mansell, Senna second, Prost fourth; and they came to Spa, where, in the wet, Senna was superb, leading the whole way. 'I had tremendous difficulty keeping the car safe on the ground. There was so much water the car was aquaplaning and you don't feel safe at all to go fast. It's difficult to motivate and to push, but as far as the car was concerned the beginning was very good for five laps or so, very stable. Then I think the front tyre pressures got too low and it started to be even harder for me. The back-markers? As usual it's always difficult in the water when you see nothing and if you wait you lose five, ten seconds. It was a very big risk and very dangerous but that was the same for everybody.' The near miraculous aspect was that, like Canada, none of this was evident to the spectator, who saw only smoothness, the ease of style.

Towards the end Senna slowed dramatically, especially on the last lap. 'There was no reason to carry on going fast,' he said, and smiling wryly, explained that his understanding of a motor race was that whoever crossed the line first had won it – the margin didn't matter.

At Spa, neither Lotus qualified for the race and Senna was moved to a great melancholy. His voice sounded heavy, almost cumbersome and he spoke the words slowly. 'If you make the wrong decisions in this business, sooner or later you have to pay but I know most of the people there and they are very nice, very good. I feel extremely sad.'

He'd never deliberately distanced himself from the Lotus personnel. 'We saw him to speak to,' Dance says, 'and he would always talk to you, same as usual, but as more and more media people were after him he got more and more shut away. The best chance one had to talk to him was if we were doing testing and, in fact, that was the last time I did talk to him, the testing at Estoril in '93. Just a chat. "How are you doing?" sort of thing. He'd always have words for you. Away from all the pressures of the races, he was a very human sort of chap.'

It is time to look at the points. Prost had 62, Senna 51, Mansell 38, Patrese 25, Boutsen 20. Five races remained. Clearly Prost would have to start dropping points soon – only your eleven best finishes counted, remember, and departing Spa he already had ten, Senna six.

Between Spa and Monza, a period of two weeks, Prost talked and Senna talked, although not to each other. Prost revealed that he had spoken to Dennis at Monaco, saying to him: 'It's with McLaren that I would still like to drive but I will drive better in another team.' Prost continued: 'I had already spoken to him about it on the telephone. I even thought of stopping then. It was close. I decided to join Ferrari in Belgium. Regrets at leaving McLaren? No. Everything I did over six years with them was positive. I leave with my conscience clear thanks to the certainty that I have given the best of myself. I was living in a fantastic atmosphere. I had the possibility to say no to Senna joining the team but I thought the team would have need of a driver of his worth when I stopped.'

(Senna told me: 'Correction. One year earlier than McLaren having Honda, both Ron and Prost even went to Japan especially to convince Honda to come to McLaren and yet Honda came to Lotus [1987]. As for 1988 I initiated the work towards Honda and Prost wouldn't have had Honda in 1988 if Senna was not part of the team! OK.')

Prost said: 'I was had. It's a lesson, that's all. At Monza he is due to have the spare car, at Estoril it's me. For the three other Grands Prix it will be decided by our positions in the Championship. We'll truly see whether we are put on an equal footing or not. If they want to advantage Senna they have that possibility.'

Someone asked Senna if friendship was possible in Formula 1? 'Evidently it is, but terribly difficult because we all come from different horizons, with different educations, different cultures.'

Will you ever speak to Prost again? 'I know that you must never say "never" but in this case I can't see what could make me change my mind. In ten years I might be able to exchange a few banalities but we won't be sincere. There will never again be any complicity between us, it's finished.' In this Senna was quite wrong.

And they came to Monza. We must start with the statistics.

Friday	Free practice	Qualifying
Senna	1:25.979	1:25.021
Prost	1:26.135	1:25.872
Saturday		
Senna	1:26.243	1:23.720
Prost	1:27.444	1:25.510

Prost now said: 'Nothing working properly – car or engine. I just don't know what to say. Sometimes the car feels good, sometimes not. This morning with a low fuel load the chassis was not bad, but the engine in qualifying was impossible low down the rev range. Very disappointing.' His hair shaggy as a mane, his face mournful, Prost began to make louder and louder noises about equal treatment and word of it spread like high voltage through the paddock; Ron Dennis was moved to hold an impromptu press conference to deny this vehemently, pointing out that each driver's car is prepared after lengthy and complex calculations. He also said: 'I think that was certainly the best pole position of Ayrton's career to date. The conditions were still very difficult and the track was still not completely dry round the back of the circuit. This is his pole, not ours.'

There was, then, a troubled backdrop to Monza and – although this was only an impression – a sense of something beginning to work its way towards a climax; not necessarily here, but surely soon. The forces in play were too strong, too entrenched for anything else.

As it happened Senna led the race for 44 laps and the engine blew up, letting Prost in. Senna summed it up like this: 'From the start I had not needed to rev the engine as high as it could have gone and about five laps before my retirement the oil pressure warning light began flashing intermittently. Then it began flashing more and more so I reduced the revs slightly but there was nothing I could really do. The engine broke coming down to Parabolica so I switched it off and coasted into the corner when I spun on my own oil.'

On the podium Prost deliberately lowered the trophy into the adoring crowd below (he was joining Ferrari, don't forget) and that gesture signalled the end of the relationship with McLaren. Dennis, measuring his words as carefully as Senna does, was speaking from the heart when he said: 'We had a relationship that was based on slow, progressive mutual respect for each other. Something took place in the Italian Grand Prix that broke that relationship. He gave to the crowd the trophy for winning the race, something which was not even his.'

Prost had been making even louder noises about equal treatment. 'I want to race and I want to compete with Ayrton with the same equipment and I think the engine was not good at all ... the engine was very bad ... I am still a bit unhappy but that is normal because in the next four races I don't know what is going to happen ... I was complaining about the engine the whole weekend and it did not improve at all. It's very easy to say luck is on my side, luck is not on his side. You have to understand they don't make engines like this for Ayrton. The chassis was not bad at all.'

These words wounded McLaren and by Portugal a statement had been drafted. It read: 'As a result of the consequences of press statements at the Italian Grand Prix, Alain Prost, Honda and McLaren have had extensive discussions and wish to put on record their intentions for creating the best possible working environment for the driver and the team for the remainder of the season. Honda and McLaren have again reassured Alain, to his satisfaction, of their commitment to equality and will continue the policy regardless of Alain's move to another team for the 1990 season.

'Alain deeply regrets the adverse publicity and the resulting embarrassment that has been caused by his actions. Honda and McLaren have accepted that these resulted from Alain's perception of his treatment by the team and were not made with malicious intent. He has agreed that in future any doubts that he might have about the parity of performance of his car will be discussed with the relevant engineers prior to comments being made to the press. The team also expresses its disdain and dissatisfaction over the inaccurate, unqualified and damaging statements made by third parties subsequent to Monza.'

At Portugal, Senna said: 'If you have God on your side, everything becomes clear: white becomes white again, and black becomes black, and you realise what is really important in life.' The other Senna said: 'I'm obviously very satisfied with another pole position although I had a slight gear selection problem during the morning which recurred again in the afternoon.'

Now a deeper chill settled. On lap 39 Mansell overshot his pit and reversed: a breach of the regulations. He emerged fourth, Senna ahead of him, then Berger and (briefly) Pierluigi Martini. For three laps Mansell was black-flagged as he hounded Senna – Mansell would strongly deny that he had seen the flag. 'Have you ever been on that part of the circuit at that time? I was trying to overtake Senna, the sun was in my eyes and I couldn't see anything.' Senna could see the flag but 'I wasn't sure about anything. I wasn't worried because the flag wasn't for me.'

On lap 49, as they crossed the line, Mansell moved to the right to overtake. Turn One, a right-hander, was flowing hard at them, the two cars abreast. Dennis realised that Senna didn't realise Mansell was out of the race and started to tell him on the radio link. 'Ayrton couldn't hear clearly so he pressed the button and said "repeat". I was in the process of repeating it when …'

… when Mansell was hugging the inside at the very mouth of Turn 1 and Senna, fractionally ahead, moved on to the racing line. He was coming across Mansell. His right rear wheel struck Mansell's left front and the McLaren skated away into the sand trap, that right rear cocked absurdly into the air, wobbling like a broken limb. For a long time Senna stood, hands resting on the rim of the tyre barrier. The Championship had almost certainly gone. 'I felt something incredible going through my head. I wanted to walk for a while, to relax, to get events in their right order once again.'

Late that afternoon he asked: 'Why did Nigel stay out after he was disqualified? Everybody can see the television transmission of what happened.'

The following morning, he was more expansive. 'In the last year and a half I have learned that in a heated situation it is best to keep quiet. Mansell was out of the race and he shouldn't have tried to overtake. Just a few instants before the accident Ron

Dennis gave me the news via radio that Mansell was disqualified. He hadn't finished telling me when the accident happened.' As Mansell drew abreast 'I didn't alter my position. I was going straight ahead. I didn't intend to get involved in a mix-up. In the position he was in it was impossible for him to get round the bend, he was too far on the inside. He did it just for the sake of trying and bumped into me.

'I have seen it again on TV. Everything is clear but I think we miss the point completely. What happened could have had a terrible ending. A disastrous ending. Mansell put in danger the life of another person. When I went off the track I managed to stop after 200 metres. There was a barrier. I could have lost my life. That is why I say that what happened is very dangerous.'

Mansell and Ferrari were fined $50,000 and Mansell excluded from the next race, Spain. He was enraged, insisted again that he had not seen the black flag and said he was prepared to swear to that on The Bible.

Enter Ron Dennis, also enraged. 'I think Nigel did know he was disqualified. It's a driver's obligations to know the regulations. The moment Nigel selected reverse gear in the pit lane he disqualified himself. I just don't accept Nigel didn't know he was disqualified. I just don't buy that horse manure. He knew. End of story. In Italy, Ferrari team manager Cesare Fiorio said Nigel asked on the radio: "Why do I have to come in?" Why ask the question when he has said he didn't see the flag? Maybe he didn't, but what about the pit board or radio?'

On the day following the race Senna gave an explosive interview to Pino Allievi which reverberated into wild headlines all over Britain when it had been relayed from Italy. The gist: *Mansell put my life in danger*. I was curious about the circumstances of this interview.

During practice Senna told Allievi where he was staying, with a friend called Carlos Braga at nearby Sintra. 'The morning after,' Allievi says, 'I went there with three other journalists and spoke with Braga, who told us Senna was still sleeping because they'd had a dinner the night before and it was a little bit early for him. I had a problem because I had to tell my newspaper what I'd be writing so I went back to my hotel in Estoril to do that. From there I also phoned Braga and Senna was now having lunch. I left my number and around two o'clock Senna rang me. I did the interview there, on the phone. If he knew you and trusted you he would ring and it was really kind. We spoke Italian because he spoke it perfectly. He used the correct grammar and spoke it as well as the average Italian, he didn't make mistakes.'

Mansell, who was due to appear before the FISA tribunal in Paris to appeal, called a press conference in Spain and robustly defended himself. He also said of the overtaking move that Senna 'saw perfectly well that I was starting to overtake. Senna even turned his head towards me but he still cut in on me.'

There was a bizarre twist, Senna black-flagged on his flying lap during qualifying for the Spanish Grand Prix, didn't slow down at all and was fined $20,000. He said he didn't see the flags. 'I made a mistake and I must pay.' He won the race comfortably and now needed to win the last two, Suzuka and Adelaide.

Suzuka. Ah, Suzuka.

'I want Prost to win the Championship as much as I don't want Senna to win it. Alain is my team-mate at Ferrari next year and for another thing I like him.' That was Mansell.

Prost said: 'I don't care about it because it will always have a bitter taste.'

Senna, who had spent the flight to Japan reading The Bible, spoke of his faith but, to reports that as a consequence he could not be hurt in a racing car, he retorted with vehemence. 'Of course I can get hurt or killed as anybody can and this feeling – or this knowledge – is what keeps you together as self preservation.' At Suzuka he did say: 'It's a blessing from Him. Other people may try to use me or destroy me but they will not succeed.' The other Senna said: 'In the car I don't even look at the rev counter because if you do that you must be a fraction less committed to your driving at that moment. So you change gear by sound. When I have finished a lap, I can recall it completely.'

Senna took pole, of course, his 12th of the season. 'I have nothing to lose. I will drive as fast as I can to win. It is the way I like to drive. I like the challenge of racing to win. It is something that stimulates me.'

Before the race, Prost made a fateful declaration: 'A lot of times, if you remember, last year and this, I opened the door and if I did not open the door we would have crashed.' This time he did not intend to open the door. It was a chilling thought so deep into that first chilled autumn, even as Honda's ten thousand guests arrived to witness what could well be the Championship decided.

Prost got away at the start and drove the way he used to handle races, as if certainty of movement had been conjured from all the uncertainties of a Formula 1 car. This, very suddenly, was the man who had once regularly outdriven Niki Lauda, who had taken a heap of pole positions, commanded and won races from the front.

At Suzuka he was quicker at the exits to each corner so that Senna, who had drawn up to him after a long chase, was squeezing himself hard to catch him again by the next corner – and Senna had to overtake or the Championship was gone. On lap 47 they were both moving towards the chicane – a proper old-fashioned chicane which twisted right then left, tight as hell – and Senna lunged down the inside. Prost turned into him and, the cars locked, they clattered on to the escape road directly ahead. Prost climbed out, Senna got a push and rejoined down the escape road. Prost walked back and as he was on the grassy verge by the pit-lane road he saw Senna – the front of the car damaged – coming in for a new nose cone.

Prost was certain Senna would be disqualified. Prost was certain he was World Champion for the third time. Senna had

had a push, hadn't he? Everybody had seen that. Senna had not rejoined the track where he had left it but taken a short cut, hadn't he? Everybody had seen that, too.

Senna 'won' the race and there was another irony in that because he overtook Alessandro Nannini at the same chicane with the same move to do it. Nannini got smartly out of the way, so smartly his tyres gave off whiffs of smoke when he hit the brakes.

Senna was disqualified.

Emotionally, Prost felt himself drawn in several different directions at once. 'The stress has been unbelievable, it has been my worst year in Formula 1. I felt very comfortable in the lead and I really didn't expect him to pass me then. A couple of times he had been much closer at that corner and yet he didn't try it. This time when I looked in my mirror he was a long way back but he just kept coming although I had the line for the corner.'

Senna also was being drawn in several different directions. 'The results as they stand provisionally do not reflect the truth of the race in either the sporting sense or the sense of the regulations. I see this result as temporary but the matter is now out of my hands. It was obvious I won the race on the track. The taste of victory was taken away.' He had judged that the chicane was 'the only place where I could overtake and somebody who shouldn't have been there just closed the door and that was that.' He would not mention Alain Prost by name: it had gone as deep as that.

Prost had sensed what might happen with great clarity. 'I was absolutely sure I would win the race or have an accident like this. I knew that he wanted to win absolutely. The problem with Ayrton is that he can't accept not to win and he can't accept that someone will resist an overtaking move.'

McLaren, who are slavishly conscious of their image, were into unfamiliar territory again, almost enemy territory. Would they protest Senna's disqualification? After all, their other man, Prost, had just won the Championship for them. If they did protest, and it was upheld, they might be taking that Championship from Prost (on the assumption that Senna won Adelaide). McLaren produced the perfect man to read out the perfect reply, Creighton Brown, a tall, co-operative, popular, approachable sort of chap who habitually thaws the ice which can surround the closed world of the McLaren motorhome.

'We feel it is important that you all know what is happening and why, so there can be no misinterpretation or misunderstanding. We think there is a possibility that Ayrton's disqualification is not consistent with some things that have happened during the rest of the year where people have missed chicanes without being disqualified. There are two things to note. It is our duty as a team to try to win every race if at all possible, and it is on that basis we have made this appeal. Also, there is absolutely no way we are doing this because we want to favour one driver against the other. We are very happy for either of them to win the Championship. We are trying to clarify the matter on the basis of finishing this race. We are only doing this to maximize our chances of winning this race.'

What really happened at that chicane admits several interpretations, not least of which is that Senna had become so controversial that rational judgement about his conduct was extremely difficult for many people, among them Prost.

It may well have been the wrong place to try to overtake but, as Senna says, it was the only place. He went to the inside, which was the only way to do it. If he counted on Prost opening the door (as Prost admits he had done before in both 1988 and '89) he was wrong this time. Senna was certainly ill advised to suggest that Prost should not have been there. Prost was leading the race and where else could Prost have been but angling his car to take the chicane in the normal way?

At Brazil, in the heat before the cold of autumn, Senna had been sandwiched between Berger and Patrese and had said the only free space available was 'up in the air'. Senna's case was further weakened because he'd cut across Mansell in Portugal and wondered whatever Mansell was doing there. Now Prost had done the same to him and he wondered whatever Prost was doing there.

But you needed to look at it another way to be fair to Senna and what he did. Here was the crucial moment in the Championship and Senna would lose that Championship if he did not find a way past Prost, however difficult that might be, whatever inherent risks that would carry. He had rationalised the possibilities of overtaking to this one corner where he might, with all his fearsome courage and speed of reaction, get himself in the right place fast enough to do it. In the matter of late braking, he was supreme.

He tried it.

In retrospect the move recalled the memorable words of the general who surrendered Berlin to the Russians in 1945: 'There are no desperate situations, only desperate men.'

The chance of decisively beating Prost to the corner was remote because Prost was already close to the corner, but Senna knew he had no other chance and he did what a racer does, balanced the risk against the logistics of the moment and went for it. FISA called the risk dangerous and their phrase for that demands to be set down: 'one who endangers the safety of others.'

The storm did not abate.

At a press conference near Heathrow Airport, between Suzuka and Adelaide, Dennis made a detailed and eloquent defence of McLaren's position – and Senna's position, too: of how Senna had re-started, of how others (including Mansell at Spa) had missed chicanes. In direct answer to the accusation that Senna had carried out a 'dangerous manoeuvre' in trying to overtake at the chicane Dennis said: 'Senna overtook on Prost's right-hand side and it would appear that FISA regard this manoeuvre as dangerous. However Chapter IV paragraph (c) of the Sporting Code (page 313) expressly permits overtaking on the right. Senna was participating in a Formula 1 race.'

Dennis was angry, also, that FISA was suddenly making other accusations, six in all, about Senna's previous behaviour, with among them his crash with Schlesser at Monza, 1988, his crash with Berger at Rio, 1989, his crash with Mansell at Portugal. It begged a question: Why hadn't FISA done anything about these at the time? Why fling them at Senna retrospectively?

Nor did FISA relent. As Senna reached Adelaide he heard that he had been fined $100,000 and given a six months suspended sentence. He was virtually in tears. 'I will drive here the way I have driven all my career. I am supposed to be a lunatic, a dangerous man breaking all the rules, but people have the wrong impression. It is a question of justice, and what has happened in Suzuka and subsequently in Paris at the appeal court is totally unfair. I have spent enough time in Formula 1 to realise you make mistakes which compromise yourself and sometimes other people but that is inevitable and you won't find another driver who won't accept that. What happened at Suzuka reflects the political situation in the sport. I never caused the accident and I'm prepared to fight to the end for my values, for justice.'

And: 'When everything goes against you, you ask yourself why you need to carry on, particularly when you have not been fairly treated. I thought about stopping, about not coming to Australia, so many things have gone through my head.'

McLaren vowed to find that justice in the French courts, although Senna's Championship was now all but gone, and gone completely in a rain-riven Adelaide Grand Prix – itself a wild thing, Prost refusing to risk his life, Senna having to risk his life. Within a few laps Senna was half a minute in the lead, spun as if he was being borne on a carousel, caught it, set off again and somewhere in walls of water did not see Brundle's Brabham. Senna struck it very hard indeed as he tried to lap it.

Brundle had an on-board camera pointing backwards and the pictures it gave seemed to capture the whole savagery of the season: the churning ball of spray and from nowhere – glimpsed like a ghostly, frantic vision – the flickering red and white of the McLaren, a hammer striking an anvil, one instant invisible, the next instant plunging into the Brabham. It was the same Brundle who had known this in 1983.

Senna limped back to the pits on three wheels – travelling at quite a respectable speed, actually – and clambered out.

Prost said 1989 had been the worst of his life. It was a sentiment shared by many other players in the big game. They all eyed 1990 warily, and wondered.

And then there was, we thought, another Ayrton Senna. This one was the child of the other Ayrton Sennas; unmistakably their progeny but The Face had softened, the eyes were no longer hunted and haunted; there was a calm about him, an ease about him, a looseness about him, a tangible, touchable tranquillity. Wasn't there?

For example, he could behave with sensitivity and magnanimity. In 1989, Mike Wilson won the World Karting Championship again. 'It was on a Sunday and I returned to Italy (where Wilson lived) on the Monday. *La Gazzetta dello Sport* said only "Mike Wilson wins World Championship in France." Senna must have seen this because he telephoned Pino Allievi and said: "all the Italian journalists think they are the best in the world, especially in motorsport, and you write practically nothing on somebody achieving a World Championship for the sixth time." Allievi phoned me on the Tuesday and asked me if I could give him an interview. I did that on the Thursday in Milan, and on the Friday I got half a page in the *Gazzetta*. I found what Senna had done for me not just so nice but absolutely incredible.' Allievi is unsure about this call, although he did interview Wilson. What Allievi does remember is that, at a subsequent Grand Prix, Senna said to him: 'Why don't you give more space to karting? It's a very good sport and you have a lot of Italians in it.'

To explore this other Senna, I'm breaking the chronology of the narrative and taking you to Silverstone at nearly mid-season in 1990. This is tyre testing and now, during the lunch break, he sits and speaks and nurses a bowl of what seems to be organic food. From time to time he feeds himself a mouthful although he is careful not to let this interrupt what he has to say. As each question is posed he hesitates, measuring his response exactly before he delivers it. Sometimes the hesitation is as long as seven seconds so that you are unsure whether he is going to answer the question at all; but he does, every time.

Are you a more contented person?

'Other than winning there was not much else positive in the past [the Prost war]. Under normal circumstances there's so much pressure, so much stress and if you have to add on top of it situations like that it is very difficult to handle. It takes away a lot of the happiness and joy of your profession. Gerhard Berger [who replaced Prost at McLaren] has been very easy-going and there's been no problem at all. We have shared some moments of fun, we've made some jokes and we spent some time together between Phoenix and Brazil [the first two Grands Prix] away from racing, enjoying the sun, sea and playing on jet skis. With Elio de Angelis at Lotus I did this at the beginning, but not with anyone else.'

He had found, as it seemed, equilibrium and that was a surprise in itself. When 1990 began we might have expected anything but that: the sense of frostbite still lingered.

FISA said that if he did not retract his allegations about how the Championship had been settled and pay his $100,000 dollar fine by Thursday, 15 February he would not be given a Superlicence.

Senna passed the close season with 'a completely open mind, just waiting. I was ready for anything. There was talk of continuing racing as well as talk of changing to America. I don't have much identification with racing other than driving so I wouldn't be a team manager. I don't think I'd be much good at it. I have come a long way fast and once you get to that level, just to throw it away is not an easy decision. I would have stopped but it would have let people down. For lots of fans we are a kind of dream, that's the way they see us. It is a different world for them and a different way of living – it is not a reality but a dream. You have some influence on the lives of those people, you get genuine enthusiasm from people you have never met. They see many positive things and it gives you a good feeling to see people like that.'

But now there was a deadline, there was Jean-Marie Balestre in one trench and across no-man's land Senna in another, both strong-willed, both with positions to defend. 'I asked myself about continuing to race. I was perfectly calm and I discussed the matter with Honda and McLaren. I said to them that I was only a driver and that McLaren and Honda would continue after me. I said that I did not want to compromise their efforts and those of the people who work to run the cars. I asked Nobuhiko Kawamoto [of Honda] and Ron Dennis to decide in my place. I said I would completely respect their wishes, that I was ready to retire or fight on as they thought fit.'

Ron Dennis, not a man given to revealing his emotions, will never forget that close season. 'Both Ayrton and I were suffering. We were the two individuals who were exposed to the Superlicence issues and the two individuals who experienced the unpleasant – I must choose my words carefully, I can't use the right words because they will only get me into more aggravation, into opening the wound again … well, let's just say it was a very unpleasant experience with lots of people not keeping their words. It had a profound effect on me and a pretty significant one on him.'

But there was the deadline and it was approaching. In late February, Balestre returned McLaren's entries for their two cars and implied that Dennis had the responsibility for making Senna retract. In early March, McLaren paid the $100,000 fine and their two entries were granted, one for G. Berger and the second for a driver 'who remains to be named.'

What followed was frankly complicated. Senna, through his promotions company, issued a statement saying that Balestre had respected his integrity, the Court of Appeal in Paris had removed the suspended sentence on his future conduct as a driver and that Dennis had 'interceded and assumed responsibility for the payment of the fine.' Surely all was well? It wasn't.

Balestre proclaimed himself 'stupefied' but quietly began negotiations with Dennis, the negotiations broke down and, that Thursday, with the FISA switchboard at the Place de la Concorde under siege by the world's press (and me), we got the one statement that nobody had expected: there would be no statement.

Overnight, common sense prevailed, something we did expect. Senna did make a statement. 'During the meeting of the FISA World Council which took place on 7 December 1989, I listened to statements and testimonies from various people and from these statements I must conclude they provide proof that no pressure group or the President of the FISA influenced the decisions regarding the result of the FIA Formula 1 World Championship.' It was as near as a proud man would get to leaving his trench with his arms up.

Balestre did make a statement. 'We acknowledge receipt of your letter of 15 February and of your application to take a part in the 1990 World Championship. We are sending you your Superlicence accordingly and wish you every success in a Championship which promises to provide us with a fine sporting season, where you will be able to give full expression to those champion qualities which nobody ever denied that you had.' It was as near as an autocrat would get to leaving his trench with a white flag.

Phoenix, Arizona and the world was back in place for the first race, 11 March. Senna reflected that 'other than being in the car driving, there was no motivation left for me. I had no feeling for the car, not even in the pit lane. In Phoenix I just couldn't understand the car or the engine. I lost all sensitivity. Even the win wasn't enough to motivate me.' The win was a good one, however much that was lost on Senna. He stalked Jean Alesi (Tyrrell), took him and instantly Alesi re-took him in a challenging thrust with no spare space at either side. After that Senna went by and finished nearly ten seconds ahead.

Dennis is candid. 'I think both of us knew that it wasn't going to be fixed in five minutes, but that's where being a real team manager starts. It's about understanding. When someone has a problem in any company, one of the functions of management is to support the weaknesses of people, not expose them to the world. If you're trying to get the best out of people, you identify their weaknesses and either assist them to come to terms with them themselves or educate themselves around the weaknesses, you position them in the organisation with a support structure. In a more refined, highly-tuned situation – such as the relationship between a racing driver and the management of the team – that becomes a more sensitive and delicate operation. I go back to the Prost situation: there was no way, no matter what he said and the press said, that we would have ever retaliated [by entering a public debate], not under any circumstances, and it was a very painful experience. It would have been counter-productive to retaliate. When a driver like Ayrton is down you don't do things to make him further down, you don't question his ability to drive. You say: "Hey come on, let's talk about it, let's have a realistic approach." You don't say: "Drink this glass of medicine and it'll all be better." My motivation was a lot longer coming back than his. I don't mean this to come out as a ham statement but we are very close as men now, meaning we have taken the time and trouble to go very much into each other's thinking.'

The Brazilian race, where Balestre reportedly had an armed guard, was at Sao Paulo, a rebuilt circuit and for Senna a homecoming, of course. 'I got my motivation back there. I had had two weeks to think about it and then I faced the challenge of driving at home and I saw the enthusiasm from all the people. That gave me the pleasure, the fire to get in the car again. It was only the people of Brazil and the positive thoughts they had for me which gave me the ingredients to re-start my career.'

He took pole, was in the lead and then tried to lap Nakajima. 'I was up behind him for four or five corners, I went to overtake him uphill to the slow corner, he opened the door and when I was halfway inside he decided to come back.' Unfortunately Nakajima had run on to dust at the side of the track and could do nothing. Senna needed a new nose cone and finished third.

At Imola he took pole, was in the lead and a stone flew up, sheared the brakes. At Monaco he took pole and won it handsomely. And he went to Montreal where, quite by chance, a respected Canadian journalist called Gerald Donaldson asked him for an interview for his book *Grand Prix People* (MRP). Since what Senna said was so staggering – even by his standards – I repeat a tract of it, with kind permission.

'Sometimes I think I know some of the reasons why I do the things the way I do in the car and sometimes I think I don't know why. There are some moments that seem to be the natural instinct that is in me. Whether I have been born with it or whether this feeling has grown in me more than other people I don't know, but it is inside me and it takes over with a great amount of space and intensity.

'When I am competing against the watch and against other competitors, the feeling of expectation, of getting it done and doing the best I can gives me a kind of power that some moments when I am driving actually detaches me completely from anything else as I am doing it ... corner after corner, lap after lap. I can give you a true example.

'Monte Carlo '88, the last qualifying session. I was already on pole and I was going faster and faster. One lap after the other, quicker and quicker and quicker. I was at one stage just on pole, then by half a second and then one second and I kept going. Suddenly I was nearly two seconds faster than anybody else, including my team-mate with the same car. And I suddenly realised I was no longer driving the car consciously.

'I was kind of driving it by instinct, only I was in a different dimension. It was like I was in a tunnel. Not only the tunnel under the hotel but the whole circuit was a tunnel.

'I was just going and going, more and more and more and more. I was way over the limit but still able to find even more. Then suddenly something just kicked me. I kind of woke up and realised that I was in a different atmosphere than you normally are. My immediate reaction was to back off, slow down. I drove back slowly to the pits and I didn't want to go out any more that day. It frightened me because I realised I was well beyond my conscious understanding. It happens rarely but I keep these experiences very much alive in me because it is something that is important for self-preservation.'

I think that Monsieur Prost's assertion about Senna thinking God would not allow him to be harmed has been finally and totally refuted by the paragraph above, despite what would subsequently happen; and you notice, too, that at no stage did Senna refer to what happened at Monte Carlo as being a religious or quasi-religious experience. It was a man taking a machine and a machine taking a man into secret places, into the subliminal.

Oh, and he won Canada, led Mexico and had a puncture.

He didn't get pole at Paul Ricard and explained that across a whole qualifying lap if you 'lift your foot by one-eighth of the play on the throttle' *once* it can make all the difference. Think about that. His chances in the race were essentially destroyed by a 16-second pitstop for tyres and he finished third. Prost won it and seemed to have rediscovered the vigour of youth to go with the wisdom of experience, something which was confirmed at Silverstone when Senna spun and inherited third place while Prost scanned developments, made incisive moves and won again.

Evening at Silverstone, a cloying, clammy heat from the embers of a burning hot day. Mansell has announced his retirement, some of the motorhomes are already packed up, some of the transporters are already lumbering towards the traffic jam directly outside the circuit. At the McLaren motorhome Senna's sister Viviane and father sit chatting with friends; Viviane disarmingly like him, the set of face, the roll of the eyes, even the position of the teeth when she smiled, which she did a lot.

Senna comes from the pits, autograph hunters closing on him and trailing him like a pack, journalists hold tape recorders to his mouth as he walks. He wears blue jeans of a careful casual cut, a white Boss shirt, trainers. A sexy Italian girl interviewer with her TV crew corners him, she uses her wide eyes to full effect and yes, he does a brief interview, moving across the lock-step of question and answer, although less than an hour before he had done the same thing three times at the official interviews (always the same questions), then come to a press conference for the journalists, where he was asked – well, the same questions. In each case he gave the same answers, varying only the odd word as he'd forgotten part of the script or he was amusing himself with variations on language to sustain his own interest.

How could he tolerate all this? Well, he was getting paid $15 million a year to tolerate it (which leads to a paradox. Normally when a human being is earning that sort of money he doesn't have to do anything he doesn't want to). And anyway, Senna put money into this context: 'A lot of people say the money is not important and it's only important to win, but I think very few of them really mean it: some because they like money and some because if they have got some already they want more, but I have never needed it and that's even more true now, because since I have been successful I have the material things.'

Or, as he has recounted when told that Dennis had described him as the shrewdest negotiator he had ever met: 'I'm not that hard. If you think that a few years ago when I was negotiating to join McLaren we got to a difficult moment right at the end trying to arrive at a figure. Instead of going for it and pushing really hard – which I could have done had I really wanted – I took a chance just to let it happen whichever way it would. We spun a coin, heads or tails, I called wrong and it cost me one and a half million dollars.'

But now at Silverstone the TV interview is over, the sexy girl gone, a gaggle of journalists call out: 'Ayrton, Ayrton,' but he won't come over. He shrugs, he's emptied, he's talked enough. He makes a racing driver's calculation, the mind moving incisively over the territory to be covered: he goes immediately to his right and through the gap at the end of the motorhome. He'll be clear before the journalists can reach him again.

It works.

He won Germany, then – inevitably perhaps – did something to imply that he hadn't fully reached equilibrium yet. The Hungarian Grand Prix was one of those rarities where many threads come together and interconnect and you have a real race. Towards the end of it, Boutsen was leading with an enormous impetus of pressure gathered behind him, Sandro Nannini, Senna, Berger, Mansell. They circled the tight, unforgiving corners nose-to-tail, nose-to-tail. All it lacked was Prost, but he'd gone in an accident on lap 36.

If this quintet had simply kept on circling it would have been no more than an interesting procession. The one place you could authentically overtake was the long straight, and lap after lap along that their speeds were evenly matched. Someone whispered to me, when there were a handful of laps left, that there was no chance, no chance whatever, that people of that disposition would all actually finish the race. He was not wrong and it happened like this: a right-hand corner, a short sharp rush to the next right-hander, an innocent back-marker up ahead, but too far away to be a factor in the pressure. Boutsen hugs the brightly striped kerbing on the left, positioned to take the ordinary racing line through the right-hander, and Nannini a car's length behind him does the same. Thirty, forty metres from the turn into the corner Senna pulls decisively out into the middle of the track. He points the snout of the McLaren at the apex but already Boutsen is turning in, Nannini is following and turning in. Boutsen threads through and still Nannini is turning in – across, of course, Senna.

Let us be clear: if you try to go inside someone at a corner and you haul yourself alongside you can justifiably claim the corner; if you are not yet alongside you lose the corner. This is a fine point and also, alas, a theoretical one. When the theory meets the reality of two racing cars contesting one portion of tarmac it is no longer a theory; it is a crash. Senna's front wheel struck Nannini's rear wheel. There is no escape from the conclusion that he was not alongside. He was substantially behind. Nannini went into the air – for an instant a long way into the air; pitched at an angle towards the critical point where he might flip. He skimmed off the circuit, landed on all four wheels.

Astonishingly, Senna's car was undamaged and he continued. While Senna tracked Boutsen, Berger tried the same move on Mansell at the same place nine laps later and Mansell went into the air. Boutsen won, Senna hounding him all the way to the line.

He came to speak afterwards and he looked, as he so often did, softened by the race, mellowed in contemplation of it as if mind and body are becalmed. A pretty and nervous Hungarian translator asked if he'd mind pausing after each answer so that she could render it into Hungarian. He smiled that deep, withdrawn, weary smile which isn't a smile at all but a mannerism and said no, really, I can't go through all that, please, I just want to speak. It was done politely but decisively. 'I was fortunate,' he said. 'Nannini closed the door and I don't think he saw me.' It was one explanation but it did not explain why he chose that corner to try it.

In the Benetton motorhome, Nannini had been crying but was now composed. He said little. There was little to say.

On the Friday before Spa, Senna duly re-signed for McLaren for 1991 although (again) he said that Ron was a tough negotiator and (again) Ron said that he was a tough negotiator. He won Spa comfortably enough from Prost and the Championship was moving decisively towards him, 63 points against Prost's 50. It was the safety margin of the next race and perhaps the one after that.

Senna won Monza from Prost and Berger. Senna sat arranged to face the press with Berger in the middle and Prost on the other side of Berger. It was a comfortable arrangement. Senna and Prost have not exchanged a word for almost a calendar year and Berger is the logistical buffer. His role seems to be minor but in fact it is very major indeed. Berger goes subconsciously straight into race-speak, the car began to slide around, chose A compound tyres and maybe that wasn't the right choice and so forth, then he stands and leaves.

The questioning moved through the lock-step of mo-race speak and when that was exhausted (it didn't take long) someone did ask a real live question. It was addressed squarely to two men who were supreme in their art – for different reasons – and who now sat within reach of each other. The question was: how much longer before you at least reach an accommodation with each other?

For a long moment Prost said nothing. It was a hell of a question and it might have involved retreat, surrender, submission, the negation of his integrity.

Prost: 'I tried to shake hands with Ayrton at the first race of the season at Phoenix. Ask him.' It was a hard point to make.

Senna: 'I did not think he was entirely sincere about it. If I had, I would have shaken his hand. It is not easy to forget what happened between us last season. However, although we don't have many things in common, we share the same passion for Formula 1 and this is very important for us. When he is able to say he is sincere in front of everyone I will accept it. I don't have a problem with that.'

Prost: 'Yes, this is very important. Ayrton is right about that: he has his ideas about what happened last year and I have my ideas. Whatever happened, I would like to forget it. We do have the same passion for the sport. I believe I have changed a lot since last year and perhaps I understand some things more clearly than I did. I think it would be good for our sport if today as we go into the last four races we could somehow go together. So if Ayrton agrees ...'

It had gone beyond words because at this extremely moving juncture (or more properly conjunction) concrete gestures were needed, too. They shook hands, there was instinctive applause and they began to slap each other on the back.

Senna 72 points, Prost 56.

Mansell won Estoril from Senna, Prost third after a frightener at the very start when Mansell veered at Prost and Prost had to hug the pit-lane wall so closely that his wheels brushed against it. Afterwards Prost rounded on the Ferrari management, rounded on their lack of organisation, said they didn't deserve the Championship and implied that he might walk away from the whole thing.

On any rostrum, you could see exhibited before your very eyes the shifting patterns of relationships which constantly evolved and dissolved (a hug might mean reconciliation, a handshake rehabilitation), Mansell put an arm round Senna (didn't they dislike each other?) but didn't put an arm round Prost (weren't they bosom buddies and team-mates?).

Senna 78, Prost 60.

Jerez and the Spanish Grand Prix were a week away, and now Prost conceded the Championship. If you followed Senna you were worried about that. (Hadn't Prost conceded it only the season before and won it?)

Senna had been taking pole after pole and was on 49. Jim Clark, as we have seen, had 33 and that had stood since 1968 until Senna beat it at Phoenix in 1989. Senna needed only one more special, squeezed lap and he had the round fifty. At 1.52 on the Friday qualifying session Martin Donnelly (Lotus) struck a barrier virtually head-on at more than 140mph. The car was torn to pieces and Donnelly lay on the track. The television camera remained on him a long time, and the first impression was that he couldn't have survived. Professor Sid Watkins, Formula 1's resident doctor, was there within two minutes.

Senna was told of Donnelly and he was close to tears. He walked to where he still lay and remained there a long time. He was not required to go. He returned to the motorhome and he asked everyone else to leave it. 'I wanted to be all with my thoughts. They were private moments and I doubt that I will ever be able to express what I felt.'

Donnelly lay on the track for twenty minutes before Professor Watkins judged he could be moved to the track hospital. Qualifying resumed, Senna didn't want to drive and then he made a fundamental decision: he'd take the McLaren to its limit. He went a full second quicker than he had done before the accident.

Why did Senna go to Donnelly? He went because, I think, his religious convictions took him there to face it. He went because, I think, he was now becoming so senior a figure in racing that one day he'd possibly be a spokesman for safety. He went because, I know, he cared very deeply about the consequences of human actions. Later that evening he visited Donnelly in hospital.

During the season, Senna gave an interview to Steve Rider of the BBC and was on his best, relaxed, whimsical form, even when asked the hard questions. A fragment.

Senna: 'Fear is an important feeling in your mind for self-preservation' (slow smile).

Rider: 'Maybe you have less fear in a cockpit than other drivers around you?'

Senna: (slow smile, smooths collar of driving overall) 'I don't know how much fear that they have. I know that I have enough to keep me in control and keep me as healthy as I am.'

I have included the smiles not because talking of fear amused Senna but because it was a way of normalising having to discuss it. In simple terms, he had found a balance between respect for danger and an acceptance that any driver must take risks. When this balance was temporarily disrupted by something like Donnelly's crash, going and facing it – he watched what Watkins was doing carefully, and even asked him about his sequence of actions later – must have been, partly, a way of restoring the balance within himself.

The following day he took the fiftieth pole although on the lap he confronted a vision which both disturbed and angered him. He had an on-board camera and what it portrayed was so fluid, something happening so fast, that he seemed to skim the whole circuit, gloved hands pump-pump-pumping the steering wheel, G-forces jud-jud-juddering the helmet, wheels fleeing across kerbing in almost brutal ferocity, corner after corner melting and rushing, melting and rushing, in a tremendous sustained surge.

He rounded a corner and halfway down a straight were two cars going very slowly indeed. One instant they were shapes in the distance – evidently arguing about who'd done what to whom – and as the Honda engine pumped in the speed he was on them fast as you can blink your eye. The sheer compression of time between Senna rounding the corner and reaching them was damn nearly beyond comprehension.

One car was full to the left, the other behind it and outside it. Two-thirds of the width of the circuit was completely filled and this by cars doing what Senna estimated at 120mph less than he was. He lifted his foot off the throttle a fraction as he placed the McLaren to the right and they vanished somewhere into the blur and the engine's shriek and the next corner was already coming, coming, coming.

He completed the lap, completed the fifty pole positions and was greeted by the mechanics in euphoria, had a touching moment with Ron Dennis, got a cake with 50 on it, but his eyes were close to tears. He spoke of what lifting from the throttle had cost in time lost, said of course that it wasn't a perfect lap – but that wasn't the point. Still Donnelly's crash was utterly vivid in the memory, it had only been the day before and here you have two cars meandering along and, Senna said, what if I'd hit one? I'd have been airborne for sure, what are these people, crazy?

It flawed the occasion, flawed the celebration of that lap of 1 minute 18.387 seconds.

Something happened in the Spanish Grand Prix, too, and it was (again we thought) another clue about the equilibrium. Senna took the lead but he sensed that Prost was quicker and after the pit stops for tyres he came out entirely by chance at a very ripe moment. Mansell was moving aside to let Prost through into the lead (bosom buddies again?) That was down the start-finish straight and Senna was travelling hard from the pit-lane exit. Mansell had gone wide and Senna nipped into the gap just as Mansell turned in to take the corner. 'It was,' Mansell said, deadpan as you like, 'an interesting moment.' Yes, and Senna's corner, too.

Ultimately a stone punctured Senna's radiator, water boiled and bubbled back and he swerved once, twice, as it smeared a tyre, naturally thought it a puncture, pitted for tyres again, retired out on the circuit. He clambered from the car and bent over it looking for the cause, was satisfied, went to the wall nearby and sat on it. He was lost in contemplation. You don't sit on the wall, you get over the wall to safety. He sat for a long time and some say he was in tears again. He turned his back on the track and talked to the people who wanted to talk to him and he remained on the action side of the wall. He was in another dimension: he couldn't have seen any spinning car which might have come at him, any errant car cavorting.

Senna 78, Prost 69.

Equilibrium? During this season he would say: 'Time shows us, as we progress, different perspectives of life. A few years ago I had no time for anything or anybody other than racing. Today I not only have the time but I need the time for my family, my friends and particularly my girlfriend. I organise myself to strike the right balance between my private and professional lives because only that way, having the equilibrium between both sides of myself, can I perform to my best.'

This was the man who, also during the season, was giving an interview when a fan approached him and offered him some little gifts. One of those gifts was a piece of ceramic with his name on it. Another was a cake from the fan's wife. 'It makes me feel embarrassed and humble. It shows how much you can touch people without knowing or even speaking to them and, as much as you try to give those people something, it is nothing compared to what they live in their own minds, in their dreams for you.'

And now it was autumn again, now it was October. They went to Suzuka. On the Thursday Prost jogged round the track and paused at the chicane, as if by standing before it he could assess its dimensions slowly, the way you never can in a racing car. His thoughts no doubt were of '89. The entrance to the chicane, he concluded, really was too narrow to be a passing point. Later, Senna was asked about that and tacitly agreed. Some observers took this as, well, something approaching a suggestion of culpability about '89.

The mathematics had become (relatively) straightforward. Senna had the 78 points, Prost 69 – as we've just seen – and both had filled their quota of eleven points finishes. This marginally favoured Prost who would only have to drop a fifth, then a fourth place. Senna had been no lower than third all season so that only victories or second places were of any material benefit to him. The permutations were also (relatively) straightforward but however you worked it out Senna remained clear favourite. If he won Suzuka he was Champion and even if he came second behind anybody but Prost he was Champion.

Prost confessed that he felt the same sort of relief he had at Adelaide in 1986 against Mansell and Piquet, when the niceties and permutations of the mathematics could be completely ignored. He'd had to go for the win then and see what happened, all the rest outside his control. Suzuka was the same in all its essentials.

There was another factor and it began to loom larger and larger. The respective situations of Senna and Prost were exactly reversed from the year before at this same Suzuka. Then Senna had had to ignore the permutations and go for the win or he was bust. So what would happen when they re-reached the chicane? With eight points for a win in those days, a crash gave Senna the Championship: even winning Adelaide, Prost would be one point short. The only calming thought was that they were friends now. Weren't they?

Pole position seemed crucial. From the lights, if either man reached that unfolding right-hand corner at the end of the start-finish straight first they could win the race from there. The other man would find it extremely difficult to overtake elsewhere, not forgetting the chicane.

This was compounded by the sure and certain knowledge that the Ferrari was now a very potent piece of machinery indeed and in it Prost had been decisively quicker at Jerez. Senna simply could not afford to let Prost get away from him at Suzuka. If he did he might not see him again until the podium. It was further compounded by the knowledge that Prost was driving as well as he had done in his life, expressed through a beautiful balancing of racecraft, calculation and prudence. From all that Prost drew great speed.

In the first grid session Berger was quickest, Senna third behind Prost. 'This morning [in the untimed session] I made a mistake on the slippery track surface and spun off,' Senna said. 'This afternoon my car was OK but it bottomed out badly at one point just as I was changing from fourth to fifth and I got a little sideways – I was glancing at the rev counter at the time. I feel quite satisfied with my performance as a whole.'

Glancing at the rev counter? Hadn't he once said: 'In the car I don't even look at the rev counter because if you do that you must be a fraction less committed to your driving at that moment. So you change gear by sound.'

In the second session he took the 51st pole position of his career although it was taut and tight. He and Prost lay in wait for each other until the last five minutes before they made their final, decisive gestures. Senna, a master of knowing *exactly* how long to wait, sensed that he needed a clear road. 'I was determined that I was going to get out on the circuit in front of Prost. The Ferrari pit was near ours and when I heard them fire his engine up I immediately gave the signal to my mechanics to do the same.' The two men circled the emptied circuit, warmed their tyres, went hard for it.

Senna 1: 36.996
Prost 1: 37.228

'The whole team,' Senna said, 'really contributed to my performance, men and machine working extremely well, but tomorrow's race is a long one and anything can happen. I'm sure it will be the most exciting race of the season. We and Ferrari are very close now but despite the pressure I am under I feel really fit. Naturally I am thinking of the Championship and this one would mean more to me than 1988.'

This was the familiar publicity-speak and did not cover what was really happening. The placing of the pole position car was on the right of the straight, but the track was 'dirty' there, and Senna argued that that negated the legitimate advantage bestowed by pole. Prost, while geometrically behind Senna because of the grid's traditional stagger, had the advantage of a clean segment of track. Senna's arguments were not accepted. He was very angry, and the anger would not subside.

Sunday, 21 October, and the clock moved towards 1.0. The parade lap had been completed, the official on the rim of the track had waved his flag now that all the cars were on the grid, and the red light flicked to green. Prost did take the lead, Senna did try to take it from him. Prost moved across onto the racing line to take the first corner, Senna went down the inside and claimed to have seen a gap. They collided. They went off. They were wreathed in a pall of dust and buried into the surface of the run-off area as if it had become a graveyard.

Senna clambered out and moved towards the track itself, plucking his driving gloves off as he went. Only once did he glance back and that seemed to be at his car, not Prost who lingered a brief moment beside the tyre-wall and he, too, was plucking his gloves off. Then he began to jog towards the track.

Would the race be stopped and re-started? The cars were in a potentially dangerous position for anyone else going off there – but both cars were promptly hoisted away. Would Ferrari protest? Even if they did and the protest was upheld it would not help Prost. He could scarcely be awarded the race by default and so would still have no points from it; Championship over.

Immediately the reverberations started. The Ferrari team manager, Cesare Fiorio, confirmed that no protest would be lodged but he did say it was a 'scandal' not to have stopped the race with the two cars positioned as they were, in the run-off area. He added: 'Prost was in front and had the right to turn into the corner.'

Balestre was not there but had seen it all on television. 'It was a scandal that the World Championship should be decided on such a collision. I leave everyone to be their own judge of who is to blame. I am sure all motor racing supporters throughout the world will feel as frustrated as I do after such an appalling end to the World Championship.'

He was asked if Senna would be disqualified but how could you disqualify a man who'd only reached the first corner? And what do you fine a man whose father is rich and who himself is earning $15 million per annum?

Senna gave Dennis a bear-hug when he returned to the pits, and later there was – however tantalising – a clue about *why* the collision had taken place.

'I had been asking the officials to move pole position to the other side of the track all weekend,' Senna said, 'and their refusal to do it created so many problems that I suppose this accident was likely to happen. But that's motor racing and a Championship title is the result of a whole season's work. This title is particularly satisfying to me as the competition from other teams has been much closer than when I won in 1988. As for the accident, it was just one of those things. I certainly wanted to win this race as much as any this season.'

There was much, much more to it than that, but we'd have to wait a calendar year to find out.

The friendship with Prost had proved very fragile indeed. Prost said: 'Anyone who understands motor racing does not have to ask what happened. He did it on purpose because he saw that I had a good start, that my car was better and he had no chance to win. So he just pushed me out. What he did was more than unsporting; it was disgusting. I have no problems with losing the World Championship, I have lost many – but not this way. Can you imagine what young drivers think when they see things like that in Formula 1? They'll think they can get away with anything.' And the fragile friendship? 'It is all over. I do not like people who show one thing but are different inside. Everything that has happened here has shown his real face. I hate this kind of situation. He has completely destroyed everything. For him it is much more important to win the Championship than it is for me. It is the only thing he has in life. He is completely screwed up.'

Nor was Prost finished yet. 'Senna is completely the opposite in character to what he wants people to believe. Technically I believe we won the World Championship. We were not even side by side. If you accept Senna's behaviour then perhaps we will get to a situation where people will start entering a team with one car specifically intended to push off the opposition to enable the other guy to win. This man has no value.'

'I don't give a damn what he says,' Senna responded. 'He took a chance going into the first corner when he couldn't afford to. He knew I was going to come down the inside. He made the biggest mistake by closing the door. He knows I always go for the gap. It has turned things upside down from last year. I cannot be responsible for Prost's actions. I know what I can do and I am happy inside.'

Ron Dennis was more pragmatic. 'This would never have happened if the officials had agreed to move pole position to the other side of the track.' And that was another clue, or rather the same clue from another mouth.

Prost's words are eminently understandable but difficult to digest. Surely he knew Senna by now, he of all people? Surely he can't have been surprised by what happened at the first corner of the Japanese Grand Prix? *But* whatever else was Prost supposed to do? Wave Senna by?

Was Senna right? That phrase comes back like an echo: there are no desperate situations, only desperate men.

It was difficult to mount a defence of Senna because he was not yet alongside Prost and, as we have seen, convention demands – absolutely demands – that you can only claim the corner if you are *at least* alongside – unless, of course, the other guy moves out of your way. Surely Senna knew Prost wasn't going to do that, not here, not now?

All these questions seemed legitimate and we'd have to wait that calendar year to find out they weren't.

There was spreading fall-out. The week after, Ferrari's chairman wrote to FISA with a straightforward request that something be done so that in future this wouldn't happen again with 'more serious and sad consequences. Everything leads one to assume that, through lack of firmness on the part of officials, certain drivers believe that crashes are now an acceptable tactic.' Fiat owned Ferrari and Fiat's managing director said: 'We are not prepared to put in so much capital and manhours building better cars just to see them shunted off the track.'

The implication was clear and enormous: Ferrari was prepared to leave Formula 1 altogether.

Dennis returned from Japan and appeared on a BBC television programme, *Sportsnight*, where he was interviewed by Steve Rider. Fragments, again.

Dennis: 'We are a team steeped in commitment to doing it well and there is nothing that tarnishes our success more than that the Championship should be decided on an incident like this.'

Rider: 'Perhaps an ingredient was that there were two very highly motivated men on the front row?'

Dennis: 'It certainly didn't help.'

Rider: 'Let's take another look at that start and get your views on it. It did seem that Prost certainly got the better start. He gets a car's length pretty early on, doesn't he?' [A re-run of the start is now being played.]

Dennis: 'That's quite right. The grip on that side of the circuit is superior to the right-hand side. It's just here where Prost moves to the left of Senna and opens the door, Senna just makes a total commitment to the corner. As regards the pre-race strategy, we had everything to lose by not winning the race. The organisers had laid down some conditions limiting the places where it would be possible to overtake, and who emerged from that corner pretty much would have won the race. Therefore, with Ayrton needing to win, Alain needing to win, there was a lot of pressure to come out of that first corner first.'

Rider: 'Shall we have another look at it and perhaps explain a bit more about that little gap Senna saw because when Senna sees a gap every driver in the field knows he goes for it.' [The re-run is being re-run.]

Dennis: 'You can see here where Prost is clearly ahead and it's just coming up now, he moves to the left, opens the gap and Senna goes for it and then it's closed again. In our briefing before the event we were actually of the opinion that Prost – knowing he had to finish the next two races in good positions – would never close the door because the resulting consequences would have lost him the World Championship, he'd leave it open – and he didn't.'

Rider: 'In general do you think rivalries in the sport are getting a bit too intense and maybe becoming a danger during the course of races?'

Dennis: 'The problem with motorsport at the moment is that there is such a shortfall in the supply of top drivers. The drivers who are recognised as being la crème de la crème struggle to come to terms with being number two and it's my view – and one shared by most people in motorsport – that Ayrton Senna is the best driver that motorsport has ever seen and therefore he becomes the subject of much criticism about his total commitment to the sport.'

In Paris, FISA formally announced that a Special Commission of Inquiry for Safety was being formed to cast a careful eye over 'incidents' during the season. It would have extensive powers enabling it to amass evidence from whichever quarter it chose and that embraced all officials (including race stewards) as well as any documents. There was a telling, almost icy phrase that 'some of the participants' – drivers – had damaged the image of Formula 1 and that the image had 'deteriorated'. There was a telling, almost icy sting: the granting of Superlicences for the 1991 season would depend on the findings of this Commission.

A British Sunday newspaper trawled deep among its records and propped up a long article with the information that since the beginning of season 1987, Senna had been disqualified three times and involved in 11 crashes whilst winning 22 races; Prost had not been disqualified at all, had crashed only three times (two of them with Senna at Suzuka) and won 19 races. I mention the article not because of the statistics, interesting though they are, but because it occupied a whole page, complete with diagrams of the crashes of '90. Senna v Prost had now become a matter of international sporting importance and well worth the whole page in a British paper, although neither of them was remotely British. The matter had grown vastly, perhaps monstrously, too big for parochialism.

Senna arrived in Adelaide trenchant and unrepentant in his logic. He said of the Commission: 'This is about a lot of drivers in a lot of races. A lot of incidents have occurred this year because of the intensity of competition between cars and drivers which was not present in 1988 and 1989. It is not directed at me. It just happened that this was announced shortly after Japan.'

He spoke of Prost: 'He made the better start and went towards the first corner just ahead of me. He moved to the inside but I knew my engine had better acceleration than his so I was not concerned. I knew there was a possibility to do it at the first corner so I chased him and as we came to the corner he moved to the outside and I went for the space. As I did so he came back at me. I was surprised because it was totally unexpected for a driver of his knowledge and experience to make such a move. Under the circumstances a crash was unavoidable. We hit each other side by side. You can see from the television cameras that it is a fact. If I had been leading under the same circumstances I would not have left room on the inside and if I had left room I would not under any circumstances have closed the door for a second time, so I think it was a major tactical mistake by him. It was really pathetic to hear him say the race should have been stopped. I don't think anyone can dispute that our cars were in a safe position.

'In the end he makes me laugh because he is the guy that complains so much and not just this year but ever since we first raced as team-mates in 1988. He complained a lot about me, then about Honda, then the following year he complained about me and Honda again, he complained about the team, and it was the team for which he won three Championships. Then he goes to a new team, Ferrari, and he criticises a tyre company for supplying us with different tyres. Then he moves on and criticises Berger, then Alesi, then his own team and management, then he ends up criticising Mansell and finishes up criticising me again, so it comes as no surprise that he criticises me over the Suzuka affair. I am used to it.

'This whole controversy has been going round a single man. If anybody gets near to him and something goes wrong he has something to say.' Senna added that the Championship had been won and lost during the whole season, not Suzuka, and Prost 'does a good job diverting people from thinking about that. His complaints in Japan were designed to ignore the other races in which we beat him. I find it amazing that an organisation like FIA and Ferrari is manipulated by one man.'

He appeared on TV with Jackie Stewart who said he (Senna) had been involved in more coming-togethers on circuits than any World Champion before. Senna betrayed anger, shifted forward on his chair, used a cocked finger to stab an accompaniment to his defence. Stewart was prepared for Senna walking out. He nearly did.

By now Prost had had enough of being pursued by media men with microphones 'stuck up my nose' trying to goad him into fuelling it all again. He did say he had been misquoted about threatening to retire and 'if I don't speak now I can't be misquoted again.'

First qualifying for the Australian Grand Prix produced a situation uncanny enough to be haunting. Senna was quickest but Prost next and if it remained so, what would happen from the green light to the first corner? Adelaide no longer carried the currency of a live championship and in theory nobody needed to take particular risks but at the personal level, who knew? Senna did get pole on the Saturday and had a tilt right at the end of the session 'just for the pure pleasure of driving and to please the spectators.' Berger and Mansell stole past Prost. Senna moved cleanly clear at the green, but eventually he went off into a tyre barrier. 'I couldn't get second gear, it was stuck in neutral.' He climbed out and walked away from 1990.

Chapter 11

THE THIRD CHAMPIONSHIP

Ayrton Senna once said his ultimate aim was to get past Fangio's total of five Championships. We had no way of knowing that in 1991 he'd win the Championship again but in something approaching a private moment he'd understand that the future was going to be difficult.

Owen O'Mahony started to work for Senna as his pilot, flying the HS125 (cost $8.5 million). 'He'd got the plane at that stage but evidently he'd had problems with Brazilian pilots. He rang British Aerospace and said: "Send an English one!" So I went out to Brazil. To be perfectly honest I wasn't really a Formula 1 fan but the name Ayrton Senna seemed vaguely familiar. *He's a driver, isn't he? I'm sure I remember that name from somewhere.* Prior to that I'd been in aviation for years.

'It took about six months for Ayrton to smile at me. After that, we'd sit and chat in the plane for long periods of time about all sorts of things. He was an endlessly fascinating man to talk to and it was endlessly fascinating to see his mind in operation. Mind you, it was never a quick brain, never ever a quick brain' (in that he thought carefully before he spoke: you cannot by definition exploit a Grand Prix car if you think slowly). Often, however, during long flights Senna would go into what O'Mahony describes as 'brain shut-off. He'd listen to music or sleep.' The eight seats on the plane could fold down into beds. 'One thing I'd like to think is that I helped him with a sense of humour. I tend to go around seeing things in funny terms, or at least the funny side. In fact I taught him an expression which he later used against me, gave it back to me, he did. It was: "How long have you been working for me *not including tomorrow?*"'

Before O'Mahony, nobody had asked Senna if he'd like to have a go at flying the plane himself and Senna never did ask O'Mahony 'can I?' They evolved a coded language with Senna wondering: 'What's the wind like at Faro?' – where he had a house – which meant *I would like a go if it is safe to do so.* 'Obviously,' O'Mahony says, 'you don't do anything silly like on the approach to somewhere like Heathrow, but Faro in the evening could be very quiet.' Flying the HS125 Senna was 'happy as a little sandboy and the interesting thing was that you only had to tell him something once. His feel was amazing.

'He didn't need the aircraft in the close season and it was kept in the UK. Occasionally I'd take people in it to keep it in working order, so to speak. It was funny because I took the ex-President of France, Valery Giscard d'Estaing, down to a weekend of shooting in Spain. Next time I was flying with Ayrton, he said: "How come you, with all your *mafia* (!!!) friends, can't get me a ride with Williams?!!!" It was at the time he was negotiating with the team and we'd had a couple of clandestine meetings with Frank Williams. The plane could fly London to Sao Paulo direct, although I once did do it in two legs, stopping at the Cape Verde Islands (off the African coast).

'The effect Ayrton had on people was amazing. I've landed him at Sao Paulo airport and had to shut the engines off because people knew he was coming and they'd break through and run towards the plane.'

The setting, moving towards the United States Grand Prix at Phoenix on 10 March: Mansell had been lured from retirement by Williams and testing implied he'd be strong. Berger, who'd joined Senna at McLaren in 1990, set himself to test and test throughout the winter to be fitter than Senna and more familiar with the car.

Senna had tested Honda's V12 at Estoril in late autumn and the week before Phoenix he returned to Estoril to try it in McLaren's new car. With complete candour he said of the engine

'I don't know what they (Honda) have been doing since, but there is not enough progress and not enough power.'

Consternation. Normally, drivers don't say those things, and certainly not in public. Moreover the widely held perception was that the Japanese, individually or collectively, might regard open criticism as a loss of face. Honda issued a statement which insisted that the V12 was already putting out more horsepower than the V10 and the engine they'd run at Estoril this early spring was in Phoenix-spec, unrepresentative of the kind you needed for Portugal.

Senna saw the perils of a season without enough power and resolved to do some hard driving in the background, urging Honda on. It produced a rich irony. He damaged his own argument by winning Phoenix and Brazil and Imola and Monaco. None of that, however, was the private moment of revelation. Before that, a revealing diversion.

Professor Watkins's two stepsons had an interesting but surely unreachable notion. They were at Loretto, the Edinburgh boarding school, and from time to time Loretto had a guest speaker on a Saturday night. The stepsons invited Senna. All else aside, the week of the requested lecture Senna was the Estoril test, itself enough for him to mutter a polite 'thanks, love to, but I can't.'

'Much to everybody's surprise, Ayrton accepted,' Watkins says.

After testing on the Friday he took his own plane from Lisbon to Heathrow, where he collected the Professor and his wife and they flew on to Edinburgh. 'He stayed at my house, which is in Coldstream. On the Saturday I took him to lunch, a pub in the Borders where nobody recognised him and that pleased him immensely. Incidentally, when he used to come and visit me at the hospital where I worked in London, we'd nip out for the odd Chinese meal in the East End. There again, he was very rarely recognised. One or two people would look at him as if it couldn't be true! And since I didn't call him by name they assumed it wasn't true.' (One time Senna was visiting Professor Watkins at the hospital and, no doubt, savouring the prospect of a Chinese meal in anonymity. As he waited for Watkins to become free, an elderly patient in a wheelchair needed moving from one department to another. Guess who volunteered to push the wheelchair and did push it?)

Watkins did something else this Loretto weekend. Discreetly he telephoned the museums officer of Berwickshire District Council, who run the Jim Clark Memorial Room in Duns, not far from Coldstream. It was closed for extensive refurbishment. Watkins explained to the officer, Jeff Taylor, that he had an important guest who didn't want to be named but who would very much like to have a look around the Room. Gently, Taylor coaxed the name out of Watkins and opened the Room specially. Taylor explained to me in an earlier book (*Champions!* by Christopher Hilton and John Blunsden, MRP) that 'without being disrespectful to Senna, he didn't seem in any way overawed by all the trophies because he'd plenty of his own, and after all, trophies are trophies. He was much more interested in what Clark was like. I imagine they were the same type of people, quiet, reflective. I looked at him and I thought: this is a very controlled man.'

At Loretto, Watkins says, 'it wasn't really a debate. Ayrton gave a talk. He'd borrowed a slide or two from the Jim Clark Room and gave his talk. He took questions for 20 minutes or so. He was absolutely super. He also had some photographs taken in the Loretto chapel, where there is a plaque to Jimmy Clark (a pupil in the 1950s). Afterwards, we went and ate supper in the headmaster's quarters with some of the Sixth Form and some of the older boys who had been invited as well. The Bishop of Truro (Michael Ball) was there and he and Ayrton got into a nice little chat about religion because, of course, they were on opposite sides of the wall: Anglican and Roman Catholic. However, they got on very well. Then Ayrton had to leave and I took him to the airport so he could fly back to Portugal. The next day, the Bishop was giving the sermon at the school and in opening it he said how very impressed he had been with Ayrton and that he felt outclassed as a preacher ...'

The Bishop of Truro, a delightful man, concurs. 'I may well have said "compared with the faith I met last night, I shouldn't be standing here at all!" Ayrton Senna struck me as forcibly as that, yes, definitely. He came over as a great sort of wave. His personality was attractive and he had a lovely sense of humour. Though we did talk about the faith, I'm not one of those people who finds it easy to talk about it unless it's spiced with humour, and he had that ability, too.

'In every way he was unlike so many people who are rich and famous and powerful. He actually did take an interest. He still retained the power to relate to other people. Without any patronisation or anything like that he remained interested in people as people, and that is rare. Loretto have some notable figures every so often to give a talk on Saturday evenings in term time and they were lucky enough to get him. The great thing proved to be not only how good he was in the talk but in the way he answered the boys' questions. He was scrupulously honest and didn't spare himself along the way.

'For instance, they said: "What about your relationship with Alain Prost? What *is* your relationship with him? The newspapers all say you hate each other." He replied: "Well, of course, I can't offer an opinion about what Prost thinks of me but, as far as I am concerned personally, our relationship is very good. But he is a competitor on the track and there we go all out to get each other." He added "Prost's remarks about me are entirely up to him." They challenged him about his relationship with his wife-who-wasn't (there were rumours of a love child). They challenged him on the lines of: "You, as a Christian." He was absolutely honest. He was prepared to answer questions in a straight and humble way. He had the boys eating from the palm of his hand. His transparent honesty and goodwill really did have them exactly where he wanted them.

'Obviously he had a very deep faith. I'd almost call him a born-again Catholic. He'd been nurtured in his faith, but somehow we all gained the impression that at some stage in his life it had become renewed and he had found a *very* deep faith. Born-again is an extreme term, but one felt somehow or other that he had recovered his faith. A very wonderful man. The other thing that came through was his care of the less fortunate. He told a story or two of the people on his continent and their degradation and he was very moving about that.

'At the dinner we got on totally. I mean by that there was no barrier of any sort. We exchanged stories as much as anything. He acknowledged me for what I was and I did the same to him. He had this amazing ability to treat you as a friend from the word go. That was the naturalness, the sheer naturalness, of the man. It was wonderful, enchanting, and it enchanted the young people as well.'

The school magazine, *The Lorettonian*, described the visit thus: 'Mr Senna gave an instructive yet informed talk to the School on his life in F1 motor racing. He was a relaxed and genial guest, yet highly professional, dealing thoroughly with possibly the longest post-lecture question session for some time. Despite an intense schedule – he had to be in Portugal early the following day – Ayrton Senna happily gave his time and attention to all whom he met during his visit.'

At Phoenix, he decisively outqualified Berger, and this exercised a profound effect on the Austrian, who needed nearly half the season to recover his confidence. Prost (at Ferrari, of course) lined up alongside Senna on the front row. At the green they lurched towards each other but that was just the power coming on, slewing the cars. Both steadied, Senna already half a length clear. Essentially he settled the race at the end of lap 1.

Two weeks later at Interlagos, Patrese held pole until the dying moments of the second session, fuelling Senna's suspicions that sooner or later the McLaren Honda would struggle against the Williams Renault. 'I realised we were in for a major challenge.' He took pole, however, 'motivated enormously by the desire to succeed in front of my home crowd. The support they gave me was inspirational. When you are moving out of the pits a billion things go through your mind and body. It's an amazingly fast process, all geared to one goal, all focused to one minor point. It's something so far away that your eyes cannot see. It's really in your mind.'

Deep into the race, Senna 'lost third and fifth gears at one point and just hooked it into sixth.' It stuck there. Patrese mounted an attack, hacking the gap to 20 seconds, but rain prohibited a final assault and Senna won by 2.991 seconds. 'I felt it was my duty to win in Brazil. (He was openly patriotic. 'My perfect day is to wake up at home in Brazil, at the farm or my beach house, with my family and friends, then go to a circuit anywhere in the world and be transported back home that evening.')

'I pushed the car regardless of the rain. I was also suffering from cramps and muscle spasms in my upper body, partly because the harness was slightly too tight, partly through emotion.' When he crossed the line and stopped he stayed in the cockpit, helmet off, head thrown back. 'I lost the engine completely and I couldn't re-start it. Then the pain was unbelievable. I tried to relax. I had such a huge pain in my shoulders and in my side I didn't know whether I should shout, cry or smile. I just didn't know what was going on.'

A few days later, after Sao Paulo, he was testing at Imola. Betise Assumpcao was there as his press person and since she was Brazilian herself I asked her about what you might call the Brazilian context.

'Like any other Latin country, you're really good when you're cool. There's an advertisement for cigarettes with Gerson, the 1970 World Cup footballer, and the translation of the slogan would be *You have to get the most out of everything*. To a Brazilian that means taking advantage, although in a good way. That's the cool way to be: take advantage of everything you possibly can in life, try to fool everybody, be smarter than them, shrewder. On the beach you adopt the laid-back way, take the mickey out of everybody and then there's sex and all that. Of course it's a macho thing. Senna is not that at all.

'Another thing. We say: "OK, see you at 7 o'clock" but everybody knows you won't. What to the Anglo-Saxons is five minutes is half an hour to Brazilians. If you arrive at the right time they'll say: "What are you doing here? I haven't even had my shower yet!" Senna is not like that at all. In fact he is exactly the opposite. He makes a point of being punctual, of doing everything he has to do in the right way. If he's late it's because he's been held up.

'Brazilians are supposed – in the eyes of other people – to laugh and be happy the whole time. Senna is not like that. It's not that he doesn't want people to like him, it's that he is not going to change the way he is just so that people will like him. The people have always liked him, but what is peculiar (in Brazil) is that a guy like Senna should be a hero. People go mad.

'When he went to his house in Sao Paulo after the Grand Prix there were 2,000 people in front of it. He couldn't get through and had to get into a police car to reach the house. The crowd stayed until one o'clock in the morning and the police asked Ayrton to come out. Otherwise the 2,000 would never have gone and the police began to fear there were bound to be some problems.

'Senna had to come out and stand on top of the three-metre wall with the trophy so that everybody could see him again, on the understanding that once they had seen him they'd disperse.

It's peculiar that the people like him the way they do, although of course he gets results.'

That Imola testing: a long-limbed girl, lycra stockings which go all the way up the limbs, wears a mini skirt not much longer than a bikini. She positions herself as near to the McLaren pit as she can get and insists she's come from Milan because she's an old friend of Ayrton. Her patience is rewarded. If he doesn't recognise her, he has the art of suggesting he does. They chat briefly while the photographers gorge. He smiles and she's thrilled. Is it – on her behalf – a publicity stunt? Has she hired one of the photographers? Has a photographer hired her? Who knows? To Senna: just another moment in just another test session.

Testing at Imola invariably attracts a crowd, which transmits the opposite of Latin warmth to Senna. Whenever he takes the McLaren out to combat the times Prost is setting in the Ferrari they jeer and taunt.

A sense of siege lay hard here. The McLaren motorhome, parked at the rear of the paddock some 30 or 40 yards from the pit, had a smoked-glass upper deck. Senna inhabited that. He didn't stray down to the cluster of tables in a cordoned off area along the flank of the motorhome. To reach the pit he emerged very suddenly, walked briskly across the paddock into a narrow valley between the transporters, passed into the bowels of the pit and instantaneously a mechanic drew a rope over the back of the pit. Senna inhabited the pit, sometimes almost in shadow. From time to time people called his name, a TV crew loomed, the long-limbed lady lingered. After his last run he raked over this and that with the engineers, emerged from the pit very suddenly and walked briskly towards the motorhome. The TV crew struggled to keep up with him – 'Ayrton, Ayrton' – and he disappeared into the smoked-glass upper-deck, refuge from the siege.

At Imola, Senna seemed more than usually preoccupied, sometimes de-briefing until past 10 in the evening. Betise explained it. 'He's trying to analyse the information the computer gives out. Now they have computers for everything, all the aerodynamics, suspension, everything – and to take an example, it gives the suspension performance in every corner. If you can't read it properly, you don't know what's happening and you can't use what the computer is saying to the full capacity. Senna wants to know everything. People show him graphics and the other day he said: "Is that good? Is that supposed to be good? Is that what it's supposed to be?" He is spending more time now in the briefings because he wants to analyse, to understand. You know what he's like. The engineers give him information but he wants to know why he goes up here and down there.'

A couple of weeks later he took pole for the San Marino Grand Prix and a wet race conjured a freakish parade lap. Prost hit water and floated off onto a grassy incline, where the Ferrari stuck. Berger also floated off but was able to use the incline to get back on. Green light. Senna tucked in behind Patrese waiting until the track improved. Ending lap 9 just before the pit lane straight he tucked inside and led. Patrese immediately pitted for slick tyres but, stationary, the engine wouldn't fire. Berger was behind Senna and they waded into back-markers. Who bothered about Patrese, who'd lost four laps in the pits, giving the Williams a run? Senna cut past him and cut past a back-marker thinking *well, I won't be seeing Patrese again for a while*. Senna accelerated. In short order Patrese took the back-marker, re-caught Senna and set fastest lap. Senna thought: *if the Williams is capable of that, what happens when it goes a full race distance?* That was the moment.

Senna won from Berger, and won Monaco from Mansell but the balance of the season began to change in Canada: Patrese and Mansell were on the front row. Senna's electrics failed but, as he'd been forecasting to anybody who'd listen, the car was not on the pace.

In Mexico he crashed heavily in first qualifying and finished the race third, Mansell won France, Senna third again, Mansell won Silverstone, Senna classified fourth but out of fuel. The first four races had given him a cushion and he still led the Championship with 51 points, Mansell 33, Patrese 22. Would the cushion be big enough?

A week before the German Grand Prix, Senna tested at Hockenheim and crashed in the first chicane at some 186mph. Evidently a rear tyre blew, the McLaren pitched 15 feet into the air, vaulting savagely. He hurt his neck and shoulder. He raced.

'I have to be honest. We haven't had much progress since Imola, both on the engine and the car despite some efforts which have been made.' The Grand Prix? A loop of film you'd seen before, Mansell wringing the Renault engine. Patrese moved up to second, and Senna and Prost contested third.

Prost came strong, eased, calculated. Eight laps remained. Prost moved into Senna's slipstream and they travelled together into a gentle right curve, together down a straight, together into the next gentle right curve towards the mouth of the chicane. Prost went left. Senna covered that. Prost went further left, abreast now but the mouth of the chicane yawned into a tight right clamp. Senna moved from mid track further across and a vice tightened on Prost as the chicane tightened towards him: he had two wheels on the edge of the track. Senna flicked clear and on to the racing line, Prost hemmed, nowhere to go except the escape road. Little plumes of smoke rose from Prost's tyres as he dipped the brake pedal. He struck a cone guarding the escape road entrance and the Ferrari chewed it. Prost parked.

Senna held fourth until the last lap when he ran out of fuel again. It enraged him; Prost enraged, too, claimed Senna had blocked him unacceptably and 'then drove across me, braking in a strange way, weaving.' If, Prost added, this happens again 'I'll just have to push him off.'

'I think everyone knows Prost by now,' Senna said. 'He is always complaining about the car or the tyres or the team or the mechanics or the other drivers or the circuit. It's always somebody else to blame. It's never his fault. He overshot under braking, he risked a lot there, he could have put himself into an accident and also involved me in that. Fortunately we didn't touch but he almost cost me an accident and almost cost himself an accident too.' Senna 51, Mansell 43, Patrese 28, Prost 21.

In Hungary, Prost and Senna made up amid chaotic scenes. They went to the Elf motorhome to watch a video of Hockenheim and emerged into a scrummage of photographers. Prost, speaking softly, said it was time to bury the past.

Senna took pole from Patrese and Mansell. In second qualifying, he climaxed at 1:16.147 compared to Patrese's 1:17.379 and Mansell's 1:17.389. After the session Senna came up to the Press Room for the mandatory conference and as he passed I couldn't help applauding, one of those instinctive reactions you have when you've witnessed something extraordinary. He smiled that slow-burning, slightly shy smile.

Senna created the race of a craftsman, taking Turn One round the outside of Patrese. 'The car was very good out of the corner onto the main straight enabling me to control the race from the front.' Mansell moved past Patrese and finished 4.599 seconds behind Senna, now on 61, Mansell 49, Patrese 32.

Senna took pole again at Spa, but a tumult of a Grand Prix: Prost challenging Senna heavily for the lead at *La Source* hairpin. Mansell took Prost but Senna held him. After the pit stops for tyres the order had become Mansell, Alesi, Senna. The electrics on the Williams let go, and Senna attacked Alesi but 'as I pulled onto his tail coming out of the hairpin I went to change into fourth and I had a major problem with the lever, similar to Brazil. I managed to get sixth and found them all from third upwards so I never tried to go slower than this again.' Alesi's engine let go on lap 30, shifting the Championship further. Senna 71, Mansell 49, Patrese 34, Berger 28.

At Monza, Senna took a third consecutive pole and in the race Mansell needed to finish in front of him to keep the

Championship alive. Mansell did, winning it – Senna second. Senna 77, Mansell 59, Patrese 34. Senna's thinking: *This second place has reduced our future problems, because every race adds more pressure to them. They cannot afford NOT to finish.*

An alarming start in Portugal, Patrese fast, Mansell bursting from behind Berger, casting the Williams into Senna's path, forcing a knee-jerk reaction. Senna had to swivel to safety. 'Nigel steered his car towards mine, I must admit I let him through too easily. If this had happened at any other race I would have let the accident happen. I braked too hard at the first corner to avoid him and even so nearly lost the nosecone. I think Nigel chose the wrong strategy for the start. Nothing happened this time but next time I don't know …'

Mansell moved past Patrese and on lap 18 came in for tyres. Essentially it decided the Championship because the nut on the right rear wheel cross-threaded and the crew on it were trying to communicate that but their signals were taken to mean all's well. Mansell launched himself without the nut, the wheel rotated clean off and Mansell sat in the cockpit beating his fists on the steering wheel in frustration. The Williams team had to scamper to Mansell with a fresh wheel and fit it in the pit lane, even though that breached regulations. He'd emerge 17th, reach sixth before the black flag was hung for the work in the pit lane. Senna finished second. Senna 83, Mansell 59, Patrese 44.

The knot tightened in Spain. The drivers' briefing resembled, according to one team manager, 'a kindergarten full of millionaires.'

Berger reportedly tapped Mansell playfully on the ankle (he'd sprained it playing in a Press versus Drivers football match) and Mansell reacted with vehemence.

Balestre addressed the drivers on the subject of the conduct at Turn One in Estoril. Mansell took this personally and, the anger in the room rising, said plaintively that if he was involved in 'incidents' it always seemed to be raised, but if Senna was involved it wasn't.

Senna took this personally and invited Balestre to have a close look at film of all the races over the past couple of years and see how many 'incidents' Mansell had been involved in. Senna also used naughty words to describe Mansell.

Ah, well.

A damp race. Berger led, Mansell challenging Senna wheel-to-wheel, man-to-man, nerve-to-nerve, willpower-to-willpower. They veered together at the end of the long straight, closer, closer, closer. Their wheels were millimetres apart. 'That was man's stuff,' Frank Williams would say. 'I wish every circuit had somewhere like that.' On lap 13 Senna spun, Mansell just missing him. Senna dropped to sixth and, while Mansell churned out the laps in the lead, he finished fifth. Senna 85, Mansell 69, Patrese 48.

The position strengthened in qualifying in Japan. On the first day Berger took provisional pole from Senna and they maintained that in the second session. That evening Ron Dennis, Senna and Berger worked on a plan to capitalise.

At the green light, Berger set off to the left side of the track, Senna nearly up with him and occupying the right: a wall of McLarens. They rounded Turn One in order Berger, Senna, Mansell then through the wriggling corners towards the cross-over Berger stole clear, Senna hemming Mansell. That was the plan. And Mansell had to win the race. 'The biggest problem,' Berger said, 'was giving the tyres too hard a time in the beginning. I wanted to get as far away as possible.'

Mansell radioed the pits. *Don't panic. I'm biding my time.* There was not too much time because Berger would soon be out of reach and victory gone with him.

	Berger	Senna	Mansell
Lap 5	1:44.582	1:45.903	1:46.273
Lap 6	1:45.824	1:46.143	1:46.106
Lap 7	1:45.265	1:45.917	1:46.192

Mansell drew back from the bounce-suck-bounce air in Senna's slip-stream. Senna knew Mansell was 'having a hell of a time in the turbulence behind me.' How long could Mansell wait? It was time to move back onto Senna.

	Berger	Senna	Mansell
Lap 8	1:45.855	1:46.209	1:45.783
Lap 9	1:44.872	1:46.093	1:45.941

That brought Mansell up and he radioed *preparing to attack*. They crossed the line to begin lap 10, feeling for position along the start-finish straight to the right-handed Turn One. No attack here, not possible. They twisted into Turn One, Mansell on the most normal line. Without warning the car jumped wide, careered with two wheels on the kerbing, crossed the kerbing and churned the gravel run-off area. The car came to rest near the tyre wall. Mansell thought the problem was brakes.

Senna saw it. 'I cannot say I was sorry.' He thought he and Berger ought to enjoy themselves in a domestic competition and he caught Berger who, once 'I heard over the radio Mansell out' slowed to protect the engine.

Late in the race Senna confronted a dilemma. 'After our tyre stops I was having to drive 99.9 per cent and we had agreed earlier that whoever led for the opening stages would be allowed to win.' Senna hesitated to radio Dennis for confirmation because to surrender any victory violated his very nature. 'Eventually I asked the question but I couldn't hear the reply clearly over the radio and I knew nobody would believe me if I didn't give way. I backed right off to reduce the engine noise and asked again. Ron said yes, he wanted us to change positions. It hurt to do it but the pain was nothing compared with the feeling from a third World Championship.'

Senna now took the opportunity to deliver two broadsides against Balestre and the events of Suzuka 1989 and 1990. Senna sanitised his remarks for the television interview, although he was pungent enough. 'It has been the most competitive World Championship that I have ever competed in. Because we fought with different cars, different engines, different drivers and not inside the same team [Senna v Prost at McLaren] it was really tough. We started the year well and then we had a tough time from the fourth race onwards and, as you all know, it was a result of a lot of push from myself, from Gerhard to the team, to McLaren and to Honda and to Shell that we managed to get steps forward time after time, bit by bit, and we caught the Williams Renaults.

'Slowly we got closer to them, put pressure on them, won a couple of races at the critical part of the Championship in Hungary and Belgium, scored the right results when we couldn't compete with the Williams at all. When it came really to the time, we were able to do one and two, fantastic. Therefore it's been a memorable Championship, not only for me but I think in Formula 1 terms over the last few years. The year 1989 had a disgraceful end when I won the race and it was taken away. I was prevented from going to the podium – I was just about to go to it – by Balestre, and I never forget that [waves finger for emphasis]. The result of that was the 1990 Championship when we fought all the way, myself and Prost, and we came to the last race and pole position was set up in the wrong place.

'We agreed before the start of qualifying with the officials that pole position would be on the outside. Then after qualifying Balestre gave the order not to change and I found myself on the wrong side on pole. I was so frustrated I promised myself that if, after the start, I lost first place I would go for it in the first corner regardless of the result. I would go for it and Prost wouldn't turn into the first corner ahead of me and that's what took place and that was a result of the politician making stupid decisions and bad decisions. This year what happened?

'We fought all the way, myself, Nigel, Riccardo, and when we got to the end it was only myself and Mansell. We had a hard time the last two races (Portugal, Spain). I think Mansell pushed a little over the limit but I was able to compensate for it and avoid incidents and a bad final for the Championship. In this race I was prepared to do my very best to fight for it. I was going to drive hard but I was still going to try to avoid any incidents.

'First corner, everything under control, nobody tried anything silly, Nigel was working properly, he was not going crazy, nothing happened. It was a good race, it was a competitive race I fought with Gerhard later, we were fighting each other all the time. It was a great race, exciting for everyone and, as I said, I hope this will stand as an example for myself and everyone who is competing now and the people who are coming in the future.'

At the Press Conference for journalists, Senna used much less restrained language. '1989 was unforgivable. I still struggle to cope with that. I had a bad time with Balestre. You all know what took place here. They decided against me and that was not justice, so what took place over that winter was (expletive).

'In 1990, before we started qualifying, Gerhard and I went to the officials and asked them to change the pole position because it was in the wrong place. The officials said "yes, no problem." I got pole and then what happened? Balestre gave an order that we don't change pole. We said that it had been agreed. They said "no, we don't think so." That was really (expletive).

'I said to myself "OK, you try to work cleanly and do the job properly and then you get (expletived) by certain people. All right, if tomorrow Prost beats me off the line, at the first corner I will go for it and he better not turn in because he is not going to make it." And it just happened. I wish it hadn't. We were both off and it was an (expletive) end to the World Championship, it was not good for me and not good for Formula 1. It was the result of the wrong decisions and partiality from the people making them. I won the Championship. So what? It was a bad example for everyone.

'We have got to have fair decisions. Now we have that possibility with new management in the sporting authority [Max Mosley had replaced Balestre]. In the drivers' briefing today there was no theatre. It was a proper, professional job. When Max stood up to say just a few words he was sensible, intelligent and fair. I think anyone there was happy because there was no bullshit.

'I don't care (if I upset Balestre). I think for once we all must say what we feel. That's how it should be. In the past there have been (expletive) rules which say you cannot speak what you're thinking, you are not allowed to say someone made a mistake. We are in a modern world! We are racing professionals! There is a lot of money involved, a lot of image and we cannot say what we feel. We are not allowed because if you say what you feel you get banned, you get penalties, you pay money, you get disqualified, you lose your licence. Is that a fair way of working? It is not. I said what I thought [in 1989] and what took place afterwards was theatre.'

The crash of 1990? 'If you get (expletived) every single time when you're trying to do your job cleanly and properly by the system, by other people taking advantage of it, what should you do? Stand behind and say "thank you, yes, thank you." No, you should fight for what you think is right. And I really felt that I was fighting for something that was correct because I was (expletived) in the winter and I was (expletived) when I got pole. I tell you, if pole had been on the good side last year, nothing would have happened. I would have got a better start. It was a result of a bad decision. And we all know why, and the result was the first corner. I did contribute to it yes, but it was not my responsibility.'

What you make of this is up to you, which is why I've quoted Senna at such length, repetitions and all. I have to say Senna at Suzuka astonished many listeners – that a perceived injustice 12 months old could still smoulder within the man and then become a fire; that, equally, Senna would allow fate to control the events at Turn One rather than control them himself.

An endnote from Senna himself: 'Sometimes when I am out jogging I say to myself: "You have won three World Championships." I say it in different ways but I have absorbed it in a healthy way. It has come from hard work from me and others. It is a great achievement but achieved with a lot of logic.'

That's how he saw himself.

Chapter 12

FAITH, HOPE AND CHARITY

In 1992 the Williams-Renault proved to be absolutely superior and Nigel Mansell, driving it, was at the height of his powers. He won the Championship at Hungary and against this there was nothing that Senna or anybody else could do. Across *the* season, Senna conjured a pole position and three wins, but was fourth in the final table: Mansell's team-mate Patrese second, young Michael Schumacher third.

I propose to examine the season in a different way, by gathering up the reflections of very different people, including Mark Blundell, journalist Joe Saward, former team owner Roger Orgee, and the landlord of the Prince of Wales at Westbury-on-Trim, Richard Ellis.

Blundell made his up towards Grand Prix racing along the orthodox route – Formula 3, Formula 3000 – and became Williams test driver in 1990. A year later he made his race debut driving a Brabham. It was an uncompetitive car and when McLaren offered him a job testing for 1992 he accepted.

'I clocked on, as you might say, in late 1991, driving the McLaren MP4/6 [that season's car] at Estoril. My relationship with Ayrton had been to say hello and we'd acknowledge each other. Obviously I'd been at circuits where he'd been and I'd done the testing at Williams. If you sit in a car like the Williams you'll make your presence felt because of the machinery, and Ayrton is going to want to know who's driving it, but when I first went to McLaren all I knew of Senna was that he was the great Ayrton Senna. I'd seen him from the Brabham, coming past me many, many times.'

I want to stress that my interview with Blundell took place in

1993 – hence his use of the present tense – and that it had a contemporary feel to it.

'When he reached Formula 1 I'd only just started motor racing so he was one of the guys I followed to see how he got on. Now I was chief test driver. At that point other guys tested as well, Allan McNish, Jonathan Palmer, but anything that was going to be done I did. It was a big role because you're talking about one of the best teams over the last 10 years and lots of things will go through your hands. It's only going to get to the race driver when you've tried it. The team will put a seal of approval on it and say: "Yeah, let's run with that." If you are handling the bulk of it you try to make sure you steer it in the right direction.

'When the McLaren MP 4/7 [the 1992 car] came out I did about 60 per cent of the work on it and I can assure you it had problems, it wasn't right straight out of the box. We put a great deal of effort into sorting it and at the point when Ayrton tried it – and ran through the first part of the season as well – I think he appreciated I was doing a reasonable job. He was – what shall I say? – quite happy with my feedback and response. He was quite happy to take a considerable amount of my say-so and my thoughts.'

Did that responsibility intimidate you?

'No, because it is not in my nature to doubt myself. That is not being cocky. It's a way of saying I am confident in what I am doing. At the same point, people can always be wrong, sure. Nine times out of ten you're on the right side but now and again you'll make a mistake. My train of thought was that I'm a race driver as well as a tester. How would I like the car to handle in a race? What will be best for Ayrton and Gerhard when they get to the Grands Prix? I always tried to keep that in mind. It gave me a high, gave me a push.'

Were you starting to get closer to Senna?

'Obviously through the year I sat down with him on a number of occasions for discussions. Going through that year, I watched what went on within McLaren and outside McLaren where Ayrton was involved, and I attended a number of Grands Prix as a member of the McLaren team. The guy is under intense pressure from everywhere. He might give a cold-shoulder feeling to a lot of people, he might seem arrogant and that sort of thing but at some point he has to close down. There is only so much he can give. At times he flusters, at times he might react in an unusual way but he is there to do his job, which is driving the car, and there is no-one presently doing the job better. You have to understand that these days there is a lot more to a driver's life than simply the driving. But he is still focused on the prime point: what it is that is driving a racing car as quickly as possible around a track. I respect him in the way he handles the many points in a driver's life.'

The temperament and the outbursts?

'I think of it this way. My upbringing is probably a lot different to his. My culture is a lot different, so our outlooks on life will be somewhat different too. For an Englishman to turn round and do what Ayrton does would be frowned upon very heavily – and maybe the other way round, too – whereas in his country it might be taken as normal. It's like watching a game of Italian football and then watching a game in our Premier League. They are completely different games, not only because of the style of the football but because of the temperaments and the mentalities.

'The thing you do have to say about Ayrton is that the guy has presence. He'll walk in somewhere and there it is, the presence. That's become bigger and bigger as he has come up through the sport and he's achieved more and more. I think he set out to achieve that from the beginning. I am sure there are a number of people who don't like the guy but I am sure that same number of people would say "we respect him 100 per cent." He was incredibly demanding and maybe some in the team got peed off at times because of his demands, but all his demands have a reason.'

Did he ever do anything magical in the car and you thought I didn't think he could do that?

'I will be perfectly honest. No. That's my feeling because when we tested together there wasn't anything out of the ordinary. However, at a Grand Prix I'd have to say he'd turn in laps which were exceptional. You know, a guy in a Grand Prix situation is always going to be more pumped up, wound up, he'll draw on everything he has – because the Grand Prix time is it, is the goal. Ayrton will go out and do what he can to the maximum because that is his make-up.

'He is very thorough in all areas. He will make sure in his mind that everything has been done as he wants. I learnt from him to make sure you were comfortable with what was going on but also to put demands on people in key areas to make sure the job does get done. That's not whingeing, it is being constructive – to reach the goal. If that peed people off, at the end of it the benefit is there for everybody, and that is something he works on. People also know that Ayrton will reward whatever effort they put in by what he does with the car on the track. If you can create that within a team you've half the job covered and he does that very well.'

There's a lovely anecdote from John Love, long out of Formula 1 but attending a test session at Silverstone. 'I was just a face in the crowd.' Love stood outside the Marlboro McLaren pit as Senna emerged from it in the car. It happens like this: always around the mouth of the pit were journalists, photographers and the curious simply wanting a look, wanting proximity. The driver, emerging, has a safe path through them because they stand back or they are held back, but the driver makes the car move at surprising speed and has already twisted it rightwards into the pit lane. He's thinking of many things, what he's supposed to be doing with the car, what the car is supposed to be doing with him, how this adjustment or that will work: a different concentration to racing. Testing is a laboratory full of endless experiments, racing is their conclusion.

So he came out and twisted the wheel to take the McLaren sharp right along the pit lane and, in the blur of faces gaping, he recognised John Love – who he hadn't seen since 1985 – and waved a gloved hand to him. 'Ayrton remembered, he remembered me.'

How can a mind do this?

But he was only human, never claimed to be more or less.

Richard Ellis, the landlord, was a good friend of Steve Lincoln who'd raced Senna in Formula Ford 1600. At Brands Hatch that year 'Steve was driving a van Diemen and Senna did a lap in it – something like one and a half seconds quicker than Steve had been. Steve said: "I'd been driving it right on the edge of the envelope: I might get to Formula 1 but this guy's going to be World Champion." He became a great Senna fan and for patriotic reasons I supported Nigel Mansell. We had some fun teasing each other and in fact, when he was ill in hospital and Mansell won the World Championship then said he was leaving the Williams team, I wrote to Steve to cheer him up: *Williams are looking for a new driver, there's still a chance for you!'*

Lincoln died at the end of 1992, leaving a widow Suzi and three sons, Charlie, Rupert and Christian.

Roger Orgee, who'd helped Lincoln in the early days, was invited to the *Autosport* dinner in London's Park Lane that winter of 1992. 'Senna was there and Lyn my wife said I've got to go and get his autograph. I said I'm not sure you're supposed to do that at these sorts of dos. She said: "Well I am." So she wanders over with a menu and he signed it, got back, said "there you are." Then somebody said: "You couldn't do it for me, could you?" so she did it again. Then another one. He said: "I'll do one more!" And then she's walking out to go to the ladies, walking past Senna's table. He turned, looked and said: "Not you again!"'

By nature, Senna was protective of his religious beliefs because 'often I was misquoted or misinterpreted.' The result was an accumulation of general statements he'd made on the subject, or endless conjecture that he spent a lot of his time on aeroplanes and at race tracks reading The Bible.

For instance, in a 1989 interview with Anne Giuntini in the French sports paper *L'Equipe* he was asked about the link between motor racing, God and himself. 'It is everything. I am permanently seeking perfection. I want to improve in every respect. I spend my time pushing back limits. I like to constantly go further, to solve problems. The big challenge for me is always to find better solutions than other people. I want to be capable of doing better than other people. At the same time I feel that I possess a kind of strength that brings me nearer to God. It is difficult to explain, but it is what I feel. And I am lucky to have found this route to such a state of harmony.

'I want to learn and to know everything that faith can bring me, and to make other people understand it in the same way. Many people don't succeed in finding contentment because, in the world in which we live, what's white is white and what's black is black. And one final point. I would like to provide concrete proof that we can really push back our limits, that this strength we can find in ourselves does enable us to improve constantly.'

Thereby hangs a tale, although it breaks the strict chronological sequence of the narrative because it began at the end of 1992 and wasn't completed until August 1993. Never mind. The tale centres round Saward, then of *Autosport*, and it happened in what might appear a curious way, although in purely journalistic terms it wasn't. Securing interviews with celebrities is by no means an exact science.

In the 8 October 1992 issue of *Autosport*, Saward wrote an open letter to Senna. During the season, Senna had tried to join Williams, who were rumoured to have lured Prost from retirement for 1993. Senna claimed Prost blocked him joining the team and claimed, too, that this had been done 'in a cowardly way,' meaning Prost is frightened of having me as a partner.

Saward wrote: 'Everything is relative in Formula 1, isn't it? Look at your talent, for example. All those blokes out there are bloody good, even the ones driving the cars which do not qualify for the races. Racing reporters (who needs them, eh?) may sit around and discuss the finer points of Formula 1 drivers and their talents, but the truth is that you are all super-talented. It is just the extra few thousandths of a second which is worth all that lovely money which you superstars collect, as opposed to the debts that some of the pay-drivers manage to bury themselves under.

'What am I trying to say? Well, let's face it, everyone is expendable. You know that Formula 1 needs you and, I suppose, this gives you bargaining power, but remember – always remember – that back in the bad old days stars died more often than they retired and there were always new stars. There are new stars standing behind you now. OK, perhaps they are pale shadows of what you are but they are stars nonetheless. I do hope you were just posturing when you said you'd quit if you didn't get a good car ...

'And another thing. I don't understand this "Prost is a coward" business. Far be it for me to remind you, but a few years ago, when a Mr Warwick wanted to join Team Lotus, you blocked his arrival. You may say that Lotus wasn't capable of running two cars at the time and you were doing Derek a favour – look, you could argue, what happened to the man who became your team-mate, Johnny Dumfries.'

Saward concluded: 'Remember when Fangio said you were a great champion but not a great sportsman. And you said you would try to achieve that. Well, I don't think this is the way to achieve that goal. See you in Australia.' That, of course, was the Australian Grand Prix on 8 November, last of the season.

During race weekend at Adelaide, Lee Guag, the long-time Goodyear tyre man, had a farewell party and Saward says 'Ayrton and I were sitting opposite one another. I'd written the Open Letter which basically said "stop messing about and get on with the driving" and this had been faxed to him about 15 times by Jo Ramirez because Jo Ramirez thought he should read it. At some point down the line Ayrton obviously had read it, as he did read things, and was upset. About halfway through the dinner – and we were supposed to be bidding goodbye to Lee, who was sitting there with pneumonia – Ayrton suddenly said: "Why do you write this rubbish?"'

Saward: 'I wrote it because it's true.'

Senna: 'No, it's not.'

Saward: 'If it's not true, prove it to me.'

Senna: 'It's not true. Why should I trust the press?'

Saward: 'Well, why don't you try? Have you tried it with me?'

Senna: 'No, I haven't.'

Saward: 'OK, try it with me sometime.'

Like a good and dogged journalist, Saward made a formal application for a personal interview with Senna (via Betise Assumpcao) 'months and months and months' in advance of it actually taking place. Very often, it is what you had to do. A mass Press Conference was a different matter, but the rarity of a one-on-one was something else and, from Senna's point of view, a genuine concession to be carved out of the valuable moments over a race weekend.

In fact, Saward only got the interview by default. 'He wouldn't do the one-on-one but Betise put me together with, I think, some Belgian journalists who really didn't have that much grasp of English. This was at the Hungaroring in August 1993, eight months after Adelaide. It must have been following a qualifying session because Senna wore his racing gear. I remember that it had been an extremely hot day, it gets clammy-hot there and so the paddock cleared very quickly. Basically, the paddock was clear of all the wombats [hangers-on constantly coming up to Senna].

'We sat at a table outside the McLaren motorhome. There were two or three questions from the others, about his feelings on McLaren and so forth, then they just sat there. I said to him at the start: "I want it to be nothing to do with motorsport, I'm not interested in that on this particular occasion." It began in a very *bristly* way, because we'd known each other for about ten years without really talking. We talked about sex, religion, education, politics and he also talked about leaving McLaren. Did I raise the matter of religion or did it just gravitate to that? We discussed the non-motor racing related topics that human beings discuss and it came up because it was a very important part of his life, and one which I think was much underestimated. What Senna was doing was trusting a journalist, and he was trusting me because I'd said: "Give me a chance before you judge me." It was good of him, it really was.' The discussion continued, as Saward remembers, 'until we ran out of time because it got dark!'

Autosport carried the interview extensively and it included these Senna words: 'I have been questioned many times about religion and often I was misquoted or misinterpreted. Sometimes it was by accident, sometimes to do me damage, but I think it is worth talking about because in this godless world there are lots and lots of people looking for religion. They are desperate for it. I am only being truthful. I am saying what I believe and what I feel. You offer religion to those who want it. If you don't do that, they will not have the opportunity to look and see. Some people may not understand you and do not have a clear opinion, some will understand because they are open enough to understand what you are talking about. It is for them that it is worth it.

'You can have it if you want. It is a question of believing it and having faith, of wanting it and being open to the experience. I think there is an area where logic applies and another where it does not. No matter how far down the road you are in understanding and experiencing religion, there are certain things which we cannot logically explain. We tend always to understand what we can see: the colours, the touch and the smell. If it is outside that, is it crazy? I had the great opportunity to experience something beyond that. Once you have experienced it, you know it is there, and that is why you have to tell people.

'You have to need it and you have to want it and you have to be open to it. It is tough, but life isn't easy. Anyone can achieve easy things: the tough ones are things that some achieve and some do not. I am still at the beginning. I am like a baby in this respect. You have to work on it. It is a difficult thing and it is much more difficult alone.' He added: 'You can be logical or stupid but you are not in control of everything that is happening with your life.'

Later in the interview Senna said: 'We go into millions of homes by way of television and people feel close to us, but at the same time they are far away. They have no idea what we are really like. They dream of watching a race live or getting to see one of us and perhaps if they had the opportunity they would see that we are just people, that there is nothing magic.'

And …

'The wealthy can no longer continue to live on an island in a sea of poverty. We are all breathing the same air. People have to have a chance, a basic chance at least.' He talked of marriage and children. 'That will happen when I have the right girl and we feel it is the right moment for us.'

Thereby hangs another tale, and one which I relate with a certain caution because it cropped up almost inadvertently in conversation with an FIA official. At the time, the official and his partner wanted a child and were considering adoption. The official was at a test session at Silverstone, was in the McLaren motorhome and mentioned it to Senna who, as he remembers, 'immediately picked up his mobile phone, rang his sister in Brazil and started to organise it!' The official quietened him, saying they were only considering adoption.

The most obvious interpretation is that Senna would instinctively try and help someone over something so important. The official and I mull it over and we conclude that, all in the moment, Senna's logic probably unfolded in two directions simultaneously. 1) Here is someone I can help. 2) In doing so, I can give one Brazilian orphan not just a chance, not just a basic chance, but a very good chance. *Therefore*, where's my phone?

There can be no doubt that Ayrton Senna experienced terrible disquiet when he surveyed the poverty of his own country, a disquiet compounded because he witnessed it getting worse. There can be no doubt either that he experienced the anguish of helplessness because even his will-power, even his multi-millions, even the use of his all-pervading name could never alleviate the plight of so many impoverished souls existing one remove from animals. That would not prevent him setting in motion an attempt to do exactly this and, after his death, others – the Foundation – making it happen.

In December, courtesy of Emerson Fittipaldi, Senna flew to the Firebird Raceway, Phoenix, to try a Penske IndyCar.

Rick Rinaman was there. 'I'm crew chief for Emerson. I had not met Senna and, of course, before you have a personal impression you take what you have heard or read. The papers over here had long written that he was a hothead, temperamental when things didn't go his way, so that was my impression going in. It was my car that was being used – Emerson's car – so I had to work on getting Senna to fit into the tub, make seat belt adjustments and so on. The thing that surprised me so much was that the guy was a gentleman to everybody. He was professional, he made sure he went up and introduced himself to everybody there. It was quite an experience for us all. Nobody was left out. You didn't have to be high on a pedestal for him to talk to you.

'Emerson went out first and did quite a few laps and got some respectable times, he came in and then I put Senna in the seat.

No, no, he hadn't had a seat fitting so he sat in Emerson's seat. The pedals, the seat belt straps were all different because he wasn't as tall as Emerson. I was ready to start adjusting everything to fit him but he said "oh, no, that's OK, don't go to any trouble." We put the seat belts on him and they were loose. I said "I'll just tighten this strap" but he repeated "oh, no, don't go to any trouble." He had to reach for the pedals – so we did very little to actually get him comfortable. He was going out to do some shakedown running to feel how the car handled.

'So out he went, warmed the car for a couple of laps, came back in and said everything was all right. Out he went again and stood on it for two laps – a track he's never been on, a car he's never been in – and in about three laps he was quicker than Emerson (chuckle). I mean, everybody was just in awe. Back he came and of course everybody, the engineers, myself, and Rick Mears (an IndyCar great) gathered round the car to hear his comments on it. Listening to this guy explain what this car was doing was unbelievable. The guy was able to tell you things about what the car was doing that I had never heard *our* drivers explain before. He was telling us when the ground effects would give up, when the suspension was working and when the downforce was working. It was an amazing amount of information he gave to us in about five minutes. He left an impression on everybody there which was like *when are you coming over here?* (chuckle).

'He left, I am sure, with a good feeling in that you want to do something but you have something else that you need to finish first (the Formula 1 career). I would have bet anything in the world that the guy would have been over here doing IndyCar within the next few years and he would have been outstanding, oh, absolutely. We talk about it nearly every day.'

Chapter 13

DONINGTON

Honda withdrew from Grand Prix racing at the end of 1992, and McLaren then ran Ford engines. Against the Williams-Renault and Alain Prost, nobody had a chance any more than they had had against Mansell the year before. The Williams-Renault would be faster, more consistent, in fact overwhelming At this juncture, Senna conjured from deep within himself something between creative and tactical genius, and it was so strong that he led the Championship to Canada, the seventh round. Few drivers in the whole history of it could have done this; perhaps only he.

Prost won South Africa by an *age* (1m 19s) from Senna and that clearly was the first overwhelming. An interesting vignette, though. Rubens Barrichello, a fellow Brazilian of course, made his debut driving a Jordan Hart. 'My first race, Kyalami, Ayrton came to me to say that if I needed anything I could go and ask him and he'd try and help. That was really good.' That perhaps begins to explain what had developed by Imola 1994, when Barrichello crashed; but all in good time.

It rained in Brazil, Prost never liked the rain, Senna always did, and he led the Championship 16–10. Senna's postview: 'This was one of my best victories, although not as good as 1991. In these conditions you need everything working for you, the whole team, to win. I didn't have a car fast enough to keep up with the Williams but it ran trouble free all the way and to see the crowd … that's something you have to experience for yourself.'

Ramirez says that 'after the race I've never seen anybody so happy. It was absolutely hilarious. We had a party in one of the discotheques and we were throwing him up in the air and Pele was there and it was … fantastic. Ayrton really, really enjoyed that.' Yes, and talked and celebrated so much he had a sore throat for a week and needed antibiotics.

Brazil was more significant than that, though. During the Grand Prix, Senna met Adriane Galisteu. She was doing promotional work there and could barely believe it when he showed an interest in her. In her book, her account of their falling in love seems to suggest he was far from a playboy/ladykiller. He proved to be a little shy and hesitant over their initial contacts.

'He used to call Adriane on the radio from the plane and I had to get the connection,' Owen O'Mahony the pilot says. 'One time she was in New York and he rang the number twice but no reply, she must have been out. I said to him, "Ayrton, this is love, isn't it?" He said "*hmmm*"' – which O'Mahony took to mean yes. 'She was a lovely girl and I have a photograph of her and I cuddling. She was very tactile and I showed the photo to Ayrton. I said: "There you are, this shows you she prefers older men" and he said: "Owen, I will remember this when it comes to your next contract!"'

Tom Wheatcroft owned and had restored Donington Park. For years he'd coveted a Grand Prix there and now he had one, called the European, third race of the season. Those who insist English weather is all four seasons on any one day would not have been disappointed. It gave Senna a chance. Wielding the creative and tactical genius, he overwhelmed Prost, and the Williams, and the mighty Renault engine, and the other 23 drivers in the race.

Naturally the Williamses of Prost and Damon Hill filled the front row of the grid, then Schumacher and Senna. Rain had fallen and then stopped before the race although only JJ Lehto (Sauber) risked dry tyres. Senna's thinking as he reached the grid and settled: *I'll really go for it before the Williams have time to settle. Because they hold technical superiority, that's the tactic.*

A fast change from red to green, Prost off securely enough, Hill close to Prost, Schumacher mid-track, Karl Wendlinger

(Sauber) surging alongside Schumacher then going to mid-track. That elbowed Schumacher who elbowed Senna, forcing him so far that he put two wheels on to the triangle which bisected the grass and the pit lane exit, a triangle painted blue and white and very slippery.

Senna twisted the McLaren back so sharply he went across the track and tried to go inside Schumacher into Redgate, a long horseshoe right. The exact positioning: Prost on the racing line and clear, Hill slotting in, Wendlinger deep to the inside behind Hill, Senna behind Wendlinger, Schumacher coming to the inside; couldn't – Senna already in occupation.

Rounding the second part of the horseshoe Prost moved to mid-track, Hill followed Prost there and Wendlinger followed Hill there, Schumacher still on the outside. It left an open channel inside. Senna turned late into that channel, the horseshoe folding from him, two wheels riding the boundary line of the circuit. He'd shed Schumacher.

They travelled downhill to the left-and-right of the Craner Curves, Senna pitching the McLaren *outside* Wendlinger and describing an enormous arc.

Third.

'I saw him in the mirrors,' Wendlinger says, 'and I could see the way he was driving. I knew his reputation in the wet and I knew precisely what he was going to do. I decided I'd better leave some room. I didn't want to go out of the race there and then.'

Ron Dennis says 'he knew the exact limit of the car and drove aggressively.'

They travelled up the incline to Starkeys Bridge, a left. Senna caught Hill. Out of Starkeys, Senna came up level but on the inside, perfect for McLeans Corner, a right. Senna had the McLaren deep to that inside and went through.

Second.

'I made a bad start,' Hill says. 'I'd actually thought I could get ahead of Alain into Redgate and if I had I'd have pushed hard to get away because in the wet the guy behind can't see while the leader has a clear track, although balanced against that is the danger of not knowing exactly how the track will be. I was a bit peeved to be behind Alain, I couldn't really see, and my concern was to stick with him and hopefully we'd pull away from the people following. You can't see what's going on behind you: you certainly see there's a car behind, and you might just make it out as a red car or a white car or something, but you don't know which car until it is alongside. I might have fought the corner but it was very early in the race for a risk like that. When he got past me I thought *for God's sake, Ayrton!* Then I thought *hold him up, Alain. Make sure you don't let him get ahead.'*

Around Coppice, a curving right, Senna gained on Prost. Along Starkeys Straight he gained on Prost, through the Esses – flick-left, flick-right – he caught him. They travelled towards the Melbourne Hairpin. Senna lined the McLaren up mid-track, Prost outside him, and seized the inside. Both cars slithered but Senna now seized the hairpin.

First.

Lap 1:	Senna	1:35.843
	Prost	1:36.541
	Hill	1:36.963

Of the millions of laps driven since the modern era of the World Championship began in 1950, no-one can or ever will know which is the best. It is too immense and subjective a matter, but no-one can reasonably doubt that this 1 minute 35.843 seconds is a prime candidate.

Ramirez, in the pits, says: 'I will never forget that lap. He'd psyched them out, demoralised the whole lot of them. He won the whole race on that first lap. I saw him go by in the lead and I thought *it can't possibly be. How can it be? How can he have that advantage? The Williamses must be on dry tyres.* I watched and no, they were on wet tyres, same as us.' Ramirez was well aware of how good Senna was in the wet – everybody knew that, 'superman in the wet' – and he had 'a lot more feeling than most other drivers in the wet. Our car was perfect for the wet conditions but even so …'

Lap 2:	Senna	1:27.882
	Prost	1:31.429
	Hill	1:32.003

'I began to think maybe I'd been mistaken about the tyres on the Williamses,' Ramirez says. 'Second lap I ran to the pit lane wall but no mistake, wet tyres same as us. I was still thinking *how can this guy have this incredible advantage?* I believe Williams had problems with the gearshift. Changing down they were locking the back wheels, meaning their cars were very difficult to drive but even so …'

Lap 3:	Senna	1:28.203
	Prost	1:30.722
	Hill	1:30.908

The order solidified – Barrichello an inspired fourth, then Alesi, then Schumacher. This order endured to lap 16 when Alesi pitted for slicks, Hill and Schumacher a lap later. Senna a lap after that, Prost a lap after that. Order: Senna, Prost, Hill, Alesi, Barrichello, Schumacher, all on dries. The lap charts would assume surreal proportions, pock-marked by pit stops in bewildering profusion – so many that the Williams team ran out of new tyres. The times, lap 20:

Senna	29m 45.973
Prost	at 5.141
Hill	at 6.913

The race might have been plucked from Senna on lap 21. Through Coppice he came upon Christian Fittipaldi and Blundell scrapping among themselves. Down Starkeys Straight, Blundell moved out to take Fittipaldi at the instant Senna moved out to take both of them. Blundell reached the flick-left of the Esses but his momentum took him fastforward and off. Fittipaldi, seeing Blundell go, twitched left into the mouth of the Esses and found Senna already there. Senna went on to the kerbing and they nudged wheels.

'Yes. I was scrapping with Fittipaldi,' Blundell says. 'It was one of those races where conditions were poor but it started to dry. There was only one dry line. Unbeknown to me Senna sat behind us, making us into a little trio. I made my manoeuvre to go by Fittipaldi, Senna ducking and diving trying to go by the pair of us. I went on to the damp patch of the circuit and, to be brutal about it, went in too deep and couldn't gather it all up. I had to continue straight on: no adhesion. Only at that point, when I was stationary sitting there in the cockpit, did I see Senna going through. I suppose he had to slow up somewhat anyway because Fittipaldi would have been in a bit of a state.

'Drivers do keep tabs on what is going on. You do look in your mirrors for an amount of the time but when you're scrapping at 180mph to 200mph the level of concentration and effort has to go up another level: you're calculating the element of risk. If there is someone behind you, or a pack behind you, with a big speed differential they'll soon be on you. And there was a big differential with Senna, as we saw when he just went off into the distance from the first lap. Things come at you within seconds so you can't always be 100 per cent on top of it.'

Raindrops fell, plump and getting plumper. Prost pitted for wets on lap 22, Hill two laps later, to steal an advantage over Senna – but this might be dangerous. How wet would the track be in another five minutes, 10, 20? How dry? England in April, remember. Senna on the roulette wheel was staying with dries as the drizzle hardened to rain. Advantage Prost? No.

	Senna	Prost	Hill
Lap 24	1:26.363	1:27.015	1:30.772
Lap 25	1:26.210	1:26.552	1:47.749
			(after his stop)
Lap 26	1:26.365	1:27.720	1:27.249
Lap 27	1:26.249	1:27.291	1:28.607
Lap 28	1:27.617	1:26.441	1:27.706

You can almost hear the continuous dialogue backwards and forwards – *Prost's just done a quicker lap than you Ayrton* – even though the order had become Senna, Alesi, Prost, Barrichello, Hill, Herbert. Senna held a lead of more than 20 seconds over Alesi, more than 30 seconds over Prost. By staying out, Senna had established enough of a lead to pit and retain that lead – and Alesi would have to stop soon, too. The rain eased to drizzle but Senna pitted for wets on lap 28 – and did retain the lead.

	Senna	Prost	Hill
Lap 30	1:28.789	1:27.040	1:28.827
Lap 31	1:29.433	1:26.221	1.30.219
Lap 32	1:27.562	1:25.544	1:29.625

Order: Senna, Prost, Barrichello, Hill, Alesi, Herbert. On lap 33, the track drying, Prost gambled and pitted for dries, and a lap later Senna followed. It cost him the lead.

'Something went wrong on the right rear-wheel but those guys are really under pressure. It's motor racing.' A wheelnut cross-threaded, holding Senna stationary for 20 seconds. Prost led by some seven seconds. And the rain returned. It forced Prost to pit for wets on lap 38, Hill on lap 41. Senna stayed out, balancing his skill against the weather, the McLaren dancing a bit but never out of overall control. It was a master at work at the crux of a race.

	Senna	Prost	Hill
Lap 42	1:25.686	1:28.293	1:45.381
Lap 43	1:26.460	1:26.119	1:25.260
Lap 44	1:24.166	1:26.503	1:25.359

By lap 46 Senna had dipped into the 1 minute 23s, Prost at the 1 minute 27s, the track drying. Prost had to gamble again or lose the race. He pitted for dries on lap 48 and stalled, the clutch misbehaving. Order when it re-settled: Senna, Barrichello, Hill, then Prost, Herbert and Patrese (Benetton) a lap down. On lap 53 Prost pitted for the sixth time to change his left rear – he'd felt a puncture – and Barrichello pitted on lap 55, so Senna led the European Grand Prix by a lap. 'Ayrton and the team worked well,' Ramirez says. 'We did less pit stops than the others so we were gaining time and when he led by a lap it was unbelievable, unbelievable.'

And the rain came back. Senna entered the pit lane for wets, ran urgently down the pit lane, waved a gloved hand at the pit crew and – kept on! 'I was calling on the radio "wets, wets, wets" and I came in but the crew weren't ready. I could see them wheeling the tyres from the garage so I went back out.' Forgive the crew. It was the only moment of disharmony in this improbable, incomparable afternoon. Mind you, by entering the pits you avoided going all the way round Goddards: a considerable economy.

Senna's pit lane run gave him fastest lap of the race, something unique and surreal of itself.

Senna covered another lap and decided to stay out 'to see if I could hang on,' but Hill unlapped himself. Senna pitted for wets on lap 66 – 'the rain got worse and I had to come in.' Hill and Prost responded by pitting themselves but by now the team had no more new sets and had to fit used ones. Forgive them. Hill changed on laps 17, 24, 34, 41, 50 and 68. Prost on 19, 22, 33, 38, 48, 53 and this lap of 69.

In the gathering murk Senna eased across the final few laps, the rain harder. The full magnitude of his achievement:

Senna 1h 50m 46.570
Hill at 1m 23.199
Prost at 1 lap
Herbert at 1 lap
Patrese at two laps
Barbazza at two laps

Dennis: 'Donington was one of the best strategic races we have ever had, one where we were in complete harmony.'

Ramirez: 'After that race Ayrton felt ever so well. He loved it, he really enjoyed it.'

Senna: 'I don't know how many times we stopped for tyres (slow smile). I think it's surely the record in any race. Driving with slicks in damp and very slippery conditions was a tremendous effort because you just don't get the feeling from the car, you have to commit yourself to certain corners and you can be off the circuit. Conditions like this is gambling and it's taking chances that pay off and we gambled well. I feel very light about it all. I wish I could go home and have another party like Brazil. Then I would have another week of bad throat and antibiotics but I would go through it again. We won as a group. So many things happened that I find it hard to remember.'

Subsequently Senna would add to this. 'That race told me everything to myself. It was what I wanted to prove to myself.' And: 'A natural tendency for a driver, as long as he is able to do his job with a team, is to learn continuously. Experience only adds to your driving, provided you can keep your motivation at a single level. I think that's the case almost every year of my career from 1984, always just a little bit better – not necessarily faster but more consistent, less susceptible to mistakes, thinking always, always, always. That experience allows you to be a step ahead all the time, ready to make the next move in a race.'

Like at Donington three pit stops ahead? 'Whatever …'

Two footnotes, the first from Barrichello. 'Donington was one of the races where I felt I was able to do something special. I had a great start and from 12th on the grid I completed the first lap fourth and I felt at home in the wet. The conditions made my car more equal with the others and I was doing really well.' He reached second place on lap 49 and held it for seven laps before a mechanical problem halted him. 'It was very sad not to finish, especially with Ayrton on the podium. I didn't have a chance to speak to him afterwards but I saw the interview he gave to Brazilian TV and he was feeling sad as well that I hadn't been on the podium.'

The second is from the pilot O'Mahony. 'Usually I'd wait at the airport for Ayrton to come back, and I'd try and watch the race on television, which I managed to do 99 times out of 100. However, if it wasn't possible and I didn't know the result when he did come back, you couldn't tell whether he had won or lost. I watched Donington on a TV in the control tower at East Midlands Airport and I had a mobile phone. We were due to take off at 6.0 or whatever. The phone rang, hell of a noise in the background. It was Ayrton from the track. He drank very rarely and when he did drink he didn't drink much but he became squiffy – not drunk, just *squiffy*. "Well done, that was bloody amazing."'

'Owen, I think we'll go tomorrow, not tonight!'

The rest of 1993 has drifted into memory, punctuated by winning Monaco. Prost took pole from Schumacher, Senna second row but directly behind Prost, despite an accident. 'It was caused by some bumps at the exit to the tunnel. The car didn't handle them too well and I lost it. More than a crash it was a scratch.' He'd hurt his hand.

At the start Prost crept a fraction before the green light and took the lead – he'd be penalised with a 10-second stop 'n' go for the crawling but not yet – Schumacher and Senna following. The hand proved 'a problem because the difference between going flat out at Monaco or only at 90 per cent is crucial. The shunt made me lose my edge a bit.' He'd thought it through the night before: 'I knew I couldn't take the lead. I had to cope with the speed of the Williams so I hoped that their tyre wear would be worse than mine. Prost jumped the start, perhaps in desperation to get to the first corner, a result of the pressure I exerted even though I was behind him. Things went my way but I had a plan and I stuck to it.'

Prost's 10-second penalty, compounded by his stalling twice trying to accelerate from it, deposited him 22nd. Schumacher, maturing, led comfortably but on lap 33 the hydraulics failed. Senna made no mistake for the rest of the race and that was his sixth Monaco win. (This total beat the record of five set by Hill's father Graham between 1963 and 1969.)

A couple of footnotes, the first from pilot O'Mahony. At Monaco he said to Senna he should take all Adriane's 'credit cards away and don't give her any of your credit cards.' He replied that it wasn't a problem. 'She's the best girl I've ever found. All she wants to do is to go to McDonald's!'

The second is from Barrichello. 'I went to him in Monaco because I didn't know the way round (no testing, because the circuit is public roads, and no chance to familiarise yourself) and we talked – but he was a busy man so I never wanted to bother him. I think he liked me because he was so good to me and many times he helped in set-ups of the car, things like that.'

The superiority of Williams was beyond even Senna to contain, and Prost took the Championship in Portugal with a couple of races to spare. The shape of Formula 1 seemed to be altering: Prost moving into retirement, Senna moving to Williams. He showed two distinct facets of his character in the last two races. At Suzuka, young Eddie Irvine (Jordan) unlapped himself by moving past Senna while Senna was trying to take Hill.

Afterwards Senna found Irvine and cuffed him. His last race for McLaren was Australia.

He found the moments before the start at Adelaide 'incredibly tough. I had to keep my feelings very much under control because in those moments the emotions were taking over. The last half hour was very hard – these emotions kept coming back, making me feel very uneasy. I wanted to do the best for the team and myself..I had to win the race. That is why I had to keep my emotions under control.' Ramirez – who Senna sensed was in similar mood – came near him two or three times with the minutes ticking and Senna 'couldn't cope.'

Ramirez says: 'Yes, I was emotional and it was sad. I tried not to think it will be the last time.' Nor can it have helped that Ramirez said he'd forgive him for leaving if he won the race.

With no more than five minutes left Senna started the process of clearing his mind and he led virtually the whole race, beating Prost by 9.259 seconds. As Senna crossed the line, a complete era ended. He'd first driven for McLaren in 1988, and between there and here had taken 46 pole positions, won 35 races and his three World Championships.

In December 1993 Senna took Adriane and competed in a kart meeting at Bercy, Paris. Former Grand Prix driver Philippe Streiff, paralysed in a 1989 testing accident, had had the idea of creating a kart meeting to raise money for charity. Streiff 'didn't really know Senna before my accident because I was competing at another level (in mid-ranking teams). I do remember one year, after the Japanese Grand Prix and before the Australian Grand Prix, we went to Bali: Boutsen, Alliott and myself. We stayed at the Club Med and we arrived in the afternoon, he arrived in the evening. We threw a surprise party for him. He seemed very tired and while we were there he slept a lot.

'When I had the idea for the karts I got Prost to agree to drive. At Monaco in 1993 I went to the McLaren motorhome – I remember it so well – and asked Ayrton if he'd compete. He said yes he would and he also said: "I began my career karting and I'll probably end it karting!" No question that he wouldn't come because Prost would be there. We did, however, have a problem because Senna was with McLaren who used Shell fuel and Elf were our main sponsors – they'd come in with Prost. Senna's advisers pointed out that his contract with McLaren ran to 1 January 1994, 15 days after Bercy. I found a way round this. I spoke to all the people concerned and it was agreed that he – only he – would run with TAG Heuer on his kart.

'It was resolved only in early December. He was due before the FIA in Paris over the Eddie Irvine incident – when he'd hit Irvine, a silly matter really and I was due to see him afterwards. The FIA meeting went on longer than foreseen and Julian Jakobi [Senna's manager] rang me to say Ayrton wouldn't be able to make our meeting. He did though manage to give a brief interview to *L'Equipe* that evening and they asked if he would be at Bercy. He explained the problem. I met him next day before he flew back to Brazil and he said: "Yes, I am coming if I can." When everything was sorted out I rang him in Brazil – it must have been midnight in Paris, nine at night over there and he'd just finished water-skiing – and it was on then. Because he would be coming specially, I sent him an aeroplane ticket but he never used it. He could have simply given it to a relative or a friend to use if he didn't want it for himself but, no, he didn't. He paid for himself, and none of the drivers were being paid for competing. This was for charity.

'When he arrived I explained that his French fan club had taken 500 seats and of course there would be the usual press coverage, which was important to the event. He was wonderful. There was no antagonism between him and Prost. They chatted about this and that, and I have some lovely photographs of them together smiling. In fact, when Prost won, Senna was applauding. The competition was on the Saturday and Sunday and Ayrton flew back to Sao Paulo that night. He was in the office at eight o'clock the next morning telling people how much he had enjoyed himself.'

Mike Wilson attended Bercy with his son and daughter. 'Ayrton and I spoke a bit but there were so many people round him all the time, young kids, even grown-up men asking for his autograph. I said: "It must be difficult to go anywhere" and he said: "Yes, but you learn to live with this. It would be nice for me to walk down the Champs Élysees, just me and my girlfriend, walk down and do some shopping, but unfortunately it is not possible. I'd be stopped every five metres."

'At Bercy each driver had his personal room upstairs where he could change. After the racing he called us up. He had three hats and he put one on me and dedicated it to me. He wrote on it *to Mike, with admiration. Ayrton Senna*. He gave one to my daughter which said to *Anna, with love* and one to my son which said to *Alex with admiration*. He also gave me a gold-plated key ring and that was touching. If people didn't know him well, they found it very difficult to understand how good a man he was. This was the other side of Senna that not many people saw.

'Since his death, there's been a lot on television about him and half the time I can't even watch because I get that feeling in my throat where you stop swallowing. I've three or four videos, one of which comes from Brazil, but I find it difficult to watch all the way through. It shows you the other side of him, when he was back in Brazil and he's playing with his nephews, he's out on the sea and he's smiling all the time and he's enjoying himself. Few people saw that side and that was the problem. I did actually know the other side of Senna. I'd go into the bar when Formula 1 was on television and people would say "oh, Senna blah blah blah" but I didn't start anything because it would have been a continual argument. They didn't know what they were saying because they didn't know him at all.'

Chapter 14

TRADING PLACES

The official presentation of Ayrton Senna after he departed Marlboro McLaren for Williams, replacing the retired Prost, was made in October 1993. There were fewer undercurrents than you might imagine. By nature, Formula 1 activists are defensive and/or outright secretive, measuring out enough information to fill a kind of façade but rarely allowing a glimpse of what lies behind it – but the presentation, in the conference centre behind the then Williams factory at Didcot, proved candid and extremely amusing. Senna allowed many glimpses of his impish, waspish sense of humour, and it really didn't matter that he happened to be in Sao Paulo at the time, not Didcot.

It was two presentations, in fact: Frank Williams and Damon Hill here, Senna there and a phone link-up between. Because what followed sometimes – tantalisingly – went behind the façade, here were the principals speaking entirely for themselves.

Ayrton Senna and Damon Hill in the Championship in 1994. Perhaps you could give us your comments on that?

Frank Williams: In my opinion it's going to be the strongest driver pairing. I feel very, very confident with the two drivers. It will depend on our technology.

How long are Ayrton's and Damon's contracts?

Williams: Ayrton's is for two years. Damon we have a long contract with. We've taken up a further year of that with an option in our favour until 1995. Regarding money I can say nothing. I've seen the speculation in the press and it is speculation.

Your feelings, Damon?

Hill: Obviously I was very relieved that Frank made the decision I hoped for. It wasn't quite as anxious a wait as it was the year before, because I knew my results had gone most of the way to making up Frank's mind.

Damon, you've driven with two of the world's finest drivers, Nigel Mansell of course when you were a test driver here and this year with four-times World Champion Alain Prost. Are you looking forward to driving alongside Ayrton?

Hill: I think that you have to have mixed emotions about facing the prospect of driving alongside someone of the calibre of Ayrton because he's fiercely competitive, but nevertheless I expect to learn quite a lot from being with him. It's a challenge to any racing driver. I welcome it and I'm thrilled to be able to have the opportunity. I don't really know Ayrton very well. I've spoken to him a few times but very little really. I'm looking forward to it but I'm not overawed. He is far and away the fastest driver currently around. You have to prepare yourself psychologically for the sort of mind games he can play. I'm not easily demoralized or crushed, so I'm well prepared for that. I'm still on the upward climb in my Formula 1 career. I still have a lot to learn and someone like Ayrton being in the team will only add to my experience.

Williams: I think I've heard the word reputation mentioned (by implication) twice in the last three questions. Alain Prost 12 months ago had a reputation for being very, very political and very divisive in a team, and in fact the opposite was true. Alain is one of the nicest guys I've ever worked with. I also believe that the reputation of the driver depends very much on the environment in which he is working. We've a happy team here and we intend to extend that into 1994 with Ayrton.

Frank, we were here in this room a year ago and you were understandably guarded about Damon. You hoped he might win a race. We're looking now at a situation where he won three and might have won five. Do you think he'll race Senna?

Williams: I think he'll give Ayrton a very hard time immediately, yes, and that's what we want.

Can we take it from that that both drivers will be driving for the Championship?

Williams: That is correct, yes.

Hill: Let's put that into context. It was only my first full season, so if I can start 1994 with the prospect of having a serious chance of becoming World Champion I can only say it's a tremendous opportunity which I will grab on to.

Williams: I've always wanted Ayrton to drive for Williams. He is an outstanding World Champion in terms of his greatest ambition, which is winning races and winning championships. Negotiations happened very quickly once it became apparent that Alain was serious about racing only until the end of 1993 and not beyond. I've been talking on and off with Ayrton for ten years. My decision to sign Ayrton had no part in Alain's decision to retire, not at all.

Hill: It's always quite sad when someone like Alain leaves the sport and I enjoyed being a team-mate with him. I found him very, very straightforward but also very committed. He seems so quiet when you meet him. I've always been aggressive but you have to learn to control it. There's a right time and a right way.

Do you consider Ayrton has been taken on as number 1 driver or are both men considered equal?

Williams: Clearly we're expecting greater things from Ayrton than we are of Damon, but Damon continues to surprise us every race he goes to – he surprises me more at each race than the previous one and the opportunity is wide open for him.

That wasn't a clear answer ...

Williams: I thought it was very charitable in every sense. I think Damon will have to push himself very, very hard to keep up with Ayrton but he's surprised me all year. I would not be surprised if he runs with him and even beats him. It could happen. (At this point, the telephone connection is established: Senna is in Sao Paulo with Betise Assumpcao translating into Portuguese for the reporters gathered there.)

Williams: Hello. We've a lot of your friends from the European media here and I'd like to welcome you to join us on their behalf. I'll pass you over to Richard [West, Williams Director of Marketing, the master of ceremonies in Didcot] who has some questions for you Ayrton. Thank you. The media are listening to every word you say. OK, this is Richard for you.

West: Ayrton, it's good to speak to you again. One of the questions that has come up today: yourself and Frank have been talking for many years, can you please give us your feelings about finally driving for the Williams team?

Senna: OK. Nice to talk to you, Richard. Good afternoon to everyone there, to Frank and all the media. This is a sort of link-up again because back in 1983 Frank was the man who gave me the first opportunity in my whole career to drive a Formula 1 car. Since then on a number of occasions we talked, we negotiated. It's been ten years since then and we finally came together now. I am very happy and I'm really looking forward to driving for Williams, to drive alongside Damon. I think 1993 was a wonderful start to Damon's career and what can I say? I'm really happy.

West: I'd like, if I may, to take some questions from the floor.

Do you expect to win the Championship?

Senna: Well, that's really tough, you know, it's been so long since I won my last one that I don't remember [laughter in Didcot] but I'll give it a chance.

Were you aware of the McLaren-Peugeot engine deal before you left McLaren?

Senna: I think I shouldn't compromise anybody. I have been in close contact this year not only with Frank but Ron and my decision was very clear in the taking, some time ago. It was something I believed was the best thing for me and the team. Therefore it is not really relevant, the Peugeot deal being through or not.

Are you disappointed you won't be driving with Alain Prost in 1994?

Senna: Alain, we miss you so much [a roar of laughter in Didcot].

Williams: A good answer, Ayrton.

Senna: The line suddenly goes dead, we cut off the line [more laughter].

If you hadn't secured this deal with Frank would you have taken next year off?

Senna: That was also a possibility but it quickly went away because I had a feeling that I should compete strongly in the future. My priority was to get something sorted out with Frank.

West: A continuation of that question. Have you at any time, Ayrton, considered a future in IndyCar racing?

Senna: Yes, last year. At the end of last year I came very close to doing so and I'm just happy that I didn't do it, that I stayed committed to Formula 1 and participated in the 1993 Championship with McLaren and therefore carried on working on my Formula 1 career, preparing myself for the future.

Do you see Damon as a serious title contender?

Senna: First of all, for obvious reasons I think without any doubt Damon today is a different driver than he was when the 1993 Championship started, or at least at the same time last year. He has now almost a full season, he has won Grands Prix, he has been on pole position and he has fought his way up in a natural way. It gives drivers a lot of confidence, which is fundamental for future success, and I believe that for next year he will be a lot more competitive right away, from the very first race – which is an important thing for the Championship. As I said earlier, he couldn't have had a better start than a first season with Alain and a second season with me, so he must be extremely motivated and faces – and faced – a tremendous challenge driving for Williams alongside Alain and myself two years in a row. He has proved he is capable of winning races, and he can only improve. It could be very interesting for him but also for me and for many English fans next year.

What effect will the new rules [no electronic aids] *have?*

Senna: Perhaps Formula 1 won't change as much as people expect but it will change because some of the technology that has been banned will lead to a situation of more driver input, not only on the set-up of the car but in driving it. I believe it's the right way as far as the drivers are concerned, so we can exploit different driving styles a little bit better. I believe and I feel that in some ways the past two years have been a limiting factor on different driving styles. I hope that it will be more competitive with other teams than Williams (prominent) but I hope Williams will stay ahead and give us the ability to have a very successful season again.

(From a reporter in Sao Paulo to Frank Williams, which Betise diplomatically translates into English) *Do you think 1994 will be as boring with Senna winning in a Williams as 1993 was with Prost winning in a Williams?*

Senna, intervening: Actually the journalist here asked: 'Don't you think the Championship will be even MORE boring with Senna?' [A roar of laughter in Didcot.] That's what he said, word by word [more laughter].

Williams: First point. I don't think the 1993 Championship has been boring. Second point. I think 1994 is going to be a much tougher Championship, partly because of the changes to the cars. No-one stays on top for ever. There will be some teams pushing us, maybe beating us. Quite likely.

Senna: OK, Frank. We are happy here with your words and we say goodbye for the moment, not only to you but everybody there in England and I'm looking forward to seeing you soon.

Williams: Thank you very much, Ayrton. It's very good to talk to you and I say that on behalf of everybody here. I'll speak to you later today.

Senna: Goodbye for now.

January, 1994. A sallow sun came sharp and sudden over the top lip of the concrete stand. A scurry of people eddied among the transporters which butted on to the pits, going nowhere in particular, milling, waiting. Ten-thirty on a winter morning, and something's happening and nothing's happening.

Someone wearing a Rothmans anorak like a uniform announces urgently: 'Don't let anyone speak to him, no questions, absolutely no questions.' Wherever he went those days there was one clear sense. Siege. He arrived, seemingly from nowhere, cloaked in a Rothmans anorak himself, his new uniform: a man of medium height, a thicket of dark, curling hair. He held a certain balanced tension even in the act of walking. He'd respond to anything unexpected instantly, never losing the balance, and you'd felt the same about Carl Lewis, Linford Christie, Muhammad Ali, Pele, Eusebio ...

He had donned his molten, melting perma-smile and as he's chaperoned towards one of the transporters he calls out 'Hi, how are you?' I have to call back: 'Sorry, can't answer any questions, not allowed!' The perma-smile opens into laughter. He sees what the siege has brought and why, and perhaps the irony of it; and still he holds the balance. Estoril, January 1994. The sun is now refracting over the flinty hillocks which rise like a backdrop of vast, broken teeth.

He has already sampled the Williams Renault the day before. Today he'll give a demonstration run or two so that some 350 journalists and photographers can witness it. He won't work himself or the car hard. Tomorrow – the siege lifted, most of the 350 gone home – he'll take the first steps on the journey to knowing the car, its engine and the team. He'll say, quietly, that each move across the decade thus far – Toleman, Lotus, McLaren – gave the career a kick, an acceleration. Here would be the next one.

Mid-morning and no car circled, the feeling of nothing and something lingering – an empty motor racing circuit is a curious contradiction.

On the grid he poses with Hill, and the new car, the arc of photographers so numerous that a photographer takes a picture of the photographers and a magazine uses it, consciously charting the extent of the siege. Then he and Hill go out and circle the track. They come past the pit lane wall in a flying formation in order that the photographers may have them in shot together.

Later he'll explain that 'it is always a temptation to go faster and push harder to make better times, but given the conditions – very cold, a car new to me and we're getting over 320kph [198mph] on the straight – it takes a lot of careful self-control not to try and exploit the potential the car really has. By that, I mean you'd be exposing yourself to a potential accident, which is not the purpose at this stage.'

Is that part of growing up, that you don't have to prove you can get a thunderous time straight away, as you would have done when you started with Toleman?

'Yes, and I'm not just speaking about ten years ago. Even six years ago I would have been trying harder at this stage, maybe taking the mental aspect a bit too far. Naturally I have been learning in these past six years and this is the biggest change I have had. Now I must use the experience.'

The choice of Estoril to launch Senna, Williams and the team's new sponsor, Rothmans, was obvious, Estoril then a favoured haunt for Formula 1 testing and in theory a warm, dry place. This January day, however, the sun warmed by implication only.

'I believe, even having done the ten years of Formula 1 and won three World Championships, that the challenge to learn and improve yourself is the biggest motivating factor for me. As you go along, every year it becomes more and more difficult to motivate yourself to do a number of things which you don't normally enjoy' (the slog of normal winter testing, for example).

'Therefore these big changes in my career are like someone moving home. You have to find out everything, adjust everything, adjust yourself to it, get to know your new neighbours and make new friends. It is a way of motivating myself to keep up with the competitive level which Formula 1 requires from you.'

Do you think you can continue the good relationship you have with Damon throughout the season?

'Perfectly possible, although it is never easy because we are always competing, but I understand your question. We have those questions before we start any partnership with any of our colleagues, and perhaps I should say one thing. The only driver I have ever had problems with as a team-mate is Alain Prost. With the others, we raced hard and so occasionally we had our different opinions, but we were able to sort it out, sit down and discuss and have respect for each other. We also had friendship. I have worked with Gerhard Berger, Michael Andretti, Elio de Angelis, Johnny Dumfries, Satoru Nakajima and Alain, so I think it is necessary for everybody who looks into this particular matter to consider the reality: as far as team-mates are concerned, I have always got on very well with all of them except one.'

There was a time, *circa* 1989–1990, when we thought we'd never hear Ayrton Senna pronounce the name Prost again, referring to him only as *he* and *him* but that lay in the bad old days, long gone as Senna moved into his mid-thirties. He'd become a businessman employing up to 100 people (importing cars and home appliances to Brazil), launching his own brand of boats and motorcycles. The brand-name? *Driven to Perfection*.

He'd become a kind of father figure to Brazilian children, investing a million dollars in an education and entertainment service for the poorest – 'they follow what I do so I like to create something for them' – and part of that involved a magazine, *Senninha* (Little Senna).

When Senna chose to wield his charm it could unbalance your equilibrium in its humble gentility so could it have been no more than three months before this chilled January day that at Suzuka, Japan, he sought out Irvine and cuffed him? Or that he'd been given a two-race suspended ban for it?

Is this thought of a ban hanging over you?

'If you hadn't mentioned it, well, I had even forgotten about it.

I don't think about it. My main objective is getting completely over that issue. My attitude is a lot more to do with the real work than to keep thinking about any political steps right now.'

Senna was asked (again!) if he regretted that Prost wouldn't be driving and he replied cryptically that if Prost did emerge from retirement 'it would be good for my bank balance.' Curiously nobody pursued Senna into that statement, because it seemed incomprehensible.

A strange affair, as it subsequently transpired. Williams had negotiated an exclusion clause with Prost, paying him £5.1 million not to drive for another team. If Prost did emerge from retirement he'd have to pay it back, and – as part of Senna's negotiations – he, Senna, would inherit the money.

That afternoon Senna sat under the awning of the Rothmans motorhome with a Japanese photographer who took pictures for him. The photographer showed his wares, a wedge of pictures. Senna handled them delicately and with infinite care ('this one with the white background is nice') and the siege assumed bizarre proportions again: the photographers gathered and took photographs of Senna and a photographer looking at photographs of himself. The whole thing seems to be folding in, feeding off itself.

Later there would be time for the British Press to have a chat with Senna. He sat under the awning of the Williams motorhome, at the end of a small table, and if there was an unstated tension – his reported objection to how the British Press covered the Irvine incident at Suzuka – it never surfaced. This was partly, I assumed, because he'd already been asked about Irvine and dealt with that, partly because he must know that if Irvine had cuffed him we'd have flayed and castigated Irvine; but also because, face-to-face, he was instinctively polite.

(In another context he'd say that 'some of the media don't really understand what it takes to drive a Formula 1 car and be successful, and some believe they are judges. We are all human beings and have our difficulties in delivering all the time. Often they criticise in a destructive sense. If it is constructive, fine, but when the goal is to destroy, that's revolting.')

The perma-smile was wan and slow-burning now. Ayrton Senna had a disconcerting habit of facing a questioner eye-to-eye and prolonging that until the end of the answer: deep eyes which assessed and penetrated rather than cut. He selected each word with laboured care and, revealingly, twice asks for a word in a question to be explained, something he didn't ordinarily do.

Your initial impressions of the car? Is the driver in you being restrained at the moment?

'Very much, because I don't feel "within" the car yet, and also the driving position isn't the best one for me yet. It will require a change to give me more of a control over the steering. Right now I don't have a good control of it. Some of that, but not all, is down to its position. Therefore you have to be very careful.'

He spoke of motivation, the favourite word. 'You learn and you tend to move your learning process on. I know the initial part of the season is going to be much more learning, a bigger learning process, so the motivation goes up.' He insisted that in general he wasn't driving faster than in the past ('I'm not driving slower, either') but had grown wiser, handling cars and situations with more precision, making more correct decisions.

The questions and answers flowed easily forward until he said: 'Hey, this was supposed to be five minutes. Look at the time!' It had been a generous half hour and the chat breaks up in good humour and handshakes and his haunting politeness. He says 'thank you' for coming when it ought to be the other way round.

The car and the 1994 season beckoned. As he walks off towards both, there it was again, the balance, the body simultaneously slack and taut, the animalism of the athlete, of Lewis and Christie, and Ali and Pele, and Eusebio who used to play just down the road. You see just such on the Savannah among hunter and prey. They too can move from the slack to the taut very, very quickly – but not at 198mph.

That chilly day, along came irreverent Johnny Herbert, largely unnoticed beyond the Senna siege. We fall to banter (the proper way to communicate with Herbert) and in the course of it I explain I'd forgotten how narrow the start-finish straight is here at Estoril, how pronounced the slope, how savage the turn into Turn One: and (true) confess that I hold an admiration for anyone who'll get into one of those goddamned cars and take it on.

The following words I wrote before Imola, and they appeared before Imola:

Whatever his rationale, the racing driver cannot escape the knowledge that dangers are always present. He witnesses others crashing and experiences crashes himself. He sees, in the pit lane, Jacques Laffite hobbling after an accident so long ago, Clay Regazzoni in a wheelchair, Philippe Streiff paralysed – and no safety regulations on earth can guarantee that the kevlar, the computers, the sand traps, the armco, the marshals and the medi-vac teams will protect you from the consequences.

Herbert limps. Donnelly speaks with a hoarse voice which literally echoes his crash. Herbert and Donnelly are lucky. The true measure: Herbert still drives, Donnelly (who runs his own racing team now) lived to prove he could get back in a Formula 1 car. How do you explain this desire? I can't because I've never felt anything so strongly.

Aspects of Senna: child-prisoner of the siege, smouldering eyes and a vulnerable amiability, a logic to daunt, a fragile man of huge strength, at peace and at war with many others, as they came, and how they came: not just Prost and Irvine but Mansell and Balestre, errant backmarkers in disarming quantities, the interview with Jackie Stewart which went seismic.

He guarded his privacy hard, although, inevitably, he'd been seen here and there with a beautiful girl on his arm – Adriane. He travelled to and from circuits in helicopters not forgetting his own jet capable of flying from Brazil. He enjoyed the perils of jet ski-ing and evidently still flew his model aeroplanes. The rest? It was hidden behind the walls of the siege.

Some people are born to fulfil themselves in a certain medium and only need to find it. When they get there they know what to do. A ballerina, a stage, my stage. Agassi at Wimbledon, centre court, striptease, my stage. Eusebio, a leopard of a footballer down the road at Benfica in the Stadium of Light – which you pass to get to Estoril – my stage.

Jo Ramirez naturally confines himself to drivers. 'I do believe it is something you have from birth. I've been in motor racing for 32 years and I've been lucky to have been associated with probably five of the best drivers ever – Fangio, Clark, Stewart, Prost and Senna. I've worked with Stewart, Prost and Senna. Those three are the same as Fangio and Clark, they had it from birth, that ability to do something better than the rest. You have drivers like Mansell, Graham Hill, and James Hunt who got there by pure, sheer determination and hard work.'

Many times we'd seen Mansell either collapse or be on the point of collapse after a race while Senna stands beside him on the podium impassive, composed, having driven the same distance.

'I've never seen Prost sweat in a race and Ayrton doesn't sweat much. The racing comes so naturally to them.'

Senna: he sits at the end of the table on the chilled January day in 1994, the wind sneaking and shivering through canvas sheets held by metal pegs driven into the tarmacadam of the paddock, sits easy although soon he'll be back in the Williams, risking it – the camber of the start-finish straight dipping to alter the composition of your stomach, the savage wrench into Turn One where your eyeballs wonder why they don't focus clearly any more – but on the big scale it's no more than another afternoon, another exploration, conducted to the rules every driver and no tennis player knows: at 198mph nothing can guarantee your self preservation.

What to ask him before he goes? More questions? More voyeurism? How much more can he give in words? He sits, homely in the antiseptic English way, deferential, sure of himself but no flaunting, a strung-out contemplation of a creed and a life: slack but still on the Savannah, taut to any move and counter-move. He will go, any minute now, to the car, the crew and the rest of his life, holding the balance as he goes. What more do you want of any human being?

A week later, McLaren unveiled their new car at their factory in Woking. It was done in the trophy room, glass shelves around the walls with ornate cups on them. The name of Alain Prost is engraved on a lot of them, the name of Ayrton Senna on a lot of them: Prost won 30 times in a McLaren, Senna 35, Prost took 10 pole positions, Senna 46; between them they took every Championship from 1985 to 1991 except 1987.

A late January day, no sallow sun even, Senna gone and Prost gone, too. Nobody knew that with both of them it was forever. Instinctively, like on the empty pit lane straight at Estoril, you looked for them, listened for Prost's glorious way of chewing English vowels, waited for Senna's way of stroking them. Instead the only driver McLaren did have, Mika Häkkinen, posed on and near the car – Häkkinen who'd yet to win a race, bring a trophy for the glass shelves. He would, all right, but we didn't know that, either.

An irony among so many ironies in 1994 was that people seriously spoke of Senna winning all 16 races. The Williams car was regarded as that good, and he was clearly that good. He'd even discussed the expectation, in however a guarded way, because it really did seem possible, if not likely. He was far, far too wise in the way of it to make predictions, of course, but that didn't prevent him discussing it. The new regulations, however, disrupted continuity and the new Williams needed work on it. As the season neared, nobody understood that better than Senna.

The fact that he took pole in Brazil proved deceptive. In the race he was decisively outpowered by young Schumacher in his Benetton, and spun out.

He took pole again at the next race, the Pacific at Aida, Japan, but moments after the start he was nudged off. Schumacher won.

By definition, as Senna flew back from Japan, pressure was gathering round him. He was being outdriven by a younger man for the first time in his life and, moreover, a man nearly a decade younger. There is, in every sport, but particularly motor racing, a moment when the next generation announces itself and the generation it is poised to replace suddenly becomes vulnerable. In 1994, that had happened in two weeks – Brazil on 27 March, Aida on 17 April. Senna now had to mount a counter-attack against the vulnerability, and Schumacher was full of running in a strong, strong car.

The third race of 1994 was two weeks away.

Chapter 15

IMOLA

The week leading to the 1994 San Marino Grand Prix at Imola began, as it seemed, in the most ordinary way. On Tuesday, 26 April, Ayrton Senna took his plane, flown by O'Mahony, from Faro to Munich. Senna had a meeting there about his Audi distributorship in Brazil.

On the Thursday, O'Mahony flew Senna from Munich to Padua, a large city 32 kilometres from Venice. During the journey, O'Mahony says, Senna was 'fine, perfectly OK.' A long day, this. Senna was due at the launch of a mountain bike – built by an Italian company, Carraro – bearing his name. He went to the factory where, naturally, the employees made a fuss of him. He shook a lot of hands and was taken to the Sheraton Hotel, a typically modern building set in its own gardens amid gentle countryside five kilometres from Padua. There, in the Congress Centre – a large room on the ground floor – he played an active part in the launch. The Sheraton was precisely the place for this: crisp, functional, accepting business meetings effortlessly.

The mountain bike bore a distinctive red S and, in white, the name Senna on its frame. For some time Senna had looked beyond his career and was engaged in creating a proper business empire. It embraced, as we have seen, the *Senninha* comic, based on his own exploits, and the proceeds from which were intended to help deprived children; the Audi cars; a joint venture with an Italian company for manufacturing domestic appliances; the manufacture of luxury yachts; a company which licensed Senna's own name and the stylised letter *S* to denote that. The bike was a further part of this empire.

When they retire, most sportspeople hold to what they know. They become coaches or managers, they write for newspapers, they commentate on radio and television. The motor racing driver can prolong his career into sports cars or touring cars until his late 40s and use his name to establish car dealerships. I do not know a single person in *any* sport who has attempted a business empire of such breadth and scope as Senna.

Senna looked perfectly groomed. He wore a crisply-cut well-fitting jacket, a creamy shirt and a sober tie nicely knotted so that the knot nestled within the flaps of the collar. Nothing garish, nothing to disturb the tone. Just this once, he'd been chewing some gum and as he took his place on the stage Betise Assumpcao gestured. He realised and whipped it smartly out.

Some tentative reports suggest he was 'nervous' as the launch began. That was when, at least in public, the ordinariness comes into question. As a young man he'd been shy, introspective, self-contained but by now moving in public, stooping and talking into microphones, shaking hands with ranks of strangers, answering questions, posing for photographs, accepting that the throng would gaze at him as in a freak show, and carrying it all off smoothly – this was something Senna had been handling for a decade. He could bring charm, praise, anger, tears, indignation, vulnerability, desperate pity to the public gaze; but not nerves. You didn't see them and you wondered if they existed. Certainly, O'Mahony attributes any suggestion of nerves to the fact that Senna wasn't *completely* comfortable in Italian (and by definition might be asked questions with unfamiliar words in them about a mountain bike: the Formula 1 words he knew by heart and could mouth just like that). Against this must be put the thoughts of Pino Allievi, who has insisted that Senna spoke Italian *as well as any ordinary Italian*. Perhaps Assumpcao is nearer the mark: Senna wasn't nervous but just plain tired. Creating a business and simultaneously meeting the demands of Formula 1 was taking its toll. Sometimes he'd be up until 1.30am phoning Brazil.

However, a few days before this launch, Senna had telephoned his sister who has said: 'We talked for a long time. He was very low, though I will not say why.'

The mystery of this endures, and will endure unless Viviane chooses to elaborate, but it surely cannot have been his personal life. He was in love with Adriane and if her account of their relationship is to be believed – and there is no reason not to, because she describes it with a soul-bearing, tenderised topsy-turvy authenticity which rings absolutely true – he was extremely happy to be in love with her.

Senna would stay evasive about actual marriage but that does not disturb the authenticity of the relationship or that one day soon, surely, marriage would become a probability. All else aside, he'd always talked of wanting children, always talked of what a fulfilling experience that would have to be, always made a fuss of children.

This Thursday, Galisteu would go to the Berlitz school in Sao Paulo to work on her English, something Senna insisted she did and for which he paid, albeit as a present to her. English, he knew, was the language you'd need in motor racing but also in the world outside, no matter where you went. She'd even sent him a saucy (well, sexy) fax one time in English to prove how much her command of the language had improved. On the morrow – the Friday – she'd board an overnight Varig flight to Lisbon and proceed to Senna's house in Faro (Portugal). She'd watch the San Marino Grand Prix on television on the Sunday and await his return, which was estimated at 8.30pm. They would spend the European season – five months to the Grand Prix at Jerez in early September – together. She could hardly wait to see him again and, he'd said on the phone, he could hardly wait to see her. Ayrton Senna did not say such things carelessly.

And yet, only a few days before Imola, he'd said: 'Even when you are beside a woman that you love, you might think she could make you unhappy in the future. The relationship between a man and a woman is the oldest thing that exists in humanity, and there are still no formulae to guarantee love, peace, and the success of a relationship. For this reason a relationship must be valued day by day. It is not only the dream that most of us have but the reality that we must evaluate.'

It's tempting to conclude that he'd chosen Faro (Portugal) for a house because it was just about as near Brazil as he could get in Europe, and whoever you are, you feel most comfortable in your own language, no matter that Senna could also speak English, Spanish and, as we have seen, Italian. Faro offered space, which his apartment in Monte Carlo could never do: four or five bedrooms, a swimming pool and of course handy proximity to all the European races in his plane. There may have been even more pragmatic reasons, however. He could jog on the beach, a favourite way of keeping fit, and not be molested. Those who wandered the beach weren't expecting to see him. There are tales of people saying *I thought I saw Ayrton Senna but I can't have done*.

As the mountain bike launch chugged along Senna appeared visibly to relax. If he was tired his physical and mental strength were overcoming that. Inevitably he had to field Formula 1 questions, specifically what he thought of his 1994 Championship chances. I've not seen a record of what he said, but we do know that the rules had been changed, banishing electronic driver aids on the cars and, as a consequence, making them more difficult to drive. Senna had spoken about this by saying *we'll be lucky if we get through the season without a big accident*. Many, many people returned to these words and found a meaning in them after Imola.

At the launch, someone raised the subject of some cars' possible illegality but Senna fended that off diplomatically. After the launch he did about six television interviews, which was quite normal. They take their place among the thousands of others he gave – each wanting to know something, each wanting a part of him revealed now and to us.

From Padua, Senna took a helicopter with his brother Leonardo and two Carraro executives direct to the Imola circuit. O'Mahony, with Senna's business manager Julian Jakobi as a passenger, flew the HS125 to the little airport of Forli, south of Imola, a journey which O'Mahony says took 'just under 20 minutes'. The landing fees here were less than the big airport of Bologna. Why pay more if you don't have to? The plane would be parked there until Senna returned to it after the race and it would take him to Faro and Adriane.

Senna might have flown with O'Mahony and gone straight to his hotel, but no such easy option ever suited him. He wanted to see what the team were doing with the car (which had been undergoing fairly fundamental aerodynamic changes since Aida, itself a reason to go and have a look; not that he needed a reason).

Throughout his career, Senna had taken a profound interest in the preparation of his car. Once upon a time you'd rarely see a driver on the Thursday except Senna, who was probing, asking, examining, staying until nightfall. What you'd glimpse was a slender chap deep in the pit, nothing unusual, situation normal, and you'd walk on. These days his arrival at a circuit loomed as an event in itself and, when he did arrive, the whole pace in pits and paddock quickened, the throng gathered. Alone, and by his presence, he could fill the emptiness of the Thursday. *He's* here ...

This Thursday he spent a few moments with the mechanics and also spoke to Richard West. Senna wanted to discuss the promotional activity he was committed to, an important matter over any Grand Prix weekend and a delicate one. Someone as experienced as West would strike the correct balance between satisfying sponsors and guests, and creating necessary space for Senna to exist in peace, concentrate on the driving. Senna also spoke to Assumpcao who had to control journalistic access to him: she had to draw her own balance between trying to make him available and trying to prevent him from being over-run.

At any Grand Prix each moment is valuable and often at Senna's level accounted for in advance. The basic format was struck in stone then, regardless of climates or continents or cultures: the free practice on the Friday morning followed by the first qualifying session (1.0 to 2.0), same on the Saturday, with the big temperature-rise on the Sunday: the morning warm-up and the race early afternoon. Only Monaco was the exception – first qualifying was on Thursday.

Each session (apart from the race) was followed by a lengthy debrief. Cumulatively it left very few of those valuable moments when the driver does interviews, chats to whoever the sponsor has brought and, in the case of Hill and Senna, treats the Williams guests to a verbal lap of the circuit after the drivers' briefing on race morning.

The talk with West over, Senna took a Renault Espace to Castel San Pietro nine kilometres from Imola. Renault had a fleet of cars at the disposal of team personnel and, understandably, were anxious for team personnel not to be seen in anything else. He went first to the Romagnola restaurant, a plain but wholesome establishment with a marble plaque on the outside wall near the door. It says:

In this house was born on the 15th of March 1839 Battista Acquaderni who died in Bologna in 1922. He was one of the founders of the Italian Catholic Youth Organisation. This man, with his word and his example, called the younger generation to the faith.

Senna booked a table for 8.30pm. He'd eaten at the Romagnola regularly since 1991. That year the hotel where he stayed, the Castello, had phoned and said: 'Can you keep a table for Senna?' The Liverani family who ran the restaurant thought *Senna! Oh my God!* He arrived with a beautiful blonde and asked only to eat in peace. The Romagnola had an advantage: a small dining room as well as a larger one. They could put him in the smaller one and not let anybody else in. They didn't serve him anything sophisticated.

At the end of the meal the family asked Senna if he really was Senna and he said yes! They asked for an autograph and proffered a block notebook. He signed every sheet. The family sensed that the tranquillity appealed to him; and so he came back. One of the family says that Senna was 'so rich he could have *bought* the San Domenico restaurant, one of the most expensive in the whole area, but instead he loved the simple things.'

Now, this Thursday, Senna made a fuss of the family and said how pleased he was to see them again. The table booked, he drove out of Castel San Pietro along a winding, descending road – a beautiful valley spread before him, the sort of softening panorama Italy suddenly offers you like a vision – to the Castello, an L-shaped building set in rolling countryside. He'd stayed there every year since 1989. Frank Williams stayed there too, and so did Ron Dennis.

Senna walked past the wishing well in the foyer: a carved stone base with a wrought-iron canopy arched over it and into which residents threw coins so that they'd have the good luck to return some time for another stay at the hotel. He went to the reception desk and enacted a familiar ritual. He wrote on a piece of paper a list of people he'd accept telephone calls from. Any other calls for him would be fielded by the reception, noted and given to him whenever he came to collect his room key or surrendered it going out. He could scan the notes and return the calls or not, as he wished.

Because Senna had stayed at the Castello so long the word had spread that he'd be there. Bouquets arrived early for him, mainly roses from female admirers. The staff arranged these in his room. He rarely tarried at the reception because people were drawn to the hotel for a peek at him, an ogle at him, a vision of the real living image of him. He took the lift nearby to the second floor. He always had the same suite, number 200, and he had that again: a small hallway, a bedroom with a TV and a curious

Previous page: *The active suspension in 1987, and a superb victory at Monaco.*

Above: *'You must isolate yourself from the distraction of the grid.' Senna prepares to win Imola, 1988.*

Below: *Rain clouds at Hockenheim in 1988, and he won.*

Right: *Dry at Hockenheim in 1989, and he won.*

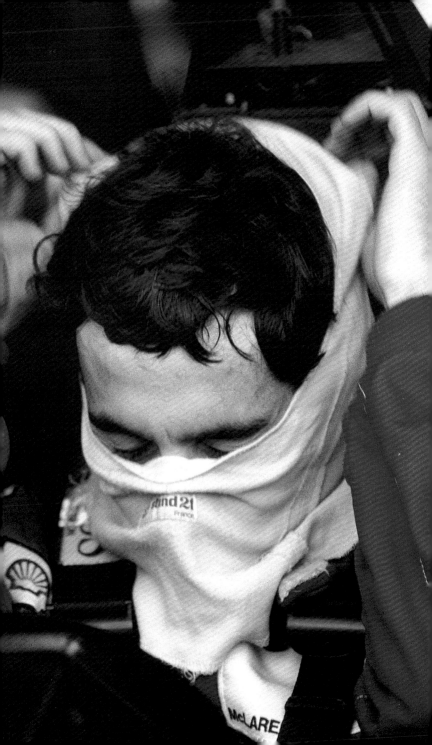

Glimpses of 1990: Senna and Ron Dennis, France. Senna was third.
Senna spins on the Friday at Spa – and wins on the Sunday.

Nightmare at Jerez. Senna goes to the scene of Martin Donnelly's crash.
A glimpse of 1991: Senna in France.

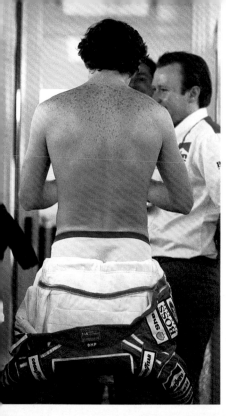

Left: *The wan, slender figure of 1984 had become a strong man by 1993. This is in Portugal.*

Below: *Chaos at the Monza chicane. Senna got through it.*

Above right: *Supreme Senna leads Donington in the wet-dry-wet-dry race, and the Williamses can't catch him.*

Middle right: *Making an impact at Imola – on the Friday.*

Bottom right: *A glimpse of the future that never was: Senna v Schumacher, here in Brazil in 1994.*

Overleaf: *The other future that never was: Senna and Adriane.*

painting above the bedhead – four Chinese-looking landscapes – a bathroom, a sitting room with another TV and sofa and chairs in day-glo purple. It cost 400,000 lire (£150) per night and was pleasant rather than extravagant. From the window he could see indoor and outdoor swimming pools and the rolling countryside.

Frank Williams had the suite below, number 100, and Ron Dennis the one above, number 300.

Ann Bradshaw of Williams explains that the whole team didn't stay in the same hotel. They tended 'to be scattered all over the place' – governed not just by cost but the availability of rooms. O'Mahony, as an example, stayed elsewhere and so did Assumpcao.

The driver naturally wants as few uncertainties as possible. Senna knew the hotel, liked his room, knew the man running it – Valentino Torsini – and the Romagnola was just up the hill, its private room giving sanctuary.

With him this weekend were those genuinely close to him (which many claimed to be and few were): Leonardo, Carlos Braga the banker from Sintra, Jakobi, Galvao Bueno (who worked for TV Globo, the Brazilian channel which covered the races), Celso Lemos (who managed Senna Licensing in Brazil), Ubirajara Guimaraes (who managed Senna Imports), and the masseur Josef Leberer. It was a larger party than usual for Senna. Ordinarily there'd be only Jakobi, Leberer and of course O'Mahony and Assumpcao.

The advantage of the small room in the Romagnola was more than privacy. It was large enough to put the tables together and accommodate whatever entourage Senna brought. This Thursday, that was himself and six others. He wore casual-chic, which he liked: smart jeans, shirt, maybe a pullover slung over his shoulders. He left before 10pm, booking again for the following evening, which he always did.

Senna was careful about what he ate and this is one of his daily menus, structured by Leberer.

BREAKFAST
Muesli, lots of fresh berries and yoghurt

Fruit tea

Multi-grain bread with strawberry jam

MID-MORNING
Carrot, orange and honey drink made of fresh ingredients

LUNCH
Fresh salad of tomato, basil, lettuce and avocado

Grilled chicken with fresh pasta and fresh tomato sauce

Fresh fruit salad

Water

DINNER
Grilled salmon with fresh green vegetable risotto

Fruit of fresh berries

Water

A note at the bottom instructed: *Always use fresh produce, olive oil for cooking and fresh herbs. Use honey instead of sugar for sweetener.*

He drove to the circuit on the Friday morning and, in the light of what would happen there, the layout will help. You entered the circuit and turned into a long, broad paddock. To one side, a dozen or more motorhomes were parked side-by-side butting onto the perimeter wall. To the other side there was a tall, imposing control tower which joined the main building. Its ground floor was divided into the pits, its upper floors contained offices, a restaurant, hospitality suites and the Media Centre. This building faced the grid and a grandstand the far side of the track. To it came the teams' transporters which, side by side, nestled into the back of the pits, disgorging the cars, spares and equipment. The paddock was broad enough to allow a walkway between the motorhomes and the transporters, but that was generally choked by mechanics wheeling tyres on trolleys, guests ambling about, friends chatting, team personnel who moved compulsively, camera crews on the look-out, not counting a hundred journalists also on the look-out and maybe, just maybe, a driver cutting a course to somewhere. Down from the main building stands the Medical Centre: low, white, with a helipad next to it and a protective mesh screen in front of it.

The track itself uncoiled from the grid and kept on coiling and uncoiling for 3.132 miles (5.05 kilometres): it curved hard-left (*Tamburello*), straightened, kinked right (*Villeneuve*), twisted left (*Tosa*), flowed left (*Piratella*), stabbed right-left-right (*Acque Minerale*), straightened a bit to a left-right stab (*Varianta Alta*), straightened to a hard-loop (*Rivazza*), straightened briefly to a fast right-left (*Variante Bassa*) which pitched the driver along a mini-straight into the 90-degree left-right (*Traguardo*) and the start-finish line in front of the pits, the main building and the grandstand. The Medical Centre was virtually level with *Traguardo*.

The surface of the track, traditionally bumpy – an alarming consideration for the margins of a Formula 1 car – had been resurfaced at strategic places.

In the Friday morning practice session, the weather hot and dry, Senna did 22 laps and expressed himself satisfied with the aerodynamic changes made to the car since Aida, and these changes were visible when the car turned in to the corners. Senna was quickest with 1 minute 21.598 seconds, Hill over a second slower, Schumacher third.

The temperature had risen to 27 degrees when first qualifying began. Wendlinger in a Sauber emerged almost immediately, then Heinz-Harald Frentzen in the other Sauber, then Gianni Morbidelli in the Footwork. The potential pole men bided their time, calculated their moment. Schumacher was the first of them and, using the full width of the track, warmed to 1:22.564.

As Schumacher travelled round the back of the circuit, Senna came out, the Williams 'bottoming' and shedding yellow sparks through *Tamburello*.

In the pits Frank Williams watched intently on the TV monitor and saw Senna's helmet bounce-stutter-bounce as the car ran across Imola's bumps. Senna thrust in 1:22.430. As Senna travelled into his second flying lap, virtually as he placed the Williams safely near the inside kerb at *Tamburello* and went crisply and cleanly round, young Rubens Barrichello came hard through *Rivazza* in his Jordan. The car missed the apex of the next right-left, Barrichello dug smoke from the rear tyres under reflex braking and tried to straighten it. He couldn't and the car rushed the far kerbing. The slope of that kerbing launched the car sideways across a tight segment of grass and it brushed the top of the tyre wall, battered the metal fencing above. It landed savaged and on its side. This looked dreadful.

Professor Watkins was there in a matter of moments. The car had been righted by marshals but Barrichello remained in the cockpit. It was just after 1.14. The red flags were hoisted immediately. Senna, touring in, did not see the accident but could not have failed to see the aftermath. He had to pass it to regain the pits.

Within five minutes Barrichello had been taken to the Medical Centre. Assumpcao went to the Jordan pit for news because she wanted to know herself and she knew Senna would want to know, too. Senna himself went to the Medical Centre. On the way there he passed the rear of the Jordan pit where he met Brian Hart, who made the engines which Jordan used. 'How is Rubens?' Senna asked urgently. Hart remembers that Senna looked 'very shocked.' Hart had seen the accident on a TV monitor and knew how bad it looked. He was able to reassure Senna, however, that Barrichello had hurt his nose but otherwise seemed fine. 'I'm going to see him,' Senna said, and strode on.

One report (Andrew Longmore in *The Times*) suggests that Senna found 'the front door of the Medical Centre blocked, and vaulted a fence to get in the back.' This appears unlikely because Professor Watkins had no objection to him visiting Barrichello and permitted it. 'Rubens was all right so I let him in.'

'I remember exactly the moment before I touched the barrier,' Barrichello would be quoted as saying, 'waiting for the crash and then everything went into darkness. The next thing I knew I was in the Medical Centre with Senna there. Senna was the first person to visit me at the hospital. He had tears in his eyes, like the accident had been his own. I had never seen that before.' Some years later, reflecting as best he could (he had been unconscious, don't forget), Barrichello said: 'I remember him being the first person I saw. I remember him saying that I was OK, just to keep calm. I don't know if he was crying, I can't remember. I read afterwards that he was speaking to someone on the telephone and crying but at that stage ... I can't remember. He didn't say much to me because I was going to be put in a helicopter to the hospital.'

Satisfied that Barrichello had suffered no more than slight injuries ('I'm off to play with the nurses and I'll be back tomorrow,' Barrichello quipped), Senna walked to the pits. Even on this short journey along the paddock the throng of some 30 to 40 pursued and hemmed him. Two hand-held television cameras probed, almost leering at his face as cameras do in close up.

The session resumed at 1.40, Senna got back in the car, and went for it. 'I don't feel that I ever drove the car properly. After the accident of Rubens I wasn't driving well – not consistent, not able to do it properly. It was just myself not being able to concentrate.' That did not prevent him recording 1:21.548, provisional pole from Schumacher on 1:22.015.

This is the sequence of events. When the accident stopped the session, Senna had been third fastest. Now he worked through a lap of 1:24.067, conservative and obviously so. He stayed away from the kerbs. On his second lap he did use the kerbs, urging the Williams much, much harder: 1:21.837 and provisional pole. Then he spun – the car reduced to a slewed standstill – but he churned it and set off again, furious wheel spin, smoke from the rears, a swathe of rubber marking the path the car took. That was 40 minutes into the session. Senna returned to the pits. He emerged onto the track with some three and a half minutes of the session remaining and urged the Williams harder still: 1:21.548. By then, Barrichello had been flown by helicopter to the Maggiore Hospital in Bologna for tests.

When the session had resumed, Hill went out and spun. How awkward were these cars to control? A few moments later Brundle, in a Marlboro McLaren Peugeot, spun at the spoon-shaped *Rivazza* corner. And Senna spun, too, of course. How awkward were these cars …?

After the session, Senna was emotionally and physically exhausted; almost irritated by some supporters in the main building above the pits who bayed their encouragement and told him he'd got the beating of Schumacher. He wasn't in the mood to hear combative calls like these. Reportedly, he attempted to do a brief interview with a television reporter over Barrichello but couldn't. He tried to speak the same sentence three times, made his excuses and vanished into one of the Williams transporters, forbidden to all but team personnel. He stayed there for half an hour and when he did come out he was able to talk, about his lack of concentration, about how 'chaotic' the whole session felt, and to a knot of Italian journalists he stressed how dangerous parts of the circuit were.

He walked to the motorhome and moved into a profound discussion with his engineer, David Brown, because Senna felt (as it emerged later, and in the words of another) there was 'a big engineering problem with the car.' Brown went briefly away and Senna came out to give a group of journalists a promised interview about his business empire. This took place in the seating area butting on to the motorhome. One of the journalists, Mark Fogarty of *Carweek*, estimated Senna answered questions for between 15 and 20 minutes but with the caveat that as soon as Brown returned the de-brief would resume. Fogarty was struck by how Senna appeared – 'extremely tired, eyes red and glassy. Drawn.' Fogarty was also struck by the difficulty Senna had in concentrating on his answers. Fogarty noticed that the gap between questions and answers became even longer than normal and those answers were 'halting,' as if Senna was trying to regain his concentration rather than selecting from his vocabulary: a powerful difference in a man accustomed to the mechanisms of absolute concentration on the topic in hand to the exclusion of all else.

Brown returned and Senna departed to the upper deck of the motorhome to resume the de-brief. He came back an hour later and told the journalists he wasn't in the mood to continue the interrupted interview, but would do so on the morrow after second qualifying. The journalists drifted off. Assumpcao went to the Maggiore to see Barrichello.

Senna left the circuit around 8.0 and dined at the Romagnola with, among others, Bueno of TV Globo. Evidently Senna was between two moods. He asked Bueno how Barrichello was, reflecting his continued anxiety, and when Bueno couldn't give him the latest bulletin ribbed him gently about being a newsman who didn't have up-to-the-minute information. The Liveranis remember Senna's mood as 'black'.

That night, too, in the hotel he and some of the support team sat round a table and Senna talked for a long time about chance, about the meaning and consequences of chance. He appeared still preoccupied by Barrichello's accident and started to mention launching safety initiatives before the next Grand Prix, at Monaco in two weeks. He went to his room shortly after 11pm. While he slept, Galisteu took off from Sao Paulo for Lisbon at 10.10 local time – 1.10am in Europe.

Seen in isolation, the impact which Barrichello's crash exercised on Senna appears difficult to comprehend, no matter that Barrichello was a Brazilian, something of a protégé and, at 22, represented the future. Barrichello had survived intact, Barrichello was chirpy. It turned out to be just another crash, just another confirmation that Formula 1 cars were so robust they'd take wild batterings and cocoon the driver from the most extreme consequences. No man had died during a Grand Prix meeting for 12 years and no man had died in a Formula 1 car for eight years.

Questions arise, and I don't think we'll ever know the answers.

Did Senna, perceptive as he was, sense that *whatever anybody claimed for the cars* Formula 1 had been very, very lucky across – respectively – the 12 years and eight, and that one day the luck wouldn't hold? That could easily have been today, Friday, 29 April 1994.

Did the accumulation of pressures – Schumacher strong, Imola pivotal, the engineering problem with the car, the rule changes, all of it, all of it – heighten his senses to an extent that something shockingly unexpected like the crash of the protégé was damn near too much? Of course, Senna had been under pressure before – every Formula 1 driver is – but not, perhaps, this peculiar and pervading conjunction of pressures. To break down and cry in a Medical Centre when you are looking at a driver who is OK and who, moreover, is poised to make quips about chasing nurses, represents a strange reaction.

Did the absence of Alain Prost increase the pressure in a subtle way? Throughout his Formula 1 career Senna had had a benchmark to measure against – Prost. Now (and begging Schumacher's pardon) Senna represented the only benchmark, and he might have felt that each time he drove he was going into the unknown, no comparisons valid.

'Ayrton was shaken, he was very much shaken,' O'Mahony says. 'He was a mentor to Barrichello.' O'Mahony accepts that it still shook Senna much more than you'd have expected, accepts that this was strange.

On the Saturday, arm in plaster, Barrichello returned to the circuit and remained chirpy. 'You OK, you OK?' Senna asked him. Barrichello talked about driving again as soon as possible. 'Don't be a fool,' Senna said. 'You think you are OK but you might not be. I know from some of my own accidents.' (Barrichello remembers Senna saying to him 'take your time,' and adds 'I understood. I did take my time, I had two weeks without driving, then I came to England to test.')

The morning free practice passed, superficially, in the most ordinary way but during it Senna did something extremely uncharacteristic.

O'Mahony stood in the back of the pits, and hereby hangs the tale which still makes O'Mahony wonder. 'Uncanny,' is his description. Before we get to that, another tale. 'I didn't have a pass for the pits,' O'Mahony says. 'I was in the paddock behind but I wasn't actually allowed into the pits without one. This 6ft, 13-stone Italian "heavy" stopped me and Ayrton saw it. He came over and said to the guy: "They're with me." So there was no problem, we just walked in. As a result of that the guy let us in all day because he recognised who we were.' Now the uncanny part. O'Mahony had worked for Senna, flying the plane, for three years and during that time – although he wanted a photograph of himself with Senna – he didn't have one. 'I thought it was a bit naff of me to ask him. I didn't really want to ask him.' Understandably so. O'Mahony was a very experienced pilot who'd flown heads of state, was old enough to be Senna's father and, anyway, Senna employed him. Senna was aware that O'Mahony wanted a photograph.

O'Mahony stood in the back of the pits because 'I aimed to be unobtrusive so if he wanted things I was there but I wasn't getting in the way. If he did want something he'd come over and ask "Owen, could you go and do so-and-so for me?" The trick was to remain out of the way but be there. During a Grand Prix weekend, he was single-minded, tunnel vision. Now he got out of the car, took his helmet off and – it was most unlike him because we never talked during sessions – he said: "Owen, I've got the photos for you." And he produced two photos.

'One was of him flying the aeroplane for the first time, and which I had taken with a fish-eye lens. We were approaching Faro after a Grand Prix, it was at night and he had a nice wry smile. By the time I'd given the camera back I thought we were too high so I had to go round again before we landed. He signed it *To Owen, that's why we missed the direct approach to Faro.*

'The second photo was on the pit lane wall at Imola and I didn't know it was being taken, just he and I talking and smiling. Nobody else around, a lovely photograph. Someone had taken it the day before and he'd remembered. It was odd. In a sense, a photographer had taken it completely by chance (in the context of O'Mahony wanting just such a photograph and happening to be with Senna on the pit lane wall) and Ayrton hadn't forgotten. He signed it *To Owen with best wishes*. It was out of character for him to think about anything but racing during a racing session, it was almost as if he wanted to tie up some loose ends.'

Galisteu landed at Lisbon at midday and travelled to Sintra, 30 kilometres from the airport, where she would spend the afternoon at the home of Braga. His wife Luiza was there but Carlos, of course, was at Imola. That evening Galisteu would fly on to Faro.

At 1.0 the second session for the grid began. At 1.18 Senna was preparing to make his first run but, before that, he watched what the others were doing on a TV monitor in the pits. He saw live coverage of the Austrian Roland Ratzenberger, a rookie in a Simtek, go off at *Villeneuve* at 200mph and smash into the concrete wall. Senna sensed instantly that the luck no longer held. He retreated to the rear of the pit and covered his face with his hands, then walked down the pit lane and commandeered an official car to take him to the crash. When he reached it, Ratzenberger was en route to the Medical Centre, but the wreckage of the Simtek and its distribution told Senna everything.

He returned to the pits in the official car and walked to the Medical Centre. This time Professor Watkins would not allow him in. 'Even when Mansell tried to get in after Berger's accident (at *Tamburello*, 1989) he was turned away because, you know, everybody's busy and the scene can be a bit of a surprise to someone who's not been in an intensive care unit before. If they are sensitive, then I'd prefer them not to see it. He arrived at the door as I happened to be walking out and I guided him away, whereas the day before Rubens was all right so I let him in.'

Ratzenberger was only clinically alive.

Watkins remembers that Senna was 'very shocked. He had never faced the reality of his profession before so starkly, because no-one had been killed during his time in Formula 1 (at a Grand Prix – he was in FF2000, remember, when Gilles Villeneuve died). He was always fatalistic about death. He was a religious man and intelligent enough to think it through. This was the first time it had come so close. He was very quiet, but he remained resolute, not questioning out loud the meaning of his sport or his own position.' This conversation took place on some grass, Senna arms folded, Watkins with his hands on his hips.

'Was there something troubling Senna even before the accidents? I think he was genuinely worried about safety,' Watkins says, 'and that was starting to preoccupy him. Mind you, it's a sign of maturity. I think he was missing McLaren, too. You've to remember it was his "family" there, wasn't it? So the whole season was very different for him: he'd gone to a new team, he'd had two unsuccessful races, one getting shunted off at Aida and in Brazil he lost it – didn't he? – lost control of the car in the dry ...'

While Senna and Watkins spoke, Martin Whitaker, Press Delegate of the FIA, waited nearby. He, too, had gone to the Medical Centre for news of Ratzenberger but clearly wouldn't intrude on the intensity of the interflow between Senna and Watkins. 'When they had finished,' Whitaker says, 'I asked Senna if he knew what had happened. He didn't reply. He just looked at me and walked away. I won't forget that look. To say it was fear would be over the top. He was just very worried. There was something different about him.'

Neither Hill nor Senna took part in this second session. From the Medical Centre, Senna walked to the pits and discreetly in a corner informed Hill and Patrick Head that Ratzenberger was dead in all but name. Frank Williams gave him the choice of continuing or not, which was the only prudent course to take. If Senna felt a need to get into the car immediately – some drivers do – as personal therapy, Frank Williams would not deny him that. If Senna felt a need to distance himself from it and reflect, Frank Williams would not deny him that, either. They are all human beings, never claimed to be more or less.

Ratzenberger was flown to the Maggiore Hospital. The second session for the grid resumed at 2.05, while the helicopter bearing Ratzenberger approached the hospital. He arrived there at 2.08 and was officially pronounced dead at 2.15.

This was the first death at a Grand Prix since Canada, on 13 June 1982. Of all the drivers at Imola on Saturday, 30 April 1994, only two – Andrea de Cesaris (Sasol Jordan) and Michele Alboreto (Minardi) – had been present that desperate, dreadful, destructive day at Montreal when the young Italian Ricardo Paletti lost his life in a startline crash. The era without a death stretched across as broad a span as that.

Senna walked to the Williams motorhome and changed from his driving overalls. He telephoned Galisteu in Sintra. She has estimated that the call lasted some 15 minutes and consisted of 'sobs, complaints, doubts'. She has written that he 'really lost control' and said he didn't want to race on the Sunday. Nobody had ever heard him say anything like that before. She also records this fragment of their conversation.

Galisteu: 'What? Isn't there going to be a race?'

Senna: 'Don't you know them?'

That demands dissection because it carries such implications. Only one Grand Prix in modern times has been cancelled when the fraternity reached the circuit, Spa, 1985. The relaid surface of the track crumbled to the point where you could lift chunks of it with your hand. There is a very important difference between that and a fatality. When Villeneuve was killed in second qualifying, the race went ahead. When Paletti crashed in Canada a month later – and was helicoptered to hospital, pronounced dead there, much like Ratzenberger – the race restarted for its full 70 laps. And then there had been the accidents during Senna's own Formula 1 career, notably Berger at *Tamburello* in 1989, the Ferrari exploding in fire. The Imola race had been stopped to rescue Berger but subsequently re-started. Donnelly was massively mauled in first qualifying at Jerez in 1990, but second qualifying and the race went ahead quite normally.

If Paletti had been the last man to die at a Grand Prix, the last man to die in a Formula 1 car was Elio de Angelis, testing a Brabham at the Paul Ricard circuit on 15 May 1986. Ten days later the Belgian Grand Prix took place at Spa, and however sombre the mood (which it certainly was) the race went ahead quite normally.

Outsiders may see this as callous, and cynics do point to the imperative of television ratings and the fact that television channels all over the world have scheduled the race; hence cancellation is a very big step and regular cancellation might call the whole thing into question. That is only one aspect. Every sane insider goes to every race knowing that something dreadful can take place there. Unless the insider finds a way of accepting this, accommodating it, he'd better stay home. That is absolutely essential to the driver because he is offering his own mortality against his desire; but whatever protective barriers he erects in his mind, whatever accommodations he reaches with his inner self, they can be stripped away very, very quickly when the dreadful does take place.

On Saturday, 30 April 1994, that is what happened to Gerhard Berger, who found himself physically shaking. Berger began to erect his barriers again, asking himself if he would continue his career or end it instantly. Once he answered this most personal of questions he returned to the pits and drove when the second qualifying session resumed.

'I was sitting in my car watching the pictures of the accident on the portable television screen. I could see how bad it was. I knew how critical the situation looked. For the first time I found myself shaking after an accident. In our job you have to be prepared to see situations like this, but because the driver was Austrian and a personal friend, it was worse.

'You shouldn't differentiate between drivers like that, but this does affect you in a different way. I felt sick. I got out of the car and went to the motorhome where I was still shaking. You ask yourself whether you want to drive or not. The question is about racing. It is not related to this afternoon and it would not make any difference to Roland. But yesterday, when I saw Rubens Barrichello's accident, it made me realise how close we are to life and death. So you ask these questions. Then you say "yes, I am going to race on Sunday." So you go out and try to concentrate on the job. It was difficult, it was very hard.'

Senna reacted in a different way to Berger. He declined the offer of Frank Williams to drive again if he wished. He returned to the motorhome. Damon Hill and Damon's wife Georgina were there and Assumpcao came in. She found Senna's spirits 'so low. I just stroked his head, talked to him a little, but he was very quiet.' She had never touched him like that. They had touched before, but only in conversation and in the natural Brazilian way, to emphasise a point, celebrate a joke, maybe.

When the qualifying session ended, no competitor bettered Senna's Friday time. He would start the San Marino Grand Prix from pole position. Under FIA rules he was obliged to attend the post-session Press Conference and, in normal times – as Martin Whitaker points out – 'it's a fineable offence if you don't.' In this case, normality had gone.

One of Ann Bradshaw's tasks as Williams PR lady was to remind her drivers they were expected at mandatory Press Conferences. She went to the motorhome and diplomatically asked Senna. 'Absolutely not,' Senna said.

Frank Williams concurred. 'Absolutely no way,' Williams said and added that if there was any question of a fine the team would simply pay it.

Bradshaw made her way to the Media Centre and Maria Bellanca, doing a similar task for Benetton, was there and said Schumacher wouldn't be attending either. Bradshaw explained the situation to Whitaker who in turn explained to her that the Press Conference had been cancelled, the drivers weren't expected and it really wasn't a problem. Bradshaw concluded that the people running it 'had hearts and they showed them.' Berger, however – there by virtue of being third quickest – did give a Press Conference, but only because he wanted to explain why he'd gone out again after Ratzenberger's crash. It had nothing to do with how or why he'd qualified third.

Meanwhile Whitaker must, by the nature of his job, give an official communiqué to the media. Official communiqués tend to be rigid and formalised, but within that structure Whitaker put it together as sensitively as he could.

The drivers required for the Pole Position Conference on Saturday, April 30th were Ayrton Senna, Michael Schumacher and Gerhard Berger. Each driver was told of his requirement to attend the Pole Position Conference, either directly or through his team manager. In the event only Gerhard Berger attended the conference. Due to the circumstances and the mood of both the teams and the media I would like to think that no further action be taken against the drivers Ayrton Senna and Michael Schumacher for not making themselves available.

No action was taken.

Around 3.0, the race Stewards summoned Senna from the motorhome about his taking the official car to Ratzenberger's accident. John Corsmit, an experienced official, was 'a consultant to the Stewards. The meeting was in the Stewards' Office on the first floor of the control building. I was there, three Stewards, Senna and someone else (Whitaker). We asked exactly what had happened and we told him "you cannot take a car from one of the officials without asking permission from the race control, you cannot go out on the track just like that when a session has been stopped under a red flag without permission. If somebody goes out onto the track, we want to know who is going where." In fact, I said to Senna "even for you, it must be very easy just to knock on the door and ask if you can go there."'(Corsmit felt, reflecting much later, that no Italian official in an official car would dare refuse that car to the great Ayrton Senna if Senna suddenly wanted to commandeer it. They are all human beings.)

Whitaker, speaking in 1999, explained that he was 'there when the Stewards talked to Ayrton and sure he was very, very low. Quite naturally so. Corsmit is a firm man but I'll tell you something. He was a bomber pilot during the war, he's seen plenty of situations which are emotionally charged and he's not a fool. He's a compassionate guy – and he has to be – to do the job he's doing. He's not oblivious to, or unaware of, the emotions of people and that was particularly true with Senna. They were very close to each other in many ways. Yes, of course, Corsmit and the Stewards did realise that Senna felt concerned. What they said was: "Yes, we understand this and we understand your desire to have a look and be aware of what is happening and so forth, but if you want to do it again please inform us and we'll give you the assistance to do it. Please don't just go and commandeer a car."'

One report suggests Senna felt such distress he shouted towards Corsmit 'at least someone is concerned about safety.' Corsmit doesn't recall this and neither does Whitaker. 'I can't remember whether he got angry or not,' Corsmit says, 'but he was not happy with the situation, the whole situation. I don't know whether he was himself or not himself, but I do know he was not happy with what we were talking about. Maybe he shouted at me. I don't know. I had never had problems with him before. Well, what am I saying, problems? Of course, we all know about the situation we had had two times with Alain Prost at Suzuka and with Senna and Prost one time at Hockenheim (in 1991).

'Senna and I had spoken to each other a lot over the years but that does not mean we were adversaries. No, never adversaries. I got on very well with Senna and, normally speaking, I had no problems at all. I think he was the best driver that we ever had. Shouting at me? He never did that. When the meeting was over, Senna just went away. There was no reprimand, no anything. We could have reprimanded him, oh yes, but the (whole) situation was bad enough for the Stewards not to do anything about it: just to let him know that he couldn't do things like that. It was the last time I spoke to him.'

Whitaker says 'I can imagine the meeting could become highly charged, but there was a point where I went out of the room.' As FIA Press Delegate, he was 'in a privileged position of being allowed in there,' but obviously couldn't 'influence anything'. Whitaker reasoned that if things got 'a bit awkward' he'd leave and then, if a story leaked to the journalists, people couldn't 'say I abused the privilege and leaked it.'

Senna's anger may have revolved around the fact that he – Senna – was sure it was a *Steward's* car he had commandeered and thus his action was de facto sanctioned.

Senna returned to the motorhome and remained there, alone, until 5.30. He emerged wearing his white *Senninha* tee-shirt, face drawn, to go to the hotel. He told a handful of journalists that at these speeds 'our reactions and our sensations are at the limit. We cannot control all the parameters of the car. I fear for the young drivers: the speeds on the circuits are higher and nothing's done about it.' He literally bumped into Mark Fogarty of *Carweek*, remembered the truncated interview of yesterday, murmured 'I don't want to talk about anything but ring me during the week and we'll do it over the phone,' and was gone.

Assumpcao had worked for Senna for five years. She hadn't been a motor racing fan nor, in a sense, had she become one. This was her job. The death of Ratzenberger hit her very hard, so hard that she couldn't eat, so she lingered at the circuit. At around 7.0 Frank Williams asked her: 'How's Ayrton? Is he OK? I want to know.' She explained that he was going out to dine with friends. That reassured Williams who said 'I was afraid he might be on his own.'

When Senna arrived at the hotel a wedding reception was under way in the restaurant and immediately he was recognised. He agreed to pose for a picture or two with the bride and groom. Whatever his feelings about Ratzenberger, whatever his state of mind, he carried this task off.

He did have an obligation that evening. It was Josef Leberer's birthday and Senna and other members of the support team dined with Leberer at the Romagnola. Senna arrived at 7.0 and ate very little. Jakobi has described this dinner as 'a sombre affair' and during it Senna asked Leberer, an Austrian, all about what kind of a person Ratzenberger had been. Ratzenberger was new to Formula 1 in 1994, hadn't qualified for the race in Brazil but finished eleventh in Aida. The way Formula 1 is, Ratzenberger was almost a complete stranger. The Liveranis heard the talk passing to and fro, heard it move to safety, to improving safety in the pit lane – Senna recounting that one time a Tyrrell had nearly crashed him in the pit lane. One of the Liveranis says that 'all evening he seemed preoccupied, very worried, much shocked.' He ate spaghetti with plain tomatoes on it and they'd prepared a special little salad but it was too salty for him. Great consternation. They hastened to make another. He drank only mineral water, as always: sparkling and at room temperature.

Shortly before he left at around 9.0 word came that Castel San Pietro's police were expressing a lively interest in the Renault car parked illegally outside the restaurant. Much further consternation, followed by a physical outpouring of Liveranis who explained *it's Ayrton Senna's car and he's going in a moment*. You see the way it is in Italy: the police would surely have *guarded* the car to keep it safe for him and parking tickets are strictly for the birds; but anyway, Senna was going soon. He shook hands with the Liveranis and they thought he was more relaxed again, quiet like usual, returning towards his old self. He said 'thank you, I'll see you next year.'

Senna returned to the hotel and the receptionist gave him a message from Frank Williams to *please come up to my room for a talk*. Senna went there and had calmed considerably. He said he would race. A little while later, Jakobi bumped into Senna who was standing outside the door to his – Senna's – room wearing pyjamas with the white tee-shirt over them.

'Ayrton, you're dressed funnily,' Jakobi said.

'That's probably true,' Senna murmured and summoned a flicker of a smile. 'I've just been speaking to Frank. Goodnight, Julian.' Senna went into his room and closed the door. Once in his room he rang Galisteu, who had flown to Faro and was now in Senna's house. He sounded 'depressed' but said he felt a little better. Galisteu writes (in *My Life With Ayrton*): 'The housekeeper interrupted us to try and motivate him by telling him what would be waiting for him on arrival; grilled chicken and steamed vegetables. She handed the phone back to me and we talked about us.'

'On race morning,' O'Mahony says, 'either I would ring him or he would ring me. That morning the phone went (around 7.0) and I knew it could only be him at that time. I picked up the phone and I said "baggage service!" He'd say something like "there are four bags to be collected and I'll be at the airport and ready to go at a certain time" – because Ayrton would leave within an hour of the end of the race, an hour and a half.' It worked like this: Senna departed for the track, O'Mahony went to the hotel, 'beat Valentino figuratively round the ears because he was such a good man and we enjoyed that sort of thing,' collected the luggage and proceeded to Forli to await the end of the race and the arrival of Senna. Then he'd fly him to Faro, a journey of 'two hours 30 after take off.' Estimated time of arrival: the 8.30 which Galisteu counted on.

That morning, Senna checked out of the hotel at around 7.30, simply surrendered the room key at the reception desk. He walked past the wishing well and didn't throw a coin in. He walked through the two electric sliding doors and down some small steps to the carpark and his Renault car. His banker friend Braga went with him. They reached the circuit shortly before 8.0.

That morning a column appeared under Senna's name in a German newspaper, *Welt am Sonntag*. He wrote: 'My car reacts a bit nervously to this kind of race surface. This stems from its special aerodynamics but it's also got to do with a difficulty in the suspension.' He also wrote: 'I pointed out to the directors of the Brazilian and Pacific Grands Prix that we should look more critically at the capabilities of young or inexperienced drivers. My fears were borne out in tragic fashion. I know from my own experience that as a young driver one goes into a race in a totally different way and accepts risks that you shake your head about later.'

(It's worth adding an explanation here because what Senna wrote is so important. Newspaper and magazine columns by celebrities may not have actually been written by them. However, in this case the newspaper faxed questions to

Assumpcao who secured the answers from Senna – or if the answers were familiar ones which had been used elsewhere, checked with Senna that they were OK – then Jakobi approved the whole. Therefore, the column was authentic Senna.)

When Senna reached the track his face still betrayed profound emotions but Frank Williams estimated he'd calmed further. Senna spoke for a while to Niki Lauda about safety then went out in the 9.30 warm-up session where he was decisively quickest (1:22.597 against Hill, next, on 1:23.449).

During it, Senna carried out a heartfelt plan he and Jakobi had hatched on the long haul back from Aida. Prost would be commentating at Imola for the French television channel *TF1*, on a programme called *Auto-Moto*. What, Senna mused to Jakobi, if I send him greetings *from the cockpit* as I'm driving round, send him greetings live onto the programme? Jakobi thought that a good idea and, unbeknown to Prost, it was arranged. In the warm-up and above the engine noise Senna suddenly said in English: 'A special hello to our dear friend Alain. We all miss you Alain.' With exquisite forethought, Senna did this on the start-finish straight which, he must have calculated, would be nearer the receivers and thus make for better clarity of reception.

Was Senna tying up more loose ends? There are people who find that conclusion too tempting to ignore; some talk of premonitions. The fact that it had been organised two weeks before Imola mitigates against such a notion. Nobody, surely, had any premonitions that Imola would be *the* dreadful weekend, or if they did there are no *facts* to prove they did. We are left with Senna's eminently understandable depression at Imola and no more than the enigmatic and incomplete words of Senna's sister – 'he was very low, though I will not say why' – before Imola; left with Senna's own words about the rule changes: 'we'll be lucky to get through the season without a major accident.'

During this warm-up also (according to Karin Sturm in *Goodbye Champion, Farewell Friend*) Betise Assumpcao claimed, heatedly, to the press that Senna had received a written warning from the Stewards the afternoon before about taking the official car to the scene of Ratzenberger's accident. Since the whole weekend was an accumulation of movements great and small which present a baffling mosaic – and since every detail seems portentous – we had better clear this up. What Assumpcao saw was the written notice to Senna to *appear* before the Stewards, which is what he did. That's not the same thing as a written reprimand which, as Corsmit and Whitaker attest, never happened.

After the warm-up, a strange minuet played itself out between Senna and Prost. Reflecting, Prost says that when he – Prost – retired and could no longer threaten Senna on the track, Senna's motivation changed. 'His reasons for living, his reasons for racing in Formula 1 were different.' Prost estimates that now the World Championships held a diminished importance for Senna and, although he didn't discuss that often, he did so from time to time with Prost. Equally, Prost estimates that Senna's message on television proved his sincerity.

The warm-up finished at 10.15 and the traditional drivers' briefing would begin at 11. Prost, touched by what Senna had said to him from the cockpit, went to the rear of the Williams pit so that they could talk. Senna was deep in conversation with Brown and Bernard Dudot of Renault, telling Brown not to change anything on the car. From the corner of his eye he noticed Prost and nodded to him, meaning *I know why you've come, I appreciate it and we'll talk when we can*. Prost understood that you don't interrupt a driver when he's deep into a discussion on race morning and, because he understood Senna's behaviour patterns so well – that this discussion might continue for a long time – Prost left. They'd talk another time.

In fact, the discussion ended fairly soon and Senna set off to find Prost; and did find him, but he was deep into a discussion of his own with Louis Schweitzer, President of Renault. Senna would certainly not be so impolite as to intrude, and went to the Williams motorhome.

Towards 11.0 Senna emerged and walked with Berger to the drivers' briefing in the control tower. Whitaker says that 'Ayrton arrived with Gerhard from the paddock and you could tell they were talking about something they wanted to achieve during the course of the briefing. I remember Ayrton's mood as very sombre, very sombre. It was well known that there would be a minute's silence at the briefing and there was. Bernie (Ecclestone, President of the Constructors' Association) doesn't play a part in the briefings but he went to the front and announced the minute's silence. They all stood and observed it.'

Senna wept quietly, privately.

'Then they started the discussion under the control of Roland Bruynseraede, the race director, who sits there and gives the briefing. If you remember, at Aida a "pace" car had been used on the parade lap (bringing the cars round in grid order for the start) for the first time – because invariably you ended up with the first few drivers waiting for the rear of the grid to arrive and settle. The idea was that the pace car would keep them more bunched. At Aida it was a Porsche 911 and Senna, on pole, felt it wasn't quick enough to allow the Formula 1 cars to heat their tyres properly (speed = friction = heat). You and I might consider a Porsche 911 to be very quick but in comparison with a Formula 1 car it isn't. At Imola they had an Opel turbo which presumably would have created the same problem. Ayrton and Gerhard drew it to the attention of Bruynseraede, it was he to whom this concern was directed. I don't know if the Stewards had already decided not to use the pace car or whether it was Senna's words in the briefing, but it wasn't used.'

Damon Hill is sure the intervention of Berger and Senna proved decisive.

Tyre temperature is by no means as trivial as it might sound. The Grand Prix car exists on fine margins. Cold tyres, when the acceleration bites, can take the car clean off the circuit or make it spin, the last thing anyone wants in the tight-packed scrummage from the grid. Following the same logic, Senna expressed disquiet about the 'safety' car, a saloon which came out in the event of an accident and which the racing cars had to follow until the accident had been cleared up. Senna insisted that the safety car didn't take them round fast enough to *keep* the tyres properly warm.

The briefing over, Senna spoke to Schumacher, Berger and Alboreto about getting all the drivers together on safety. 'You'd find,' Whitaker says, 'that there were many occasions when drivers remained behind to discuss a couple of points. Ayrton was one of those. He was a perfectionist, and if he wanted to discuss something he would discuss it. If somebody else had something for him to do they'd just have to wait.' These drivers tentatively agreed to meet about safety on the Friday of the next race, Monaco, the only race on the calendar where the usual routine was broken: first qualifying on the Thursday, the Friday being kept free for promotional activities.

The newspaper *Motoring News*, in its issue after Imola, carried this paragraph: 'Several drivers reportedly felt the urge to go up to him (Senna) and touch his arm or shoulder at the drivers' briefing, without being able to say quite why.' The paragraph was written by David Tremayne, an experienced journalist, and he confirmed to me that some of the drivers had told him this.

Senna went to the Williams motorhome then he and Hill, however reluctantly, went to the Paddock Club and gave some Williams guests in the hospitality area their verbal laps of the circuit and chatted as best they could about the weekend. That done, some time past midday, Senna re-entered the motorhome and ate a light lunch. There was a discussion about the race and Frank Williams remembers Senna picking up some spare driving overalls and heading off with them to meet Berger. Williams didn't see him again.

Quite by chance, Prost ate his lunch in the Renault motorhome virtually next to the Williams motorhome – the Williams cars had Renault engines – and, the lunch digested, came out precisely when Senna came out. Prost sensed that this was not the moment: Senna moving into his concentration for the race, wishing absolutely no distractions. The minutes ticked by lockstep to the start.

It was 1.30, and so 30 minutes to go. Senna saw Prost and waved, again meaning *we'll talk when we can*. Prost noted how astonished bystanders were. Normally Senna and Prost exchanged little niceties when they met and could hardly avoid doing so, but waving affectionately hadn't been seen for years. Prost would remember Senna's look as strange, 'bizarre', almost haunted.

When Senna reached the Williams pit a Brazilian journalist, Jayme Brito, asked him to sign three photographs. Brito has been quoted as saying that 'the photos were so sad. I remarked about it.' This was even more peculiar than the O'Mahony photographs: not just that they were sad, but in the folklore of Formula 1, less than 30 minutes before a race, Senna isolated himself in his concentration of other-worldly intensity. He once explained to me that in those moments it is *wrong* to recognise anybody except perhaps your race mechanic. Over the past few years he had become more relaxed, however, and, superficially, this one time, he scanned the photos, signed them and listened to Brito talk about them.

Brito remembers Senna 'did something I had never seen him do before. He walked round the car, looked at the tyres and rested on the rear wing, almost as if he was suspicious of the car.'

Assumpcao says that *ordinarily* Senna 'had a particular way of pulling on his balaclava and helmet, determined and strong as if he was looking forward to the race. That day, you could feel just from the way he was putting on his helmet that he was different. He'd have preferred not to race. He was not thinking he was going to die, he really thought he would win that race, but he just wanted to get it over with and go home. He wasn't there, he was miles away.'

At Faro, Adriane Galisteu settled down to watch on television.

At Forli, Owen O'Mahony settled down at the airport to watch on television.

At Sao Paulo, the president of Senna's fan club, Adilson Carvalho de Almeida, and many other members of the 1,600-strong club settled down in Senna's business skyscraper to watch on television. They felt close to him in the skyscraper, not a continent and the width of the Atlantic distant.

At Imola, Martin Whitaker settled down in an office adjoining the Media Centre to watch on television. The room, like the Media Centre, was directly above the pits.

At Silverstone, Lyn Patey – aspiring journalist covering the British Formula 3 meeting there, and as we've seen a long-time Senna admirer who'd met him in F3 days – sipped coffee in the Marlboro motorhome and settled down to watch on television. She had a very uneasy feeling that 'Ratzenberger hadn't been enough of a sacrifice.'

At Imola, Assumpcao settled down in the Media Centre to watch on television.

At Newport, in Wales, Mrs Susan Nichols – who had never met Senna but followed his career avidly since 1983, and may be regarded as an atypical supporter – would only watch the warm-up lap.

Once the car had been fired up, Senna completed a lap of the circuit and nosed the car onto his grid position, front and to the left. There, he removed his helmet and balaclava, placing the helmet on the bodywork immediately in front of the cockpit. *Ordinarily* he did not remove his helmet once he'd reached the grid. Each driver prepares in his own way. Some get out of their cars and stand around; some like to wave to the roving television camera which side-steps between the mechanics and the cars;

others, like Berger, are just as likely to wander over to the grass beside the track and have a sit-down, a last gorge of mineral water. Invariably Senna remained as near as you can get to motionless inside the cockpit, his daunting eyes locked onto the stretch of circuit ahead. To fiddle around taking the helmet off and putting it back on again could only break the concentration.

Is this trying to fit theory to fact? After all, he'd changed, was more relaxed these days, more likely to do something like that. Whatever, Assumpcao glimpsed Senna's eyes and felt a certain sense of reassurance. Senna, she imagined, was now prepared to do what he did best and do it as well as any man had ever done it. Race.

He summoned a watery smile when the drivers were introduced over the public address and Berger – driving the Ferrari, of course – got a wild cheer. Senna understood about that, the Italian chauvinism, and it seems to have amused him, however many times he had heard it before here, and at Monza for the Italian Grand Prix. He also smiled when Patrick Head, the Williams Technical Director, said something to him (about the pace car, as it happens). He never, as far as we can ever know, smiled again.

In the pits Frank Williams felt confident. Refuelling stops had been introduced this season, bringing with them a tactical question: how many pit stops a team chose to make. 'Ayrton was on a two-stop run, which was going to be quicker than three stops. We did not know Benetton's strategy [for Schumacher] but Ayrton, we believed, was going to drive away from the others to the point where it didn't matter what they did.'

Just before the 1-minute board was hoisted, Senna put the balaclava on and adjusted it carefully, his strong hands tucking it into the collar of his overalls, smoothing it to his neck. His face seemed morose but that might have been the concentration. It is true he looked miles away, looked to be … somewhere else. Maybe he always appeared like that with a minute to go but all these years it had been hidden under the helmet. Maybe not. He put the helmet on and the 25 cars covered the parade lap, felt for their places on the grid in their twin columns.

Susan Nichols felt 'what I can only describe as a mounting sense of panic. I said to my husband and daughter: "I can't watch any more because I don't want to see what is going to happen." It was the first time in over 12 years that I couldn't watch the race. They both thought I'd gone mad. I went into the garden.'

When the red light flicked to green Senna made a classic start, onto the power instantly, strongly holding the Williams which wanted to wrestle from him as the power tried to break free. Laying broad, equidistant burn-marks of rubber scrubbed from the tyres by the power, he was already good and clear of the grid and neatly, neatly into the first little left-hander; already decisively ahead of Schumacher.

Behind him, JJ Lehto's Benetton stalled three grid ranks from the one Senna started on. Car after car twisted, darted and missed Lehto. Pedro Lamy (Lotus), unsighted and coming over from the second last rank of the other column, struck the Benetton's rear a mighty blow, so mighty that a wheel was hurled as far as the spectators, causing injury, and the Lotus was hurled across the track. Lehto and Lamy escaped largely unscathed. With debris everywhere, the safety car came out and took the remaining 23 cars round for three laps, overall the 'fourth' of the Grand Prix. On the next lap the safety car signalled – by illuminating the rotating lights on its roof – that it would be pulling off and the race could resume at full bore. Senna's race engineer David Brown radioed what was about to happen and Senna acknowledged it.

The safety car did peel off and again Senna made a classic 'start', onto the power instantly, Schumacher behind, then Berger but already Berger some distance away.

At Silverstone, Patey 'sickened by the first incident, waited long enough to see Ayrton safely into the lead after the safety car pulled off and I went to sit outside, unable to shake off a feeling of deep depression.'

Now Senna had the powerful, pervading, pounding pressure of Schumacher in pursuit, Schumacher whose Benetton would do 0–60mph in 3.6 seconds, 60–100mph in 1.5 seconds and 100–203mph, its top speed, in 15 seconds; would brake from 203–100mph in 2.3 seconds, 100–60mph in 0.6 of a second, 60–0mph in one second. Schumacher could handle all this with complete confidence. Here, already, was a pivotal position in the race which might be pivotal to the whole World Championship.

On that lap six Schumacher thought the Williams looked nervous in *Tamburello* and was bottoming. Senna led into lap seven, urging the Williams through the hard-right onto the start-finish straight, his hands firm but flexible on the wheel. The white bays of the grid fled beneath the car. He took it over to the right at the little left-hander and kept it on the right along the tree-lined straight towards *Tamburello*. The creamy-milky coloured concrete wall in front of the trees seemed to flicker by because of the car's sheer speed. This wall curved round the outside of *Tamburello*, a looping left which went on and on. Into the mouth of the corner, Senna brought the Williams over towards the red and white painted kerbing on the inside, the classical position for going round.

A camera, and particularly a television camera, distorts distance in width and depth. The television camera which captured Senna assuming this classical position, and whose images would flood round the world, presented *Tamburello* as a broad, deep place. It was not. It was tight, cramped and narrow. If you stood on the rim of the track and walked directly to the outside wall it was 14 paces.

Senna could see, in panorama.

To his left: the tall, verdant trees, then a wall with mesh fencing above it, then a thin strip of grass, then the red and white kerbing which ended just into the corner.

Directly in front: the width of the track which unfolded out of sight.

To his right: a white boundary line, then a thin strip of grass, then the concrete run-off area, then the low concrete wall with mesh fencing above it, then more trees.

As the loop tightened he placed the car a little further over to the left and passed before a large advertising hoarding for Kronenburg beer. At the point where the red and white kerbing ended, the loop still tightening, he was travelling at 192 miles an hour. The car straightened, which – the loop unfolding left-left-left away from it – took it clean off the circuit.

Schumacher would say: 'Ayrton took two or three bumps. I was behind and, the lap before, I saw he was a little unstable and skittish in that corner. The next time he went sideways and then he lost it.'

The car shrieked over the thin strip of grass, over the concrete run-off area. It bisected the run-off area and, in the 1.8 seconds before it struck the wall, Senna had clawed the speed down to 131 miles an hour. It was not enough. He sustained devastating head injuries. The distance from the end of the kerbing across the track, grass and concrete to the wall at the angle he went: 102 paces. From 192 miles an hour, and even plough-plough-ploughing the fearsome stopping power of the brakes, 102 paces is a very short distance.

It was 2.18 of the hot, dry, sunny afternoon which remains yesterday afternoon.

The Williams bounced from the wall with such force that it reached the rim of the track spinning savagely, thrashed back onto the run-off area and came to rest there.

If what he believed was true, he met the God he felt he had known for so long then. Of the physical world he would know nothing more.

Immediately after this impact, the world *we* had known grew darker, moment by moment. The golden helmet did move within the cockpit, and movement – any movement – is what you look for first because it means life. It moved, a convulsive twitch, and moved no more. Reportedly, the first marshal to reach Senna, called Stefano Bounaiuto and with 20 years experience, leant towards the cockpit and felt himself recoiling. Afterwards, he wouldn't say publicly what he saw.

Whitaker watched on the television. 'There was an aerial shot and you could see Senna sitting in the cockpit and his head moved slightly. My first thought: *he's had a bad accident but this is his usual way of coming to terms with it*. Normally, if he'd had a big accident or something had happened, he would try and compose himself. Automatically I thought that was what he was doing.'

It was the saddest misreading, and one shared.

Adriane Galisteu saw and thought Ayrton would be home to her sooner.

Lelio Benetti, a marshal, told *F1 Racing* magazine: 'The accident was so hard and fast it happened like lightning. We are not allowed to touch the car or drivers until medical help arrives, but as I ran over I could see the car had stood up well. It was similar to Berger's crash [in 1989] but his car exploded and broke in two – Senna's hadn't. Berger and Senna hit at different angles.'

Giuseppe Bezzi, also quoted in *F1 Racing*, was the first doctor to attend to Senna. 'I didn't see the accident because I was in the medical car, but you could see it was bad. I could tell he was alive but badly injured. He was unconscious and losing a lot of blood. He was still alive – his heart was beating and his blood pressure was at 120 (over 80), a normal reading. But he was very badly injured. We got him out of the car and laid him on the track. We attempted to resuscitate him with all the normal procedures.'

An ambulance waited to take him to the Medical Centre, the normal route to examination, recuperation, rehabilitation. The careful hands did not put him in the ambulance. They waited: he would go by helicopter direct to the Maggiore Hospital in Bologna.

I think I knew then.

At Forli airport, O'Mahony 'simply didn't know Senna's condition' but didn't like the implications of what he was seeing at all.

In Sao Paulo the communal feeling of the fan club found expression in de Almeida. 'We were shocked, but we were sure we would soon see him walking away from his car with an angry look on his face. He'd been in other accidents that seemed far worse than this one and always walked away.'

In Gwent, Susan Nichols 'knew instantly what had happened when my daughter told me through her tears that Ayrton had been involved in a horrific accident. I didn't need confirmation that Ayrton had been killed. I already knew.'

At Silverstone, Patey sat and 'someone gave me the news, almost falling out of the motorhome in his urgency. I leapt to my feet desperate for a TV and more information. As I started to run towards the awning opposite I caught my toe in the bar at the bottom of the Marlboro unit entrance. I fell very heavily on my left side, hitting my head on the concrete and hurting my arm.'

In the Media Centre, Assumpcao had seen Senna's head move and went down to the Williams pit where the mechanics were watching on a big screen. She tried to peer between them. His brother Leonardo arrived soon after.

Whitaker would, within moments, find himself the only official conduit between the tragedy at *Tamburello* and the assembled media relaying it to the world. 'If there is an accident, the first thing I do is leave the Media Centre and go straight to the Stewards' Office because, if you like, that becomes the nerve centre. There's a long corridor between the two which is usually so packed with people you can hardly walk along it. I met Alan Henry there (*Guardian* journalist and author) and we were the only people in that corridor. As I saw Alan, I could see he had this look on his face. He looked at me and said: "He's dead." There was nothing I could reply.'

The medical team, Watkins playing a prominent role, tended Senna and removed him from the cockpit, laid him on the ground, continued to tend him. He was alive, but only clinically. The medi-vac helicopter belonging to the Maggiore Hospital, a BK 117, had just dealt with an emergency call at Castel San Pietro – which Senna had left that morning – and was re-routed to *Tamburello*. It landed on the track five minutes later. Ordinarily this helicopter would be staffed by a doctor and two nurses but now three specialist doctors boarded it to take Senna to the Maggiore. He was lifted carefully inside but it was cramped because the helicopter carried so much life-saving equipment.

At 2.34 it rose above the trees and reached towards its maximum speed of 140 miles an hour. It would take no more than 18 minutes to reach the Maggiore, following the most direct route to Bologna, which was a straight line passing directly over Castel San Pietro. During the flight Senna had a cardiac arrest but the doctors brought him back from that.

O'Mahony knew 'as soon as he was put into the helicopter something was seriously wrong.' The world did, too.

At Silverstone, Patey had reached a TV in time to see the 'feverish activity' before Senna was put into the helicopter, but after her fall 'a friend took one look at me and despatched me to the Medical Centre where I was inspected and sent on to Northampton General Hospital.'

At Imola, Professor Watkins was driven back to the Medical Centre.

Whitaker 'told the Stewards I would now be going to the Medical Centre. I had a long-standing agreement with Professor Watkins about how we would cope with such eventualities. At the Medical Centre he would give me a very brief statement on the driver and say if the driver required hospitalisation and which hospital he had been taken to. I would issue that to the media.' By then Assumpcao and Leonardo had arrived there and seen Watkins go in, not seeming to recognise anybody. They asked Whitaker: 'What's happened? What's happened?' but Whitaker knew no more than they.

Whitaker 'asked for Professor Watkins and was shown into a big office. He was sitting there on his own looking at the helmet on the table. I'd seen everything going on, but this was the first time I became aware, the first time I really, really realised something was desperately wrong. Watkins is a professor of medicine, he's seen a lot of things but he was numbed by the whole thing. He looked at the helmet, turned it upside down and walked to the corner of the room and put it down there. He didn't show it to me but I saw the hole in the visor.'

Outside, Assumpcao heard someone asking what Senna's blood group was. Jakobi had arrived and suggested it might be in his passport, which was in his briefcase in the Williams motorhome. Assumpcao went there immediately and returned with the briefcase and Senna's mobile phone. No blood group in the passport. Leonardo tried to make a call on the mobile but couldn't get a line. (He had phoned Viviane in Brazil, however, to say Senna had had an accident. Her 'initial reaction' – quoted in *F1 Racing* – was that 'it wasn't too bad.' She made that judgement based on what she'd just seen on television. 'But when I saw the doctors working on him I knew it wasn't good.')

Inside, Whitaker explained that a statement was necessary, Watkins said Senna had received a 'head injury' and Whitaker would draft this into a short, simple press communiqué. Whitaker asked if he wanted to add anything and Watkins said 'No, that's it.'

Whitaker left the Medical Centre and Assumpcao asked again: 'What's happened?' Whitaker was faced with an immediate dilemma. Here was Senna's *brother*. Whitaker suggested they went to the Stewards' Office. 'They asked: "Shall we come with you?" I said "it's probably better that I go up the pit lane and you go through the paddock because if we are all seen together people may start drawing conclusions." We did that.' They reached the Stewards' Office and Whitaker asked Leonardo and Assumpcao to wait outside. She realised that she'd left both Senna's briefcase and her handbag at the Medical Centre and hastened to retrieve them. They were exactly where she had set them down.

Inside the Stewards' Office, as Whitaker remembers, 'there was complete silence. Bear in mind that at this point I was the only person who had had contact with Professor Watkins. The information he'd given wasn't the sort of thing you'd send over the radio (from the scene). The Stewards were sitting round a table. I said: "I have a statement which I am going to issue but not until I have read it to you so that you know the details of it." I read the statement – including the phrase *head injury* (author's italics) – and asked if they were in agreement. "Yes, yes, yes."

'Bernie was in there. I told him Ayrton's brother and others were outside and suggested somebody should look after him. "Leave it to me, I'll take them to my motorhome," Bernie said.' (FOCA had a motorhome to rival any other in facilities and privacy.) Whitaker said he would go there after he had issued the statement in the Media Centre. Whitaker read the statement to a 'hushed audience' of the media and although more and more questions were fired at him he didn't elaborate because he couldn't. He was telling them all he knew.

At some point, Leonardo rang Viviane again to say it looked bad.

The helicopter touched down on the Maggiore's helipad, a broad concrete area some 300 metres from the main hospital building with a white painted cross in the middle of it. Ordinarily the staff on the helicopter would transfer their patient to the waiting ambulance but they'd radioed ahead and another specialist team were in the ambulance so that he could be transferred in as little time as possible. As they prepared to transfer him he had a second cardiac arrest, but they brought him back from that. Beyond the high fence which separated the helipad from the adjoining road a few people had already gathered and gazed mute. The ambulance reached the Maggiore, a 16-storey L-shaped building, in one minute, reversing up a ramp to the mouth of the intensive care unit.

Under the head of intensive care, Dr Maria Teresa Fiandri, the staff managed to bring his pulse back to somewhere near normal. 'With the first aid at the track, during transport here and in the hospital we did all we could,' she said. They put him on a respirator.

At Northampton General Hospital, Patey was 'dizzy and in a lot of pain. I was cushioned by the shift in reality facing me. There was a perpetual motion of sick and noisy children, a constant stream of bandaged feet, be-slinged arms like mine, drunk, angry, brawling teenagers and, seemingly ignored by Everyone except me, a large TV and video pumping out endless Bugs Bunny cartoons. I suppose I was praying but mainly my mind was blank. I'd had several phone calls from worried friends at the track but only to talk about me and arrange a lift back.'

Braga rang his wife Luiza in Sintra, who in turn rang Adriane in Faro, explained how serious Braga had told her it was and that they must go to Bologna. Luiza said she'd hire a plane in Lisbon, come to Faro and together they'd fly on to Bologna.

From Forli, O'Mahony began to telephone the hospital 'but it was difficult to make them understand I was Ayrton's pilot and not just another fan ringing up.' He kept on ringing.

Whitaker went from the Media Centre to the FOCA bus nearby in the paddock. 'As I got there Bernie came out to meet me. He said: "What are we going to do now?" Bear in mind we've got camera crews and journalists all around. I said quietly: "First of all we need to get an official statement from the hospital as to what Ayrton's condition is." He said: "What condition?" He looked at me with that look which says *what are you talking about?*'

Ecclestone: 'I thought you said he was dead.'

Whitaker (heart sinking): 'I didn't say he was dead.'

Ecclestone: 'You said he was dead.'

Whitaker: 'No, I said he has an injury to his head.'

Ecclestone: 'Oh my Good God.'

Whitaker realised 'this has gone wrong. I thought the "family" were in the motorhome because Bernie was looking after them. This would have been Bernie's reaction: to take them under his wing. And also Ayrton was an incredibly important part of Bernie's life. They'd been close friends and not many people know that Ayrton had been ski-ing with him and things of this nature' – albeit a long time before.

They agreed that it would be more prudent to enter the motorhome away from the camera crews and journalists. Everybody, Whitaker remembers, 'was in there, including Bernie's wife, and they were numb. People were in tears but I think numbed is the better word. Bernie started to explain that there had been a misunderstanding – Bernie knew the situation didn't look good because he'd heard the original statement I'd read out in the Stewards' Office – but it became apparent that he'd told them Ayrton was dead. Leonardo was sitting in Bernie's chair and was visibly very, very upset. Bernie started to explain and didn't seem to be having a lot of success so I thought that – as the link, if you like, with Professor Watkins – I should try. I said "in good faith, Bernie has obviously told you something which in actual fact is not quite correct and, although a tragic one, it is a misunderstanding. Here is my notebook and I can show you and read to you what I did say in the Stewards' room." I read them the statement.'

Assumpcao said: 'I don't want to know what you said in the Press Room, I want to know the truth.'

Whitaker 'looked at her and said: "I've never told you a word of a lie in my life and I'm not about to start right now. Here is my notepad, here is what I wrote down."'

She looked and saw the two words *head injury*.

Whitaker remembers that she said: 'You're a liar, you're a liar, you're just doing it to cover it up.' Assumpcao does not remember saying this but frankly, in the circumstances, it's entirely natural for the participants to find difficulty in retracing exact dialogue. Whitaker left the motorhome, Ecclestone organising for the Senna entourage to go by helicopter to the Maggiore. That also involved organising a car to take them to the helicopter because the track's helipad, on a football field, was some distance away.

The misunderstanding would subsequently assume bitter proportions culminating in the Senna family advising Ecclestone not to attend the funeral in Sao Paulo because he wouldn't be welcome. How did the misunderstanding arise? In the circumstances, every person at Imola on Sunday, 1 May 1994 found themselves in a shifting, cascading nightmare of global consequences and with minimal factual information to go on. Those closest to it felt the weight most. Whitaker is 'convinced that although Bernie listened while I read the statement out in the Stewards' room, under the overbearing enormity of the situation, he took the word head for dead. And that was the only word he really heard. I'm sure about that. When I'd said to him that Leonardo and entourage were outside and needed looking after, he assumed it was to comfort them (for a bereavement).' Beyond question, Ecclestone acted with propriety and compassion.

The race had re-started at 2.55, more or less as the helicopter touched down at the Maggiore. Berger, Senna's great friend among the drivers, led from Schumacher. At 3.15, 20 minutes into the re-started race, Berger lost the lead after nine laps and drifted back. The Ferrari was awkward-handling but Berger had

had enough. He retired after 11 laps. His thoughts were on getting to the hospital. At the Maggiore, Dr Fiandri spoke of Senna's 'desperate condition'.

Whitaker had returned to the Stewards' Office and moved into another nightmare. 'The Stewards were there and the director of the circuit and his secretary and a bank of TV monitors and they were watching replays of the incident. We needed the director of the circuit to establish lines of communication with the hospital.' What the hospital did have was direct communication with *RAI*, the Italian television channel, who were broadcasting up-to-the-minute information and inevitably it was looming on some of the screens on the bank of monitors, Whitaker having the words translated. There was a groundswell of rumours suggesting that information was being withheld. Since Whitaker had no official word from the Maggiore, and since in his position he could only relay official words, the nightmare darkened within the wider nightmare.

'We don't have any jurisdiction over a country's medical authorities. To all intents and purposes we are just a racing circuit who want information from a hospital on a racing accident. They don't have to give it to us, and they didn't, they didn't.' They did, however, continue to give it to *RAI*, leading to further confusion. Two laps before the end of the race the following was issued in the Media Centre in an attempt at clarification:

As you will be well aware there are numerous rumours circulating the paddock and here in the Media Centre over the condition of Ayrton Senna. The organisers of the San Marino Grand Prix are in the hands of the Maggiore Hospital in Bologna and only the hospital can issue an official statement on the condition of the driver. Until we receive an official statement from the hospital there is nothing further we can add. As soon as any official statement is available we will make sure that you receive it.

By now TV Globo in Brazil were moving into extreme emotion, with broadcasters struggling to control themselves.

At 4.0 Dr Fiandri announced Senna as 'clinically dead'. At 4.05 Father Amedeo Zuffa administered the Last Rites. By now a crowd of some 300 people – who, on the radio or *RAI* or by word of mouth, had heard where he was – crowded the hospital reception area. It remains staggering that this throng felt a compulsion to go to the hospital. They can't have been active race supporters or they'd surely have been down the road at Imola.

Leonardo, Assumpcao, Lemos and Leberer arrived in the helicopter. Leonardo could have gone in to see Senna but, in the circumstances, decided not to do so.

O'Mahony 'eventually got through to the hospital and spoke to Julian Jakobi. Then I flew the plane to Bologna in case Ayrton needed to be taken anywhere.' He took off from Forli at 4.15.

At 4.20 the race ended, Schumacher winning it from Nicola Larini (Ferrari) and Mika Häkkinen. The crowd, unaware of Senna's true condition, grouped under the podium, waved Ferrari flags and chanted to salute Larini. Then he, Schumacher and Häkkinen attended the mandatory Press Conference. They sat side by side and their faces betrayed that they were lost in another dimension.

At 5.30 at the circuit Martin Whitaker issued a similar verbal statement to the one issued before the end of the race. This again stressed that there were still many rumours circulating about the condition of Ayrton Senna but that no official statement had been forthcoming from the Maggiore Hospital and until this happened there was nothing to add.

At 6.0 Berger arrived at the hospital and was permitted to see Senna. Berger later told Nigel Roebuck of *Autosport* that Senna was still alive when he saw him and 'I want that to be known, because various accusations were made at the time, against Bernie Ecclestone, that Ayrton was already dead at the circuit, and Bernie knew about it. That's absolutely not true. I saw Ayrton with my own eyes.' Berger flew by helicopter to Bologna airport and 'we landed near my plane, which was parked next to his. (In fact where O'Mahony had parked it.) Even though I'd just left him, it hit me hard.'

At 6.40 Dr Fiandri announced that 'Ayrton Senna died a few seconds ago.' The machinery keeping him alive had not been switched off because Italian law forbade it. The plane which Luiza Braga had hired reached Faro and Galisteu boarded it. Galisteu constantly repeated to herself 'be strong, be strong' because that is what Senna had taught her to be. The pilot took it to the end of the runway but while he waited for permission to take off for Bologna a message came through. He swivelled the plane and returned to the terminal building. When they deplaned Galisteu started shivering 'from head to toe'. Luiza Braga received and gave the message and they sat in the terminal for a long time or a short time. Luiza said they'd better go to the house in Faro. There was nothing else they could do. Bologna, a routine hop of maybe three hours, might have been the far side of the moon from them or an infinity further on; and was.

The finality had not been announced at Imola because the fact of it had not been transmitted to there. Whitaker, impatience rising around him, hammered at the officials in the Stewards' Office 'who were totally embarrassed to even pick up the phone and dial the hospital by this stage.' Whitaker found Professor Watkins and between them they fashioned another statement, issued at 7.20.

Ayrton Senna suffered severe head injuries which produced a deep coma. His condition is grave and the electrical brain test shows brain death. His condition is deteriorating.

Whitaker qualified it by adding:

This statement was issued by Professor Watkins from his hotel room in Bologna some minutes ago. I stress that the information given is his assessment of the situation before leaving the Maggiore Hospital and travelling back to his hotel.

The fax from the Maggiore did not come through to the Stewards' Office until 7.23. It bore the hospital's headed notepaper and, pre-printed, who it was from and how many pages (Pages, 1, including This Page). The typed message:

Alle ore 18.40 cessa l'activita cardiaca.
Si constata il decesso.
(At 6.40 the heart stopped.
We verify his death.)

It was signed-off, in typed block capitals:

IL PRIMARIO DEL SERVIZIO RIANIMAZIONE
DOTT. M. TERESA FIANDRI

but not signed or initialled. Nowhere did it say whose heart had stopped. Ayrton Senna did not need to be named.

All the hospital could do now was set in motion the autopsy, which under law they were obliged to do. However so many people were gathering – reports speak of thousands – that transferring him to where the autopsy would take place proved temporarily impossible.

At 7.40 Whitaker read out:

The circuit has just received the following official statement from the Maggiore Hospital in Bologna. 'We verify the death of Ayrton Senna. The time of death is registered as 18.40.'

In Sao Paulo, normally a mass of humanity, the streets were emptied. Conjure that image: the 20 million inhabitants absent. Instead, they listened to radios or watched television where, one report says, 'newscasters were unable to hide their emotion as they read the tragic news from Italy, but there was also anger in their voices.' The presenter who announced the finality said: 'All Brazilians feel this as if it were a relative.' A few of the millions began to drift to the house of Senna's parents in a wealthy suburb. A fraction of the millions began to drift to a soccer match where the crowd observed a minute's silence and some of the players sank to their knees for the duration of that, hands clasped in prayer. The silence over, the crowd chanted Senna's name and waved in ripples.

President Itamar Franco sent his condolences to the Senna family. Senna's Brazilian trainer, Nuno Cobra, broke down during a television interview and murmured 'how can this be?'

Police mounted guard over Senna's office block in Sao Paulo in case anybody tried to get souvenirs.

At Northampton General Hospital, Patey says that about 'four hours after I arrived I received my last phone call of the day.' A friend in London 'had heard of my plight and called to see how I was. I quickly assured her that I would be fine and then asked the question. "What's happened to him?" There was silence at the other end of the phone, then … "I'm sorry, I thought you knew. We've lost him …"'

The toll from the Imola week-end:

Friday – Barrichello's crash at 1.14. Saturday – Ratzenberger's crash at 1.18. Sunday – Frenchman Jacques Heuclin injured in a Porsche race before the Grand Prix; Lamy and Lehto crash at the start of the Grand Prix, a tyre injures seven spectators and a policeman; Senna's crash at 2.18; three Ferrari mechanics and a member of the Lotus team injured when a wheel came off Alboreto's Minardi in the pit lane.

Chapter 16

AFTERMATH

O wen O'Mahony made his way to an hotel in Bologna and 'we stayed there, Leonardo, Julian and I. Leonardo was the senior family member present, of course, and the Brazilian ambassador came about the arrangements.'

However routine and necessary these arrangements may have seemed on this Sunday night, they would come to reveal the true scale of what Senna meant. Even those close to Formula 1 were unprepared for the scale: not just Brazil brought to open grief but that rarest of human conjunctions which transcends climates, continents and cultures *and unites*. Self-appointed world statesmen might hope for this but they don't get it.

While the initial arrangements were being made, O'Mahony says, 'there was some talk that I was going to have to fly Ayrton back to Brazil.' He phoned an engineering company in England who explained that the aircraft's side-hatch wasn't big enough. 'I would have wished to fly him back, oh yes, oh yes. The last part of my contract would have been to deliver him safely home. Put it this way, it would have been a very painful trip, a very painful trip, but it would have been an honour.'

Monday, 2 May

Mourners were so numerous they provoked traffic jams outside the Instituto Di Medicina Legale, where Senna had been taken at 9.0 the night before and would lay there until the autopsy was ordered. Police ensured the mourners could not enter, but a stretcher was brought out so that they could lay flowers upon it. The stretcher quickly overflowed. No statement would be made after the autopsy.

At *Tamburello* flowers were laid.

At the gates of the Williams factory in Didcot, near London, flowers were laid. Richard West observed that many of them must have come from people who had never met Senna, never spoken a word to him and maybe never been to a race.

O'Mahony flew the HS125 to Paris, taking Leonardo there so he could board a Varig flight to Sao Paulo. 'I parked by the side of the Varig 747. He got out, got into the Varig and I departed. Leonardo was stunned. He did speak a bit but he was stunned. There had been so much responsibility on him, apart from the grief.' O'Mahony flew the HS125 to Southampton, its usual base and where it was serviced. He left it and went home, prepared to fly to the funeral.

Members of the Williams team had flown back to England on Sunday night, landing shortly after midnight. Ann Bradshaw faced a television camera 'because you have to. You can't run away from what happened.' She spoke a few sombre words but her face betrayed her feelings. She looked as if she had come from another planet.

That morning the British headlines brushed aside news of the first full South African election, regarded as a turning point in 20th century democracy. That was equally true in Italy where, with very little restraint, newspapers apportioned blame, passing judgement on the circuit, the crash helmets, the Williams team.

That morning, too, mourners made their way to the Williams factory to position bouquets on the gates. West said: 'A little boy arrived here first thing with some flowers. He'd probably only ever seen Ayrton on TV, but Ayrton meant everything to him. When sport loses someone like Ayrton, millions of people around the world feel it even though they have never met him.'

Frank Williams, who'd remained in Italy, arrived in the early afternoon, his eyes reddened, and were driven into the factory without stopping. He'd need time to choose his words. When he was ready he said: 'Williams Grand Prix Engineering is a family, and although Ayrton had only joined us this season, he and I enjoyed a longstanding relationship, and I am proud that the first Formula 1 car he ever drove was indeed a Williams. He gave us his total commitment, and we gave him ours. He loved his motor racing and shared this passion with every one of our employees at Didcot. We are a Grand Prix team, committed to the sport, and will continue our work, which I am sure is exactly what Ayrton would have wanted. He became a key member of our team in a very short time, and I hope that what we achieve in the future will be an honour to his memory.

'His loss is impossible to quantify. Everyone who has ever met him in whatever capacity feels they have lost someone very special. All of us in the Rothmans Williams Renault team will remember him with respect, admiration and affection. Our sincere condolences go to his family and many friends around the world.

'We are at this moment studying data available to us to ascertain the cause of the accident. The FIA, motorsport's governing body, as a matter of policy, investigates all accidents and they too will be examining all the relevant information.'

The FIA announced that they had arranged a meeting in Paris for Wednesday. They said that 'the FIA is gathering reports from its technical, medical, safety and supervisory staff, as well as from the relevant team and circuit personnel. As soon as these reports are received, they will be studied as a matter of urgency.'

Jean Todt, manager of Ferrari, said in Italy that work would begin immediately on improved crash helmets, not just to protect the driver's head but his neck as well. 'We will give twice what it costs, it is as important as that. At the moment we know that the driver's body is protected by a strong chassis, and there has been a great improvement in circuit safety. It is obvious that the weak point is the driver's head. Helmets are heavy and subject to enormous deceleration, and nothing has been done to protect the back of the neck. For me, that is a major concern.'

Before the San Marino Grand Prix, Prost had spoken of how in Formula 1 'everything is done for business, for money, and nothing for the sport.' Max Mosley, President of the FIA, countered that. 'The truth of the matter is that, generally speaking, drivers are interested in having the fastest car. They are not really interested in safety. That is our responsibility, and something to which we give constant thought and attention.'

In Italy, magistrates ordered the autopsies on Senna and Ratzenberger to be carried out, impounded the cars, and sealed the circuit. They confiscated all film of the race. There was talk of possible criminal proceedings, embracing the track manager, Williams officials, and Simtek.

Grief hung over Brazil. President Franco declared three days of national mourning and cancelled his official engagements. The Foreign Minister, Celso Amorim, tried to hasten the release of Senna's body and offered his plane to bring it home, but the Bologna magistrates insisted on the autopsy on Tuesday morning.

One of Senna's former girlfriends, Marcella Praddo, claimed her baby daughter was Senna's love child. It seemed like the first taking up of positions for Senna's millions.

Tuesday, 3 May

Senna's body was flown to Brazil via Paris. An Italian military aircraft had taken him from Bologna to Paris, where he was transferred to a Varig flight. As a mark of respect, the Varig flight cleared a section of their business class for him rather than, as is normal airline practice, find space in the hold.

Headlines shrieked again, like SENNA: HIS FATAL ERROR. Patrick Head had been quoted by Italian and Brazilian newspapers as saying: 'Ayrton Senna made a mistake. We have checked the telemetry. He slightly lifted his foot just at the dip in the place where the tarmac changes. That caused a loss of downforce on the rear wing which meant the car went straight on.'

Quietly, in the background, Damon Hill paid his tribute. 'For all his concerns about safety, Ayrton never played safe in the cockpit. He performed at a hundred per cent all the time and for that he commanded admiration from every driver. I will never forget my short period working with him, and consider myself immensely privileged to have been a team-mate. The loss of Roland and Ayrton has affected everyone deeply.'

In Sao Paulo, word spread that he would lie in state at the city's legislature and a column of those wishing to pay their respects began to form.

Wednesday, 4 May

In Brazil, Charles Marzanasco, a spokesman for the Senna family, made an appeal on the radio for people not to go to Sao Paulo airport when the Varig flight landed at dawn. There were fears that the city would cease to function if, literally, millions descended on the airport. 'The best way to show your love and respect is to go, in an orderly fashion, to the legislature,' Marzanasco said. The column would stretch a mile.

Towards dawn, as the Varig entered Brazilian air space, a flight of jets joined it and fanned out in formation across a leaden sky in salute and, unconsciously, to protect the one who no longer needed their protection. As he was brought from the Varig many people wept but some applauded. To applaud a coffin is a poignant act, a last gesture of appreciation, but surely also a denial that Senna had died, a denial that he was here but no longer here.

A guard of honour waited. Six air force cadets loaded the coffin on to a large hearse – in fact a fire engine – and it began its dignified procession to the legislative assembly. Six motorcycle riders formed a phalanx around it, others formed an arrowhead before it. As the cortege reached the city, uniformed cavalry replaced the bike riders, and now it moved so slowly that thousands upon thousands ran parallel to it as if they wanted to hold the moment, couldn't let it go. Nobody can ever know how many people gathered to watch the cortege pass but it was certainly in the millions. At the legislative assembly an immense crowd waited, many waving flags in mute salute. Here, 16 uniformed men carried the coffin slowly along a red carpet and between massive white pillars into the building. The coffin was draped in the blue, green and gold of Brazil. Some quarter of a million people were expected to file past the coffin before the funeral on Thursday.

Almost unnoticed among them was Liliane, the woman who had been his wife, who had shared briefly his life and who he had divorced more than a decade before because he'd concluded that his career over-rode his marriage. She made no special arrangements for priority, simply filed by among the throng.

At Didcot, Williams issued a statement. 'Following reports in the Press that the Rothmans Williams Renault team blames Ayrton Senna for Sunday's accident, Technical Director Patrick Head has commented: "We are still studying the data, still gathering the information, and at this stage we have reached no conclusions. All the relevant information is not available at present. I believe that any initial conversations I had at the circuit have been taken out of context, and would point out that I have not spoken to any journalists on the subject since leaving the circuit. At no time did I ever say Ayrton Senna was to blame."'

In Paris the FIA met, and then Mosley faced the Press. Shouldn't the remainder of the season be called off? 'It would be, I think, over-reacting in the absence of some evidence. Everyone has been deeply affected by what happened over the weekend at Imola. We are confronted with problems in motorsport, but we have to keep our calm and *sang-froid*. We need to examine the cars to be able to come to precise conclusions as to the causes of the accidents. This will only be available in about a month from now. What I can tell you now is that each of the three accidents of the weekend – Barrichello, Ratzenberger and Senna – is unconnected.

'Alain Prost has suggested, among other people, that the Federation has no contact with the drivers and is in some way distant from the drivers. This is completely untrue. This suggestion has only been made by people seeking to make trouble. We have worked constantly on means to improve safety for the last three years and next year. One of the areas under examination is airbags for front impact.

'The immediate safety measures we can make for the Monaco Grand Prix (two weeks after Imola) will concern the pit lanes. They are the following: 1) The entrance and exit to the pit lane will be shaped to decelerate the cars, thus reducing the number of pit stops because of the time loss. 2) It will be prohibited for anyone to stand in the pit lane unless they are about to work on a car or have just finished. 3) We will ensure that the number of cars that come in on each lap is very limited. The unscheduled stops will not be for changing tyres or refuelling.'

Thursday, 5 May

The funeral, after the lying-in-state, made the most profound impression on all who attended it. 'I had never seen two million people crying before,' O'Mahony says. 'You have to remember that Ayrton was all that Brazil had, Ayrton and a soccer team which wasn't doing that well.'

They laid him to rest with great dignity. Berger and Prost and Stewart and Emerson Fittipaldi and Hill helped bear the coffin, their faces drawn, sombre, perhaps still uncomprehending. Others of his life were here also, Frank Williams, Ron Dennis of McLaren. Petals were strewn over the coffin before its lowering. Field guns fired a salute and far, far overhead, jets carved a huge *S* in the sky. Ayrton Senna da Silva was buried in the Morumbi Cemetery in the centre of a large, circular plot.

It is precisely the shape of a wheel.

Derek Warwick was there, but only after making a very personal decision. 'I'd known Roland Ratzenberger but I could not find a way of getting to his funeral (in Salzburg) the following day if I went to Sao Paulo. I ended up ringing Roland's family and I said: "Look, I am very, very sorry. I am not favouring one driver over another, but please understand I raced Ayrton Senna for over a hundred Grands Prix – he had become a friend, an enemy – and I had more respect for that man than any other racing driver I have ever known. I cannot not go to Ayrton's funeral." I almost went to Roland's because I thought that was the right thing to do and, at the eleventh hour, I said *no, I have to say goodbye to Ayrton*. It was a difficult decision.

'It was very, very special to be a part of the funeral [as a coffin bearer]. In myself I felt numb, I felt it wasn't actually happening. It was all a bit of a nightmare. I felt such sadness, and at the same time a kind of happiness to see so many, many people saying farewell to a great driver. Did we fully appreciate the extent of what Ayrton meant to people before that? I'll give you an example. A friend of mine [in Jersey, where Warwick lives] was having some building work done and the day after the accident my friend was showing me round this building. I went into one of the rooms and the workmen were having a tea-break. Each one of them was sniffling. I thought that was strange. None of them were racing people – all football and cricket – but they'd just been reading about the accident.'

In fact, quite unknown to Warwick, it would have been possible to attend both funerals because Johnny Herbert and Berger managed that. Berger felt an eerie sense that Senna was watching the extraordinary vastness of the funeral, on a presidential scale but with the emotion on top, and that Senna the perfectionist would have been annoyed if anyone had put a single step out of place.

Herbert was 'a bit disappointed' that more drivers did not go because 'there was only really a handful of us who went to either.

I know it affects different people in different ways and I understand that but to me it was a matter of showing respect. I knew Senna well enough to joke around with him and have little chats with him. He'd joke around with me. I got on well with him. I'd known him a little bit in karting, I'd raced with him twice there – once in Italy and once in Sweden: 1982, he'd reached Formula Ford 2000 but he was so desperate to win the World Championships he competed in that one event.'

Winners are often desperate to win, but none more so than Ayrton Senna.

Once upon a time, many years before the circuit of Imola was built, the parkland in which it stands was a favoured walking place on a Sunday. In those days people gathered in a quiet corner by a fountain and listened to a little band which played a special kind of drum, a tamburello. Its sound has long gone from there. On Sunday, 1 May 1994, in the looping corner which bears the name of the drum and close to the old fountain, it was replaced by a sound from hell.

On the Wednesday before Monaco, ten days beyond Imola and as the gathering for the Grand Prix began, the Senna family issued a statement to answer the thousands upon thousands of messages of condolence they had received, some from as far as Afghanistan.

For many years people from all over the world have shared with us their great admiration for our dear Ayrton Senna; someone who worked to make dreams come true, someone who always tried to improve in every aspect of his life; someone to whom life was filled with happiness; someone who deeply loved his country. With the green and yellow flag of Brazil in his hands after each victory, Ayrton demonstrated with pride how much he believed in his country, and in his fellow Brazilian citizens who always loved and supported him. We now find comfort in our deepest belief that Ayrton's same ideals will endure throughout the world; ideals of solidarity and faith. God bless our friends from all nations who have demonstrated so much love and sympathy for us at this moment of pain and sorrow.

The banners began to appear at Monaco, as they would at every circuit before the long year ended. On the cliffs above the Principality, the first of them said AYRTON SENNA FOREVER. Down by the harbour, the usual vending stalls sold their souvenirs but Senna dominated them. One stall, devoted to tee-shirts of him – with the profits going to a Brazilian children's charity – sold out fast.

Joseph White of the *Associated Press* conducted a survey of the stalls and quoted a saleslady, Rachel Duffy, as saying: 'I disagree with it, I disagree with making money on tee-shirts which are more expensive than the others just because it's Senna.' White noted that Duffy was selling tee-shirts 'emblazoned with the former three-times World Champion for $14 apiece – because her boss said she had to.' White moved on and noted that other vendors lacked Duffy's inhibitions. Senna was everywhere: on hats, in photos, on scarves, his portrait woven into Brazilian flags. One stall estimated he accounted for 70 per cent of what they were selling. A vendor said: 'It's money. It's sad, but people want to pay their money. It's business.' White concluded that 'Ratzenberger, who lived in Monte Carlo, seemed to be the forgotten driver.' He asked more than 12 vendors if they had *anything* on Ratzenberger and they told him, 'No, not at all.'

Approaching Monaco, drivers kept their personal barriers up in their own ways but two of them – Berger and Schumacher – publicly confessed they felt a pressing need to demonstrate to themselves that they could still drive a Formula 1 as they had done before Imola. Berger had not fundamentally tampered with the decision he made at Imola to continue, although he'd missed a Ferrari testing session before Monaco because he didn't feel he could get in a car again yet; and Schumacher reacted by asking himself a series of profound questions about what he'd do if the feeling was wrong.

If either judged that something subconscious was holding them back, that the precious thousandths of a second were no longer there, they'd have to reconsider. Those thousandths are hewn from *absolute* commitment of the kind Senna had always shown everywhere but especially at Monaco. And Monaco hammered and haunted, anyway, as if time hadn't begun its healing process but had reversed it. In the Thursday morning free practice, Wendlinger crashed in his Sauber, sustained serious head injuries and would lie for days in a coma at a Nice hospital, his life in danger.

And somehow they forced themselves through qualifying, forced themselves to the absolute commitment, went in search of the thousandths.

In the background, moves on safety intensified and would come to represent one of the legacies of Senna and, however unprovable, the legacy of Ratzenberger. Some things have to be faced. I do not believe the death of Ratzenberger alone would have lent such urgency to this, or made it such an imperative, but Senna and *Tamburello* had become a worldwide matter, and what had passed for 12 years as another sporting activity among many, found itself under ferocious scrutiny.

After Imola, the Italian defence minister, Fabio Fabbri, was quoted as saying: 'I hope the murder of Imola is punished. The Formula 1 world is worse than the gladiator's circus.' Italian President Oscar Luigi Scalfaro sent a telegram to the President of Brazil stating his disapproval that the race had not been abandoned after Senna's crash. The Vatican newspaper, *L'Osservatore Romano*, wrote that 'the show at Imola went on despite everything and death itself was made into a brutal spectacle.' In a sense, these were instant reactions, however understandable. How could these people suddenly grasp that *it had always been like this, that the risks weren't new but eternal, that deep down every driver knew the score, that Grand Prix racing could be wonderfully rewarding but horrifically hard?*

At Monaco, amidst the grim, sombre, withdrawn faces, Niki Lauda announced the reformation of the Grand Prix Drivers' Association to occupy itself with safety. Max Mosley said firmly that whatever was necessary would be done.

Before the start of the race, the drivers stood across the grid and observed a minute's silence. Two drivers held a large, square Brazilian motif: a green background, Senna's face against a segment of yellow and the simple message *adeus Ayrton*. When the cars formed up for the green light, the front row of the grid was left empty as a mark of respect. Williams ran only one car, for Hill. Brazilian flags hung limp from balconies.

As these cars formed up for the green light, an uncounted number of regular tele-spectators around the world could not bring themselves to watch. Something had gone, and wasn't coming back: Senna's five pole positions here, some extraordinary, some challenging credulity; Senna's six victories here, some lusty and brave, some soothed by finesse. Many people, to judge from the letters I've received, would take months to watch again. Some perhaps never would.

Schumacher won Monaco, came second in Spain, won Canada on 12 June. The World Football Cup Finals began in the United States five days later. Romario's goal-scoring partner Bebeto was asked who he'd dedicate ultimate victory to if Brazil achieved that. He replied, 'to my wife, my children, my family and above all to the Brazilian people. These suffering people have to have some happiness in their lives. Here in the United States, in the concentrated situation we find ourselves in, we never forget Brazil and I never forget Rio, which I love. More often than not, the players talk about it. Our people have had only blows – inflation, violence and corruption. Ah, I almost forgot. I will also dedicate the title to Ayrton Senna, a great idol who the people will never forget.'

And it happened thus, not just from Bebeto but other players as well. The World Cup Final, between Brazil and Italy at the Rose Bowl, Pasadena, California, lurched to a penalty shoot-out and Roberto Baggio of Italy crucially missed his. In the commentary area, Pele – an icon like Senna – danced up and down in delight and shook his fist in triumph. The Brazilian players spilt onto the pitch and abandoned themselves. Romario, close to tears, was wrapped in a Brazilian flag. Then four, five, six players held a banner up to the crowd. It was white with a message in black full across. *Senna: we accelerate together. The fourth title is yours.* Brazil won the World Cup in 1958, 1962 and 1970 so this was the fourth. Senna won the World Championship in 1988, 1990 and 1991 so 1994 might have been his fourth.

The long year limped on and at race after race the Senna flags and banners fluttered, plaques were set up, statues unveiled, homage paid because each race was the first in each place without him, the grief and void coming afresh to each group of supporters: Magny-Cours, Silverstone, Hockenheim, the Hungaroring, Spa; and at Spa, wonderfully, Barrichello took pole position in the Jordan. He had not been on pole before and neither had Jordan. In a wet-but-drying session he timed his most important run perfectly and dedicated the pole to Senna.

Schumacher took the title in Adelaide and, in turn, dedicated it to Senna. Schumacher and Hill had crashed, of course, but by tradition Schumacher, as the new champion, took his place with the first three in the Australian Grand Prix, Mansell, Berger and Brundle.

Afterwards, Schumacher spoke about the crash then reviewed the season. 'It started quite well in Brazil, even Aida it was a good race, and then we came up to Imola [shakes head]. What happened at Imola is just a … [purses lips, shakes head again] … all of us know what kind of feelings we had to make about this, particularly for Ayrton but also for Roland and as well for Karl – what happened in Monte Carlo. For me it was always clear that I was not going to win the Championship and it was Ayrton who was going to win the Championship, but he hasn't been there for the last races. I'd like to take this Championship and give it to him because he is the driver who should have earned it. He had the best car, he was the best driver ...'

That was mid-November. A month later the second Elf Master Karting took place at Bercy. Sometimes, time passed quickly in the long year. Could it have been a whole 12 months since Senna was here with Adriane?

Philippe Streiff says 'every driver wore the *Senninha* logo as a mark of respect.' Prost had the distinctive S on his left arm and, throughout the event when he wasn't driving, sported a *Senninha* cap. Good men and true attended Bercy and drove there: Prost, Schumacher, David Coulthard, Herbert, Alessandro Zanardi, Olivier Panis and several young hopefuls. The indoor course, so tight that the racing was nip and tuck and nudge, proved ideal for real racing, just as Ayrton Senna would have wished. Schumacher, who reportedly brought a team of mechanics from Germany, won, Prost third.

'Before the presentations,' Streiff says, 'all the lights were switched off and we had three minutes of absolute silence – 15,000 people and no sound. Then Alain Prost paid a very touching homage about how Ayrton was here only last year and how much he was missed.'

Prost said: 'Last year, Ayrton was in our midst, competing here. He was here because he had a passion for the sport, a very deep passion, which drove him to look for perfection. We all have a similar feeling, which helps us to go on when terrible things happen.'

Streiff ruminates on the three minutes of silence. 'The event was televised by *Eurosport* and obviously because we were to switch all the lights off, you can't very well have three minutes of the silence and what would have been a blank screen. So we'd compiled our tribute in pictures and that was transmitted. It was condensed from 32 minutes of film from the year before and you can see how happy he was, how full of happiness. That's strange, because in all the pictures of him I saw in 1994 – at the Brazilian Grand Prix, at Aida, before the race at Imola – he looked ... sad. At Imola, he looked ... very sad.

'After Bercy in December 1994 his sister Viviane gave me a card, a card of good wishes. It had a picture of *Senninha* with the S large and a light coming from above it. On the card was written *Life is a gift from God every morning, and it is necessary for each and every person to rediscover the magic and mystery of life itself.*'

Owen O'Mahony refracts this, distils it into eight words, this same Owen O'Mahony who'd flown him so far and come to know him so well. 'Ayrton Senna was big enough to be little.'

An example of that. Senna would try with the *Senninha* comic to give kids something to strive for, maybe convince them that they could not only strive but succeed whatever odds were heaped against them in the wreckage and ruin of the slums, the *favelas*. A certain logic here, too. Virtually the only exit from these *favelas* was petty crime or becoming a footballer, the latter much easier at the outset than motor racing because you only really need boots (and could even play barefoot) but even football is not an easy path once it starts to get serious.

Romario would say: 'I come from a poor family. Sometimes I had to miss training so that my brother could go. We couldn't both afford to go. We had very little money. I'm sure this is still the case today. There are many young players who are not seen at the clubs because they can't afford the bus fare to get to the training.'

Senna knew, as everybody knows, that if you can't raise a bus fare the prospect of buying a kart is beyond imagination, but he must also have known that his career represented something else beyond money. If you set out to achieve and you are determined enough, you can achieve it virtually whatever obstacles are put in your way. True, he'd had more than enough money to get the kart, enough to come to England for the single-seaters, but thereafter many obstacles stood in his way: homesickness, an active dislike of the soggy English climate, learning a foreign language, the choice of sustaining his marriage or his career. Higher obstacles followed: the struggles with Piquet, Prost and Mansell for the World Championship and becoming the man every other driver wanted to beat. Money always helps in daily life, just as a British Aerospace HS125 helps, but no amount of money could bring Brazil closer to England or make England a sunny, jet-ski place or make Piquet, Prost and Mansell and the others easier to beat; but he did win and it came from himself.

Chapter 17

THE LEGEND

Everything which followed 1 May 1994 moved in two dimensions, foreground and background: the foreground was the continuation of the World Championship, and we've just seen Schumacher win it. The background was why he'd crashed and what was happening about that. This did not end with the completion of the official report into what befell Senna. That report, available in February 1995, was of some 500 pages and prolonged a mystery as well as launching a further step: it was passed to magistrates in Bologna and they initiated a process of questioning participants and witnesses. Later, a trial judge would consider whether prosecutions be brought.

Nobody, surely, had anticipated a clean, swift conclusion and there were precedents. Two racing accidents involving fatalities in Italy – Wolfgang von Trips and 13 spectators in 1961, Jochen Rindt in 1970 – begat investigations which lingered and lumbered for years; but the death of Senna was different. He was arguably the most famous, and certainly the most fascinating, sportsman on the planet. His face was universally familiar. There had been many, many hundred million viewers who had watched the catastrophe at the San Marino Grand Prix, or seen replays of it. A very great imperative existed to know what had happened and why.

After the accident, as we have seen, the car had been impounded at the circuit where it remained while a magistrate, Maurizio Passarini, launched the official investigation. He brought a wide-ranging group of experts in to help and advise, because much of the investigation would penetrate the extremely technical. Whatever Passarini's deliberations and discoveries, however, several theories already existed about the cause, notably that the steering column on the Williams had failed, rendering Senna helpless.

A Grand Prix racing car is a highly complex creation. Sheer technology allows the most astonishing and exact information about its every movement – telemetry – to be relayed to the pits. Patrick Head had had limited access to the crashed car but he and the Williams team tried to help, albeit from their factory in England. 'We gave a comprehensive report on the telemetry from the steering wheel and did a lot of tests which we recorded on video. We presented documentation within a month of the accident which pretty much showed that we couldn't get any of the data that was recorded without the wheel being attached to the column.

'We then produced a report about two months later because, although we had given quite a lot about what we didn't think had happened, we thought it was important to give an opinion on what we did think happened. I asked our [Italian] lawyer what the response was on those reports and he said: "The problem is that both reports are too technical to be understood." Well, the first had a few numbers in, but the second was deliberately put into layman's terms.' Head, incidentally, saw the impounded wreckage only twice in the months after Imola, and then only for between five and ten minutes.

In August, two French newspapers – *L'Equipe* and *Info-matin* – claimed to have a leak from the University of Bologna, which was active in the investigation, implying (it's an imprecise leak, don't forget) that a fracture in the steering column had been found or a quality flaw or a lack of thickness in the metal used. The Williams team responded within hours. 'Current media reports giving information regarding the possible cause of Ayrton Senna's accident are not based on the official findings of the technical experts investigating the matter. They have not yet reached any conclusions and have asked the magistrates for a delay until the end of September. Therefore any speculation prior to this date is unfounded. We have no further comment.'

The end of September 1994 came and went, and Passarini talked of his experts meeting 'after the end of November.' That came and went too, and so did Christmas, and so did January 1995. In early February, Max Mosley said: 'I expect the report will give an explanation for the causes of the accident and say that the steering column was broken. It will also probably mention the bumps on the track, which we all know about, but not much more. I expect it will blame some people, but I am satisfied in my own mind that no-one did anything that could be seen as deliberate or reckless with Senna's car. Everything was done with the best of intentions and no-one should be blamed for anything on moral grounds.' Mosley added that he saw 'no possibility of [Frank] Williams going to jail or the Williams team being put out of business.' Quite how Mosley could say this is unclear.

In mid-February, Head said: 'We have a copy of what is supposedly the experts' report going to the magistrate. I hesitate to make too much comment, but I cannot actually believe that the technical people who I am aware were involved had any influence on it. It does not appear to have anything like the structure of somebody with a technically-trained mind.'

A few days later, word leaked from Italy that the report contained a conclusion: the steering column had been shortened before the race – so that Senna had a better driving position and perhaps a better view of the cockpit instruments – and a length of tubing welded to the column. This snapped at the entry to *Tamburello*. Williams's Italian lawyer responded: 'Our data shows the steering was working until the moment of impact.'

And there it lay, as the final sequence of interviewing the participants and witnesses began. There it lay while so many people waited to know conclusively the what and the why of *Tamburello*, and could never find peace within themselves until they did.

As we saw in the introduction to this book, Head and Adrian Newey were acquitted of all charges in December 1997. It seemed the prosecution had failed to prove that the steering column failed, but that, of course, merely reopened all the other speculative theories about the reason for the crash. Some were strange, some absurd, some at least plausible. For example, Damon Hill felt the cause might have been oversteer, but that wouldn't explain why Senna did not – the instant the oversteer became apparent – turn the car away from the wall. That would equally apply to the car bottoming over the bumps and snapping out of control. He'd *still* have turned it away from the wall.

This is something you can do endlessly and it takes you nowhere, just as it has taken the Italian legal system nowhere. The prosecution appealed the 1997 verdict, and this appeal was dismissed in 1999. This, evidently, was not enough and in 2003 a court announced that the whole process would have to be gone through again because there had been 'errors' the first two times around.

In that sense we are exactly where we were on the night of 1 May 1994. It is as if you really do spend your life running every minute hard against time and you do miss its deceptive sweeps, its long and silent passages, its subtle elongations. Because of that, and because this book is an updated compilation, I want to finish on the timeless dimension.

As 1994 moved to its conclusion, and Schumacher was the new World Champion, Darryl Reach, then the Editorial Director of publishers Haynes, and I both felt strongly that we should do something to mark the first anniversary of Imola. The result was *The Legend Grows* and almost a decade later I don't feel the need to change the way it ended. Here it is.

Late January-early February 1995 and the long year would complete itself in just a few weeks. The Liveranis were reluctant to speak about Senna because, I sensed, they felt close to him and maybe were expecting to see him in that small, private dining room again. They were extremely unanxious to promote the Romagnola restaurant through his association with it. Paolo, one of the two brothers running it, did speak and in a few moments he was very close to breaking down. His eyes looked away, then at the floor as he composed himself. When he'd done that he recounted an anecdote which still amused him.

Once, just once, Senna arrived – it was a test session at Imola – and they couldn't give him the private room because it was already full. For some reason Senna hadn't forewarned them he'd be coming. They asked if he'd mind going into the main dining room and he said he wouldn't mind. Of course, the other diners there wanted his autograph and he handled that with his usual grace. However, one of the autograph hunters tried to lure him into signing a blank cheque.

'Sorry, no chance!'

I imagine the place shook with laughter.

The walls of the Romagnola were full of pictures of disabled push-chair races around Castel San Pietro, but no pictures of Senna, no proclamations that the great Ayrton Senna was a patron, nothing except, discreetly on one wall, his autograph on a sheet of the block notepad. 'It's a photocopy,' Paolo said. 'I've got the original locked safely away.'

Apart from the privacy of the small room, apart from the food, apart from the family embrace which the Liveranis exuded, I wonder if Senna kept going there *because* it did not have pictures and proclamations of himself; didn't have posters of that yellow helmet and the red and white Marlboro McLaren or the blue and white Rothmans Williams leaping off the walls at him – as they did in so many other places on earth, cafés, bars, factories, bedrooms, living rooms, airports, magazine stands, hoardings.

We'll never know now.

The Hotel Castello had experienced a sharp dilemma over Room 200. A lot of people rang up and said they wanted to stay in it. Others, when told its significance, said they didn't. If someone arrived and wanted a suite and obviously didn't know, the reception was drawn between telling them and not telling them. I sensed they hadn't quite resolved this dilemma yet.

The circuit of Imola was deserted that winter's day. A few of the permanent staff were working in offices in the long building above the pits, next to the control tower. There was a map of the revised circuit, the alterations intended to be in place when the year ended. The San Marino Grand Prix would fall, in 1995, on 30 April, a day short of the calendar completion.

The map showed alterations to about half the circuit but helplessly your eye was drawn to *Tamburello*. It would become an S-bend – left-right-left – and the new section of track coil away from the wall; there'd be a proper gravel trap, deep enough to stop a car in good time; and, anyway, the cars would be passing through at the reduced speed an S-bend demands. The old *Tamburello* would be a memory, seared and searing, but a memory.

This deserted winter's day, you could walk from the grid to *Tamburello* as it still was. It wasn't not a long walk. You passed under the gantry bestriding the track which housed the red stop lights and the green go lights, the last ones he saw. You followed the little left-hand corner where, at the start of the race yesterday afternoon, he had already taken the lead for the last time. You're out into the country, which is actually a public park, the track slicing through. On the other side of the wire fencing, a group of old men chuckle and argue at an intersection. Ordinary cars pass quietly by because a normal road runs there, just the other side. Joggers pass, too. A man in a woollen hat whistles for his dog and it scampers through undergrowth towards him.

Just for a moment, the contrast is difficult to take. Five or six yards away, the most normal, mundane, everyday form of life is going on. *Here* the ribbon of track so accustomed to unimaginable ferocity is entirely empty. Yes, *here* are the verdant trees he saw, the strips of grass, the white boundary line whose coats of paint have crusted and cracked a bit. And up *there* ahead, *there* a couple of hundred yards away is the red and white kerbing to the left, the advertising hoardings to the right and the tightness, the narrowness, the on-and-on out-of-sight final twist of *Tamburello*.

I suppose, during those 200 yards, I was walking towards him and walking back to myself and, just for a moment, that contrast was difficult to take, too. I started writing about Formula 1 in 1982, started writing about him in 1983 as a man I'd soon be writing about in Formula 1. As I'm nearing *Tamburello* I have in my pocket a little green book for telephone numbers and his is in there, *circa* 1983, a Tilehurst, Berkshire, number. I hadn't taken the book deliberately, because I take it everywhere, but somehow the phone number returned me virtually to when I'd begun: I'd spent every year except 1982 writing about him.

As I'm nearing *Tamburello*, a little flurry of memories came back. Silly memories, mostly. Stowe corner, Silverstone, one time and we're discussing his braking point in the Marlboro McLaren and where mine would be in my Ford Sierra. I indicate mine. 'That's a long way back,' he says. 'Funny,' I say, 'I thought it was too close.' Another time I've scribbled some practice lap times in a notebook and he beckons me over, wants to see what the others are doing. My scribble is spaghetti carbonara with a felt-tipped pen but he locks onto the numerals and dissects them as if he's moved into another world: of analysis, received information, conclusions. He nods and hands the notebook back. He *knows* now and he's stored it.

Another time I'm putting together a Grand Prix supplement for the *Daily Express* prior to the British Grand Prix and wouldn't it be interesting to get him *batting at cricket*? I'm curious to see how fast he masters the mechanisms of something completely unfamiliar, how his co-ordination copes with pads, gloves, a bat and a moving ball. I explain this and he says, 'sure, ring me.' The supplement didn't have enough space for the article and so the cricket never happened.

It's normal, I believe, with any bereavement that you remember what had been and equally mourn what hadn't been and now never would be.

Another time further on down the road, Donington 1993, the Thursday before the European Grand Prix when, on the Sunday in the wet, he will make his own contribution to Einstein's Theory of Relativity. He espies me lurking and, as usual, moves to shake hands because he was, all else aside, an instinctively polite man. I shoo him off because I'm streaming and steaming with influenza of the virulent weak-at-the-knees kind and the last thing I want is for him to catch it. What if we had shaken hands and he had caught it? What if *even he* was too weakened-at-the-knees to construct the great, majestic, mental arithmetic race which he did, a race so enormous in execution and accomplishment that it takes its place among the greatest ever driven by anyone?

Ah, well.

Like I say, mostly silly memories.

It's a crisp, cloudless winter's day, a little wind stirring the parched leaves which have gathered, nestling, against the wall at *Tamburello*. In the wall there is a gouge mark, the sort you'd expect shrapnel to make: not symmetrical but a frantic, shapeless burst into the eight inches of concrete. It is not very large. On the wall, like a form of graffiti touched with grace, are messages of salute and condolence and devotion in several languages. A man and a woman from Holland have inscribed in English *Senna for always in our minds 26–1–95*. Above the wall, slotted into the wire mesh, are bouquets. The most touching is a single tulip whose stem has been crudely hand-wrapped in a twist of ordinary tinfoil. It's easy to buy a bouquet but to pick a tulip and arrange it yourself seems quite different: humble and thoughtful and entirely personal, *my gesture to you*. There's no card attached to it, no message, just the tulip bending to the wind.

A bouquet has fallen into the leaves and they partially camouflage it, rustling and whispering around it; some leaves scrape over the concrete run-off area away from the wall. The wind rises to a gusting flurry so that, in unison, all the bouquets except the one which has fallen, are beating hard against the wire-mesh above the wall.

It was a long walk back.

When I get home, I'm speaking on the telephone to Barrichello and, however painful Imola might be to discuss, he readily agrees to help get some of the detail correct. During this conversation, my daughter is trying to get through to say she's had a car crash. She keeps on trying and the moment I put the phone down on Barrichello it rings and there she is. She's OK, but the car isn't. On a left-right section of a country road the car may have hit black ice. She wrestled it and it clipped kerbing, was airborne, ran across a corner of a field, burst a substantial wooden fence and reared up a bank towards a concrete wall. The ground was heavy, muddy, cloying. The car stopped just short of the wall.

A few days further on, I'm chatting to O'Mahony and he's remembered another anecdote. It centres on Imola and the traditional testing there well before the San Marino Grand Prix. Senna had a hire car, O'Mahony had a hire car and, the testing over, Senna wanted his baggage transferred from his to O'Mahony's for transport to the aeroplane. Senna would be coming along to the plane later, after a debrief. The baggage comprised a suitcase, a holdall and Senna's briefcase. *Don't take your eyes off the briefcase*, Senna instructed. O'Mahony began the transfer, lugging the suitcase, then the holdall, but when he returned to the boot of Senna's car a third time it was empty. Someone had stolen the briefcase. Seeing his career as Senna's pilot passing before his very eyes, as drowning men see their whole lives, he looked up and a *lot* of people were looking at him and his visible anxiety. Any of them might have done it, or an accomplice, or someone who'd run off – run off with Senna's money and passport and credit cards and helicopter pilot's licence and all else which the briefcase contained. Slowly, slowly those who looked at O'Mahony began to smile and that turned to laughter. Behind the bonnet of Senna's hire car a familiar figure bobbed up to have a swift savour of O'Mahony's anxiety, ducked down, bobbed up again. It was, of course, Senna and he had, of course, the briefcase he'd lifted unseen as O'Mahony did the lugging and he was, of course, grinning hugely. *I won't forget this*, O'Mahony said, *and I've a long memory*.

Ayrton Senna da Silva had a grin you'll never forget, anyway, and it always conveyed the same thing: sunshine.

In February, the investigation into the crash still awaited, Frank Williams spoke of Senna, sought out the Senna context. He wasn't sure about ultimate speed because 'I've always thought Jochen Rindt (the Austrian World Champion, posthumously, 1970) was the quickest human being God ever created.' Rindt drove for Lotus and, confining himself to his own drivers, Williams estimates: 'Ayrton was certainly the most competitive. In my opinion, Alain Prost was just as skilful – very, very skilful, immensely precise – but the difference was the commitment.'

Question: Did you feel Senna had a strong shell with a brittle centre?

'Effectively, he only drove for Williams for two races and did some testing so I can't tell you very well. He was definitely the best driver who's ever driven for Williams. His mental application was remarkable, his ability to understand and improve the car was better than anybody else we've ever had, and in saying that I'm not denigrating the other drivers who came before him.'

How did you cope as a person with Imola?

'You have to get on with your life.'

I'm not sure I could cope.

'You would, if it happened to you. You've just got to get up in the morning and get on with it. Being busy is always the best antidote to events like that, the best antidote to mental distress.'

Some time after yesterday afternoon, when the long year began, the children of Imola wrote poems and they were gathered into a book. It bears a simple title.

In paradise there are no walls.

COMPLETE RACING CAR RECORD

O ne late winter's day in 1981 a shoal of little cars fled towards an adverse camber corner called Paddock Hill. The wan, slender, shy young man with the yellow helmet was lost in the shoal; and that was the beginning. Between this corner and another – *Tamburello* – 13 years later, Ayrton Senna drove in 235 races. Some were ordinary, some flawed, some cunning, many magnificent, most turbulent. Here they are in numerical order.

I have tried to give something from each qualifying session as well as the races, because the endless complexities of racing are revealed there.

To preserve authenticity, wherever I have quoted contemporary sources in the early days – before he changed his name from Da Silva to Senna – I've left it the way it was reported, mis-spellings and all.

Before each Formula 1 race report there are the basic statistics. For example:

RACE 137

Brazil, Rio, 3 April. Q 1:30.218 (1);

1:28.096 (1). P. Overcast. W: 1:45.165 (1).

Disq, 31 laps.

This means it was his 137th race, the Brazilian Grand Prix at Rio on 3 April. **Q** is Senna's best qualifying times in the two sessions, with his position in brackets. **P** means he took pole. If Senna didn't get pole, I give whoever did and their time. **Overcast** is the weather on race day. **W:** is the Sunday morning warm-up, with Senna's time and his position in brackets. The final entry is where he finished in the race, in this case **Disqualified after 31 laps.**

Under each race report is a summary. For example:

Pd Senna 2h 00m 28.006s, Alboreto @ 1m 02.978, Tambay @ 1 lap. **FL** Senna 1:44.121. Ch Alboreto 12, Prost and Senna 9.

Pd is the podium, with times. **FL** is Fastest Lap and its time. In the races where someone else set it, I have given Senna's best time in brackets. **Ch** is the Championship points. Note that in seasons where Senna was not in contention for championships I have not given the points race-by-race.

I have not attempted to collate his karting career – which began in 1973 – except the major races, because so many have, by definition, to be minor and virtually impossible to trace. The majors: 1974: Sao Paulo Junior Champion; 1976: Sao Paulo Champion; 1977: South American Champion; 1978: World Championship, Le Mans, 6; 1979: World Championship, Estoril, 2; 1980: World Championship, Nivelles, 2; 1981: World Championship, Parma, 4; 1982 World Championship, Kalmar, 14.

1981 Formula Ford 1600

The front-runners apart from Senna were Enrique Mansilla from Argentina, Mexicans Alfonso Toledano and Ricardo Valerio, Britons Rick Morris (who had a Royale car), Andy Ackerley and Dave Coyne. 'It was more friendly then than it is now,' Coyne says, 'although the racing was hard. A 1600 car was the most difficult of all to drive correctly and FF1600 was never a pleasure! Every corner was an accident waiting to happen.'

Senna contested three championships, the Townsend-Thoresen, the RAC, and just once, the P&O Ferries. The Townsend-Thoresen scoring descended 20–15–12–10–8–6–4–3–2–1 with 2 for fastest lap and 11 best finishes counting; the same scoring applied in the RAC but with nothing for fastest lap.

RACE 1
P&O round 1. Brands Hatch, 1 March. 5.
At the time it seemed ordinary, the race, one of seven on the programme. Coyne (regarded as the coming man) led into Paddock Hill Bend, Senna sixth. *Autosport* reported that 'Toledano climbed back to fourth at the expense of former kart sensation de Silva, who will definitely be all the better for the race.'

Pd Mansilla, Morris, Coyne. **FL** Toledano.

RACE 2
T-T round 1. Thruxton, 8 March. 3.
Morris and David Wheeler contested the lead throughout but 'all eyes were on Ayerton de Silva who engaged and got the better of the recovering Mansilla in a thrilling all-angles tussle' *(Autosport)* after 'dicing' with Howard Groos.

Pd Morris 14m 41.5s, Wheeler @ 2.1, Senna @ 9.4. **FL** Morris.

RACE 3
T-T round 2. Brands Hatch, 15 March. 1.
Senna now had the latest van Diemen and exploited it. There were two heats and a final. In the second heat a downpour flooded the track but he beat Mansilla by a second after holding off a heavy attack. This is the first recorded instance of Senna's control in the wet. The final, over 15 laps, began in another downpour and Senna resisted pressure from Ackerley, who 'bravely' drove round him at Paddock on lap 4. They surged abreast up the incline to the horseshoe of Druids, Ackerley trying to out-brake Senna on the outside and going off. As Senna won, Liliane was almost in tears.

Pd Senna 15m 07.2s, Toledano @ 9.4, Lincoln @ 10.4. **FL** Kevin Gillen.
Ch Senna 32, Morris 26.

RACE 4
T-T round 3. Mallory Park, 22 March. P. 2.
The very first pole but Mansilla made the better start. Senna caught him and drove so forcefully that he went onto the grass several times trying to overtake. Into the final lap he emerged from the long loop of Gerard's Bend faster, drew alongside but was unceremoniously edged off onto the grass.

Pd Mansilla 12m 44.3s, Senna @ 1.2, Toledano @ 1.6. **FL** Toledano. **Ch** Senna 47, Morris 34.

RACE 5
T-T round 4. Mallory Park, 5 April. 2.
A tight finish behind Morris. Senna went round Toledano at the esses at the back of the circuit to lead but Morris came through and Senna held off Toledano – although Toledano broke the lap record.

Pd Morris 12m 38.1s, Senna @ 0.1, Toledano @ 1.2. **FL** Toledano. **Ch** Senna 62, Morris 54.

RACE 6
T-T round 5. Snetterton, 3 May. P. 2.
Two heats, aggregate to count. Toledano led the first from Morris but Senna overtook Morris and two laps later Toledano. Senna won by 2.3 seconds. In the second heat Morris led from Senna but after both had been on the grass they touched and spun at the esses on lap 3. Senna accepted responsibility. Morris beat him by 6.2 seconds.

Pd (on agg) Morris 28m 45.8s, Senna @ 3.9, Toledano @ 8.3. **FL** (heat 1) Toledano, (heat 2) Morris. **Ch** Senna 77, Morris 74.

RACE 7
RAC round 1. Oulton Park, 24 May. P. 1.
Senna equalled the two-year-old track record in taking pole. Toledano led from Morris, Senna and Mansilla but Senna was through by lap 2. Often he had the car virtually sideways but caught it each time.

Pd Senna 16m 48.0s, Morris @ 1.7, Mansilla @ 9.0. **FL** Senna. **Ch** Senna 20, Morris 15, Mansilla 12.

RACE 8
T-T round 6. Mallory Park, 25 May. 1.
Senna made a sure start and led into Gerard's from Toledano, who may well have jumped the flag and settled to blocking Morris, third. Senna built a lead. *Motoring News* wrote of him 'stamping his authority.' Valerio crashed with Toledano, Senna made no semblance of a mistake and ticked the laps off.

Pd Senna 12m 43.9s, Morris @ 5.8, Chris Marsh @ 15.7. **FL** Morris. **Ch** Senna 97, Morris 91.

RACE 9
T-T round 7. Snetterton, 7 June. 1.
Senna dominant. *Autosport* reported that 'the works van Diemen driver looked very assured throughout and Rick Morris had to drive much less tidily to separate the Brazilian from his team-mate Toledano in third.' *Motoring News* set the context. 'Morris is the season's yardstick to gauge new talent by. It thus augurs well for Ayerton da Silva … the only runner in the T-T series to consistently beat the experienced Englishman.'

Pd Senna 18m 16.5s, Morris @ 0.7, Toledano @ 5.5. **FL** Senna. **Ch** Senna 119, Morris 106.

RACE 10
RAC round 2. Silverstone, 21 June. 2.
Morris made a poor start, Senna away clear, but Morris, dogged, pursued and by lap 5 caught him. Morris had five laps to plot an overtaking move. On lap 9 into the tight curve of Stowe he 'scrabbled' by on the inside but under braking at the Woodcote chicane Senna retook him. Morris made a gambler's throw at Woodcote chicane. A contemporary account says that Morris braked as late as he could to 'bounce his Royale RF29 over the chicane and come out a clear winner.' Morris remembers Senna's 'unbearable' anger.

Pd Morris 17m 01.8s, Senna @ 0.9, Mansilla @ 6.3. **FL** Morris. **Ch** Senna and Morris 35, Mansilla 24.

RACE 11
T-T round 8. Oulton Park, 27 June. 1.
In practice Senna went 0.1 of a second inside the track's long-standing FF1600 record and so did Morris but a shower before the race sponged away any chance of beating the official record. Senna led from Morris, who spun on lap 2. Toledano bustled late on.

Pd Senna 16m 49.5s, Toledano @ 0.6, Fernando Macedo (Brazil) @ 45.9. **FL** Senna. **Ch** Senna 141, Morris 106, Toledano 94.

RACE 12
RAC round 3. Donington Park, 4 July. 1.
Senna and Morris went in sharing the championship lead, of course, but now Senna moved ahead. He led the race and though Morris moved on him towards the end of the 15 laps he couldn't get close enough to conjure a proper attack.

Pd Senna 20m 35.6s, Morris @ 2.8, Mansilla @ 14.3. **FL** Senna and Morris (1:21.5s). **Ch** Senna 55, Morris 50, Mansilla 36.

RACE 13
RAC round 4. Brands Hatch, 12 July. 4.
Senna suffered problems setting the car up in practice and started from the third row. He made 'a truly sensational' start and reached Paddock level with Mansilla for the lead 'having displaced four cars instantly, seemingly without contact!' Mansilla resisted but 'had to relent at the hairpin, da Silva forging ahead immediately. The brilliance of the former karter, once free, was a joy to behold. Deft flicks of opposite lock through Paddock – such elegant car control can only be natural talent – took him ever further out of reach until, dramatically, the van Diemen slewed sideways beyond instantaneous recall at Clearways with three laps remaining, Ayrton resuming fourth with a water hose adrift' *(Autosport).*

Pd Morris, Toledano, Mansilla. **FL** Senna.
Ch Morris 70, Senna 65, Mansilla 48.

RACE 14
T-T round 9. Oulton Park, 25 July. 1.
A potentially explosive front row, Toledano,
Senna and Macedo, but it didn't detonate:
Toledano faster away than Senna who
overtook him on the opening lap. Senna
fashioned 'an impressive lead' while Morris
needed until lap 6 to move into second place.

Pd Senna 16m 59.7s, Morris @ 2.9,
Toledano @ 8.6. **FL** Senna. **Ch** Senna 163,
Morris 121.

RACE 15
RAC round 5. Mallory Park, 26 July. 1.
Autosport reported that 'a tremendous race
eclipsed everything that had gone before' –
six other races of various kinds on the day's
programme. Senna had pole and the lead but
behind him a 'monumental second place
struggle' between Toledano, Mansilla and
Morris lasted the whole 15 laps.

Pd Senna 12m 44.4s, Morris @ 1.6,
Mansilla @ 2.2. **FL** Senna, Mansilla and
Morris (50.1s). **Ch** Senna, Morris 85,
Mansilla 60.

RACE 16
T-T round 10. Brands Hatch, 2 August. 1.
Senna stormed into the lead and never lost it.
He completed the opening lap with at least a
six-length lead. On that lap Toledano and
Morris crashed at Druids but recovered. Their
crash removed any distant threat.

Pd Senna 12m 58.0s, Morris @ 0.1,
Toledano @ 2.4. **FL** Toledano. **Ch** Senna 183,
Morris 136.

RACE 17
RAC round 6. Snetterton, 9 August. 1.
Drizzle fell during race morning practice but
the surface dried for the race although it was
treacherous. Toledano led until Senna
overtook him on lap 2. By half distance rain
drifted over and 'the pace slowed
dramatically. At the Esses, where the wet
track was first encountered, da Silva went
wide and tiptoed through. Mansilla was off
into the rough but regained the track and then
the next bunch imitated a bomb-burst,

shooting off in all directions' (Autosport).
Senna was RAC champion.

Pd Senna 19m 19.8s, Mansilla @ 1.1,
Toledano @t 18.9. **FL** Senna. **Ch** Senna 95,
Morris 85, Mansilla 63.

RACE 18
T-T Euroseries. Donington Park, 15 August. 1.
Senna was a late entrant but led and only
Morris could compete with him. Autosport said
he was 'really is in a class of his own in FF1600
this season and his fellow competitors must
have been dismayed when his van Diemen
appeared as an additional entry. Sure enough
Ayrton rushed off as he pleased.'

Pd Senna 16m 13.7s, Morris @ 0.9,
John Booth @ 8.0. **FL** Morris.

RACE 19
T-T round 11. Thruxton, 31 August. P. 1.
Senna took pole by 0.5 and took his second
championship. He seized the lead, Morris
third and, crossing the line to complete the
first lap, led narrowly from Toledano. Morris
probed for second place but dropped out
with mechanical problems. By lap 3 Senna
was in complete command from Toledano.

Pd Senna 14m 25.4s, Toledano @ 3.3,
Atkinson @ 19.7. **FL** Senna. **Ch** Senna 205,
Morris 136.

RACE 20
T-T round 12. Brands Hatch, 29 September. 2.
The contemporary accounts capture it exactly.
Autosport reported that 'two incidents on the
first lap put the brilliant Ayrton de Silva way
down the field but his drive through to second
place was undoubtedly the talk of the race.'
Motoring News reported his performance as
'incredible. After a slow practice, he made a
good start but clipped Morris and spun down
the field and then he was chopped by a back-
marker, spinning again. All this didn't prevent
him from eventually finishing second and
setting fastest lap by nearly two seconds! Da
Silva's antics virtually defied belief.'

Pd Morris 23m 20.1s, Senna @ 6.4,
Toledano @ 9.2. **FL** Senna. **Ch** Senna 222
(210 counting), Morris 156.

1982 Formula Ford 2000

Senna took up an offer from Dennis Rushen of the Rushen-Green team. The Formula Ford 2000 cars had wings, allowing sophisticated permutations. Senna would be in a van Diemen and his main competitor, Englishman Calvin Fish, initially in a Royale. The other front-runners: Senna's team-mate Kenny Andrews (van Diemen), Russell Spence (van Diemen), Frank Bradley (van Diemen) and Tim Davies (Royale). Scoring in the Pace British Championship: 20–15–12–10–8–6–4– 3–2–1, plus 1 for pole, 1 for fastest lap; scoring in the EFDA Euroseries the same but 2 points for fastest lap. Some confusion remains over the points totals and it may be that these can never be resolved because records were incomplete, not kept or destroyed. As a consequence I give only the totals of Senna and Fish in the Pace British.

RACE 21
Pace British round 1, Brands Hatch, 7 March. P. 1.

Senna arrived in England late and Rushen explained the possibilities of adjusting wing settings. In practice Senna went 1.3 seconds faster than anybody else and at the start of the race 'simply rushed off into the distance' while 'Fish came back from a slow start to take Spence' (*Motoring News*).

    Pd Senna 11m 57.4s, Fish @ 9.8, Spence @ 10.7. **FL** Senna. **Ch** Senna 22, Fish 15.

RACE 22
Pace British round 2. Oulton Park, 27 March. P. 1.

Senna 'rocketed' from the green light so that as the others reached for their rhythm he'd already found his and was a long way in front. He gave a 'masterful display of his undoubted ability and headed into the distance. Da Silva polished off the race with a new lap record, his only problem coming when he lapped back-markers' (*Motoring News*). He beat the two-year-old track record by 0.2 of a second.

    Pd Senna 15m 37.6s, Fish @ 10.1, Mike Taylor @ 14.4. **FL** Senna. **Ch** Senna 44, Fish 30.

RACE 23
Pace British round 3. Silverstone, 28 March. P. 1.

Senna was majestic in his manipulation of the car. He bestrode practice and took pole by 0.9. In the race he took an immediate lead and before the end broke the track record.

    Pd Senna 14m 30.8s, Colin Jack @ 17.1, Spence @ 18.5. **FL** Senna. **Ch** Senna 66, Fish 40.

RACE 24
Pace British round 4. Donington Park, 4 April. P. 1.

A poser from *Motoring News*. 'The question hanging over event four [of the race day programme] was "Will Ayrton da Silva walk away with another win?" The answer was "Yes!"'

    Pd Senna 18m 49.1s, Fish @ 18.3, Spence @ 21.9. **FL** Senna. Ch Senna 88, Fish 55.

RACE 25
Pace British round 5. Snetterton, 9 April. P. 1.

Senna went into the lead unimpeded by a considerable crash behind to give a first lap order of Senna, Andrews, Bradley, Spence, Fish. Moving into lap 2 Senna picked through the debris of the crash and suddenly slowed. Andrews and Spence immediately closed and went by. Senna had lost front brakes but adjusted to that and retook them both.

    Pd Senna 17m 07.1s, Andrews @ 12.6, Victor Rosso @ 17.3. **FL** Senna. **Ch** Senna 110, Fish 55.

RACE 26
Pace British round 6. Silverstone, 12 April. P. 1.

Senna equalled the record he had set on 28 March. *Motoring News* reported that he 'romped off into the distance right from the start and lapped within 0.40 of the record from his first flying lap. Halfway through the 15-lap event he equalled the FF2000 record and may have bettered it on the next circuit had he not had to lift whilst lapping a backmarker. Not even a misfire held back the ragged but incredibly quick da Silva.'

Pd Senna 14m 31.5s, Rosso @ 14.2, Spence @ 15.0. **FL** Senna. **Ch** Senna 132, Fish 63.

RACE 27

EFDA round 1. Zolder, Belgium, 18 April. P. R, 3 laps, engine.

Senna's first car race outside Britain. The anticipation was of a battle between him and Dutchman Cor Euser, the reigning European Champion. In qualifying, Senna went quickest in both sessions and took pole by a clear second. Euser had a two-year-old Delta car which he managed to put on the front row. The start was delayed through oil on the track and Senna's engine overheated. He led in spite of that and in a couple of laps built a two second lead over Euser. Then he felt the engine tightening.

Pd Euser, Jesper Villumsen, Maarten Henneman. **FL** Euser.

RACE 28

EFDA round 2. Donington Park, 2 May. P. 1.

Contemporary reports suggest that Spence looked capable of getting closer to matching Senna. Wrong. In the race, Senna suffered a misfire, which did not prevent him winning or breaking his own lap record by 0.11s.

Pd Senna 24m 57.5s, Spence @ 7.1, Kristian Nissen @ 25.8. **FL** Senna. **Ch** Senna 24, Spence 15, Bradley 10.

RACE 29

Pace British round 7. Mallory Park, 3 May. 1.

Victor Rosso (van Diemen) took pole from Senna, who had an engine which wasn't delivering enough power. It had to be changed at lunchtime. Rosso made a poor start and Senna capitalised, going through and dragging Spence with him. Senna pulled clear while Rosso, recovering, overtook Spence on the third lap.

Pd Senna 15m 44.3s, Rosso @ 8.0, Andrews @ 18.6. **FL** Senna. **Ch** Senna 153, Fish 73.

RACE 30

EFDA round 3. Zolder, 9 May. P. R, spin.

The weekend Gilles Villeneuve was killed near the end of Saturday second qualifying. What impact this made on Senna is unknown. He took pole but in the race made a rare error when he was leading by 13 seconds and spun into the catch fencing.

Pd Huub Vermeulen, Villumsen, Rob Leeuwenburgh. **FL** Senna. **Ch** Villumsen 34, Senna 27, Vermeulen 20.

RACE 31

Shell Super Sunbeam for celebrities. Oulton Park, 30 May. 1.

Nine cars contested this event, run before round 8 of the British FF2000. Evidently the entrants were decided by the fastest qualifiers in selected races but however it was done Senna qualified. He led from an experienced driver, John Brindley, and moved from him at a second a lap setting a class record. Another experienced driver, Chuck Nicholson, guards a vivid semi-memory of the race: he didn't see Senna at all!

Pd Senna 9m 50.2s, Brindley @ 7.1, Nicholson @ 9.6. **FL** Senna.

RACE 32

Pace British round 8. Oulton Park, 30 May. R, 11 laps, puncture.

Fish now had a van Diemen and took pole, Senna on the front row although (again) his engine hadn't been delivering enough power. Fish led from Senna but Senna was in trouble almost immediately when his right rear tyre exploded in the downhill Cascades lefthander at 125mph. Fish beat Senna's lap record by 0.1.

Pd Fish, Andrews, Neil Myers. **FL** Fish. **Ch** Senna 153, Fish 95.

RACE 33

Pace British round 9. Brands Hatch, 31 May. 1.

Fish took pole from Senna but Senna was determined to have the lead and into Paddock he and Fish touched, Fish losing some of his nose-cone. Somehow Fish stayed with Senna for the 20 laps but could do no more.

Pd Senna 15m 54.8s, Fish @ 1.6, Spence @ 14.5. **FL** Senna. **Ch** Senna 174, Fish 111.

RACE 34
Pace British round 10. Mallory Park, 6 June. 1.

Tim Davies took pole but Senna took the lead in the race. Andrews attacked Davies and overtook him on lap 3 (of the 15) and Fish overtook Davies too. By half-distance they were chasing Senna but didn't catch him.

Pd Senna 11m 47.2s, Andrews @ 9.2, Fish @ 10.9. **FL** Senna. **Ch** Senna 195, Fish 123.

RACE 35
Pace British round 11. Brands Hatch, 13 June. P. 1.

During qualifying Senna equalled the track record and said: 'First I think about winning then maybe the record.' The race had to be stopped after two laps because Sigurd Krane, a Norwegian, lost control at Paddock and hammered the fencing. At the re-start Senna led, Fish matching him and the intensity was such that Senna did break the record and Fish did too. They averaged 93.98mph.

Pd Senna 11m 44.8s, Fish @ 1.0, Andrews @ 7.8. **FL** Senna and Fish (46.4s). **Ch** Senna 217, Fish 139.

RACE 36
EFDA round 4. Hockenheim, 20 June. P. R, lap 1, accident.

Senna cooked his clutch on the start line and then Euser, in the lead, misjudged the chicane and his Delta was flung into a series of barrel-rolls. Everyone behind darted and dived to avoid him, causing a major crash, Senna in the midst of it. The car was so badly damaged he didn't go to the re-start.

Pd Rosso, Fish, Bradley. **FL** Henrik Larsen. **Ch** Villumsen 34, Euser 30, Senna 28.

RACE 37
Pace British round 12. Oulton Park, 26 June. 1.

The track was damp, although drying, and Andrews led but on lap 2 Senna overtook him. By lap 4 he commanded the race but on

lap 9 (of 15) Fish overtook Andrews and set off in pursuit. Fish pushed himself so hard he set fastest lap then Senna went faster than that.

Pd Senna 16m 10.4s, Fish @ 4.2, Andrews @ 8.3. **FL** Senna. **Ch** Senna 238, Fish 154.

RACE 38
EFDA round 5. Zandvoort, 3 July. P. 1.

Senna took pole despite missing the opening practice because of a clutch problem and it left him 30 minutes to learn a new circuit. He followed a Dutchman, Ron Kluit, for a couple of laps then set the time. He made a crisp start but missed second gear which allowed a driver called Jaap van Silfhout in a Lola to dodge ahead into the lead. Euser ran third, Fish fourth. On lap 2 at the curve at the end of the start-finish straight, Senna out-braked van Silfhout and stayed in front for the remaining 10 laps.

Pd Senna 20m 08.0s, Fish @ 2.3, Euser @ 2.7. **FL** Kluit. **Ch** Senna 49, Euser 42, Villumsen 34.

RACE 39
Pace British round 13. Snetterton, 4 July. 2.

Senna didn't have pole. Heavy rain fell by the second race on the card so that the fourth – the FF2000 – was wet. Bradley gambled on dry tyres and 'wallowed in midfield' while Fish led. Senna caught and overtook Fish but Bradley charged. Before half distance, with the track drying, the leaders – especially Senna – were conserving their tyres. Fish harried, however. In the background Bradley came on strongly and by the second last lap had reached them. He took Fish at Coram [a curve] and, on the last lap, Senna at Sear [a right-hander].

Pd Bradley 24m 46.4s, Senna @ 3.6, Fish @ 4.1. **FL** Bradley. **Ch** Senna 253, Fish 166.

RACE 40
Pace British round 14. Castle Combe, 10 July. P. 1.

Senna took 0.9 off the record to have pole from Fish by a tenth. Marcus Pye wrote in *Autosport* that 'practice form was repeated in the race, quite the most tedious I've ever seen in this formula, with da Silva just out of Fish's reach throughout and the rest, headed by Spence, following on.' Senna and Fish both broke the record.

Pd Senna 15m 47.2s, Fish @ 3.0, Spence @ 16.2. **FL** Senna and Fish (1m 02.6). **Ch** Senna 275, Fish 182.

RACE 41
Pace British round 15. Snetterton, 1 August. 1.

Fish pole, Senna alongside and they diced as the race unfolded – Senna leading – but by lap 4 Fish challenged. Past the pits Senna firmly blocked and weaved down the straight. Fish went to the inside, Senna squeezed him and Fish went onto the grass. Fish's car went 10 feet in the air and the day culminated in a marshal's report condemning Senna.

Pd Senna 16m 52.0s, Andrews @ 17.8, Max Busslinger @ 18.3. **FL** Senna. **Ch** Senna 296, Fish 183.

RACE 42
EFDA round 6. Hockenheim, 8 August. P. 1.

The crowd were evidently astonished by Senna in qualifying. It rained although one practice session was dry and Senna exploited that, taking pole by three seconds.

Three cars crashed at the start but at the re-start Senna led and didn't lose it. Fish ran evenly in second, no threat to Senna – who broke the lap record.

Pd Senna 26m 59.2s, Fish @ 4.2, Volker Weidler @ 20.5. **FL** Senna. **Ch** Senna 72, Euser 52, Fish 45.

RACE 43
EFDA round 7. Österreichring, 15 August. P. 1.

This race supported the Austrian Grand Prix. Senna took pole by a 'staggering' 1.561 seconds. In first practice he set fastest lap with 1m 59.814s (110.946 mph) to take pole from Fish. Senna got the start of the race right and won at a canter.

Pd Senna 24m 21.3s, Fish @ 24.3, Nissen @ 37.7. **FL** Senna. **Ch** Senna 95, Fish 60, Euser 53.

RACE 44
EFDA round 8. Jyllandsring, 22 August. P. 1.

The championship decider. Pole, inevitably, and a smooth, soothed race with the Dane Nissen struggling to stay with him – and failing – early on. Fish, initially third, soon took Nissen but Senna hammered the lap record and finished an age from Fish.

Pd Senna 19m 35.0s, Fish @ 2.6, Nissen @ 5.4. **FL** Senna. **Ch** Senna 118, Fish 75, Euser 57.

RACE 45
Pace British round 16. Thruxton, 30 August. 1.

Fish took pole by 0.3 from Senna, and Senna 1.3 from the rest. Spitting rain made conditions dubious for the start. Fish led, Senna harrying him, crowding him at each corner. On lap 4 Senna slowed – the oil pressure gauge giving alarming readings – and Fish eased out to perhaps 50 metres. Fish held the gap at around 0.5 until lap 13 (of the 15) when, baulked by a back-marker, he couldn't prevent Senna going by even with oil smoke billowing from the engine. Fish attacked, Senna defended and broke the lap record in his defence.

Pd Senna 20m 00.7s, Fish @ 1.3, Spence @ 16.6. **FL** Senna. **Ch** Senna 317, Fish 199.

RACE 46
Pace British round 17. Oulton Park, 4 September. P. 1.

Senna and Fish shared the front row. Fish stormed into the lead, drawing Senna with him. Senna pressured, Fish made a slight error on lap 9 and Senna went by.

Pd Senna 20m 40.9s, Fish @ 2.9, Spence @ 18.4. **FL** Fish. **Ch** Senna 338, Fish 215.

RACE 47
Pace British round 18. Silverstone, 5 September. P. 1.

Senna and Fish set identical times in practice. Senna led but Fish hovered and hung for the first five laps. From laps 5 to 10 (of the 15) Senna siphoned a lead of around a second. Fish came back at him but never close enough to mount an overtaking move.

Pd Senna 14m 33.6s, Fish @ 0.6, Rosso @ 13.5. **FL** Senna and Fish (57.6s). **Ch** Senna 360, Fish 231.

RACE 48
EFDA round 9. Mondello Park, 12 September. 1.

'[Joey] Greenan led da Silva away on the green. For two laps the Irish driver led but missed a gear change and the Brazilian swept by on the outside. Once in front da Silva raced away into the distance [and broke the lap record] to win by the huge margin of over 20 secs. Greenan held station behind da Silva, totally out of touch with the leader' – *Autosport*.

Pd Senna 19m 32.7s, Greenan @ 18.5, Nissen @ 20.5. **FL** Senna. **Ch** Senna 140, Fish 83, Euser 57.

RACE 49
Pace British round 20. Brands Hatch, 26 September. 2.

Two meetings on consecutive weekends here. Senna did not compete in the first (on 19 September, round 19, which Fish won). He was contesting the World Karting Championships. Next weekend Rosso, Fish and Senna all did 46.5 in qualifying, but Senna on the second row. Fish made a monumental start, overtaking Rosso on the outside at Paddock and led by six lengths. Senna dived inside Rosso at Clearways but Fish continued untroubled until back-markers hampered him. Senna was 'quick to pounce' but Fish 'clung grimly' to the lead and kept it.

Pd Fish 11m 46.7s, Senna @ 0.8, Rosso @ 3.7. **FL** Senna. **Ch** Senna 376, Fish 271.

RACE 50
F3, Thruxton, 13 November.
Q: 1:13.34 (1); 1:13.54 (1). P. 1.

Senna needed to step upwards again. That would be Formula 3 with a team called West Surrey. 'I went home to Brazil in order to enjoy a little bit of the summer, the sunshine, and also to meet my sponsors and talk about this race and about next season. I arrived back in England two weeks ago and did some tests at Thruxton and Snetterton. I went well in the car and I found it very good to work with Dick Bennetts.' In Senna's first qualifying in a Formula 3 car he broke the lap record.

The race: He judged the start exquisitely and led through the first corner. 'I kept a close watch in my mirrors to see if anybody was going to do anything stupid under braking.' They didn't.

Pd Senna 18m 37.4s, Tragardh @ 13.1, Fish @ 17.4. **FL** Senna.

1983 Formula 3

Senna drove for West Surrey Racing. Ralt was the car to have and West Surrey Racing had them. The championship was the Marlboro British. Among others Senna would meet Martin Brundle, an ambitious, fresh-faced young man from Norfolk being run by Eddie Jordan. The Senna versus Brundle combat reached such a pitch that it attracted attention far beyond the motorsport community. The other front-runners: American Davy Jones, Fish, David Leslie and Johnny Dumfries. Fewer strangers would come and go now. This season Senna wished to be known simply as Ayrton Senna. Points scoring: 9–6–4–3–2–1 plus 1 for fastest lap.

RACE 51
Marlboro British round 1. Silverstone, 6 March. Q: 53.90 (2); 53.77 (1). Row 1.
P: Leslie (53.54). 1.

Senna seemed more uptight than at the end of 1982. Bennetts explained it was 'just because this is the first race. He's been looking forward to it for a long time and there's quite a lot of pressure on him.'

Leslie and Senna ran wheel-to-wheel to Copse where Senna drove round the outside and led, leaving the others to pick up what they could. 'I knew I had to try and pass round the outside but I was worried about the grip on coldish tyres. I kept the power on and the car gripped.'

Pd Senna 18m 07.14s, Brundle @ 6.43, Jones @ 7.26. **FL** Senna.

RACE 52
Marlboro British round 2. Thruxton, 13 March. Q: 1:13.46 (1); 1:19.22 (2). P. 1.
Before this race Senna tested at Donington Park and on the full Silverstone Grand Prix circuit and beat the records at both. Now in the first session he broke the record here. The second session was wet, the first time Senna had driven Formula 3 in such conditions and Brundle did a 1:19.15, quickest.

The rain stopped before the race and although Senna made a lovely start Brundle stayed with him. 'I could see that I was faster through the corners but I also knew that I had to conserve my tyres. Whoever could make their tyres last longer would win.' Senna gained in the corners, Brundle regained on the straights.

Pd Senna 26m 26.31s, Brundle @ 0.83, Mario Hytten @ 47.94. **FL** Brundle. **Ch** Senna 19, Brundle 13, Hytten 6.

RACE 53
Marlboro British round 3. Silverstone, 20 March. Q: 1:34.74 (1); 1:25.14 (1). P. 1.
Although Senna had had a heavy mid-week accident testing at Snetterton he took provisional pole on a wet Saturday morning and confirmed pole in a dry afternoon session.

Spotting rain forced nearly everyone onto wet tyres for the race. Senna took an immediate lead, Brundle second but into Becketts Senna adopted a wide line and Brundle went through. Senna overtook on the outside at Stowe. The rain fell heavier. A back-marker slithered and almost collected Senna, who was lapping him.

The race was halted and restarted for a further six laps, aggregate to count. Brundle led but at Becketts Senna braked particularly late and went outside. 'Incredible,' Brundle said. 'He had two wheels on the grass but he still kept going.' Senna held the inside for Chapel so that he led down the Hangar Straight. The spray his wheels churned made any overtaking by Brundle beyond the possible. On the last lap Senna's fire extinguisher bottle exploded ('bloody cold in there'). He kept on.

Pd Senna 19m 36.51s, Brundle @ 1.96, Fish @ 7.01. **FL** Senna. **Ch** Senna 29, Brundle 19, Jones and Fish 7.

RACE 54
Marlboro British round 4. Donington Park, 27 March. Q: 1:19.66 (1); 1:18.06 (1). P. 1.
Drizzle for the first session and Senna had new Avon wet tyres, which evidently the Jordan team couldn't afford. In the afternoon, dry, Senna and Brundle traded times in the last 10 minutes but Senna had it by 0.13. 'It was terrible out there, it was like you were driving on oil all the way.' Dry for the race, Senna and Brundle level but Senna inside for the long Redgate horseshoe and ahead. By lap 4 he'd magnified that to a couple of seconds.

Pd Senna 23m 23.35s, Brundle @ 5.63, Jones @ 6.36. **FL** Senna and Jones (1m 09.52). **Ch** Senna 39, Brundle 25, Jones 12.

RACE 55
Marlboro British round 5. Thruxton, 4 April. Q: 1:13.07 (1); 1:13.80 (3). P. 1.
Senna had 'flu and Bennetts wondered about letting him race. 'I did not feel good but I was not making mistakes in the car so I felt it was OK. I'm not sure whether I was going as well as I should have done.'

He missed second gear at the start. Jones led, Brundle passed Senna too. Senna muscled Brundle outside at Campbell and they crossed the line in a chain, Jones-Senna-Brundle. Into the chicane on lap 2 Brundle tried a move but Senna resisted that and overtook Jones on lap 3.

Pd Senna 25m 03.29s, Brundle @ 01.24, Fish @ 22.04. **FL** Brundle. **Ch** Senna 48, Brundle 32, Jones and Hytten 12.

RACE 56
Marlboro British round 6. Silverstone, 24 April. Q: 53.30 (1); 53.38 (1). P. 1.
Senna had been to Brazil to relax and felt better. It showed. He beat his own lap record in both sessions. Race: Brundle led towards

Copse but, changing down, missed a gear and floated into midfield. He struggled to third, Senna alone at the front and breaking the official lap record (only set in races).

Pd Senna 22m 33.59s, Jones @ 5.14, Brundle @ 5.41. **FL** Senna. **Ch** Senna 58, Brundle 36, Jones 18.

RACE 57
Marlboro British round 7. Thruxton, 2 May. Q: 1:33.55 (1); 1:14.08 (1). P. 1.
In the first session Senna could 'only' beat the record by 0.01. 'The wind is making it impossible to make the car perfect at both the Complex and the chicane. That is why we cannot get near the record.'

Senna led although a 'cautious' exit from the Complex let Brundle close enough to slip-stream throughout the opening lap. Brundle got alongside but that left him with the outside line at the chicane. Senna drew away at the end of lap 2.

Pd Senna 24m 51.88s, Brundle @ 3.40, Jones @ 4.07. **FL** Senna. **Ch** Senna 68, Brundle 42, Jones 22.

RACE 58
Marlboro British round 8. Brands Hatch, 8 May. Q: 43.35 (1); 43.14 (1). P. 1.
Senna was sensational through Paddock Hill Bend in qualifying. In both sessions he went under the qualifying record (as did Brundle, Jones and Fish.)

A deluge delayed the race. Senna emerged from Paddock ahead, Brundle reasoning it would be 'silly' to try anything there. Senna wasn't to be caught and insisted the win was his best of the season so far: clean, accomplished, assured.

Pd Senna 17m 21.6s, Brundle @ 2.4, Jones @ 9.5. **FL** Senna. **Ch** Senna 78, Brundle 48, Jones 26.

RACE 59
Marlboro British round 9. Silverstone, 30 May. Q: 53.05 (1); 53.39 (2). P. 1.
Senna covered a lot of fast laps in first qualifying, dipping below his own record. At the green light he moved decisively and by Copse seemed to have the race at his mercy. Leslie followed him through Copse but his clutch failed and Brundle suffered extreme oversteer. On lap 3 Senna led by two seconds and increased it over the 30 laps.

Pd Senna 27m 00.98s, Brundle @ 10.10, Berg @ 22.49. **FL** Senna. **Ch** Senna 88, Brundle 54, Jones 28.

RACE 60
Marlboro British round 10/European Championship round 6. Silverstone, 12 June. Q: 1:32.27 (1); 1:24.08 (2). Row 1. P: Brundle 1:23.99. R, 7 laps, accident.
The race brought some leading Continentals, including Gerhard Berger. A wet first session but Senna seemed to have pole in the second, dry. However with 15 minutes left Brundle put on a new set of Yokohama tyres and stole it.

Brundle finished lap 1 with Senna behind and pressing, and Dumfries pressing him. On lap 3 Dumfries tried to pass at Stowe. Senna reportedly had gambled on three different compound tyres on the car to have a set which would last the 20 laps. He soon had oversteer. 'After two laps the left rear wasn't working at all. There was just no grip.' Dumfries says that 'I was alongside him down Hangar Straight and he put me on the grass.' On lap 6 Senna lost control at Club and spun off. He rejoined ninth, went off backwards at Woodcote.

Pd (British): Allen Berg, Jones, Fish. **Pd** (European): Brundle, Tommy Byrne, Theys. **FL** Dumfries. **Ch** Senna 88, Brundle 54, Jones 35.

RACE 61
Marlboro British round 11. Cadwell Park, 19 June. Q: 1:22.57 (1); did not take part. P: Brundle 1:22.58. DNS.
In first qualifying Senna and Brundle duelled and were within that fraction of each other – 0.01 – but, lapping a second under Mansilla's year-old record, Senna went wide at one point, kept the power on to try to regain the track but instead hit a marshals' post. His car was a sorry mess.

Pd Brundle, Fish, Jones. **FL** Brundle. **Ch** Senna 88, Brundle 64, Jones 39.

RACE 62

Marlboro British round 12. Snetterton, 3 July. Q: 61.89 (5); 61.81 (2). R 2. P: Brundle 61.59. R, 23 laps, accident.
Senna not on the front row: that hadn't happened in 1983 before. 'I don't know what is wrong. We have changed many things and yet there is no real improvement.'

Race: Brundle led. Dumfries had crashed in qualifying and Senna, lined up on the grid behind where Dumfries would have been, enjoyed a clear run. He was quickly up to Brundle – at lap 12 it was only six metres. Brundle held him there. Out of Sear on the 24th lap (of the 25) Brundle kept the inside line. They moved along the straight with Senna 'creeping' towards him. Into the left-hand kink Brundle moved on to the racing line but Senna's front wheel ran over Brundle's rear. Senna spun off.

Pd Brundle, Jones, Fish. **FL** Senna. **Ch** Senna 89, Brundle 73, Jones 45.

RACE 63

Marlboro British round 13. Silverstone, 16 July. Q: 1:26.57 (3); 1:26.13 (1). P. 1.
Senna tested before the meeting and the car was 'much more consistent.' After the first session the team changed the set-up and he took the pole by 0.04.

Brundle accelerated ahead but Senna took the inside at Copse, rattled and rode the kerbs, Brundle hanging on. After two laps the gap stood at a second. They drew away from the bunch but Brundle was briefly baulked by a back-marker and, a lap later, lost more time when Senna thrust inside two back-markers at the chicane, obliging Brundle to follow them. It created a gap Brundle could not close.

Pd Senna 28m 59.55s, Brundle @ 1.61, Fish @ 19.03. **FL** Senna. **Ch** Senna 99, Brundle 79, Jones 45.

RACE 64

Marlboro British round 14. Donington Park, 24 July. Q: 1:08.42 (1); 1:10.41 (4). P. 2.
A dry first session proved decisive. 'We had been out on old tyres at the beginning and I was just getting the car balanced. Then we put on some new tyres and I went out and set a time. On the second lap I was already in pole position.' A dry-wet second session left it undisturbed.

Brundle made an incisive start and commanded Redgate, Jones hard in third. Now Brundle had to handle the heat. On lap 8 he made a supreme effort to shed Senna and squeezed a gap of a second but Senna closed and set fastest lap. Brundle kept his nerve.

Pd Brundle 35m 09.21s, Senna @ 00.40, Jones @ 03.17. **FL** Senna. **Ch** Senna 106, Brundle 88, Jones 49.

RACE 65

Marlboro British round 15. Oulton Park, 6 August. Q: 57.38 (2); 57.43 (1). R 1. P: Brundle (57.04). R, 28 laps, accident.
Senna crashed heavily in testing on the Thursday – the rear stub axle failed at Druids – and that brought extensive work before Saturday qualifying. After the first session Senna confessed that the car was 'very difficult to drive. Very dangerous. I couldn't drive it on the limit.' The weather warmed for second qualifying, precluding improvement despite a 'heart-stopping' moment when he braked too late.

Brundle and Senna went hard and banged wheels. Brundle led Senna by a whisker completing the opening lap but Brundle had problems braking. On lap 28 Senna 'went right up his gearbox into Cascades and I was going much quicker than him. I braked late and went for the inside. I'm sure he didn't see me and he closed in on me when we were already going into the corner.' They met, Senna's car riding over Brundle's as they came to rest off the circuit.

Pd Fish, Jones, Berg. **FL** Senna. **Ch** Senna 107, Brundle 88, Jones 55.

RACE 66

Marlboro British round 16. Silverstone, 29 August. Q: 53.18 (1); 53.43 (2). P. 1.
Senna managed a couple of days testing with the repaired car. 'It is exactly the same as the last race here.' Is it perfect? 'No, no but quite close.'

He forced a small lead from Brundle by Copse before they reached 'stalemate,' Senna stretching on the straight (this the Club circuit) to prevent Brundle trying a move at Woodcote.

Pd Senna 27m 02.45s, Brundle @ 1.44, Jones @ 2.83. **FL** Jones. **Ch** Senna 116, Brundle 94, Jones 60.

RACE 67

Marlboro British round 17. Oulton Park, 11 September. Q: 59.62 (1); 57.24 (1). P. R, 7 laps, accident.

Pole turned on the second session, in drying conditions. Senna explored the track surface and after 15 minutes pitted for slick tyres. He couldn't get a clear lap but he did get pole.

Brundle led, Senna pressing, Jones third. On lap 8 Senna made his move, outside at Druids. It took him off the racing line and he lost adhesion and slithered into the barrier.

Pd Brundle, Fish, Leslie. **FL** Jones. **Ch** Senna 116, Brundle 103, Jones 61.

RACE 68

Marlboro British round 18. Thruxton, 18 Sep. Q: 1:17.79 (1); 1:14.01 (1). P. R, 2 laps, engine.

Senna had a new car and could have taken the Championship but complained of lack of balance – despite taking pole.

Brundle led but Senna attacked. Brundle locked a brake and Senna led. On this opening lap, Brundle went inside to the chicane, Senna went off line through and Brundle had him on the exit. Then Senna's engine let go, a blown head gasket.

Pd Brundle, Jones, Fish. **FL** Brundle. **Ch** Senna 116, Brundle 113, Jones 67.

RACE 69

Marlboro British round 19. Silverstone, 2 October. Q: 1:30.62 (4); 1:35.44 (1) R 2. P: Jones (1:29.16.) 2.

Drizzle fell at the beginning of the first session and Jones set a time. As Senna came out the drizzle hardened. On Senna's second lap he lost control at Abbey. The car spun wildly across the track and nudged the barrier backwards. No improvement in the second session in the wet.

Jones crept the start and missed third gear, Brundle into the lead from Senna. At half distance the gap was 1.5 seconds. They lapped back-markers and Senna drew up. On the last lap he made a lunge at Becketts but Brundle resisted.

Pd Brundle 28m 55.23s, Senna @ 0.64, Jones @ 17.16. **FL** Brundle. **Ch** Brundle 123, Senna 122, Jones 71.

RACE 70

Marlboro British round 20. Thruxton, 23 October. Q: 1:13.55 (1); 1:13.36 (1). P. 1.

The shoot-out. In the first session Senna took provisional pole. 'I came across a couple of cars stopped at the Complex on the lap and although the car felt good it wasn't perfect for the conditions.' The temperature rose for the second session, Senna and Brundle (third overall) improving.

The race was anti-climactic, Senna leading by two lengths. His team had taped over the oil radiator outlet to heat the oil more quickly. 'It was perfect. The oil was up to proper temperature within a lap or so rather than the usual six or seven.' On lap 6, as anticipated, the water temperature climbed. Senna loosened his seat belts enough to reach out and tear the tape away. 'By the time I looked back up I was almost at the chicane. I thought I had lost it for a minute.' He got through and settled the race and the Championship.

Pd Senna 18m 39.78s, Jones @ 5.43, Brundle @ 8.53. **FL** Senna. **Ch** Senna 132, Brundle 127 (123 counting), Jones 77.

RACE 71

Macau GP, Macau, 20 November. Q: 2:23.47 (2); 2:22.02 (1). P. 1.

Senna's first time at a street circuit. Roberto Guerrero went quickest in the first session. After three laps Senna had been third quickest before wrecking all four wheels in two brushes with the barriers. In the second session he bent a gear selector but the session was red flagged and that gave time for repairs. In three more laps Senna had pole.

He dominated the two heats (aggregate counting). He led the opening lap of both by

2.5 seconds. In the first heat, Guerrero took the initial corner tight then Senna 'came past me down the alley between the two corners. I couldn't believe what he was able to do on cold tyres.'

Heat 1: Senna 35m 44.65s, Guerrero @ 06.00, Berger @ 20.83. **Heat 2:** Senna 35m 50.31s, Guerrero @ 01.32, Berger @ 16.85. **Pd** Senna 1h 11m 34.96s, Guerrero @ 7.32, Berger @ 1m 14.38. **FL** Senna, both heats.

1984 Formula 1: Toleman

He signed for Toleman, a small and ambitious team, in December 1983. Johnny Cecotto, 1975 World 350 Motorcycle Champion, would partner him. Toleman had Hart engines and initially Pirelli tyres. Other front-runners: Lauda and Prost (McLaren), Piquet (Brabham), Rosberg (Williams), de Angelis and Mansell (Lotus), Alboreto and Arnoux (Ferrari), Warwick and Tambay (Renault).

RACE 72
Brazil, Rio, 25 March. Q 1:36.867 (21); 1:33.525 (17). R 8. P: de Angelis 1:28.392. Hot. W: 1:39.746 (12). R, 8 laps, turbo.
Senna could cope with the Toleman but, in qualifying, sustained speed chewed chunks of tread from the Pirellis.

He gained four places on lap 1 but under the sheer pace fell away: 14th on laps 2 and 3, 15th on 4, 5 and 6, 16th on 7 before the turbo choked.

Pd Prost, Rosberg, de Angelis.
FL Prost 1:36.499 (Senna 1:42.286).

RACE 73
South Africa, Kyalami, 7 April. Q 1:07.657 (14); 1:06.981 (11). R 7. P: Piquet 1:04.871. Hot. W: 1:11.944 (14). 6.
Senna judged 'overall, the car feels pretty good.' After the Friday session he estimated he'd go seven-tenths quicker on the morrow – and did. 'If we have no mechanical problems I'm quite confident we can finish in the points.'

Part of the Toleman's nose cone wrenched off but he didn't pit. Fifteenth on lap 1, he ran solidly in 16th. Retirements mounted and he rose to ninth on lap 42, unlapping himself on 49, lapped again on 53. Exhausted, he summoned a 1:12 on his final lap. He had to be helped from the cockpit.

Pd Lauda, Prost, Warwick.
FL Tambay 1:08.877 (Senna 1:12.124).

RACE 74
Belgium, Zolder, 29 April. Q 1:18.914 (15); 1:18.876 (18). R 10. P: Alboreto 1:14.846. Sunny. W: 1:21.282 (14). 6.
Only two laps on the Friday, an electrical problem in the morning session forcing him into the spare car. The next day a misfire coughed and a back pain stabbed – he'd hurt himself testing.

Race: he got the start wrong, completing lap 1 24th. He slogged again: lap 2 23rd; lap 3 22nd; lap 5 21st; lap 9 18th; lap 12 17th … rising to tenth on lap 50, then lap 52 ninth, 59 eighth, 67 sixth.

Pd Alboreto, Warwick, Arnoux.
FL Arnoux 1:19.294 (Senna 1:22.633).

RACE 75
San Marino, Imola, 6 May. Q did not run; 1:41.585 (26). DNQ.
Toleman were in dispute with Pirelli, so Senna didn't have tyres on Friday. He was new to Imola and rain in the Saturday untimed restricted his chance to learn it. In the afternoon 'I suffered a problem with the fuel system. The car just wasn't working at all, the engine misfiring all the time.' He did 10 laps, the 1:41.585 too slow to make the race.

RACE 76
Mercedes-Benz Cup, Nürburgring, 12 May. No qual. Murky. 1.
The old Nürburgring had a new circuit added. To celebrate, Mercedes-Benz – who'd unveiled their 190 saloon – invited 20 drivers for a 12-lap race, including Lauda, Prost, Rosberg, John Watson, James Hunt, Jody Scheckter, Stirling Moss, Alan Jones, Carlos

Reutemann, Jack Brabham and John Surtees.

Reutemann led early lead from Jones, who dropped out. Senna took Reutemann but came under pressure from Lauda, Watson and Scheckter. He held on.

Pd Senna 26m 57.7s, Lauda at 1.4, Reutemann at 3.7. **FL** Scheckter.

RACE 77
France, Dijon, 20 May. Q 1:05.744 (13); 1:28.225 (16). R 7. P: Tambay 1:02.200. Overcast. W: 1:09.530 (14). R, 35 laps, turbo.

Toleman introduced their new car and on Friday Senna said: 'Really you cannot compare it with the old one. It seemed to me that I could gain on anybody through the corners but we lose out on power up the hill and onto the straight past the pits.' A wet Saturday.

Race: up to ninth when the turbo failed.

Pd Lauda, Tambay, Mansell.

FL Prost 1:05.257 (Senna 1:10.100).

RACE 78
Monaco, Monte Carlo, 3 June. Q 1:27.865 (15); 1:25.009 (13). R 7. P: Prost 1:22.661. Heavy rain. W: 1:59.892 (7). 2.

Brian Hart produced a new engine management system which gave, Senna insisted, better response. Early in first qualifying he hit a barrier, retreated to the spare and set his best time in that. The next day, learning, he did 25 laps – more than anyone else.

Race: a vicious rain, three cars gone on the opening lap. Senna was ninth. Prost led from Mansell who overtook and crashed. Senna found the Toleman difficult with full turbo boost and progressively turned the boost down until it was completely off. He was catching Prost who said: 'In the cockpit it was hell. The rain, big problems with the brakes, Senna and his Toleman/Hart on my heels – I was on the limit everywhere.'

	Prost	Senna	Gap
lap 31	2:03.766	1:59.433	7.446

At this point the race director, Jacky Ickx, decided enough was enough. The race officially ended at this point.

Pd Prost 1h 1m 7.740s, Senna @ 7.446, Bellof @ 21.141. **FL** Senna 1:54.334.

RACE 79
Canada, Montreal, 17 June. Q 1:29.282 (9); 1:27.448 (9). R 5. P: Piquet 1:25.442. Hot, dry. W: 1:33.062 (12). 7.

Nigel Roebuck wrote in *Autosport*: 'Only a fraction slower than the second McLaren (Lauda) was the first Toleman/Hart, Ayrton Senna qualifying in the top 10 for the first time. As in Monte Carlo, the Brazilian … ran with the Hart engine management system on the opening day, reverting to normal mechanical injection thereafter. If we accept that the Hart engine does not have the power of BMW, Renault or Ferrari then it becomes clear – in the light of Ayrton's overall lap time – that the TG184 chassis is working extremely well. Into corners Senna looked as quick as Prost, with the same fluent ease that we see from the Frenchman.'

In the race Senna rose to sixth on lap 15, fell back to ninth, rose to seventh but two laps adrift of the winner.

Pd Piquet, Lauda, Prost.

FL Piquet 1:28.763 (Senna 1:31.822).

RACE 80
USA-East, Detroit, 24 June. Q 1:47.188 (7); 1:42.651 (7). R 4. P: Piquet (1:40.980). Hot, dry. W: 1:49.347 (9). R, 21 laps, accident.

On the Friday, Senna clipped the kerbing on the entry to the chicane before the pits. It looked nasty, a flash fire and the Toleman bouncing from barrier to barrier like a pinball. Toleman repaired it overnight and Senna used it for the seventh place, his highest in any qualifying so far. Meanwhile Toleman kept the car with the management system – the only car they had with it – for the race.

A multiple-crash at the start, Piquet striking a wall and wrenching his right front wheel off. It flew towards Senna, who was accelerating, and landed on the Toleman with such ferocity that it wrecked the front suspension. Senna took the spare to the re-start and ran tenth for 13 laps, up to eighth by lap 20 but skimmed the tyre wall into turn one.

Pd Piquet, Brundle (later disqualified), de Angelis. **FL** Warwick 1:46.221 (Senna 1:47.444).

RACE 81
USA, Dallas, 8 July. Q 1:38.256 (5); did not run. R 3. P: Mansell (1:37.041). Hot, dry. No warm-up. R, 48 laps, driveshaft.

On the Friday the track began to break up under immense heat – over 100 degrees, so hot the Toleman mechanics poured ice cubes into Senna's overalls. In the Saturday morning untimed session 'I didn't tighten my helmet strap enough in the pits and when I went out the helmet slipped over my eyes the first time I braked hard!' By second qualifying the track surface was disintegrating.

He completed the opening lap fourth but hit a wall next lap and pitted for tyres, dropping him to 21st. Nine laps later he hit a wall again, pitted and ran last until lap 38 when he overtook Palmer. By lap 47 he'd taken Manfred Winkelhock (ATS). Then the driveshaft failed.

Pd Rosberg, Arnoux, de Angelis.
FL Lauda 1:45.353 (Senna 1:46.419).

RACE 82
World Sportscar Championship round 4. Nürburgring, 15 July. Partnering Johansson, Henri Pescarolo. Q 1:32.07 (9); 1:37.27 (6). P: Bellof/Derek Bell (1:28.68). Becoming wet. 8.

Senna told a friend he'd like to try sportscar racing and the friend organised it with the Joest Racing Porsche 956 team. While Johansson and Pescarolo monopolised qualifying in the dry, Senna had a go in the wet and completed his first lap, came in and asked what all the dashboard dials meant. Senna set a quick time in the wet.

A wet race, too, the car had problems and Senna couldn't run full boost when his turn at the wheel came. They lost eight laps in the pits when the clutch failed.

Pd Bell/Bellof, Thierry Boutsen/David Hobbs, Sandro Nannini/Paolo Barilla.

RACE 83
Britain, Brands Hatch, 22 July. Q 1:11.890 (4); 1:13.991 (13). R 4. P: Piquet (1:10.869). Hot, dry. W: 1:16.256 (8). 3.

Ten minutes into the Friday morning session Cecotto struck a guardrail virtually head on. When the session resumed Senna went fastest. On the Saturday he couldn't sustain his Friday pace.

Race: within five laps he was sixth, past Mansell and Alboreto, but Palmer crashed. The re-start: aggregate times to count. Senna overtook Alboreto again and ran seventh to lap 34 when Tambay pitted. It made him sixth. He settled to a long pursuit. This lasted until lap 66 when he overtook de Angelis at Paddock. Prost, leading, retired on lap 38, gearbox, so Senna became fourth. On lap 67 Piquet toured, the turbo gone, Senna third.

Pd Lauda 1h 29m 28.532s, Warwick @ 42.123, Senna @ 1m 03.328.
FL Lauda 1:13.191 (Senna 1:13.951).

RACE 84
Germany, Hockenheim, 5 August. Q 1:49.395 (5); 1:49.831 (9). R 5. P: Prost (1:47.012). Dry. W: 1:58.553 (2). R, 4 laps, accident.

Rumours abounded that Lotus wanted Senna and these intensified over the weekend. Senna did not permit this to affect his driving, although on the Saturday the engine was 1,000 revs adrift and he could do no more than the fifth row.

On the second lap he moved smoothly past Tambay and ran fifth for the next three laps. Approaching the first chicane on lap 5 'I was flat in fifth but the speed was steady, not accelerating. Then I felt something happen behind me. I didn't want to brake hard to unsettle the car but it spun anyway, twice. Then I was off the road.'

Pd Prost, Lauda, Warwick.
FL Prost 1:53.538 (Senna 1:55.712).

RACE 85
Austria, Österreichring, 19 August. Q 1:29.463 (10); 1:29.200 (10). R 5. P: Piquet (1:26.173). Warm, dry. W: 1:32.978 (6). R, 35 laps, engine.

In both qualifying sessions Senna's car was down on revs despite having larger turbos.

Race: seventh for the first four laps, three of them behind de Angelis. At the Hella Licht chicane Senna suddenly darted through catching de Angelis by surprise; a move which de Angelis repeated on him three laps later. De Angelis took Warwick, who Senna caught by lap 15. Next lap Senna tried to take Warwick at the chicane but Warwick blocked; Warwick's engine failed, leaving Senna fifth, to become fourth on lap 28 when de Angelis pitted, engine expired. A lap later that became third when Prost spun on oil de Angelis had deposited. Senna felt the Hart engine tightening, race over.

Pd Lauda, Piquet, Alboreto.
FL Lauda 1:32.882 (Senna 1:34.348).

RACE 86
Holland, Zandvoort, 26 August.
Q 1:16.951 (13); 1:15.960 (13). R 7.
P: Prost (1:13.567). Dry. W: 1:20.607 (5).
R, 19 laps, engine.
We can dispense with qualifying quickly, a misfire on Friday, a blown engine on Saturday morning. On the Sunday morning Senna warned the Toleman team-members closest to him that there would be some action this day, and not just on the track. Lotus announced that Senna would be joining them in 1985 and Toleman were enraged.

Not much of a race to balance that, Senna working up to ninth before the turbo blew. He pulled off after Tarzan and all that remained was a short stroll to the pits.

Pd Prost, Lauda, Mansell.
FL Arnoux 1:19.465 (Senna 1:21.683).

RACE – no number
Italy, Monza, 9 September.
Did not take part.
Strictly speaking, this 'race' ought not to be included. Toleman, threatening litigation against Senna, took the car off him because they felt the only way to reach Senna was to do that. Senna went to Monza and, seeming wearied and saddened, said: 'I intended to keep quiet about the whole thing and deal with the people who were involved at

Toleman. I don't want any more aggravation. I just want to go motor racing.'

Pd Lauda, Alboreto, Riccardo Patrese (Benetton).

RACE 87
Europe, Nürburgring, 7 October.
Q 1:22.439 (12); 1:43.747 (12). R 6.
P: Piquet (1:18.871). Cool. W: 1:25.066
(6). R, 0 laps, accident.
The Hart engine had newer and bigger turbos and Senna said he was pleased with how much speed they gave him exiting the corners. He had a difficult Friday untimed session because a wire in the electronic control box severed, forcing him to the spare car. He covered no more than a lap and a half in that before the engine failed. The wiring was repaired in time for first qualifying. It rained on the Saturday.

In the first corner, a right-left already notorious, he claimed that Eddie Cheever (Alfa Romeo) pincered him and he had no option but to go into Rosberg's Williams. Some felt Senna had braked too late, others that he'd been tapped by another car.

Pd Prost, Alboreto, Piquet.
FL Alboreto and Piquet 1:23.146.
Senna: no laps.

RACE 88
Portugal, Estoril, 21 October. Q 1:30.077
(6); 1:21.936 (3). R 2. P: Piquet (1:21.703).
Hot, dry. W: 1:26.147 (5). 3.
The Championship decider between Lauda and Prost. Senna was fifth in the Sunday morning warm-up. Prost led by lap 9, Senna fourth, Lauda ninth and coming. On lap 19 Senna took Rosberg for third, where he remained until lap 33. Lauda wrote in *To Hell and Back* 'things are moving along nicely now. I am reeling them in one after the other every second round. Finally, I overtake Senna. I think I am in second position' Senna, hampered by a misfire, ran unobtrusively to the end.

Pd Prost 1h 41m 11.753s, Lauda @ 13.425, Senna @ 20.042. **FL** Lauda 1:22.996 (Senna 1:24.373). **Ch** Lauda 72, Prost 71.5, de Angelis 34, Senna joint ninth 13.

1985 Formula 1: Lotus

Senna joined de Angelis at Lotus and their relationship seems to have been one of content. They even holidayed together and Senna wouldn't do that again for years, until he partnered Berger. Lotus, once a great team but now trying to arrest decline, believed Senna was the man around whom to build the effort. They had Renault turbo engines. The other front-runners: Lauda and Prost (Marlboro McLaren), Rosberg and Mansell (Williams), Piquet (Brabham), Alboreto and Arnoux (Ferrari), Tambay and Warwick (Renault). Note: I have only included the Championship positions when Senna was in the top three.

RACE 89
Brazil, Rio, 7 April. Q 1:28.705 (2); 1:28.389 (3). R 2. P: Alboreto (1:27.768). Hot, dry. W: 1:38.194 (8). R, 48 laps, engine electronics.
Lotus went strongly for pole and de Angelis took it provisionally from Senna on the Friday. He'd start from the second row, however.

Race: he ran fourth, third when Rosberg's turbocharger failed. Lauda took Senna in an exquisite move of late braking – but Lauda's electronics failed after 27 laps, leaving Senna a long thrust towards the end. He didn't make it.

Pd Prost, Alboreto, de Angelis.
FL Prost 1:36.702 (Senna 1:38.440).

RACE 90
Portugal, Estoril, 21 April. Q 1:21.708 (1), 1:21.007 (1). P. Very wet. W:1:27.337 (7). 1.
He dominated qualifying: this was the first of Senna's 65 poles and achieved with an economy of effort.

The race was aquatic. Senna made a smooth start, de Angelis up past Prost but Senna lapping a clear second quicker. By lap 10 Senna led de Angelis by 12 seconds, cars spinning everywhere like a crazed carousel. Alboreto took de Angelis for second place on lap 43, the gap 58.066 to Senna. Senna did not permit this gap to close. Of the 26 starters, 17 didn't finish.

Pd Senna 2h 00m 28.006s, Alboreto @ 1m 02.978, Tambay @ 1 lap.
FL Senna 1:44.121. **Ch** Alboreto 12, Prost and Senna 9.

RACE 91
San Marino, Imola, 5 May. Q 1:27.589 (1); 1:27.327 (1). P. Overcast. W: 1:53.317 (11). R, 57 laps, out of fuel.
Senna expressed 'surprise' to be on pole. On the Saturday 'there was rain, but the biggest problem was we couldn't get enough heat into the qualifiers. I was driving very hard – any harder would have been verging on the dangerous. I only improved because the track was a bit faster.' Fuel regulations limited each car to 220 litres and Imola was thirsty.

He soon duelled with Prost until Prost was hemmed in behind Tambay. 'I hadn't been pushing before that because the car was too heavy on fuel. After I made my break I turned the boost down and cut my revs, thinking only of saving fuel. I never expected to run out.'

Pd Prost (later disqualified), de Angelis, Thierry Boutsen (Arrows).
FL Alboreto 1:30.961 (Senna 1:31.549).

RACE 92
Monaco, Monte Carlo, 19 May. Q 1:21.630 (1); 1:20.450 (1). P. Overcast. W: 1:25.195 (7). R, 13 laps, engine.
On the Saturday, Senna set his time early and defended it by holding up Lauda and Alboreto – which enraged Alboreto. Senna confessed he 'felt bad' about Lauda. Senna said: 'I drove closer to the limit on my quick laps than ever before.'

Just before the race, the electric blankets warming Senna's tyres short-circuited, blistering the fronts, which had to be replaced. Senna started on cold fronts and warm rears. He led but 'until the fronts came properly up to temperature the car was very unbalanced.' The engine failed.

Pd Prost, Alboreto, de Angelis.
FL Alboreto 1:22.637 (Senna 1:24.803).

RACE 93

Canada, Montreal, 16 June. Q 1:25.399 (2); 1:24.816 (2). R 1. P: de Angelis 1:24.567. Overcast. W: 1:30.530 (7). 16.

'I like this place,' Senna said: 'Very hard to go quickly and save the car.' De Angelis took the third and last pole of his life on the Saturday.

De Angelis led. Senna had to pit on lap 6, a turbo problem. He lost five laps and when he emerged diced with Rosberg (although in laps far behind him). Rosberg said: 'He's really good. I was impressed, but Jesus, he takes some risks ...'

Pd Alboreto, Johansson, Prost.
FL Senna 1:27.445.

RACE 94

USA-East, Detroit, 23 June. Q 1:42.051 (1); did not run. P. Hot, dry. W: 1:44.877 (1). R, 51 laps, accident.

Senna complained that the infamous bumps (and manhole covers) were worse than the year before. He set his time on his fourth lap, a stunning thing a full second faster than Mansell, next. Rain on Saturday brought standing water.

Senna led but pitted on lap eight, the surface gnawing the tyres. That made him 13th. Within six laps he'd risen to eighth, seventh when he pitted for more tyres. He constructed a monumental assault: he passed Bellof and set off after Alboreto. By lap 51 – Senna setting fastest lap of the race – he was full on Alboreto Then he 'hit the tyre barrier and it was my own fault.'

Pd Rosberg, Johansson, Alboreto.
FL Senna 1:45.612.

RACE 95

France, Paul Ricard, 7 July. Q 1:32.835 (1); 1:33.677 (4). R 1. P: Rosberg 1:32.462. Hot, dry. W: 1:41.020 (8). R, 26 laps, accident.

Friday: 'I missed a gearchange on my first run and at the end of the lap the tyres were still in good shape so obviously I wasn't driving hard enough. The second run was better.' Saturday: trying to better Rosberg's time, the engine blew.

In the race he ran second to Rosberg for six laps before Piquet slipstreamed past.

Senna slowed on lap 9 and pitted, the gear selectors jammed, came out 20th and gained five places by lap 26 before the engine blew.

Pd Piquet, Rosberg, Prost.
FL Rosberg 1:39.914 (Senna 1:41.552).

RACE 96

Britain, Silverstone, 21 July. Q 1:06.324 (3); 1:06.794 (4). R 2. P: Rosberg 1:05.591. Overcast. W: 1:12.065 (7). R, 60 laps, out of fuel.

Rosberg became the first man to lap Silverstone at 160mph. On the Friday Senna suffered engine problems on his qualifying car and had to use the spare. He went into a vast slide at Woodcote on oil. On the Saturday he suffered fuel feed problems.

He made a massive start and drew away but eventually the engine misfired, allowing Prost by, and with five laps left he parked it, the fuel gone.

Pd Prost, Alboreto, Laffite.
FL Prost 1:09.886 (Senna 1:10.032).

RACE 97

Germany, Nürburgring, 4 August. Q 1:18.792 (5); 1:36.471 (4). R 3. P: Teo Fabi (Toleman) 1:17.429. Overcast. W: 1:23.398 (3). R, 27 laps, CV joint.

A rubber washer came loose and went into the mechanical fuel pump, allowing Senna only one run on the Friday; a wet Saturday.

Race: Rosberg led, Senna in tandem, both drawing away. On lap 16 Senna pressed the power at the hairpin, went inside and forced Rosberg to concede. Senna maximised that then raised an arm – I'm slowing – and headed to the pits.

Pd Alboreto, Prost, Laffite.
FL Lauda 1:22.806 (Senna 1:24.270).

RACE 98

Austria, Österreichring, 18 August. Q 1:28.123 (10); 3:04.856 (22). R 7. P: Prost 1:25.490. Overcast. W: 1:32.352 (5). 2.

Friday. 'If we cannot get the balance of the car better I may as well stop after five laps in the race.' Saturday: he wanted a time fast – rain threatened. He did one lap and a turbo failed. Rain fell ...

The race had to be re-started after a crash. Senna worked his way up so effectively that when Lauda, leading, dropped out after 39 laps (turbo) he ran second behind Prost.

Pd Prost 1h 20m 12.583s, Senna at 30.002, Alboreto at 34.356. **FL** Prost 1:29.241 (Senna 1:31.666).

RACE 99
Holland, Zandvoort, 25 August.
Q 1:11.837 (4); did not run. R 2. P: Piquet 1:11.074. Warm, dry. W: 1:17.997 (7). 3.
In the Friday untimed session the Lotus caught fire and took a short cut to the paddock. He was fined $5,000. A wet Saturday.

Piquet stalled on the grid, Rosberg leading from Senna. Prost and Lauda went by but Rosberg's engine failed and Lauda pitted for tyres: Senna second to Prost. Eventually Lauda had the lead back, from Prost. Senna ran third and Alboreto wanted that. They 'met' at the chicane. 'He just drove straight into the back of me,' Senna said, 'trying to push me straight on. For sure it was deliberate.'

Pd Lauda 1h 32m 29.263, Prost at 0.232, Senna at 48.491. **FL** Prost 1:16.538 (Senna 1:17.835).

RACE 100
Italy, Monza, 8 September. Q 1:27.009 (4); 1:25.084 (1). P. Overcast. W: 1:32.639 (11). 3.
Senna hadn't driven Monza before and went seventh fastest in the Friday untimed. 'I arrived at the chicane flat in fifth on one lap simply because I'd forgotten it was there!' On the Saturday he made an early and late run – and on that almost lost control.

Senna led but Rosberg contested that at the first chicane and got in front. The Williams Honda power was too much and Mansell went by, then Prost. Rosberg and Mansell dropped out, and Senna completed a quiet race.

Pd Prost 1h 17m 59.451s, Piquet at 51.635, Senna at 1m 00.390.
FL Mansell 1:28.283 (Senna 1:31.703).

RACE 101
Belgium, Spa, 15 September. Q 2:00.710 (18); 1:55.403 (2). R 1. P: Prost 1:55.306. Wet, drying. W: 2:26.732 (3). 1.
On the Friday 'my car was having an engine change so I decided to run in the spare on race tyres, then run qualifiers on my own when it was ready. We had a fire in the pits which burned an oil line. They changed that, I went out and the left-hand turbo broke.' Saturday was better.

A wet race, and Senna made a gorgeous start. He led clearly on the climb after *Eau Rouge* while Prost decided on playing percentages, particularly when the clutch on Alboreto's Ferrari failed after only three laps. 'The engine started missing occasionally halfway through.' It lasted.

Pd Senna 1h 34m 19.893s, Mansell @ 28.422, Prost @ 55.109. **FL** Prost 2:01.730 (Senna 2:03.700). **Ch** Prost 69, Alboreto 53, Senna 32.

RACE 102
Europe, Brands Hatch, 6 October. Q 1:08.020 (1); 1:07.169 (1). Pole. Cool, dry. W: 1:14.995 (9). 2.
Provisional pole on the Friday and decisively, Piquet next on 1:09.204 – a difference of 1.184. On the Saturday he dipped into the 1m 7s and only Piquet could follow him there. Senna made a second run and when he crossed the line he'd averaged 140.100mph – nobody had done that at Brands before.

Senna led, Rosberg after him. Repeatedly Rosberg tried to overtake and on lap 7 spun. Piquet rammed him. Rosberg pitted and emerged, a lap down, as Senna was coming round followed by Rosberg's team-mate Mansell. Rosberg decided to help Mansell and show Senna what blocking looked like.

Pd Mansell 1h 32m 58.109s, Senna @ 21.396, Rosberg @ 58.533. **FL** Laffite (Ligier) 1:11.526 (Senna 1:12.601). **Ch** Prost 72, Alboreto 53, Senna 38.

RACE 103
South Africa, Kyalami, 19 October. Q 1:04.517 (4); 1:02.825 (4). R 2. P: Mansell 1:02.366. Hot, dry. W: 1:08.296 (2). R, 8 laps, engine.

The Renault engine wasn't giving enough straight line speed, a crippling disadvantage because Kyalami had an enormous straight. On the Friday Senna was down on boost but felt better after the Saturday: more boost and the car better balanced.

A nothing of a race, fourth on the first two laps, fifth for the next three, fourth on lap 6, third on lap 7; and that was it.

Pd Mansell, Rosberg, Prost. **FL** Rosberg 1:08.149 (Senna 1:10.077). **Ch** Prost 73, Alboreto 53, Senna 38.

RACE 104
Australia, Adelaide, 3 November.
Q 1:22.403 (2), 1:19.843 (1). P. Hot, dry.
W: 1:23.854 (1). R, 63 laps, engine.
He went out early on the Friday, 'made a few mistakes' and claimed Mansell blocked him on his second run. On the Saturday he was sure 'I couldn't have gone 100th of a second quicker.'

Mansell led but Senna lunged down in the inside and hoofed him off. Rosberg led, Senna trying to hold Alboreto at bay. Suddenly, Rosberg went to pit and Senna couldn't react fast enough. The Lotus lost its front right wing. Senna rushed on and plunged off at the hairpin. He did pit for a new nose cone, caught and passed Lauda for second place and set off after Rosberg – who pitted, Senna leading from Lauda who took him. Lauda crashed, Senna led again until blue smoke and dribbling oil announced the end.

Pd Rosberg, Laffite, Philippe Streiff (Ligier). **FL** Rosberg 1:23.758 (Senna 1:24.140). **Ch** Prost 76 (73 counting), Alboreto 53, Rosberg 40, Senna 38.

1986 Formula 1: Lotus

De Angelis departed for Brabham and Senna invoked the wrath of many by making sure Lotus did not sign Warwick to replace him but Dumfries, a debutant, instead. The other front runners: Prost and Rosberg (Marlboro McLaren), Mansell and Piquet (Williams), Teo Fabi and Berger (Benetton), Alboreto and Johansson (Ferrari).

RACE 105
Brazil, Rio, 23 March. Q 1:26.983 (2)
1:25.501 (1). P. Hot, dry. W: 1:36.556 (10). 2.
Friday: Piquet did the fastest lap ever at the circuit. Saturday: Senna sat contemplating for a long time, emerged and stole pole on the final lap of the session.

A front row of Senna and Piquet: Senna away quickest from Mansell, and Mansell pulled out to take the inside line at the fast left-hander. Senna granted him just enough space and they went in side-by-side. They touched but Senna steadied the Lotus. Piquet went through on lap 3 and that was it.

Pd Piquet 1h 39m 32.583s, Senna @ 34.827, Laffite @ 59.759. **FL** Piquet 1:33.546 (Senna 1:34.785).

RACE 106
Spain, Jerez, 13 April. Q 1:21.605 (1);
1:21.924 (1). P. Hot, dry. W: 1:28.964 (3). 1.
Friday: Senna insisted the Lotus was 'bottoming everywhere.' He watched most of the Saturday session on a television in the Lotus motorhome. With 20 minutes left Mansell did 1:22.760. Senna strode to the Lotus and did 1:21.924.

Senna led to lap 39, Mansell taking him as they came upon a back-marker. Mansell led for 10 laps. They grappled and Senna overtook Mansell at the uphill hairpin. Mansell risked pitting for fresh tyres and devoured the circuit. One lap to go: Mansell closed, closed, closed and crossing the line they were so close that Mansell imagined he'd won.

Pd Senna 1h 48m 47.735s, Mansell @ 0.014, Prost @ 21.552. **FL** Mansell 1:27.176 (Senna 1:28.801) **Ch** Senna 15, Piquet 9, Mansell 6.

RACE 107
San Marino, Imola, 27 April. Q 1:25.050
(1); 1:25.286 (1). P. Overcast. W: 1:32.225
(2). R, 11 laps, wheel bearing.

Senna wasn't completely happy with the brakes on the Friday and said he hadn't driven well. He was quickest (by 0.840 from Piquet). Traffic hampered him on the Saturday.

He moved swiftly away from the green but Piquet overtook. On lap 4 Prost went by into *Tosa* and Rosberg went by on the exit. On lap 12 the failed wheel bearing brought a smoke-cloud from the Lotus.

Pd Prost, Piquet, Berger.
FL Piquet 1:28.667 (Senna 1:31.999).
Ch Senna and Piquet 15, Prost 13.

RACE 108

Monaco, Monte Carlo, 11 May.
Q 1:25.222 (1); 1:23.175 (3). R 2. P: Prost
1:22.627. Warm, sunny. W: 1:28.376 (6). 3.
Thursday: he 'missed a gear at the chicane and on my second run I got held up by Johansson.' Saturday: each lap was hampered by traffic.

Prost led from Senna and Mansell, Senna holding second until Prost pitted for tyres on lap 35. Quickly, Prost caught Senna, waited until Senna pitted on lap 42, Rosberg up to second. It remained static.

Pd Prost 1h 55m 41.060s, Rosberg @ 25.022, Senna @ 53.646. **FL** Prost 1:26.607 (Senna 1:26.843). **Ch** Prost 22, Senna 19, Piquet 15.

RACE 109

Belgium, Spa, 25 May. Q 1:55.776 (5);
1:54.576 (3). R 2. P: Piquet 1:54.331. Hot,
dry. W: 2:01.950 (10). 2.
Friday: Rosberg was on a flying lap and Senna held him up out of *Eau Rouge.* Rosberg found Senna afterwards to explain the facts of life. Saturday: balance changes improved the Lotus but third gear jumped out twice.

Senna tracked Piquet early but Piquet departed (engine). After the pit stops Mansell led from Senna. 'I had big understeer all through.'

Pd Mansell 1h 27m 57.925s, Senna @ 19.827, Johansson @ 26.592.
FL Prost 1:59.282 (Senna 1:59.867).
Ch Senna 25, Prost 23, Mansell 18.

RACE 110

Canada, Montreal, 15 June. Q 1:27.422
(1); 1:24.188 (2). R 1. P: Mansell 1:24.118.
Hot, dry. W: 1:30.168 (11). 5.
A wet but drying Friday. In the final minutes he went out to gauge conditions and returned for qualifiers – only to have a random weight check. That meant he began his lap less than one second before session's end. He took provisional pole. Next day he couldn't find quite enough speed.

Mansell led from Senna but into lap five Prost pressed the McLaren alongside in the sweepers and gained the racing line. It forced Senna to lift and skitter over the kerbing – Rosberg, Piquet and Arnoux through, Senna sixth. He took Arnoux and spent the rest of the race fending him off.

Pd Mansell, Prost, Piquet.
FL Piquet 1:25.443 (Senna 1:27.503).
Ch Prost 29, Mansell and Senna 27.

RACE 111

USA-East, Detroit, 22 June. Q 1:40.301
(2); 1:38.301 (1). P. Hot. W: 1:42.499 (3). 1.
Senna couldn't match Mansell on the Friday but did on the Saturday.

Senna chose B compound tyres. 'There was no doubt that the Cs gave better grip for a few laps but after that they started to go off.' Senna led but into lap 3 missed a gear, ceding it to Mansell. Brake problems crippled Mansell and in a flurry Senna, Arnoux and Laffite overtook. Senna pitted for tyres on lap 14. Order at lap 30: Laffite, Piquet, Senna. Laffite pitted next lap, Piquet nine laps later and Senna led to the end.

Pd Senna 1h 51m 12.847s, Laffite at 31.017, Prost at 31.824. **FL** Piquet 1:41.233 (Senna 1:41.981.) **Ch** Senna 36, Prost 33, Mansell 29.

RACE 112

France, Paul Ricard, 6 July. Q 1:06.526
(1); 1:06.807 (1). P. Overcast. W: 1:11.982
(6). R, 3 laps, accident.
He had a revised Renault engine and covered a lot of laps in both untimed sessions in his race car. By Saturday he expressed satisfaction.

Senna led immediately but Mansell out-braked him into the first corner. On lap 4 de Cesaris's engine blew on his Minardi and laid oil in Signes. Senna cuffed the tyre barrier. 'I didn't see the oil in time and I lost it. No excuses.'

Pd Mansell, Prost, Piquet.
FL Mansell 1:09.993 (Senna 1:12.882)
Ch Prost 39, Mansell 38, Senna 36.

RACE 113
Britain, Brands Hatch 13 July. Q 1:09.042 (4); 1:07.524 (3). R 2. P: Piquet 1:06.961. Hot, dry. W: 1:13.095 (4). R, 27 laps, gearbox.

For once, he was ragged in qualifying and the Lotus looked a handful.

The race had to be re-started after a crash and Mansell fought a mind-over-matter contest with Piquet, Senna fourth until the gearbox failed.

Pd Mansell, Piquet, Prost.
FL Mansell 1:09.593 (Senna 1:14.024).
Ch Mansell 47, Prost 43, Senna 36.

RACE 114
Germany, Hockenheim 27 July. Q 1:45.212 (8); 1:42.329 (3). R 2. P: Rosberg 1:42.013. Hot, dry. W: 1:51.863 (9). Hot, dry. 2.

On the Friday the balance of the Lotus wasn't quite right, but better on the Saturday.

At the green, Senna bored between the McLarens and led for a lap before Rosberg went through, then Piquet, then Prost. Rosberg ran out of fuel and Senna risked some of his in overtaking Prost – who also ran out. Approaching the finishing line Senna weaved the Lotus from side to side to slosh whatever fuel remained into the engine.

Pd Piquet 1h 22m 08.263s, Senna @ 15.437, Mansell @ 44.580.
FL Berger 1:46.604 (Senna 1:49.424).
Ch Mansell 51, Prost 44, Senna 42.

RACE 115
Hungary, Hungaroring, 10 August. Q 1:32.281 (3); 1:29.450 (1). P. Hot, dry. W: 1:35.048 (6). 2.

The new circuit lacked rubber on it and in the Thursday introductory session cars spun

everywhere, Senna quickest, however. On the Saturday most teams ran on race tyres then qualifiers – except Senna who chose qualifiers both times. He was right.

Senna led from Mansell into turn one. Piquet took Mansell on lap 3 and took Senna on the straight on lap 12. 'That was really the problem for me through the whole race. The Lotus was as quick as the Williams in the corners … but Piquet was much faster in the straights.'

Pd Piquet 2h 00m 34.508s, Senna @ 17.673, Mansell @ 1 lap. **FL** Piquet 1:31.001 (Senna 1:31.261). **Ch** Mansell 55, Senna 48, Piquet 47.

RACE 116
Austria, Österreichring, 17 August. Q 1:26.650 (9); 1:25.249 (7). R 4. P: Fabi 1:23.549. Hot, dry. W: 1:31.824 (12). R, 13 laps, engine.

Friday: he had engine problems and used Dumfries's car. Saturday: he had his own car but was unhappy with its balance and grip.

He ran seventh early on, pitted for tyres on lap 8, pitted again three laps later with a misfire, managed a 1:52.440 (an eternity off the pace), struggled round in 3:35.788 and pitted again, game over.

Pd Prost, Alboreto, Johansson.
FL Berger 1:29.444 (Senna 1:33.437).
Ch Mansell 55, Prost 53, Senna 48.

RACE 117
Italy, Monza, 7 September. Q 1:25.363 (1); 1:24.916 (5). R 3. P: Fabi 1:24.078. Hot, dry. W: 1:30.482 (10). R, no laps, clutch.

Fastest on the Friday, Senna couldn't hold on to that. On the Saturday an engine blew.

At the green, the clutch broke and the Lotus edged slowly forward, going nowhere.

Pd Piquet, Mansell, Johansson.
FL Fabi 1:28.099. **Ch** Mansell 61, Piquet 56, Prost 53, Senna 48.

RACE 118
Portugal, Estoril, 21 September. Q 1:19.943 (5); 1:16.673 (1). P. Overcast. W: 1:22.844 (4). 4.

Friday: he didn't like the balance of the car. Saturday: a spectacular lap.

Mansell claimed the first corner, then Senna flirted with a move on him out at the back of the circuit. Piquet spent a long afternoon trying to get at Senna, Senna cutting past back-markers at places where he knew Piquet couldn't follow. Into the final lap Senna ran out of fuel but was classified fourth.

Pd Mansell, Prost, Piquet.
FL Mansell 1:20.943 (Senna 1:21.283).
Ch Mansell 70, Piquet 60, Prost 59, Senna 51.

RACE 119
Mexico, Mexico City, 12 October.
Q 1:18.367 (4); 1:16.990 (1). P. Hot, dry.
W: 1:20.962 (3). 3.
The previous Mexican Grand Prix had been 16 years before and the surface remained corrugated with bumps. Senna couldn't avoid one on his pole lap. 'I could have been half a second quicker.'

Mansell struggled to get first gear, Piquet fast away from Senna who challenged him at the first corner, Piquet ceding nothing. It stayed like that until 31 laps when Piquet pitted, Senna leading until he pitted, too. Berger completed the race without a stop and led, Senna behind.

Pd Berger 1h 33m 18.700s, Prost @ 25.438, Senna @ 52.513. **FL** Piquet 1:19.360 (Senna 1:20.237). **Ch** Mansell 72 (70 counting), Prost 65 (64 counting), Piquet 63, Senna 55.

RACE 120
Australia, Adelaide, 26 October.
Q 1:21.302 (6); 1:18.906 (3). R 2.
P: Mansell 1:18.403. Overcast.
W: 1:22.698 (1). R, 43 laps, engine.
Friday: he crashed in the special qualifying car and set his time in the race car. Saturday: he improved using race tyres but during the session the track lost grip.

Mansell made the better start, Senna harrying then following. They moved through the left-sprint-right and Senna went inside. Piquet broke through and on lap 2 Rosberg took Senna as well. Mansell made his move on lap 4 and overtook, then Prost on lap 7. Senna ran fifth to lap 42 when the engine went.

Pd Prost, Piquet, Johansson. **FL** Piquet 1:20.787 (Senna 1:24.149). **Ch** Prost 74 (72 counting), Mansell 72 (70 counting), Piquet 69, Senna 55.

1987 Formula 1: Lotus

Dumfries, who had scored three points in 1986, departed Lotus to be replaced by Satoru Nakajima, a pleasant Japanese who, we assumed, came as part of a package: Lotus secured Honda engines. The other front-runners: Prost and Johansson (Marlboro McLaren), Piquet and Mansell (Williams), Patrese and de Cesaris (Brabham), Boutsen and Fabi (Benetton), Alboreto and Berger (Ferrari).

RACE 121
Brazil, Rio, 12 April. Q 1:29.002 (3); 1:28.408 (3). R 2. P: Mansell 1:26.128. Hot, dry. W: 1:33.547 (3). R, 50 laps, engine.
Senna had an active suspension car and said they'd decided two weeks ago they'd only run

it – 'and I agree completely. In fact, I don't want to drive a car with a normal suspension again.' Friday: he complained that the car felt terrible and not much better on the Saturday.

Piquet led Senna by three seconds after a couple of laps, Mansell moving up. Piquet pitted because he'd picked up some waste paper which coated his radiators and threatened to boil the engine. Senna led, pitted for tyres on lap 13 and worked up to second place, slipped back. 'I felt the engine was going to seize.'

Pd Prost, Piquet, Johansson.
FL Piquet 1:33.861 (Senna 1:35.312).

RACE 122
San Marino, Imola, 3 May. Q 1:27.543 (3); 1:25.826 (1). P. Hot, dry. W: 1:32.416 (7). 2.

Senna was surprised to be on pole, pointing to the complexities of the 'active' system. 'We have so much to learn about it. The car is really not handling that well.'

He led through *Tamburello* but Mansell slotted out approaching *Villeneuve* and overtook. Senna resisted Prost for three laps and drifted into a swap shop sort of afternoon: third, second, fourth and when Patrese fell away on lap 50, third. A lap later he overtook Alboreto, the Ferrari losing boost.

Pd Mansell 1h 31m 24.076s, Senna @ 27.545, Alboreto @ 39.144. **FL** Fabi 1:29.246 (Senna 1:30.851). **Ch** Mansell 10, Prost 9, Johansson 7, Senna and Piquet 6.

RACE 123
Belgium, Spa, 17 May. Q 2:08.450 (5); 1:53.426 (3). R 2. P: Mansell 1:52.026. Overcast. W: 2:02.000 (12). R, no laps, accident.

Friday: wet and cold. Saturday: wet and dry. 'Yes, I am quick in the wet but that doesn't mean I like it. The balance of the car is not too bad but it doesn't feel as stable as I would like at a circuit as quick as this.'

Senna led from Mansell but at a right-hander out in the country Mansell came alongside and they touched, pirouetted. Mansell was able to rejoin, Senna not. When Mansell retired after 17 laps he strode to the Lotus pit and grasped Senna round the throat.

Pd Prost, Johansson, de Cesaris. **FL** Prost 1:57.153 (Senna no laps). **Ch** Prost 18, Johansson 13, Mansell 10, Senna and Piquet 6.

RACE 124
Monaco, Monte Carlo, 31 May. Q 1:25.255 (2); 1:23.711 (2). R 1. P: Mansell 1:23.039. Warm, dry. W: 1:26.796 (1). 1.

After the drivers' meeting Senna and Mansell had a talk and although neither retracted from their position over the Spa crash they decided to let it rest. Mansell couldn't be caught in either session.

Mansell travelled clean through Ste Devote followed by Senna who concentrated on finding 'a pace, a rhythm I could sustain for the whole race.' He let Mansell go, attacked later: on lap 28 Mansell led by 11 seconds, down to 6 next lap, Senna through the lap after that, Mansell out with a broken exhaust.

Pd Senna 1h 57m 54.085s, Piquet @ 33.212, Alboreto @ 1m 12.839. **FL** Senna 1:27.685. **Ch** Prost 18, Senna 15, Johansson 13.

RACE 125
USA-East, Detroit, 21 June. Q 1:42.985 (2); 1:40.607 (2). R 1. P: Mansell 1:39.264. Overcast. W: 2:12.754 (12). 1.

Mansell bestrode the Friday and Saturday, fastest in both. Senna (briefly) held pole on the Saturday but Mansell battered that.

Mansell led by five seconds after 10 laps, Alboreto almost half a minute distant in third. 'Early in the race I was in trouble with a soft brake pedal and I backed off. And maybe slowing helped me on tyre wear.' Mansell pitted for tyres, Senna led, and mounted his assault. Senna resisted and didn't make a pit stop at all.

Pd Senna 1h 50m 16.358, Piquet @ 33.819, Prost @ 45.327. **FL** Senna 1:40.464. **Ch** Senna 24, Prost 22, Piquet 18.

RACE 126
France, Paul Ricard, 5 July. Q 1:07.303 (4); 1:07.024 (2). R 2. P: Mansell 1:06.454. Hot, dry. W: 1:10.797 (3). 4.

Friday: a troubled session, although quickest at the timing beam on the Mistral Straight with 205.664mph. Saturday: he liked the car's balance better but, chasing Prost's Friday time of 1:06.877 the engine tightened.

He ran fourth from the start and remained there until the pit stops, ran fourth again. The balance of the car, evidently, had been the problem.

Pd Mansell, Piquet, Prost. **FL** Piquet 1:09.548 (Senna 1:12.231). **Ch** Senna 27, Prost 26, Piquet 24.

RACE 127
Britain, Silverstone, 12 July. Q 1:09.255 (4); 1:08.181 (3). R 2. P: Piquet 1:07.110. Hot, dry. W: 1:13.450 (7). 3.

Friday: Senna remained unhappy about the balance and the team experimented with different settings. The car felt better on the Saturday.

Piquet and Mansell made strong starts, Senna fourth. Prost took the lead, Piquet and Mansell retook him and Senna probed. On lap 2 Senna went inside at Copse and took Prost – who did it back three laps later. Senna circled fourth. Prost pitted for tyres on lap 29 and Senna ran third to the end.

Pd Mansell 1h 19m 11.780s, Piquet @ 1.918, Senna @ 1 lap. **FL** Mansell 1:09.832 (Senna 1:11.605). **Ch** Senna 31, Mansell and Piquet 30.

RACE 128
Germany, Hockenheim, 26 July.
Q 1:42.873 (2); no time. R 1. P: Mansell
1:42.616. Overcast. W: 1:49.718 (7). 3.
Senna liked the balance better on the Friday – evidently the 'active' suspension had a new programme – although he damaged the underside of the qualifying car. He transferred to the race car but it bottomed so badly he spun. On the Saturday, in terrible weather, he did a single (uncompleted) lap.

He made a superb start, Mansell tardy, but out into the country Mansell screamed by and Senna had Prost behind him. On lap 2 Prost flicked inside into the Stadium entry. A lap later Piquet sailed by and Senna settled for the art of the possible: fourth, becoming third when Prost's alternator failed.

Pd Piquet 1h 21m 25.091, Johansson @ 1m 39.591, Senna @ 1 lap. **FL** Mansell 1:45.716 (Senna 1:49.187). **Ch** Piquet 39, Senna 35, Mansell 30.

RACE 129
Hungary, Hungaroring, 9 August.
Q 1:31.387 (8); 1:30.387 (6). R 3.
P: Mansell 1:28.047. Hot, dry. W: 1:35.096 (8). 2.
An unhappy qualifying despite Lotus's revised rear bodywork to improve the airflow. Senna couldn't find enough grip and on the Saturday his engine cut in too quickly.

He ran fifth early, fourth when Berger went (differential), and third when Alboreto went (engine). That was lap 44. Senna lay 12.312 seconds behind Piquet who was in second place. Six laps to go and Mansell went (a

loose wheel nut). Piquet first and Senna second.

Pd Piquet 1h 59m 26.793s, Senna @ 37.727, Prost @ 1m 27.456.
FL Piquet 1:30.149 (Senna 1:32.426).
Ch Piquet 48, Senna 41, Mansell and Prost 30.

RACE 130
Austria, Österreichring, 16 August.
Q 1:25.492 (7); 1:39.647 (4). R 4.
P: Piquet 1:23.357. Hot, dry. W: 1:29.153 (6). 5.
A difficult qualifying, the elusive search for balance continuing. 'It is poor here and the car feels unstable on some parts of the circuit.'

A shambolic sequence of starts on the narrow grid. Cars crashed three times before they finally got away, Senna 18th and in the spare. After the pit stops he ran sixth, caught Alboreto and they quarrelled, touched. Senna pitted for new front wings. Ninth, he stampeded again to fifth.

Pd Mansell, Piquet, Fabi.
FL Mansell 1:28.318 (Senna 1:28.559).
Ch Piquet 54, Senna 43, Mansell 39.

RACE 131
Italy, Monza, 6 September. Q 1:25.535 (7);
1:24.907 (4). R 2. P: Piquet 1:23.460. Hot,
dry. W: 1:29.308 (3). 2.
McLaren announced that Senna was joining them to partner Prost in 1988, and McLaren would have Honda engines. In qualifying Senna could only get to slightly less than a second from Berger, who was third on the Saturday.

A poor start, sixth across the opening four laps before he opened up. 'I wanted to win this one or be nowhere.' He took Prost on lap 5 and gambled on no pit stop (or 'the race was lost'). On lap 25, the other pit stops completed, Senna had a gap of 14.084 to Piquet. On lap 43, Senna pushed hard toward Parabolica, drawing up to Piercarlo Ghinzani (Ligier) but the Lotus bounded over the run-off area. Piquet was through.

Pd Piquet 1h 14m 47.707s, Senna @ 1.806, Mansell @ 49.036.
FL Senna 1:26.796. **Ch** Piquet 63, Senna 49, Mansell 43.

RACE 132

Portugal, Estoril, 20 September.
Q 1:18.382 (3); 1:18.354 (4). R 3.
P: Berger 1:17.620. Hot, dry. W: 1:22.877
(8). 7.

On the Friday he spun twice, one of them to avoid a spinning car, and on the Saturday he had an engine fire. He retreated to the spare. It rained.

The race was re-started after a crash. Into turn one Senna was third behind Mansell and Berger. Piquet harassed and on lap 11 sneaked by. Senna pitted on lap 14 – an intermittent engine cutout – and emerged 22nd. He produced an insistent charge to finish only four seconds behind Eddie Cheever (Arrows), sixth.

Pd Prost, Berger, Piquet.
FL Berger 1:19.282 (Senna 1:20.217).
Ch Piquet 67, Senna 49, Mansell 43.

RACE 133

Spain, Jerez, 27 September. Q 1:25.162
(6); 1:24.320 (2). R 3. P: Piquet 1:22.461.
Hot, dry. W: 1:31.170 (14). 5.

Friday: the engine on Senna's qualifying car misbehaved. Saturday: in the morning he damaged the underbelly over a kerb. In the afternoon he did 24 laps shaving off fractions as best he could.

Mansell led from Piquet, Senna third and clearly holding the others up. Mansell pitted for tyres on lap 42, Piquet on lap 45, Senna now second behind Mansell. 'I knew that if I came in the best I could hope for was maybe fourth or fifth. I decided to stay out, fight, and hope that the tyres would last.' Late on he couldn't resist moves by Piquet, Johansson and Prost.

Pd Mansell, Prost, Johansson.
FL Berger 1:26.986 (Senna 1:30.088).
Ch Piquet 70, Mansell 52, Senna 51.

RACE 134

Mexico, Mexico City, 18 October.
Q 1:21.361 (7); 1:19.089 (7). R 4.
P: Mansell 1:18.383. Hot, dry. W: 1:25.367
(18). R, 54 laps, spin.

The 'active' suspension helped over the Mexican corrugation but the Lotus lacked grip. On the Saturday and with only moments of the session left, he bounded over a bump and the car rammed the tyre wall.

He ran consistently in the race, rising to second behind Mansell on lap 21 before Piquet overtook him on lap 38. The clutch failed and, nine laps to go, he tried to change down without it. His brakes locked and he spun, the car stalling.

Pd Mansell, Piquet, Patrese.
FL Piquet 1:19.132 (Senna 1:20.586).
Ch Piquet 73, Mansell 61, Senna 51.

RACE 135

Japan, Suzuka, 1 November. Q 1:44.026
(9); 1:42.723 (7). R 4. P: Berger 1:40.042.
Overcast. W: 1:47.740 (6). 2.

A crash by Mansell on the Friday gave the Championship to Piquet. For Senna the familiar fate: lack of balance, lack of grip.

Berger led from Boutsen, Senna third, Piquet fourth. The dislike between Senna and Piquet no doubt deepened because Senna had expressed the hope that Mansell would be Champion. Now Piquet complained that Senna went off the track and returned to it with less than decorum. After the pit stops Senna ran third behind Berger and Johansson until, on the final lap, fuel problems slowed Johansson.

Pd Berger 1h 32m 58.072s, Senna @ 17.384, Johansson @ 17.694.
FL Prost 1:43.844 (Senna 1:45.805).
Ch Piquet 73, Mansell 61, Senna 57.

RACE 136

Australia, Adelaide, 15 November.
Q 1:18.508 (4); 1:18.488 (4). R 2.
P: Berger 1:17.267. Hot. W: 1:23.701 (8).
Disq.

Senna savoured the prospect of a street race and second row of the grid opened up possibilities.

A sad, angered end to three years with Lotus. Senna didn't make a pit stop, enabling him to finish second to Berger. Benetton successfully protested the brake-ducting on the Lotus.

Pd Berger, Senna (later disqualified), Alboreto. **FL** Berger 1:20.416 (Senna 1:20.456). **Ch** Piquet 76 (73 counting), Mansell 61, Senna 57.

1988 Formula 1: McLaren

Prost, World Champion in 1985 and 1986, had been in Grand Prix racing since 1980. How would he cope with Senna as a team-mate? Would he cope? None had so far, but none had had the stature of Prost. It became the central question of the season, and the next season, too. McLaren had Honda turbo engines. The other front-runners: Mansell and Patrese (Williams); Piquet (Lotus); Boutsen and Alessandro Nannini (Benetton); Alboreto and Berger (Ferrari).

RACE 137
Brazil, Rio, 3 April. Q 1:30.218 (1); 1:28.096 (1). P. Overcast. W: 1:45.165 (1). Disq, 31 laps.
In first qualifying, Senna took provisional pole – Prost fourth. A vast, exuberant crowd saw Senna improve by two seconds on the Saturday.

On the grid, Senna began to wave his arms: the gear linkage had broken. The start was aborted, and Senna began it from the pit lane in the spare. He reached sixth but the Stewards decided to disqualify him for changing cars after the first start.

Pd Prost, Berger, Piquet.
FL Berger 1:32.943 (Senna 1:34.657).

RACE 138
San Marino, Imola, 1 May. Q 1:41.597 (2); 1:27.148 (1). P. Warm, dry. W: 1:32.544 (2). 1.
The Friday was wet, the Saturday overcast but dry. Senna had a problem before he set the pole time on Saturday. 'The pop-off valve was giving trouble, obliging the Honda engineers to fit a new one.'

At the green, Prost almost stalled – Senna crisp into the lead. Prost completed the lap sixth. What would Prost do? By lap three he was fifth, by lap 5 fourth, by lap 8 second. Prost knew 'Ayrton would be very difficult to beat.' And was.

Pd Senna 1h 32m 41.264s, Prost @ 2.334, Piquet @ 1 lap. **FL** Prost 1:29.685 (Senna 1:29.815). **Ch** Prost 15, Senna 9, Piquet and Berger 8.

RACE 139
Monaco, Monte Carlo, 15 May. Q 1:26.464 (1); 1:23.998 (1). P. Warm, dry. W: 1:44.159 (1). R, 66 laps, accident.
Stunning Senna in second qualifying: he went faster and faster to the point where 'I suddenly realised that I was no longer driving the car consciously.'

Senna led, Berger uncompromising on the inside into *Ste Devote*, Prost third. By the time Prost took Berger (lap 54!) Senna led by more than 46 seconds. Dennis radioed Senna and Prost to relay the position but on lap 67 Senna lost concentration in the right-hander before the tunnel and punted the barrier.

Pd Prost, Berger, Alboreto.
FL Senna 1:26.321. **Ch** Prost 24, Berger 14, Senna 9.

RACE 140
Mexico, Mexico City, 29 May. Q 1:17.468 (1); 1:17.666 (1). P. Overcast. W: 1:20.121 (1). 2.
Senna set the pace in the Friday untimed session, Prost next. In fact the only session when Senna wasn't quickest was Saturday morning untimed – Prost first, Senna fourth.

The race was settled at the start, Prost and Piquet off faster. Senna tracked Piquet to *Peraltada* and overtook him on the start-finish straight, but – the McLarens evenly matched – such a short delay proved too much to recapture.

Pd Prost 1h 30m 15.737s, Senna @ 7.104, Berger @ 57.314. **FL** Prost 1:18.608 (Senna 1:18.776.) **Ch** Prost 33, Berger 18, Senna 15.

RACE 141
Canada, Montreal, 12 June. Q 1:22.392 (1); 1:21.681 (1). P. Dry. W: 1:26.645 (6). 1.
Senna's fifth consecutive pole. He took it provisionally on the Friday (from Prost, of course) and set the decisive time early in the Saturday session.

Prost made the more assertive start, Senna angry that he'd been given the wrong side of the grid for pole: on the right, but the first corner a left, favouring Prost. Senna got to within striking distance of Prost. On lap 19 he out-braked him at the hairpin.

Pd Senna 1h 39m 46.618s, Prost @ 5.934, Boutsen @ 51.409.
FL Senna 1:24.973. **Ch** Prost 39, Senna 24, Berger 18.

RACE 142
USA-East, Detroit, 19 June. Q 1:40.606 (1); 1:41.719 (3). P. Hot, dry. W: 1:42.409 (2). 1.

Senna didn't venture out for most of the Friday session and complained about the difficulty of getting a clear lap. The track, recently resurfaced, broke up on the Saturday.

Senna's chances were spiced by Berger and Alboreto lining up between himself and Prost. Berger almost outdragged Senna into turn one but Senna responded to that and led. Any hopes of a race within the race, Prost catching Senna, ebbed as gearbox problems hampered Prost.

Pd Senna 1h 54m 56.035s, Prost @ 38.713, Boutsen @ 1 lap. **FL** Prost 1:44.836 (Senna 1:44.992). **Ch** Prost 45, Senna 33, Berger 18.

RACE 143
France, Paul Ricard, 3 July. Q 1:08.456 (2); 1:08.067 (2). R 1. P: Prost 1:07.589. Hot, dry. W: 1:10.135 (1). 2.

Prost quickest both sessions, the first pole Senna hadn't taken this season. Senna held it fleetingly on the Saturday before Prost countered.

Prost led, Senna swiftly overtaking Berger. Prost siphoned a gap of a second, Berger lurking around Senna. Prost had a long stop (10.68), Senna led. Prost caught him. From a long way back Prost mounted an enormous run down the inside channel, hugging the kerbing and was through.

Pd Prost 1h 37m 37.328s, Senna @ 31.752, Alboreto @ 1:06.505.
FL Prost 1:11.737 (Senna 1:11.856).
Ch Prost 54, Senna 39, Berger 21.

RACE 144
Britain, Silverstone, 10 July. Q 1:10.787 (3); 1:10.616 (3). R 2. P: Berger 1:10.133. Wet. W: 1:17.264 (1). 1.

A Ferrari festival in qualifying, both days. 'Because of trying to get the handling right we haven't done as much "fuel running" as usual so we don't really know what the position is with consumption.' On the Saturday Senna spun through 360 degrees twice, rotations of absolute ferocity, and both times he continued at tremendous speed.

Officially a wet race. Berger led, Senna manipulating wide around Alboreto at Maggotts for second place. Senna attacked into Stowe but Berger blocked that and Senna existed within the spray Berger cast back. On lap 14 Senna took Berger towards Woodcote.

Pd Senna 1h 33m 16.367s, Mansell @ 23.344, Nannini @ 51.214.
FL Mansell 1:23.308 (Senna 1:23.595).
Ch Prost 54, Senna 48, Berger 21.

RACE 145
Germany, Hockenheim, 24 July. Q 1:44.596 (1); 1:50.002 (10). P. Damp, cloudy. W: 1:48.674 (1). 1.

On the Friday the Honda engines were down on power. Saturday was hot and humid, no improvement possible.

On a damp track virtually everyone began on wet tyres. Senna led but Prost, fourth, needed 11 laps to reach second place. By then Senna was an unassailable 13 seconds ahead.

Pd Senna 1h 32m 54.188s, Prost @ 13.609, Berger @ 52.095.
FL Alessandro Nannini (Benetton) 2:03.032. (Senna 2:05.001). **Ch** Prost 60, Senna 57, Berger 25.

RACE 146
Hungary, Hungaroring, 7 August. Q 1:30.422 (5); 1:27.635 (1). P. Hot, dry. W: 1:32.379 (8). 1.

A dank Friday and a cut and thrust Saturday not settled until five minutes from the end when Senna finally took pole from Prost. 'Hard work.'

Senna out-rushed Mansell into turn one, Prost tenth. Prost gained places and Mansell drifted back. On lap 47 Prost darted past Boutsen and set about catching Senna. Prost caught him, challenged into turn one – got in front, went wide and Senna had the lead back. 'For an instant I thought we could both go off the road.' Soon after Prost felt a 'huge vibration' from the front of his car.

Pd Senna 1h 57m 47.081s, Prost @ 0.529, Boutsen @ 31.410. **FL** Prost 1:30.639 (Senna 1:30.964.) **Ch** Senna and Prost 66, Berger 28.

RACE 147
Belgium, Spa, 28 August. Q 1:53.718 (1); 2:15.196 (4). P. Dry, sunny. W: 1:59.988 (1). 1.
Senna got pole on the Friday and Saturday was wet.

Senna and Prost, filling the front row, made a pact not to take each other off at *La Source* in the jostle from the lights. Once through they'd race. Senna churned too much wheelspin, giving *La Source* to Prost but out in the country Senna went by. Prost spent the race trying to stay with Senna and couldn't.

Pd Senna 1h 28m 00.549s, Prost @ 30.470, Boutsen @ 59.681.
FL Berger 2:00.772 (Senna 2:01.061).
Ch Senna 75, Prost 72, Berger 28.

RACE 148
Italy, Monza 11 September. Q 1:26.160 (1); 1:25.974 (1). P. Hot, dry. W: 1:29.820 (1). R, 49 laps, accident.
On the Friday Senna used one set of tyres on the race car because he wanted to check the spare, which he had for the weekend. On the Saturday he improved by two-tenths for his tenth pole of the season, beating the record nine of Piquet (1984), Ronnie Peterson (1973) and Lauda (1974 and 1975).

By lap 2, Senna led by 3.4 seconds from Prost, who had a misfire. Prost sensed the engine wouldn't last and decided to push Senna, making him use too much fuel. Prost did 34 laps and went out. The Ferraris took up the chase and closed. At the first chicane on lap 50, second to last lap, Senna tried to lap Jean-Louis Schlesser but they crashed.

Pd Berger, Alboreto, Cheever.
FL Alboreto 1:29.070 (Senna: 1:29.569).
Ch Senna 75, Prost 72, Berger 37.

RACE 149
Portugal, Estoril, 25 September. Q 1:18.032 (1); 1:17.869 (2). R 1. P: Prost 1:17.411. Hot, dry. W: 1:22.601 (9). 6.
On the Saturday Prost said: 'I wasn't terribly interested in getting pole – no point in taking any more risks just for the sake of a tenth of a second.' But he did. Senna said his car was working well although he'd had a repeat of an electrical failure.

The race had to be re-started after a crash. Along the start-finish straight Prost positioned himself directly behind Senna, jinked right as they accelerated towards 190mph and Senna jinked at him. Their wheels virtually touched, Prost wedged between Senna and the pit lane wall. Senna's fuel read-out soon gave alarming readings and he settled to an economy run.

Pd Prost, Capelli, Boutsen.
FL Berger 1:21.961 (Senna 1:22.852).
Ch Prost 81, Senna 76, Berger 37.

RACE 150
Spain, Jerez, 2 October. Q 1:24.775 (1); 1:24.067 (1). P. Hot, dry. W: 1:29.299 (5). 4.
On the Friday he found it 'quite difficult to get the car to work.' He and Prost improved on the Saturday.

Prost made an instantaneous start, Senna hesitant, Mansell into second. Senna attacked Mansell, wove a path through at a right-hander, drifted wide and Mansell nipped back at him. The McLaren used too much fuel and by lap 39 was fourth. Senna pitted late for tyres – seventh – and flogged into the points.

Pd Prost, Mansell, Nannini.
FL Prost 1:27.845 (Senna 1:28.273).
Ch Prost 90 (84 counting), Senna 79, Berger 38.

RACE 151
Japan, Suzuka, 30 October. Q 1:42.157 (1); 1:41.853 (1). P. Wet, dry. W: 1:46.372 (1). 1.

They say he read The Bible on the flight as he prepared to vindicate his life. Prost stated his intentions by going fastest in the Friday morning untimed session, Senna second. Senna took provisional pole in the afternoon, and confirmed it the following day.

The start went wrong: he stalled. The track sloped and as the McLaren dribbled forward he fired it up. He was eighth after lap 1. The rest was a long pursuit towards Prost. When he reached him he probed for eight laps, got by. Prost dug a warrior's effort towards the end, cutting the gap to 1.5 but, in heavy rain, had no further chance. Senna had his first World Championship.

Pd Senna 1h 33m 26.173s, Prost @ 13.363, Boutsen @ 36.109.
FL Senna 1:46.326. **Ch** Senna 88 (87 counting), Prost 96 (84 counting), Berger 41.

RACE 152
Australia, Adelaide, 13 November.
Q 1:18.332 (2); 1:17.748 (1). P. Warm, overcast. W: 1:21.011 (2). 2.
On the Friday 'I made a mistake at the hairpin when I went a bit wide under braking.' A frantic Saturday finale: as the flag was to fall to end the session, Senna shaved Prost's time and had his thirteenth pole of the season.

Prost made the better start and Berger overtook Senna on lap 3. Berger even overtook Prost on lap 14 but crashed into Arnoux while lapping him. Prost led and increased the gap.

Pd Prost 1h 53m 14.676s, Senna @ 36.787, Piquet @ 47.546. **FL** Prost 1:21.216 (Senna 1:21.668). **Ch** Senna 94 (90 counting), Prost 105 (87 counting), Berger 41.

1989 Formula 1: McLaren

Could Prost survive Senna? The question sharpened and quickly. The other front-runners: Boutsen and Patrese (Williams), Piquet (Lotus), Nannini and Herbert (Benetton), Mansell and Berger (Ferrari). Turbos and the fuel restriction had been banned.

RACE 153
Brazil, Rio, 26 March. Q 1:26.205 (2); 1:25.302 (1). P. Hot, dry. W: 1:32.797 (2). 11.
The pole came on the Saturday. 'I wouldn't say I took any risks, because the car felt safe to drive. The most difficult thing is to believe that you can go through the corners at the sort of speeds you need.'

At the green, Senna moved to mid-track, Berger out from behind, Senna flicking towards Berger forcing Berger to flick clear, two wheels off the track. They reached the first corner, a right, three abreast: Berger, Senna, Patrese. The Ferrari and the McLaren clouted each other. Senna pitted for a new nose cone, making him last. He ran to the end two laps down.

Pd Mansell, Prost, Mauricio Gugelmin (March). **FL** Patrese 1:32.507. (Senna: 1:33.685).

RACE 154
San Marino, Imola, 23 April. Q 1:42.939 (2); 1:26.010 (1). P. Warm, sunny. W: 1:28.571 (2). 1.
On the Friday 'it was all a question of being out and ready for a quick lap in the last few minutes because the circuit was getting drier all the time.' On the Saturday 'on qualifying tyres I came up behind two other cars – the Arrows, I think – running slowly on the straight down towards *Tosa*. I found myself taking a "confidence" lift.'

Senna led Prost but on lap 4 Berger crashed at *Tamburello*, the Ferrari exploding in flames. At the re-start Prost out-gunned Senna onto the power and led through *Tamburello* but, into *Tosa*, Senna curved round the outside. Afterwards Prost could not conceal his anger – claiming Senna had broken a pact that whichever led initially wouldn't be attacked by the other.

Pd Senna 1h 26m 51.245s, Prost @ 40.225, Nannini @ 1 lap. **FL** Prost 1:26.795 (Senna 1:27.273). **Ch** Prost 12, Senna and Mansell 9.

RACE 155
Monaco, Monte Carlo, 7 May. Q 1:24.126 (1); 1:22.308 (1). P. Warm, sunny. W: 1:26.214 (1). 1.

On the Saturday Senna confessed to 'a slight mistake at Casino Square' but got a clear run and took pole. No-one had ever driven a lap of the circuit quicker.

The race needed two starts – Warwick stalled, aborting the first – and Senna reacted to the green light superbly. For the first three laps he fashioned a gap but Prost set fastest lap and drew up. Deep into the race Senna lost 'second then first gears. It made the car extremely difficult to drive in traffic but I kept pressing on as hard as I could because I didn't want to give Alain any indication that I was in trouble.'

Pd Senna 1h 53m 33.251s, Prost @ 52.529, Stefano Modena (Brabham) @ 1 lap. **FL** Prost 1:25.501 (Senna 1:26.017). **Ch** Prost, Senna 18, Mansell 9.

RACE 156
Mexico, Mexico City, 28 May. Q 1:19.112 (1); 1:17.876 (1). P. Hot, sunny. W: 1:21.461 (3). 1.

Friday: 'It's a lot easier in a way than driving a turbo because the altitude means we have less power than normally so to compensate we have run less wing and the car is obviously much lighter in the corners.' Saturday: he equalled Jim Clark's record of 33 poles.

At the green, Senna went full over to the left and hugged the kerbing to turn perfectly into turn one, the right. A tale of tyres, Senna correct, Prost incorrect. Prost would finish fifth.

Pd Senna 1h 35m 21.431s, Patrese @ 15.560, Alboreto @ 31.254. **FL** Mansell 1:20.420 (Senna 1:20.585). **Ch** Senna 27, Prost 20, Mansell 9.

RACE 157
USA, Phoenix, 4 June. Q 1:30.108 (1); 1:30.710 (1). P. Hot, sunny. W: 1:33.949 (1). R, 44 laps, electrics.

He moved past Clark's 33. Friday: 'extremely hard work on what was a very low grip surface.' It proved sufficient, the track markedly slower on the Saturday.

Prost almost headed Senna into the first corner but hit a bad bump. Senna: 'Everything was perfect from the start. I was leading quite comfortably, keeping a cushion over Alain when the engine began to misfire slightly.' It would prove terminal.

Pd Prost, Patrese, Cheever (Arrows). **FL** Senna 1:33.969. **Ch** Prost 29, Senna 27, Patrese 12.

RACE 158
Canada, Montreal, 18 June. Q 1:21.049 (2); 1:21.269 (1). Row 1. P: Prost 1:20.973. Wet. W: 1:47.149 (4). 7.

Friday: 'I could not go any quicker and on my last run I had a slight problem with third gear jumping out a couple of times.' Saturday: 'the circuit conditions were a lot worse so the fact that I almost equalled my Friday time indicates how well the car was working.'

A drying track. Prost slithered across Senna for the lead but on lap 2 Senna surged by. Senna pitted for dry tyres – and rain fell from lap 5, Senna fifth. He was second by lap 11 and caught Patrese, leading and on wet tyres. At the hairpin Senna skimmed off – on the dry tyres. He pitted and led but with three laps to go he felt the engine tighten.

Pd Boutsen, Patrese, de Cesaris. **FL** Palmer (Tyrrell) 1:31.925 (Senna 1:32.143). **Ch** Prost 29, Senna 27, Patrese 18.

RACE 159
France, Paul Ricard, 9 July. Q 1:07.920 (1); 1:07.228 (2). R 1. P: Prost 1:07.203. Hot, sunny. W: 1:10.951 (3). R, no laps, differential.

Friday: 'I made a mistake and dropped a wheel over one of the kerbs. That spoilt my chances .' Saturday: the wind dropped and his second run was 'fine but just a shade away.'

A re-start (after Gugelmin crashes). 'I was just about changing from first to second gear when the drive simply vanished.'

Pd Prost, Mansell, Patrese. **FL** Gugelmin (Leyton House) 1:12.090 (Senna no laps). **Ch** Prost 38, Senna 27, Patrese 22.

RACE 160

Britain, Silverstone, 16 July. Q 1:09.124 (1); 1:09.099 (1). P. Warm, sunny. W: 1:12.530 (3). R, 11 laps, gearbox/spin.

A strong run on the Friday 'but I had to ease off slightly for yellow flags at Woodcote when Alesi spun his Tyrrell. I had lots of problems throughout both days, all involving problems with the engine oil system.'

Prost away hard enough to judge that by the entry to Copse he could safely turn in across Senna. Wrong. Senna went inside and gripped the corner. At Becketts into lap 12 he slewed and spun onto the gravel trap.

Pd Prost, Mansell, Nannini.
FL Mansell 1:12.017 (Senna 1:13.737).
Ch Prost 47, Senna 27, Patrese 22.

RACE 161

Germany, Hockenheim, 30 July. Q 1:42.300 (1); 1:42.790 (1). P. Warm, cloudy. W: 1:46.433 (1). 1.

In the Friday untimed Senna made a mistake and spun. 'I damaged the car and the mechanics had to work very hard to repair it.' Pole on the Saturday? 'No problem!'

Berger flung the Ferrari diagonally left round Senna on the outside into the lead. It couldn't last and didn't. In the country Senna went by and Prost went by. Senna led to lap 19 when he pitted for tyres, a long stop. Senna emerged behind Prost – but eventually Prost lost first gear.

Pd Senna 1h 21m 43.302s, Prost @ 18.151, Mansell @ 1m 23.254.
FL Senna 1:45.884. **Ch** Prost 53, Senna 36, Mansell and Patrese 25.

RACE 162

Hungary, Hungaroring, 13 August. Q 1:21.576 (6); 1:20.039 (1). R 1. P: Patrese 1:19.726. Warm, overcast. W: 1:24.176 (3). 2.

Friday: he had 'balance problems,' his best lap spoiled by traffic. Saturday: he congratulated Patrese on his 'super time from yesterday. It was impossible to beat.'

Patrese got the start right, fending off Senna: Patrese would hold this lead for 52 laps until Senna feinted by. Mansell took Patrese, too, and swarmed Senna for five laps. Out at the back of the circuit they came upon the Onyx of Johansson. Instantaneously Mansell saw a gap full on the right and corkscrewed the Ferrari into it.

Pd Mansell 1h 49m 38.650, Senna @ 25.967, Boutsen @ 38.354.
FL Mansell 1:22.637 (Senna 1:23.313).
Ch Prost 56, Senna 42, Mansell 34.

RACE 163

Belgium, Spa, 27 August. Q 2:11.171 (2); 1:50.867 (1). P. Cold, wet. W: 2:16.252 (5). 1.

Friday: 'On my first run the car felt better and better. I ended up only a fraction slower than Berger.' Saturday: 'It was obviously a very busy session after yesterday was effectively rained out. My first run felt good but not as good as my second.'

A wet race and at the green Senna moved from Prost. He built an immediate gap, Prost lost in the spray. This opening lap decided the whole thing: after three laps Senna led by more than five seconds and although Prost drew up – the track drying – overtaking was unreachable.

Pd Senna 1h 40m 54.196s, Prost @ 1.304, Mansell @ 1.824. **FL** Prost 2:11.571 (Senna 2:12.890). **Ch** Prost 62, Senna 51, Mansell 38.

RACE 164

Italy, Monza, 10 September. Q 1:25.021 (3); 1:23.720 (1). P. Warm, sunny. W: 1:27.637 (1). R, 44 laps, engine.

Friday: Berger provisional pole from Mansell. Senna: 'I think my absolute best would have been a 1m 24.8, nothing quicker.' Saturday: 'I missed a gear again on my first run but at least it gave me a reference point for my second try.'

A big start, Senna nicely in front of the Ferraris, Prost fourth. It solidified in mid-race, Senna from Berger. On lap 21 Prost took Mansell and advanced on Berger. On lap 41 – Senna 22 seconds ahead – Prost out-powered Berger. Three laps later Senna was gone: smoke from the engine.

Pd Prost, Berger, Boutsen.
FL Prost 1:28.107 (Senna 1:28.179).
Ch Prost 71, Senna 51, Mansell 38.

RACE 165

Portugal, Estoril, 24 September.
Q 1:15.496 (1); 1:15.468 (1). P. Hot, sunny.
W: 1:19.795 (1). R, 48 laps, accident.

He had a 'slight problem which I was unable specifically to pinpoint' on the Friday but still did a time good enough to remain on pole.

The race was lost in controversy and confusion. Berger led, Mansell hustling Senna, Prost fourth. On lap 8 Mansell got a 'tow' down the start-finish straight and slotted by. Mansell pitted for tyres on lap 40 but overshot his pit. The mechanics prepared to haul the Ferrari to the bay but Mansell reversed. He'd be black-flagged for that but pressed Senna. They crashed.

Pd Berger, Prost, Johansson.
FL Berger 1:18.986 (Senna 1:19.490).
Ch Prost 77 (75 counting), Senna 51, Mansell 38.

RACE 166

Spain, Jerez, 1 October. Q 1:21.855 (1);
1:20.291 (1). P. Warm, sunny. W: 1:25.552
(3). 1.

Senna needed a win or a second place to keep the Championship alive. He converted provisional pole to pole itself on the Saturday when 'I got a clear run on my second set of qualifiers.'

At the green, Senna was away, Berger tracking, Prost third. Senna would not lose the lead. 'It was a very long race on an extremely stressful circuit and that stress was intensified by Gerhard keeping up the pressure from second place in the early stages.'

Pd Senna 1h 47m 48.264s, Berger @ 27.051, Prost @ 53.788. **FL** Senna 1:25.779.
Ch Prost 81 (76 counting), Senna 60, Mansell 38.

RACE 167

Japan, Suzuka, 22 October. Q 1:39.493
(1); 1:38.041 (1). P. Mild, overcast.
W: 1:44.801 (3). 1, disqualified.

Friday: 'I missed second gear coming out of the hairpin. Without that I think I could have managed a 1:39 dead.' Saturday: 'My fastest lap wasn't a smooth one but quick, believe me.'

Prost had made a pact, but with himself. He'd moved aside rather than crash with Senna before. Not now. Prost led, from Senna. Lonely duellists they were, measuring the distance between themselves. On lap 47 Senna tried a long thrust towards the chicane, Prost following the orthodox line, into where Senna now had the McLaren. The inescapable laws of geometry decreed the crash. Senna continued after a push and was subsequently disqualified.

Pd Nannini, Patrese, Boutsen.
FL Prost 1:43.506 (Senna 1:43.025).
Ch Prost 81 (76 counting), Senna 60, Mansell 38.

RACE 168

Australia, Adelaide 5 November.
Q 1:17.712 (2); 1:16.665 (1). P. Wet.
W: 1:21.306 (1). R, 13 laps, accident.

Saturday: 'My first run was not as smooth as I would have liked but my second produced no problems. That was as much as I could do. If anybody had been able to go faster then so be it.'

A deluge descended on Adelaide, the start delayed by half an hour. On lap 2 the race was stopped, re-started 30 minutes later. Senna led again, the car moving like a nervous breakdown. He had 28 seconds over Boutsen by lap 6. He spun. On lap 14, unsighted by the spray, he hammered the rear of Brundle's Brabham.

Pd Boutsen, Nannini, Patrese.
FL Nakajima 1:38.480 (Senna 1:41.159).
Ch Prost 81 (76 counting), Senna 60, Patrese 40.

1990 Formula 1: McLaren

Berger came to McLaren and after a brief misunderstanding with Senna they grew to like each other. The other front-runners: Prost and Mansell (Ferrari), Boutsen and Patrese (Williams), Piquet and Nannini (Benetton), Alesi (Tyrrell).

RACE 169
USA, Phoenix, 11 March. Q 1:29.431 (5); 1:52.015 (3). R 3. P: Berger 1:28.664. Cool, overcast. W: 1:30.458 (1). 1.
Friday: 'We had some electrical problems in the morning so we changed the cockpit computer but the engine still misfired slightly in the afternoon.' Rain smothered Saturday.

Into the first right-hander Jean Alesi sliced his Tyrrell between Berger and de Cesaris, Senna fourth. By lap 11 Alesi led by eight seconds – from Senna. He tracked. On lap 34 into a right-hander Senna sneaked the inside line but Alesi elbowed Senna aside. Next lap Senna repeated the move and it settled the race.

Pd Senna 1h 52m 32.829s, Alesi @ 8.685, Boutsen @ 54.080. **FL** Berger 1:31.050 (Senna 1:32.178).

RACE 170
Brazil, Sao Paulo, 25 March. Q 1:17.769 (1); 1:17.277 (1). P. Hot, sunny. W: 1:20.990 (2). 3.
Friday: 'On my first set of tyres I didn't drive very well. The car felt too light. On my second set I put a little bit more wing on but I still didn't drive very well.' Saturday: 'A few minutes before the end I changed to my second set [of tyres] because I felt the conditions were on the verge of improving. It was a good lap.'

Senna led to his pit stop on lap 33 and led again to lap 41 when he reached Nakajima (Tyrrell). They crashed, Senna pitted for a new nose-cone and that cost 23.61 seconds stationary.

Pd Prost 1h 37m 21.258s, Berger @ 13.564, Senna @ 37.722. **FL** Berger 1:19.899 (Senna 1:20.067). **Ch** Senna 13, Prost 9, Alesi, Berger and Boutsen 6.

RACE 171
San Marino, Imola, 13 May. Q 1:24.079 (2); 1:23.220 (1). P. Hot, sunny. W: 1:27.497 (1). R, 3 laps, broken wheel.
Friday: 'I had done about half a lap when [Pierluigi] Martini [Minardi] had his accident and the session was stopped. I went out again but my tyres had lost some of their grip.' Saturday: 'I believe it would have been possible to be even quicker.'

Senna took Berger for the lead but into the fourth lap 'I thought I had a deflating tyre but I realised I was losing my brakes.' The right rear wheel had broken.

Pd Patrese, Berger, Nannini.
FL Nannini 1:27.156 (Senna: 1:30.615)
Ch Senna 13, Prost and Berger 12.

RACE 172
Monaco, Monte Carlo, 27 May. Q: 1:21.797 (1); 1:21.314 (1). P. Warm, overcast. W: 1:24.814 (1). 1.
He didn't quite feel 'that I produced my maximum on my first run' on the Friday 'so I really had to give it everything on the second just in case we had problems on the Saturday.'

After a re-start he led from Prost and dealt with the traffic with brutal finesse. When Prost dropped out – 30 laps, battery – Alesi ran second. Midway through Senna led him by 22 seconds: enough.

Pd Senna 1h 52m 46.982s, Alesi @ 1.087, Berger @ 2.073. **FL** Senna 1:24.468.
Ch Senna 22, Berger 16, Alesi 13.

RACE 173
Canada, Montreal, 10 June. Q 1:20.399 (1); 1:30.514 (5). P. Wet, drying. W: 1:37.394 (3). 1.
Friday: he thought he was on a very good lap when 'I lost fifth gear coming out of the fast chicane' Saturday was drying, no improvement.

Berger jumped the start but amidst plumes of spray Senna led. They would pit for dry tyres and it settled. 'They radioed me very early to say Gerhard had been penalised a minute. That reduced the pressure on me.'

Pd Senna 1h 42m 56.400s, Piquet @ 10.497, Mansell @ 13.385.
FL Berger 1:22.077 (Senna 1:23.375)
Ch Senna 31, Berger 19, Prost 14.

RACE 174
Mexico, Mexico City, 24 June. Q 1:18.417 (4); 1:17.670 (2). R 2. P: Berger 1:17.227. Cool, overcast. W: 1:19.930 (2). R, 63 laps, puncture.
Friday: 'I only tried one set of qualifying tyres, at the end of the afternoon session when I went for my time. I think I was a little too conservative early in the lap.' No pole on the Saturday. 'We made a slight improvement.'

Patrese reached turn one before Senna, who used the lap to close and take him on the start-finish straight. 'About 25 laps from the end I felt the car getting unstable and I thought it was a tyre problem.' He had a slow puncture in the right-rear.

Pd Prost, Mansell, Berger.
FL Prost 1:17.958 (Senna 1:19.062).
Ch Senna 31, Prost and Berger 23.

RACE 175
France, Paul Ricard, 8 July. Q 1:04.549 (2); 1:08.886 (30). R 2. P: Mansell 1:04.402. Hot, sunny. W: 1:08.711 (5). 3.
Friday: 'My best lap was clear of traffic, very good, but on my second set of tyres I had to back off a little on the double right-hander beyond Signes when my left front lost grip.' Saturday: 'We ran in race conditions, mainly to gain as much data as possible and it proved productive.'

Senna made a hesitant start, third behind Mansell and Berger. On the opening lap Berger took Mansell and next lap Senna followed. It remained like that until Berger pitted for tyres after 27 laps. Senna led for two laps 'then I made my tyre stop which is where we lost the race' – it lasted 16 seconds, a problem with the left rear.

Pd Prost 1h 33m 29.606s, Capelli (Leyton House) @ 8.626, Senna @ 11.606.
FL Mansell 1.08.012 (Senna 1:08.573)
Ch Senna 35, Prost 32, Berger 25.

RACE 176
Britain, Silverstone, 15 July. Q 1:08.071 (1); 1:09.055 (8). R 1. P: Mansell 1:07.428. Hot, sunny. W: 1:11.840 (5). 3.
Friday: 'on my first run I was slightly baulked going into Copse at the start of the lap.' Saturday: he 'badly blistered the front tyres' on his first run. He adjusted the downforce but the car felt 'dangerously nervous'.

At the green, Mansell went to mid-track and Senna, coming hard, nearly nudged him. Senna led into Copse and Mansell would need 12 laps to overhaul him. Senna touched a kerb, spun, pitted. He was tenth and handled the remainder gently.

Pd Prost 1h 18m 30.999s, Boutsen @ 39.092, Senna @ 43.088.
FL Mansell 1:11.291 (Senna 1:12.250).
Ch Prost 41, Senna 39, Berger 25.

RACE 177
Germany, Hockenheim, 29 July. Q 1:40.198 (1); 1:46.843 (22). P. Hot, humid. W: 1:44.734 (1). 1.
Friday: he 'made a small mistake on my second run when I hit the bump on the exit of the last chicane.' He devoted the Saturday to work on the race set-up.

A tight start, Berger – sharing the front row – making a powerful bid to take the first corner. 'I came in for tyres at the end of lap 17. It proved to be the right choice.' He emerged, tracked Nannini – leading – 'got closer and picked up a very good tow.'

Pd Senna 1h 20m 47.164s, Nannini @ 6.520, Berger @ 8.553. **FL** Boutsen 1:45.602 (Senna 1:45.711). **Ch** Senna 48, Prost 44, Berger 29.

RACE 178
Hungary, Hungaroring, 12 August. Q 1:20.389 (8); 1:18.162 (3). R 2. P: Boutsen 1:17.919. Hot, sunny. W: 1:22.618 (3). 2.
A fraught Friday. 'On my qualifying lap I came up behind [Gregor] Foitek [Monteverdi] whose tyres I could see were badly blistered and I naturally assumed he would move over but when he saw me he just accelerated hard, holding me up.' Saturday: on his big lap 'I just didn't have any grip from my tyres.'

Boutsen made a big start, Berger round the outside of Patrese into second, Senna sixth. He picked up a puncture – lap 22 – rejoining eleventh after the stop. In time, he'd catch Nannini in second place and on lap 64 he rushed the 90 degree right at the back of the circuit: he crudely punted Nannini into the air. Senna continued and drew up to Boutsen, who sailed stately on to the end.

Pd Boutsen 1h 49m 30.597s, Senna @ 0.288, Piquet @ 27.893. **FL** Patrese 1:22.058 (Senna 1:22.577). **Ch** Senna 54, Prost 44, Berger 29.

RACE 179
Belgium, Spa, 26 August. Q 1:52.278 (3); 1:50.365 (1). P. Overcast, humid. W: 1:56.401 (3). 1.
Senna survived a freak accident on the Friday. Martin Donnelly (Lotus) went into the barrier and his right rear wheel was flung back at Senna who was arriving quickly. He liked the Saturday lap.

Two re-starts (after crashes) so Senna led for the third time and initially couldn't shed Berger. Prost ran third until Berger's tyres wore, ran second facing a five-second gap to Senna and attacked. They both pitted on lap 22 for tyres but Prost was stationary four seconds longer.

Pd Senna 1h 26m 31.997s, Prost @ 3.550, Berger @ 28.462. **FL** Prost 1:55.087 (Senna 1:55.132). **Ch** Senna 63, Prost 50, Berger 33.

RACE 180
Italy, Monza, 9 September. Q 1:22.972 (1); 1:22.533 (1). P. Hot, sunny. W: 1:27.396 (2). 1.
Friday: 'My left front tyre was absolutely on the limit going through *Parabolica* and I had to back off slightly on the exit at a point where you should be hard on the throttle.'. He adjusted the chassis twice on the Saturday and set the pole time.

After a re-start, Senna led from Berger and Prost, who stalked Berger for 20 laps before overtaking him – Senna 3.5 seconds up the road. They exchanged fastest laps. 'It was a question of keeping the right pace lap after lap.'

Pd Senna 1h 17m 57.878s, Prost @ 6.054, Berger @ 7.404. **FL** Senna 1:26.254. **Ch** Senna 72, Prost 56, Berger 37.

RACE 181
Portugal, Estoril, 23 September. Q 1:14.246 (1); 1:13.601 (3). R 2. P: Mansell 1:13.557. Warm, dry. W: 1:19.306 (4). 2.
He judged his Friday lap 'rough, not a quick one. The car was understeering generally.' Saturday: he accepted the Ferraris had more power.

Mansell slewed and almost sandwiched Prost, Senna put the nose of the McLaren into the gap, Berger jinked in front of Mansell: Senna, Berger, Mansell, Piquet, Prost through turn one. The front trio ran in tandem until the tyre stops. Senna led from Mansell who inevitably attacked, paused to get his breath back, attacked again. On lap 50 Mansell nestled up for a 'tow' down the start-finish straight and classically went inside.

Pd Mansell 1h 22m 11.014s, Senna @ 2.808, Prost @ 4.189. **FL** Patrese 1:18.306 (Senna 1:18.936). **Ch** Senna 78, Prost 60, Berger 40.

RACE 182
Spain, Jerez, 30 September. Q 1:18.900 (1); 1:18.387 (1). P. Hot, sunny. W: 1:24.713 (2). R, 53 laps, engine.
Donnelly crashed horrifically with eight minutes of the Friday qualifying remaining and lay unconscious on the track. 'I went to the place where he was on the ground and when I saw the consequences I thought about not running anymore.' He did – provisional pole. Saturday: he was angry that two back-markers had a slow-motion argument when he was on his flyer. 'That was very dangerous.' Anyway, he had his fiftieth pole.

He led to his pit stop on lap 27. 'I thought I had a problem with my tyres but it was water leaking from the right-hand radiator onto the right rear tyre.' He pursued Prost but 'when I saw the oil warning light come on as the temperature rose I decided to switch off and park it.'

Pd Prost, Mansell, Nannini.
FL Patrese 1:24.513 (Senna 1:27.430).
Ch Senna 78, Prost 69, Berger 40.

RACE 183
Japan, Suzuka, 21 October. Q 1:38.828 (3); 1:36.996 (1). P. Hot, sunny. W: 1:43.353 (3). R, no lap, accident.
Friday morning: he 'made a mistake on the slippery track surface and spun off. This afternoon my car was OK but it bottomed out badly at one point just as I was changing from fourth to fifth and I got a little sideways.' Saturday: 'The whole team really contributed: men and machine working extremely well.' Senna had pole, on the right. He wanted it moved and the officials wouldn't.

Prost to the left and his Ferrari looked strong enough to be uncatchable if he led through turn one. Senna made a decision. He would allow Fate to decide. Prost led into turn one, Senna went down the inside and they crashed. The recriminations began immediately.

Pd Piquet, Roberto Moreno (Benetton), Aguri Suzuki (Lola). **FL** Patrese 1:44.233 (Senna no laps). **Ch** Senna 78, Prost 69, Berger 40.

RACE 184
Australia, Adelaide, 4 November. Q 1:15.671 (1); 1:15.693 (1). P. Hot, sunny. W: 1:19.516 (2). R, 61 laps, accident.
On the Friday he said the balance of the car improved, on the Saturday 'I went out for my second run for the pure pleasure of driving even though my pole position was under no threat.'

He led from Mansell and then Piquet. 'I had to be careful with the brakes from the start. I had too much brake balance on the rear to save the front brakes, which was a problem so I was on the absolute limit everywhere. Then I couldn't get second gear. I came to a left-hander stuck in neutral and I went straight into the tyre barrier.'

Pd Piquet, Mansell, Prost.
FL Mansell 1:18.203 (Senna 1:19.302).
Ch Senna 78, Prost 73 (71 counting), Piquet 44 (43 counting) and Berger 43.

1991 Formula 1: McLaren

Berger stayed at McLaren, the friendship with Senna deepening. The other front-runners: Mansell and Patrese (Williams), Piquet and Michael Schumacher (Benetton), Prost and Alesi (Ferrari). A rule change opened up the season, 10 points for a win and all 16 races to count.

RACE 185
USA, Phoenix 10 March. Q: 1:23.530 (2); 1:21.434 (1). P. Overcast. W: 1:27.747 (1). 1.
Berger spent the winter doing tracts of testing while Senna rested in Brazil. Berger reasoned he'd know the car better but Senna arrived and his qualifying times almost destroyed Berger.

Senna made a broad brush-stroke of a sweep into turn one, a right-hander. For the next two hours he turned left and right as the geometry of Phoenix demanded and at no stage lost the lead, even during his pit stop.

Pd Senna 2h 00m 47.828s, Prost @ 16.322, Piquet @ 17.376. **FL** Alesi 1:26.758 (Senna 1:27.153).

RACE 186
Brazil, Sao Paulo, 24 March. Q 1:18.711 (1); 1:16.392 (1). P. Wet. W: 1:21.000 (4). 1.
Rain made it 'very difficult to get it right' on the Friday. On the Saturday he spoke of the inspiration of driving in front of his own people. 'At one point on my second run I went well over the limit, riding one of the kerbs.'

The race pressed at the boundaries of the possible. Senna led from Mansell and deep into it Mansell stopped when the gearbox failed. On lap 60 of the 71 Senna led Patrese by 40 seconds. Rain spattered and spat and from around lap 50 Senna suffered 'serious gearbox trouble. I lost third and fifth and one point just hooked it into sixth. I saw Patrese coming for me and I really didn't think I'd make it.' He did.

Pd Senna 1h 38m 28.128s, Patrese @ 2.991, Berger @ 5.416. **FL** Mansell 1:20.436 (Senna 1:20.841). **Ch** Senna 20, Prost 9, Patrese and Piquet 6.

RACE 187
San Marino, Imola, 28 April. Q 1:21.877 (1); 1:43.633 (9). P. Wet, drying. W: 1:27.115 (2). 1.

Friday: he 'got a gear change slightly wrong on my first run so I knew it would not be quick enough. We made a few changes and I dipped below 1:22 on my second run.' Saturday: an engine problem in the morning and wanted the spare car – Berger's turn for that and he insisted.

Patrese made a crackling start, Senna following, staying far enough behind to give him some vision through Patrese's spray. Patrese pitted on lap 9, Senna slotting easily by as Patrese peeled into the pit lane. Berger cut the gap to Senna and they traded fastest laps. They pitted within a lap for dry tyres and when they'd reached racing speed Senna led by 1.4 and extended that. 'Halfway through, my oil pressure dropped, the warning light came on and I thought I wouldn't finish so I slowed until Gerhard started to catch me.'

Pd Senna 1h 35m 14.750s, Berger @ 1.675, JJ Lehto (Dallara) @ 1 lap. **FL** Berger 1:26.531 (Senna 1:27.168). **Ch** Senna 30, Berger 10, Prost 9.

RACE 188
Monaco, Monte Carlo, 12 May. Q 1:20.508 (1); 1:20.344 (1). P. Warm, overcast. W: 1:24.312 (2). 1.

On the Thursday 'I lost some time on the fast right-hander going into the tunnel so I waited until just before the end for my second try. I got a good clean lap.' On the Saturday 'the track conditions changed a lot but I managed to keep pole which is all that really matters.'

Stefano Modena (Tyrrell) shared the front row but Senna maximised the advantage of the stagger. Modena tracked, Senna settling to his pace and rhythm. Modena went to lap 43 (engine failure) and the race as an unresolved competition ended then, Mansell too far back.

Pd Senna 1h 53m 02.334s, Mansell @ 18.348, Alesi @ 47.455. **FL** Prost 1:24.368 (Senna 1:25.250). **Ch** Senna 40, Prost 11, Berger 10.

RACE 189
Canada, Montreal, 2 June. Q 1:35.843 (3); 1:20.318 (3). R 2. P: Patrese 1:19.837. Hot, sunny. W: 1:23.271 (3). R, 25 laps, alternator.

Saturday: 'Up until now people think we have had it easy with four pole positions and four wins but my performance today shows how competitive it really is out there.'

Mansell led from Patrese, Senna third, Prost hustling. Senna ran third to nearly half distance. 'I stopped with an electrical problem.'

Pd Piquet, Stefano Modena (Tyrrell), Patrese. **FL** Mansell 1:22.385 (Senna 1:24.647) **Ch** Senna 40, Piquet 16, Prost 11.

RACE 190
Mexico, Mexico City, 16 June. Q 1:17.264 (3); 1:18.711 (5). R 2. P: Patrese 1:16.696. Overcast, then sunny. W: 1:20.719 (3). 3.

'A big shunt' on Friday qualifying at *Peraltada*. 'I went in too wide and too fast.' He'd recovered by the Saturday.

He ran second early on, then third to the end behind Patrese and Mansell. 'The Williamses were very fast and it was difficult to get more power from our engine.'

Pd Patrese 1h 29m 52.205s, Mansell @ 1.336, Senna @ 57.356. **FL** Mansell 1:16.788 (Senna 1:18.570). **Ch** Senna 44, Patrese 20, Piquet 16.

RACE 191
France, Magny-Cours, 7 July. Q 1:16.557 (1); 1:14.857 (3). R 2. P: Patrese 1:14.559. Warm, overcast. W: 1:21.170 (9). 3.

Friday: 'My qualifying lap was very hard work. I could not have kept up that level of performance for much longer.' Saturday: 'I had a clear lap on both runs with just a little bit of oil which caused me to slide wide midway round the second lap.'

Senna made a 'poor start and knew I could not go with Prost or Mansell.' Apart from the tyre stops, he ran third the whole race.

Pd Mansell 1h 38m 00.056s, Prost @ 5.003, Senna @ 34.934. **FL** Mansell 1:19.168 (Senna 1:20.570). **Ch** Senna 48, Mansell 23, Patrese 22.

RACE 192

Britain, Silverstone, 14 July. Q 1:23.277 (3); 1:21.618 (2). R 1. P: Mansell 1:20.939. Warm, sunny. W: 1:29.281 (11). R, out of fuel, classified fourth.
Friday: 'The engine is not working well.' Saturday: 'I did my best, it was a good lap but the Williams team is really strong at the moment.'

Senna drew ahead into Copse. Mansell harried to Hangar Straight, got a 'tow', sprang out, led. He would not lose it. 'On the last lap the engine started to die as I went down the Hangar Straight.'

Pd Mansell, Berger, Prost.
FL Mansell 1:26.379 (Senna 1:27.509).
Ch Senna 51, Mansell 33, Patrese 22.

RACE 193

Germany, Hockenheim, 28 July. Q 1:38.208 (4); 1:37.274 (2). R 1. P: Mansell 1:37.087. Warm, sunny. W: 1:44.747 (3). R, 44 laps, out of fuel.
Friday: 'We haven't had much progress since Imola. We are just not quick enough to compete with the Williamses.' Saturday: 'Maybe I could have gone one-tenth quicker but I was really on the limit.'

Mansell off to a stormer, Berger past Senna, Prost fourth. After the pit stops Senna ran fourth, Prost fifth. The combat endured from lap 22 to lap 38, when Prost tried it at the first chicane and Senna elbowed him. Senna kept on; retired out of fuel on the final lap. 'I am too disappointed to make any comment.'

Pd Mansell, Patrese, Alesi.
FL Patrese 1:43.569 (Senna 1:44.213).
Ch Senna 51, Mansell 43, Patrese 28.

RACE 194

Hungary, Hungaroring, 11 August. Q 1:18.549 (2); 1:16.147 (1). P. Hot, sunny. W: 1:23.229 (6). 1.
Friday: 'It's very hot and my tyres were going off before the end of the lap so I had to be careful.' Saturday: two runs in the 1:16s. He radiated speed without rawness, drawing harmony from the car and himself.

At the green, Senna was sweetly away but Patrese, inside, abreast into turn one. Senna out-braked him. 'My tyre choice was a calculated risk [Cs left, Ds right] and after two laps I thought I had a puncture. The team told me they were ready for me to come in but I tried one more lap and the problem disappeared.'

Pd Senna 1h 49m 12.796s, Mansell @ 4.599, Patrese @ 15.594.
FL Bertrand Gachot (Jordan) 1:21.547 (Senna 1:22.392). **Ch** Senna 61, Mansell 49, Patrese 32.

RACE 195

Belgium, Spa, 25 August. Q 1:49.100 (1); 1:47.811 (1). P. Hot, sunny. W: 1:56.752 (3). 1.
Friday: he had two 'clean, good laps.' Saturday: 'I really had to push everything to the limit.'

Senna alongside Prost and on the sprint to *La Source* they waved front wheels at each other, Senna leading. Senna had a slow pit stop 'due to a problem refitting one of the rear tyres.' That made him third behind Mansell and Alesi. Mansell's electrics failed, Alesi's engine failed.

Pd Senna 1h 27m 17.669, Berger @ 1.901, Piquet @ 32.176. **FL** Moreno 1:55.161 (Senna 1:56.471). **Ch** Senna 71, Mansell 49, Patrese 34.

RACE 196

Italy, Monza, 8 September. Q 1:21.114 (1); 1:21.245 (1). P. Warm, breezy. W: 1:26.355 (4). 2.
Friday: Senna spoke of improving the chassis balance. Saturday 'at the start of my second quick lap I heard over the radio about Mansell's best time so I knew it was just between me and Gerhard for the pole.'

Mansell needed to win. He followed Senna and at one point let Patrese through to have a tilt at him. Patrese did overtake, spun. Senna: 'My set-up was not good so I used up my tyres and lost grip. Then my left front began to vibrate and locked under braking. Soon after that [lap 14] Mansell passed me and I decided to stop for fresh rubber. If I had not I could not have finished second.'

Pd Mansell 1h 17m 54.319s, Senna @ 16.262, Prost @ 16.829. **FL** Senna 1:26.061. **Ch** Senna 77, Mansell 59, Patrese 34.

RACE 197
Portugal, Estoril, 22 September.
Q 1:13.752 (2); 1:13.444 (3). R 2.
P: Patrese 1:13.001. Warm, sunny.
W: 1:19.798 (6). 2.
Friday: Berger took provisional pole. Saturday: Senna felt it 'a shame I could not get onto the front row with Gerhard but Riccardo deserved pole.'

From row 2 Mansell pulled over in front of Senna. 'If I hadn't braked hard and pulled my car to the inside Mansell and I would have had a big accident.' Patrese led from Mansell, Berger, Senna. When Mansell pitted the stop went wrong – he'd be disqualified – and Senna took Berger for second.

Pd Patrese 1h 35m 42.304s, Senna @ 20.941, Alesi @ 53.554. **FL** Mansell 1:18.179 (Senna 1:18.929). **Ch** Senna 83, Mansell 59, Patrese 44.

RACE 198
Spain, Barcelona, 29 September.
Q 1:19.474 (3); 1:19.064 (1). R 2.
P: Berger 1:18.751. Overcast, drizzle.
W: 1:46.561. (6). 5.
Friday: 'I could have done slightly better because when I changed cars I really wanted to use a mixed set of worn tyres but due to a slight misunderstanding they fitted my original set.' Saturday: 'When I started my second run the engine didn't feel quite right on the start-line straight and after a couple more corners it broke.'

Berger led from Senna, though Mansell took him on lap 3. On lap 13 Senna spun. 'I feel I spun because the slicks we fitted to the left-hand wheels were too hard and I was

fighting for grip in the wet. After the spin the left-hand tyres were blistered and I couldn't go any quicker.'

Pd Mansell, Prost, Patrese.
FL Patrese 1:22.837 (Senna: 1:24.771).
Ch Senna 85, Mansell 69, Patrese 48.

RACE 199
Japan, Suzuka, 20 October. Q 1:36.490 (2); 1:34.898 (2). R 1. P: Berger 1:34.700. Warm, sunny. W: 1:41.442 (1). 2.
After qualifying Senna said: 'As far as the World Championship is concerned I feel good but I am under no illusions. The race is going to be very tough but I think things are coming our way step by step.' The McLarens had the front row.

McLaren decided that Berger would build a big lead while Senna restrained Mansell – Mansell had to win. It worked. Trying to take Senna, Mansell went off. Senna and Berger raced, Senna led but the team instructed him to give it to Berger.

Pd Berger 1h 32m 10.695s, Senna @ 0.344, Patrese @ 56.731. **FL** Senna 1:41.532. **Ch** Senna 91, Mansell 69, Patrese 52.

RACE 200
Australia, Adelaide, 3 November.
Q 1:14.210 (1); 1:14.041 (1). P. Wet.
W: 1:18.964 (3). 1.
On the Saturday he took his 60th pole, 'a target I set myself this season and we just made it at the last minute.'

The race degenerated into a sodden shambles. 'I only started because I felt a strong obligation to the team and with the Constructors' Championship in mind.' He led from Berger. So many cars crashed that it was stopped at 14 laps.

Pd Senna 24m 34.899s, Mansell @ 1.259, Berger @ 5.120. **FL** Berger 1:41.141 (Senna 1:42.545) **Ch** Senna 96, Mansell 72, Patrese 53.

1992 Formula 1: McLaren

Berger remained with Senna at Marlboro McLaren. The other front-runners: Mansell and Patrese (Williams), Schumacher and Brundle (Benetton), Alesi (Ferrari). A rule change banned qualifying tyres.

RACE 201
South Africa, Kyalami, 1 March.
Q 1:16.815 (3); 1:16.227 (2). R 1.
P: Mansell 1:15.486. Warm, overcast.
W: 1:20.347 4). 3.
Friday: 'without qualifying tyres it's impossible to really go for it on a single lap with maximum grip.' On the Saturday he managed a clear lap.

Mansell led throughout, Patrese nestling between the McLarens from the green light. 'I knew right from the start after such a good getaway from Riccardo it would be almost impossible to pass him.'

Pd Mansell 1h 36m 45.320s, Patrese @ 24.360, Senna @ 34.675.
FL Mansell 1:17.578 (Senna 1:18.140).

RACE 202
Mexico, Mexico City, 22 March.
Q 1:23.063 (27); 1:18.791 (6). R 3.
P: Mansell 1:16.346. Hot, sunny.
W: 1:19.420 (5). R, 11 laps, transmission.
Friday: he insisted the bumpy track was 'very, very dangerous. An accident is inevitable.' He crashed heavily 18 minutes into the session. On the Saturday, 'sore and in pain' he couldn't get near the Williamses.

He ran third to lap 12. 'I had some sort of problem with the clutch or the transmission, not a problem I have had before.'

Pd Mansell, Patrese, Schumacher.
FL Berger 1:17.711 (Senna 1:20.721)
Ch Mansell 20, Patrese 12, Schumacher 7, Berger 5, Senna 4.

RACE 203
Brazil, Interlagos, 5 April. Q 1:19.358 (9);
1:17.902 (3). R 2. P: Mansell 1:15.703.
Hot, sunny. W: 1:21.146 (9). R, 17 laps,
electrics.
New McLaren cars but Senna felt it was 'premature to make any comment' on the

Friday. Saturday: 'We registered a significant improvement.'

He ran third, descending to sixth. 'During the early stages my car suffered a serious and intermittent engine cut-out. The effect of this was totally unpredictable and could occur four or five times on one lap and not at all on the next. At times the cut-out was so bad that it felt as if I had applied the brakes.'

Pd Mansell, Patrese, Schumacher.
FL Patrese 1:19.490 (Senna 1:23.101).
Ch Mansell 30, Patrese 18, Schumacher 11, Berger 5, Senna 4.

RACE 204
Spain, Barcelona, 3 May. Q 1:21.209 (3);
1:46.581 (3). R 2. P: Mansell 1:20.190.
Cool, wet. W: 1:44.964 (10). R, 62 laps,
spin.
He said 'We have made some progress since Brazil, we have a better understanding of the car and how it works.' On the Saturday it rained and 'the car works better in the wet than it does in the dry partly because we are a little bit down on power and that matters less in the wet.'

Mansell led throughout, Senna fifth to lap 8, fourth to lap 20 and third to lap 63. 'When I spun the first time I was lucky to get back on the circuit but the car was aquaplaning everywhere and the second time I just couldn't hold it.'

Pd Mansell, Schumacher, Alesi.
FL Mansell 1:42.503 (Senna 1:43.176).
Ch Mansell 40, Patrese 18, Schumacher 17, Berger 8, Alesi 7, Senna 4.

RACE 205
San Marino, Imola 17 May. Q 1:23.086 (2);
1:23.151 (3). R 2. P: Mansell 1:21.842.
Hot, sunny. W: 1:26.665 (4). 3.
Saturday: 'We have not made as much progress since yesterday as I would have hoped and the fact that the track conditions were slower didn't help.'

Mansell led throughout, Senna third to lap 26 (his pit stop) then chasing and overtaking Alesi for third again on lap 40. And that was it.

Pd Mansell 1h 28m 40.927s, Patrese @ 9.451, Senna @ 48.984. **FL** Patrese 1:26.100 (Senna 1:27.615). **Ch** Mansell 50, Patrese 24, Schumacher 17, Senna and Berger 8.

RACE 206

Monaco, Monte Carlo, 31 May.
Q 1:21.467 (2); 1:20.608 (3). R 2.
P: Mansell 1:19.495. Warm, overcast.
W: 1:25.116 (3). 1.

Saturday: 'I spun my race car on my first quick lap. It was going to be a good one. I was driving over the limit trying to make up the time somehow.'

Mansell clean into *Ste Devote*, Senna going for it 'at the last moment so as not to give Riccardo [on the front row] any indication because otherwise he would have closed the door, of course. After that I tried to keep the gap [to Mansell] as small as possible.' On lap 71 Mansell thought he had a puncture (a wheel nut was loose) and pitted for tyres. It cost him the race.

Pd Senna 1h 50m 59.372s, Mansell @ 0.215, Patrese @ 31.843.
FL Mansell 1:21.598 (Senna 1:23.470).
Ch Mansell 56, Patrese 28, Schumacher 20, Senna 18.

RACE 207

Canada, Montreal, 14 June. Q: 1:19.775 (1); 1:20.590 (2). P. Hot, sunny.
W: 1:23.964 (5). R, 37 laps, electrics.

Friday: 'I am not really convinced about the Williams team's performance (Patrese second, Mansell fourth).' Saturday: 'It has been a long time since I can remember being on pole position! Conditions were more difficult and I was unable to improve but it is good to be fastest.'

Senna led, holding Mansell captive for 14 laps. Coming to the chicane Mansell tried the inside, went broadside across the run-off area and ended on the start-finish straight pointing the wrong way. Mansell sat in the cockpit and as Senna passed next time stuck an accusing finger towards him. Senna didn't let that disturb him but 'eventually the engine just cut out.'

Pd Berger, Schumacher, Alesi.
FL Berger 1:22.325 (Senna 1:23.728).

Ch Mansell 56, Patrese 28, Schumacher 26, Senna and Berger 18.

RACE 208

France, Magny-Cours, 5 July. Q 1:16.892 (3); 1:15.199 (3). R 2. Pole: Mansell 1:13.864. Showers. W: 1:32.516 (6). R, no laps, accident.

Friday: 'When the tyres were good, the engine wasn't – and when the engine was, the tyres weren't.' Saturday: 'Basically, I did the best I could with the machinery.'

Senna made 'a bad start. Gerhard and I ended up side by side at the first corner. It was close but OK. I followed him down the straight, he braked very late so I was being careful and then Schumacher hit me from behind.'

Pd Mansell, Patrese, Brundle.
FL Mansell 1:17.070 (Senna no laps).
Ch Mansell 66, Patrese 34, Schumacher 26, Senna and Berger 18.

RACE 209

Britain, Silverstone, 12 July. Q 1:21.706 (3); 1:41.912 (11). R 2. P: Mansell 1:18.965. Warm. W: 1:26.606 (5). R, 52 laps, gearbox.

Senna estimated 'the gap between us and the Williamses is bigger here than normal, reflecting their strengths and our weaknesses.' Drizzle fell on the Saturday.

Senna ran fourth behind Brundle. 'I had a good clean fight with Martin. I was pushing like hell the whole race and it was really tiring. I had a lot of vibration and for the last 15 laps I could hardly see the track.'

Pd Mansell, Patrese, Brundle.
FL Mansell 1:22.539 (Senna 1:25.825).
Ch Mansell 76, Patrese 40, Schumacher 29, Berger 20, Senna 18.

RACE 210

Germany, Hockenheim, 26 July.
Q 1:40.331 (2); 1:39.106 (3). R 2.
P: Mansell 1:37.960. Hot, sunny.
W: 1:44.251 (4). 2.

Saturday: 'I was right over the limit and that was as fast as I could go.'

The race settled Mansell, Patrese, Senna, each stretching from the other. During the pit stops a ploy revealed itself: Senna wouldn't be stopping. Mansell came out behind him and attacked, on a straight Mansell powered by.

Pd Mansell 1h 18m 22.032s, Senna @ 4.500, Schumacher @ 34.462.
FL Patrese 1:41.591 (Senna 1:42.272).
Ch Mansell 86, Patrese 40, Schumacher 33, Senna 24.

RACE 211
Hungary, Hungaroring, 16 August.
Q 1:16.467 (3); 1:16.267 (3). R 2.
P: Patrese 1:15.476. Hot, sunny.
W: 1:19.408 (1). 1.
Friday: 'it was very difficult to get a clear lap. There seemed to be cars going off everywhere.' Saturday: everybody, it seemed, was spinning, including Senna.

Patrese led from Senna, who'd made an awesome getaway outside Mansell into turn one. Patrese spun off on lap 39 and a slow puncture made Mansell pit.

Pd Senna 1h 46m 19.216s, Mansell @ 40.139, Berger @ 50.782.
FL Mansell 1:18.308 (Senna 1:19.588).
Ch Mansell 92, Patrese 40, Senna 34.

RACE 212
Belgium, Spa, 30 August. Q 1:52.743 (2);
2:14.983 (14). R 1. P: Mansell 1:50.545.
Wet, dry. W: 1:57.243 (4). 5.
Friday: 'The car seems to be the same as ever but I am still trying as hard as ever!' Saturday was typically wet.

Senna went outside Mansell into *La Source*. In the country Mansell crowded, overtook on lap 2; and drizzle dripped. At the *Bus Stop* Patrese overtook. Schumacher bustled around Senna. The leaders pitted for wet tyres – except Senna. 'Gambling on staying out was my only chance.' He was on dries in heavy rain. On their wet tyres Mansell and Patrese shredded Senna's lead and eventually he had to pit.

Pd Schumacher, Mansell, Patrese.
FL Schumacher 1:53.791 (Senna 1:54.088).
Ch Mansell 98, Patrese 44, Schumacher 43, Senna 36.

RACE 213
Italy, Monza, 13 September. Q 1:22.822
(2); 1:24.122 (6). R 1. P: Mansell 1:22.221.
Hot, sunny. W: 1:27.088 (4). 1.
Saturday: 'A bad failure with my race car, I'm not quite sure what it was. It's difficult to say whether I could have matched Mansell.'

Mansell made a big start but Alesi slotted his Ferrari between Senna and Mansell. Senna dealt with him. 'I didn't think I could maintain my position but Nigel only pulled out a relatively small advantage and I was able to stay in touch.' Patrese took Senna, Mansell retired after 46 laps (hydraulic failure), and Patrese slowed, the active suspension playing tricks.

Pd Senna 1h 18m 15.349s, Brundle @ 17.050, Schumacher @ 24.373.
FL Mansell 1:26.119 (Senna 1:27.190)
Ch Mansell 98, Schumacher 47, Patrese and Senna 46.

RACE 214
Portugal, Estoril, 27 September.
Q 1:15.343 (4); 1:14.258 (2). R 2.
P: Mansell 1:13.041. Hot, sunny.
W: 1:20.531 (6). 3.
A 'moment' on the Friday. 'The rear wing on the spare car broke just as I was down-changing for the first corner.' Saturday: 'I ended with three or four really good laps.'

Mansell led throughout. Senna ran third behind, inevitably, Patrese. Senna pitted four times. 'The circuit conditions were abnormal and therefore the tyre wear and the performance of the tyres was also abnormal.'

Pd Mansell 1h 34m 46.659, Berger @ 37.533, Senna @ 1 lap. **FL** Senna 1:16.272.
Ch Mansell 108, Senna 50, Schumacher 47.

RACE 215
Japan, Suzuka, 25 October. Q 1:38.375
(3); did not run. R 2. P: Mansell 1:37.360.
Warm, sunny. W: 1:44.520 (5). R, 2 laps,
engine.
Senna hoped that 'coming here we would have been able to close the gap to the Williamses but although the engines are running well they are not as quick as we expected.' Torrential rain washed over the Saturday.

Senna ran third but 'I felt the engine begin to fail and decided to park the car to avoid destroying the engine.'

Pd Patrese, Berger, Brundle.
FL Mansell 1:40.646 (Senna 1:46.229).
Ch Mansell 108, Patrese 56, Senna 50.

RACE 216
Australia, Adelaide, 8 November.
Q 1:14.202 (2); 1:14.416 (1). R 1.
P: Mansell 1:13.732. Cool, overcast.
W: 1:17.651 (3). R, 18 laps, accident.

Friday: 'You are always working hard. To get under the 1:15s takes tremendous effort and concentration.' Saturday: 'Strategically, I drove a little bit better but the circuit was certainly more than half a second slower.'

Into lap 19, Senna pressed Mansell. At the corner before the pit lane straight they collided nose to tail.

Pd Berger, Schumacher, Brundle.
FL Schumacher 1:16.078 (Senna 1:17.818).
Ch Mansell 108, Patrese 56, Schumacher 53, Senna 50.

1993 Formula 1: McLaren

Honda withdrew from Grand Prix racing and McLaren had to reach for Ford engines. That seemed to condemn McLaren to a season of impotence against Williams and Renault, for whom Prost returned after a year off. Berger departed McLaren for Ferrari when he received an offer no man could refuse. It made him one of the highest paid people in the world. Michael Andretti crossed the Atlantic to partner Senna who, dubious about spending 16 Grands Prix of futility half a lap behind Prost, competed during the early part of the season on a race-by-race basis. Rule changes: no use of the spare car in qualifying and, from Brazil, a limit of 12 laps per driver in each qualifying session. The other front-runners: Damon Hill (Williams), Schumacher and Patrese (Benetton), Alesi (Ferrari).

RACE 217
South Africa, Kyalami, 14 March.
Q 1:17.152 (2); 1:15.784 (2). R 1. P: Prost 1:15.696. Hot, overcast. W: 1:19.475 (2). 2.

On the Friday, he didn't feel well. On the Saturday, he went out early and pitched the McLaren to the edge, drawing dust as he rode over the kerbing. 1:16.683. Prost responded – 1:16.604. Senna responded – 1:15.784. Seven minutes remained when Prost settled it by an eye-blink.

Prost made a hesitant start and nearly stalled. Senna sprang on that and led Schumacher by 1.7 seconds on the opening

lap. Soon enough Prost – overtook Schumacher and, after the pit stops, led, Senna literally powerless to do anything but follow.

Pd Prost 1h 38m 45.082s, Senna @ 1m 19.824, Mark Blundell (Ligier) @ 1 lap.
FL Prost 1:19.492 (Senna 1:20.755).

RACE 218
Brazil, Interlagos, 28 March. Q 1:18.639 (3); 1:17.697 (3). R 2. P: Prost 1:15.866. Dry, wet. W: 1:21.518 (3). 1.

'We are in a closed circle – the power we have is not great. To compensate you drop the wing level a lot but you are still slow on the straight and you compromise the car a lot round the corners.'

Prost led from Senna until, on lap 11, Hill overtook him. On lap 24 Senna was brought in for a 10-second stop 'n' go penalty for overtaking Erik Comas (Larrousse) under a yellow flag. As Senna emerged a downpour fell. He pitted for wets, Prost ran over debris and was out and Hill led – but the track dried. Senna pitted for slick tyres first and that settled the race.

Pd Senna 1h 51m 15.485s, Hill @ 16.625, Schumacher @ 45.436.
FL Schumacher 1:20.024 (Senna: 1:20.187).
Ch Senna 16, Prost 10, Hill, Blundell 6.

RACE 219
Europe, Donington Park, 11 April.
Q 1:23.976 (1); 1:12.107 (4). R 2. P: Prost 1:10.458. Damp, wet. W: 1:30.206 (3). 1.

A wet Friday. Senna mastered the rain and was majestic, then mounted a late run but had a hydraulic failure. Saturday was dry and he mounted another late run but a vast slide out of Goddard cost him too many fractions.

For a full race description, see the chapter titled Donington.

Pd Senna 1h 50m 46.570s, Hill @ 1m 23.199, Prost @ 1 lap. **FL** Senna 1:18.029. **Ch** Senna 26, Prost 14, Hill 12.

RACE 220
San Marino, Imola, 25 April. Q 1:24.042 (4); 1:24.007 (4). R 2. P: Prost 1:22.070. Overcast, wet. W: 1:26.752 (3). R, 42 laps, hydraulics.

He arrived 15 minutes before the Friday untimed session and spun off at Tosa; at the end of first qualifying he spun coming out of the *Variante Bassa*. Twenty-two minutes into the Saturday session he spun into the wall at *Acque Minerale*.

Hill led, Senna holding Prost and, after the pit stops, he ran second to Prost. Approaching *Tosa* at more than 205mph he felt the car losing its hydraulics.

Pd Prost, Schumacher, Brundle. **FL** Prost 1:26.128 (Senna: 1:27.490). **Ch** Senna 26, Prost 24, Hill 12.

RACE 221
Spain, Barcelona, 9 May. Q 1:20.221 (2); 1:19.722 (3). R 2. P: Prost 1:17.809. Hot, sunny. W: 1:24.066 (3). 2.

On the Friday 'there is nothing more to come out of me. Now we have to get more out of the car.' Saturday: the car was pulling to the right.

Hill made the better start. Senna tucked to the inside of Prost into turn one – but Prost held him. After 41 laps Hill's engine let go, Senna second and facing a long passage home.

Pd Prost 1h 32m 27.685s, Senna @ 16.873, Schumacher @ 27.125. **FL** Schumacher 1:20.989 (Senna: 1:21.717). **Ch** Prost 34, Senna 32, Schumacher 14.

RACE 222
Monaco, Monte Carlo, 23 May. Q 1:42.127 (5); 1:21.552 (3). R 2. P: Prost 1:20.557. Hot, sunny. W: 1:24.283 (3). 1.

Was he having to push too hard? On the Thursday morning at *Ste Devote* the McLaren was pitched hard left by a bump and hit the barrier virtually head on. On the Saturday he reached the harbour chicane and slithered down the escape road, battering the barrier there.

'I was thinking hard before going to bed on Saturday and when I got up on race morning I was thinking positively. When I couldn't make the front row [Prost and Schumacher] I knew I couldn't take the lead. I had to cope with their speeds and hope that their tyre wear would be worse than mine.' Prost 'jumped the start, perhaps in desperation to get to the first corner, a result of the pressure I exerted even though I was behind him.' Schumacher led from Senna until Schumacher's active hydraulics failed on lap 33. The victory, Senna's sixth here, beat Graham Hill's record of five.

Pd Senna 1h 52m 10.947s, Hill @ 52.118, Alesi @ 1m 03.362. **FL** Prost 1:23.604 (Senna: 1:23.737). **Ch** Senna 42, Prost 37, Hill 18.

RACE 223
Canada, Montreal, 13 June. Q 1:21.706 (8); 1:21.891 (7). R 4. P: Prost 1:18.987. Hot, sunny. W: 1:24.170 (5). Result: R, 62 laps, alternator.

'I will race defensively, waiting for the length of the race and the peculiarities of the circuit to take their toll. That is the best I can do.' Thus said Senna on the Saturday.

He ran third behind Prost and Hill although somehow he managed to pressure Hill briefly. Schumacher advanced on him. Hill had a chaotic pit stop and Senna inherited second place, something he consolidated. Schumacher advanced again and 'the car suddenly started cutting out.'

Pd Prost, Schumacher, Hill. **FL** Schumacher 1:21.500 (Senna 1:22.015). **Ch** Prost 47, Senna 42, Hill 22.

RACE 224
France, Magny-Cours, 4 July. Q 1:16.782 (4); 1:16.264 (5). R 3. P: Hill 1:14.382. Hot, sunny. W: 1:19.819 (3). 4.

Senna had problems with the car's balance on the Friday and although it was 'much better'on the Saturday he couldn't force it to the front of the grid.

He ran fifth, Schumacher behind him but Schumacher made two pit stops, Senna only one.

Pd Prost, Hill, Schumacher.
FL Schumacher 1:19.256 (Senna 1:20.521).
Ch Prost 57, Senna 45, Hill 28.

RACE 225
Britain, Silverstone, 11 July. Q 1:37.050 (3); 1:21.986 (4). R 2. P: Prost 1:19.006. Cool, overcast. W: 1:28.468 (17). 5.
On the Friday 'it was hard to get a clear lap' and on the Saturday 'the car is undoubtedly better but we still seem to have some trouble in balancing it.'

At the green light Senna pitched the car level with Prost and he shifted Prost virtually onto the grass. For six laps they grappled. It was so dangerous that Prost wouldn't discuss it afterwards. Eventually Prost did get by. On the last lap Senna stopped, fuel gone, although he was classified fifth.

Pd Prost, Schumacher, Patrese.
FL Hill 1:22.515 (Senna: 1:24.886)
Ch Prost 67, Senna 47, Schumacher 30.

RACE 226
Germany, Hockenheim, 25 July. Q 1:40.642 (5); 1:39.616 (4). R 2. P: Prost 1:38.748. Warm, sunny. W: 1:58.997 (2). 4.
In the Friday morning session 'I went in too long at the first chicane, spun and then stalled the engine, so in the afternoon we had to start from scratch. It was better but still not quite right.' The car was better on the Saturday.

Hill led from Schumacher, Senna and Prost contesting third. They weaved together – another alarming instant. At the first chicane Prost had the inside line and held it, Senna – turning in – realised Prost wouldn't give way. Senna skittered around the rim of the gravel run-off area and spun onto the track. He was 24th. By lap 8 he was tenth, by lap 28 in the points; and, a mere five laps remaining, he pitted. 'The car felt funny and the last thing I wanted was to risk a blow-out at 300kph.'

Pd Prost, Schumacher, Blundell.
FL Schumacher 1:41.859 (Senna 1:42.162).
Ch Prost 77, Senna 50, Schumacher 36.

RACE 227
Hungary, Hungaroring, 15 August. Q 1:18.260 (5); 1:16.451 (4). R 2. P: Prost 1:14.631. Hot, sunny. W: 1:20.208 (4). R, 17 laps, throttle.
Friday: 'On my first set of tyres we tried to find a little more speed by reducing the size of the rear wing. That did not work so we went back to the larger wing.' Next day: 'significant improvements'.

Prost stalled on the parade lap, and had to start from the back of the grid. With pole vacant Senna made a hesitant start. 'I opted for a more cautious approach because the car felt near the limit. Quite soon I started to experience problems with the throttle.'

Pd Hill, Patrese, Berger. **FL** Prost 1:19.633 (Senna: 1:22.838). **Ch** Prost 77, Senna 50, Hill 38.

RACE 228
Belgium, Spa, 29 August. Q 1:51.385 (4); 1:49.934 (5). R 3. Pole: Prost 1:47.571. Hot, sunny. W: 1:54.802 (4). 4.
Friday: 'The car is not very good.' Saturday: 'We have improved the car from yesterday but unfortunately it wasn't good enough to maintain our position.'

Schumacher stalled, Senna instantly to mid-track to go round him. At that instant: Prost clear on the right, Hill on the left, Alesi in mid-track, Senna behind Alesi – a massive, compressed movement. On the descent to *Eau Rouge* Senna held left and overtook Hill. Anyway, 'ten laps from the end the car started to vibrate. It felt as if it was coming from the gearbox or the engine.'

Pd Hill, Schumacher, Prost.
FL Prost 1:51.095 (Senna 1:54.185).
Ch Prost 81, Senna 53, Hill 48.

RACE 229
Italy, Monza, 12 September. Q 1:23.310 (4); 1:22.633 (4). R 2. P: Prost 1:21.179. Warm, sunny. W: 1:26.533 (5). R, 8 laps, accident.
Senna was quite pleased on the Friday, and on Saturday preferred to talk about the race and the 'many unknown factors'.

At the start, Senna followed Alesi and they took Hill 'but Damon insisted on trying to stay on the outside and we touched. It was quite a hit but I landed more or less in the right direction and could carry on.' Senna completed the opening lap tenth and rose to eighth when he ran into the back of Martin Brundle.

Pd Hill, Alesi, Andretti. **FL** Hill 1:23.575. Senna: 1:27.939. **Ch** Prost 81, Hill 58, Senna 53.

RACE 230
Portugal, Estoril, 26 September.
Q 1:12.954 (3); 1:12.491 (3). R 2.
P: Hill 1:11.494. Warm, sunny. W: 1:16.493
(3). R, 19 laps, engine.
Häkkinen joined Senna at McLaren, Andretti retreating to the United States. Häkkinen astonished everyone by out-qualifying Senna, who complained of oversteer on the Friday. On the Saturday he had traffic on his fast laps.

Alesi led, Senna chasing but 'the engine blew suddenly, with a big bang. I feared it might catch fire.'

Pd Schumacher, Prost, Hill.
FL Hill 1:14.859 (Senna: 1:18.365)
Ch Prost 87, Hill 62, Senna 53.

RACE 231
Japan, Suzuka, 24 October. Q 1:38.942
(4); 1:37.284 (2). R 1. P: Prost 1:37.154.
Changeable. W: 1:43.694 (4). 1.
After his first flying lap on the Friday he felt 'a lot more to come' but on his second set of tyres 'the engine broke.' On the Saturday 'we decided that although I had five laps left I would only carry enough fuel for two fast ones. Unfortunately, the tyres were not quite right on what should have been the first fast lap so I only had one lap to set my time.'

Senna won turn one, Prost following. Senna pitted on lap 13 and on lap 21 he had to stop for wets. He led, Prost chasing. He came up to lap Hill and Eddie Irvine (Jordan). Irvine re-took Senna. After the final stops for slick tyres Senna went comfy to the end, then marched to the Jordan team and explained the facts of life to Irvine.

Pd Senna 1h 40m 27.912s, Prost @ 11.435, Häkkinen @ 26.129.
FL Prost 1:41.176 (Senna 1:43.217).
Ch Prost 93, Hill 65, Senna 63.

RACE 232
Australia, Adelaide, 7 November.
Q 1:13.371 (1); 1:14.779 (5). P. Cool,
overcast. W: 1:16.642 (1). 1.
'It was a tremendous lap, a pretty special one' on the Friday. Warmer Saturday weather made improvements rare, giving Senna pole.

The last race for McLaren. 'The last half hour before the race was very hard on me: these emotions kept coming back to me making me feel very uneasy.' He led from start to finish (except briefly during the pit stops).

Pd Senna 1h 43m 27.476s, Prost @ 9.259, Hill @ 33.902. **FL** Hill 1:15.381 (Senna 1:16.128) **Ch** Prost 99, Senna 73, Hill 69.

1994 Formula 1: Williams

1994 Formula 1: Williams
It seemed the logical move to a proven, winning car and a proven, winning engine; and it seemed like Senna's fourth championship won before he'd turned a wheel. He'd partner Hill. The other front-runners: Schumacher (Benetton), Berger and Alesi (Ferrari): not many. Rule changes banned many electronic driver aids. I have not given the Championship positions.

RACE 233
Brazil, Interlagos, 27 March. Q 1:16.386
(1); 1:15.962 (1). P. Warm, overcast.
W: 1:18.667 (1). R, 55 laps, spin.
Senna was immediately quickest on the Friday morning but Schumacher closed in the afternoon. A downpour dampened a Senna-Schumacher shoot-out for pole on the Saturday.

Senna led, but by lap 17 Schumacher was within a second of him. They pitted on lap 21 – Schumacher getting a quicker stop to lead.

The order didn't change after the second stops. Senna pressed. 'I was driving right on my limit and I was caught out at the exit of the third gear corner onto the main straight.' He went off.

Pd Schumacher, Hill, Alesi.
FL Schumacher 1:18.455 (Senna 1:18.764).

RACE 234
Pacific, Aida, Japan, 17 April. Q 1:10.218 (1); 1:19.304 (24). P. Warm, sunny. W: 1:12.872 (1). R, no laps, accident.
On the Friday 'here the problem is very low speed in several corners. We have to deal with it. Everybody uses a lot of wing, which compensates a little bit.' Saturday was slower.

Schumacher made the better start. Senna might have tried inside him but in an 83-lap race 'there was no point'. Häkkinen prodded into him and spun the Williams. As it rotated onto the run-off area Nicola Larini's Ferrari rammed it.

Pd Schumacher, Berger, Rubens Barrichello (Jordan).
FL Schumacher 1:14.023 (Senna no laps).

RACE 235
San Marino, Imola, 1 May. Q 1:21.548 (1); did not run. P. Hot, dry. W: 1:22.597 (1). R, 6 laps, accident.
As long as anyone cares about racing motor cars, and the consequences of racing motor cars, the three days of Imola will remain static in time. Friday: Barrichello, Senna's protégé, crashed and went to hospital. Senna somehow put together a lap good enough for provisional pole. Saturday: Roland Ratzenberger, in a Simtek, crashed fatally.

He raced. From the conflicts and confusions of his emotions he drew a beautiful beginning from himself. On the opening lap he tried to break Schumacher but a startline crash produced the Safety Car which they all followed until the debris had been cleared. At the end of 'lap 5' they raced again: Senna against Schumacher, skill against skill, man against man, the eternal combat bearing eternal consequences. Through the corner called *Tamburello* Schumacher noticed the Williams 'bottoming'. Through *Tamburello* next time round the Williams went straight off and pounded a concrete wall. In the final 1.8 seconds of his life Ayrton Senna was able to reduce the speed of the car from 192 to 136mph. It was not enough.

I do not propose to give the podium at Imola and I do not propose to give who set fastest lap or their time. I offer you one statistic. It is Ayrton Senna's best lap – 1:44.068.

Appendix 2

STATISTICS

First car race: FF1600: Brands Hatch 1 March 1981
First win: Brands Hatch: 15 March 1981
First pole: Mallory Park: 22 March 1981
First fastest lap: Oulton Park: 24 May 1981

1981: Townsend-Thoresen and RAC Champion
1982: Pace British and EFDA European Champion
1983: Marlboro British F3 Champion

First Grand Prix: Brazil, 1984
First fastest lap: Monaco 1984
First pole, win: Portugal, 1985
First World Championship: McLaren 1988
World Champion: 1988, 1990, 1991

THE ALL-TIME RECORDS, AS AT 1 MAY 1994

Total points per driver:

Prost – 798.5

Senna – 614

Piquet – 485.5

Mansell – 469

Lauda – 420.5

Most poles:

Senna – 65

Clark – 33

Prost – 33

Mansell – 31

Fangio – 29

Most poles in a season:

14 – Mansell 1992

13 – Senna 1988, 1989

13 – Prost 1993

10 – Senna 1990

9 – Lauda 1974, 1975

9 – Peterson 1973

9 – Piquet 1984

Most successive poles:

8 – Senna 1988/89

7 – Senna 1990/91

7 – Prost 1993

Most wins:

Prost – 51

Senna – 41

Mansell – 30

Stewart – 27

Clark – 25

Lauda – 25

Most wins in a season:

9 – Mansell 1992

8 – Senna 1988

7 – Prost 1984, 1988, 1993

7 – Clark 1963

7 – Senna 1991

Most fastest laps:

Prost – 41

Mansell – 30

Clark – 28

Lauda – 24

Fangio – 23

Piquet – 23

Moss – 19

Senna – 19

INDEX